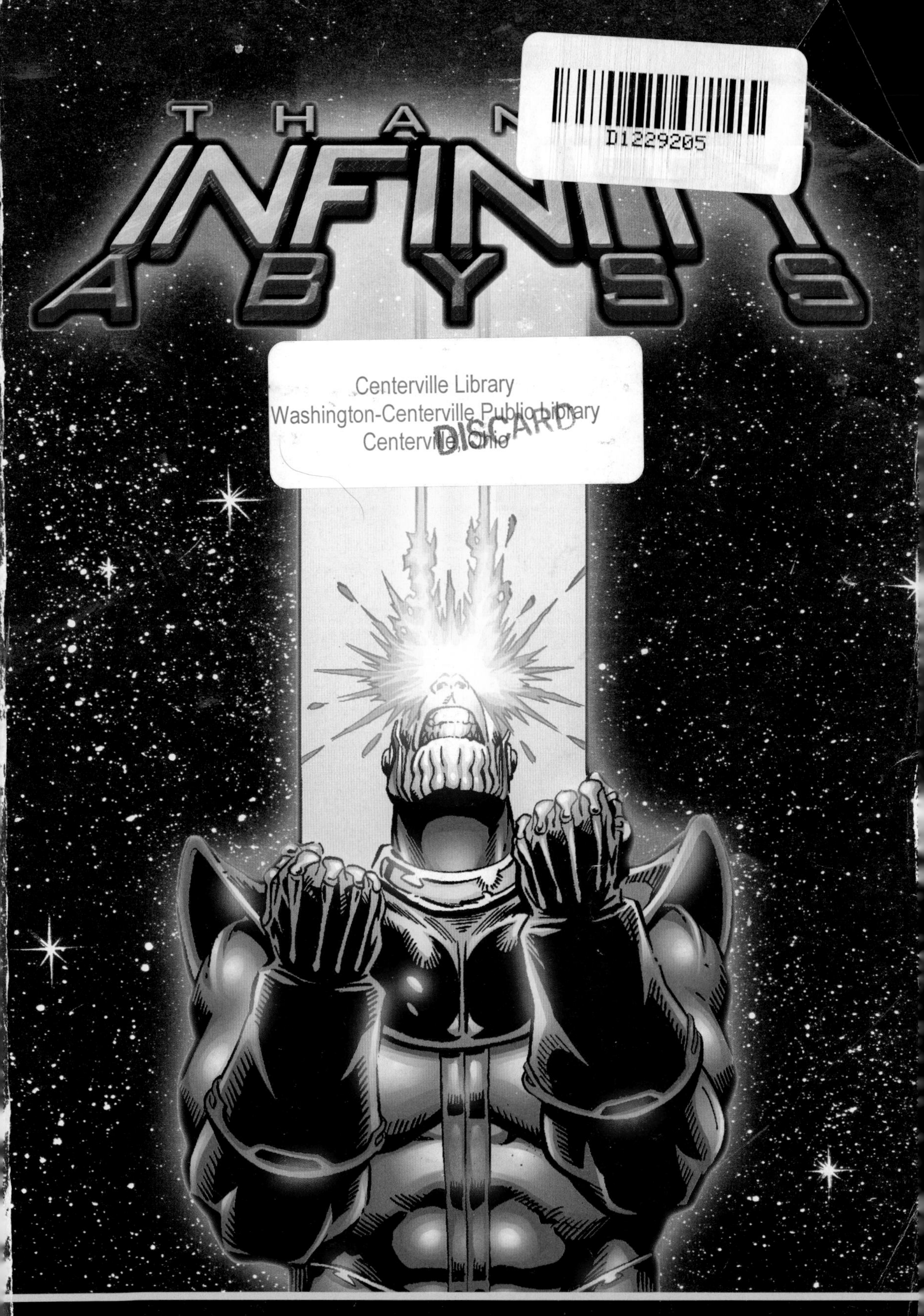
ABYSS

THANOS: INFINITY ABYSS. Contains material originally published in magazine form as INFINITY ABYSS #1-6. Second edition. First printing 2013. ISBN# 978-0-7851-8512-3. Published by MARVEL WORLDWIDE, INC., a subsidiary of MARVEL ENTERTAINMENT, LLC. OFFICE OF PUBLICATION: 135 West 50th Street, New York, NY 10020. **Printed in the U.S.A.** ALAN FINE, EVP - Office of the President, Marvel Worldwide, Inc. and EVP & CMO Marvel Characters B.V.; DAN BUCKLEY, Publisher & President - Print, Animation & Digital Divisions; JOE QUESADA, Chief Creative Officer; TOM BREVOORT, SVP of Publishing; DAVID BOGART, SVP of Op[illegible] & Procurement, Publishing; C.B. CEBULSKI, SVP of Creator & Content Development; DAVID GABRIEL, SVP of Print & Digital Publishing Sales; JIM O'KEEFE, VP of Operations & Logistics; DAN CAR[illegible] Publishing Technology; SUSAN CRESPI, Editorial Operations Manager; ALEX MORALES, Publishing Operations Manager; STAN LEE, Chairman Emeritus. For information regarding advertising in Mar[illegible] com, please contact Niza Disla, Director of Marvel Partnerships, at ndisla@marvel.com. For Marvel subscription inquiries, please call 800-217-9158. **Manufactured between 10/18/2013 and** [illegible] **GRAPHICS, VERSAILLES, KY, USA.**

10 9 8 7 6 5 4 3 2 1

THANOS: INFINITY ABYSS

WRITER & PENCILER
Jim Starlin

INKER
Al Milgrom

COLORISTS
Christie Scheele & Heroic Age

LETTERER
Jack Morelli

ASSISTANT EDITOR
Marc Sumerak

EDITOR
Tom Brevoort

COVER ARTISTS
Jim Starlin, Al Milgrom, Christie Scheele & Heroic Age

RESEARCH: Daron Jensen **LAYOUT:** Jeph York
COLLECTION EDITOR: Nelson Ribeiro
ASSISTANT EDITOR: Alex Starbuck
EDITORS, SPECIAL PROJECTS:
Mark D. Beazley & Jennifer Grünwald
SENIOR EDITOR, SPECIAL PROJECTS:
Jeff Youngquist
SVP OF PRINT & DIGITAL PUBLISHING SALES:
David Gabriel

EDITOR IN CHIEF: Axel Alonso
CHIEF CREATIVE OFFICER: Joe Quesada
PUBLISHER: Dan Buckley
EXECUTIVE PRODUCER: Alan Fine

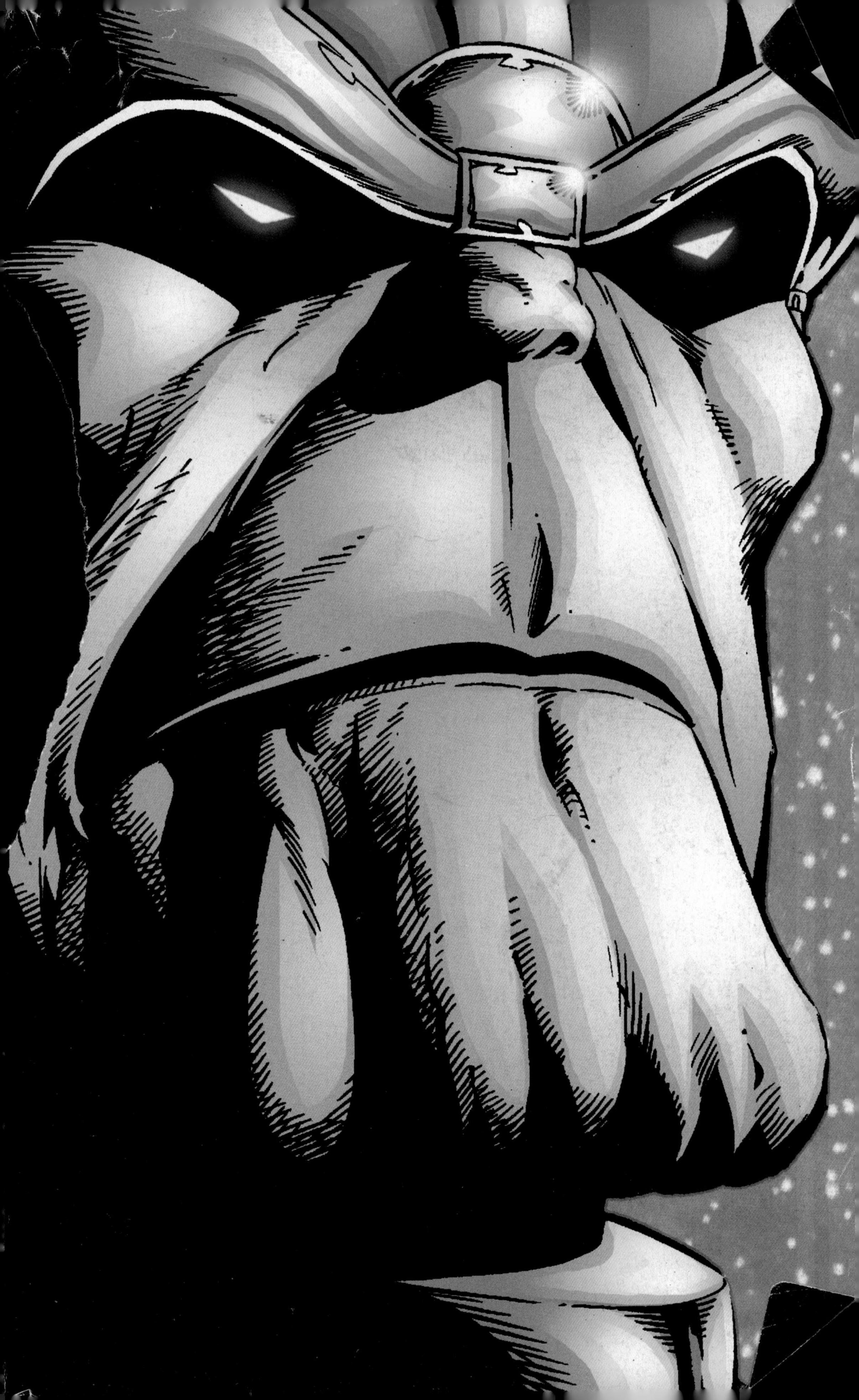

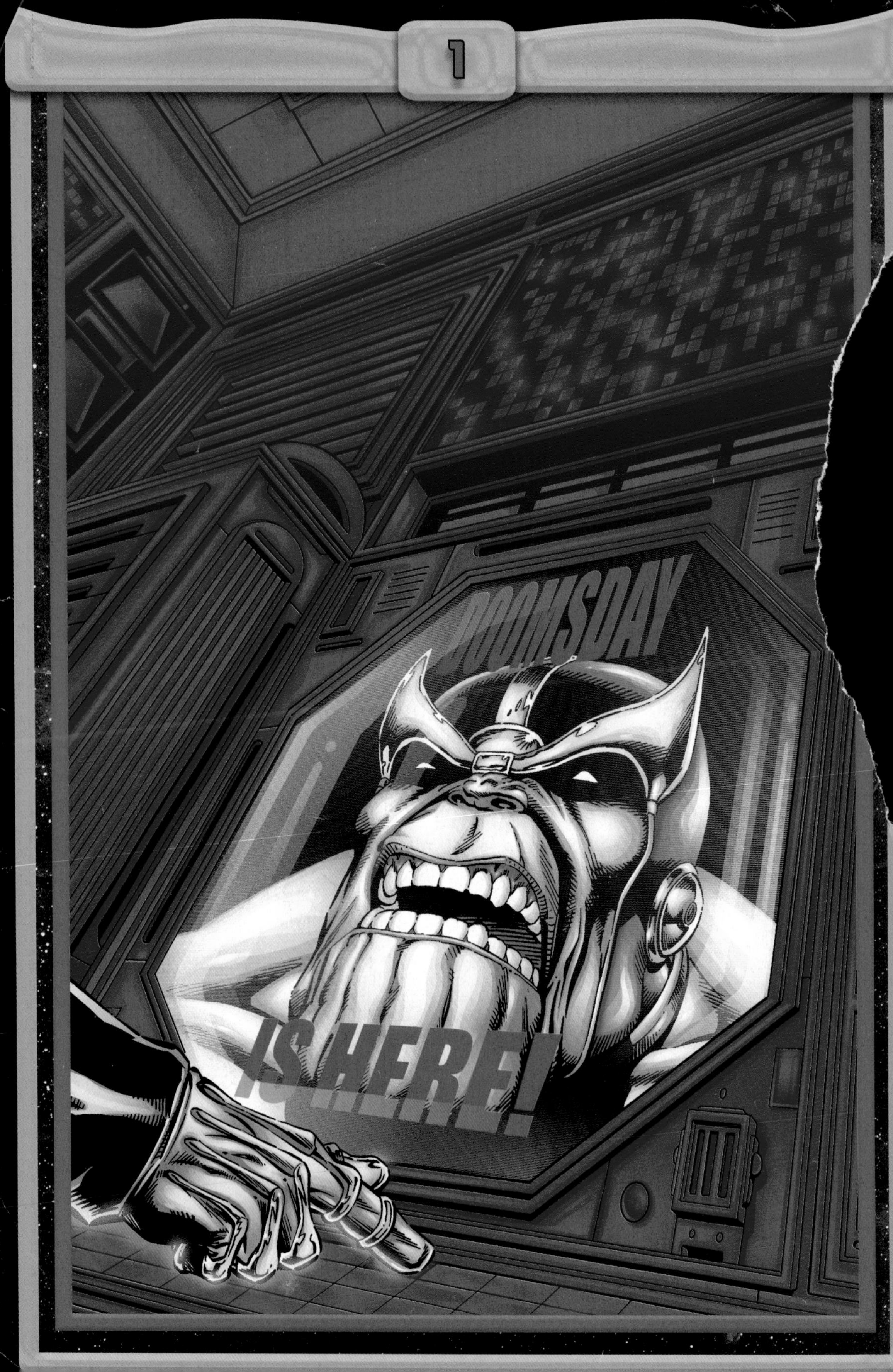
1
DOOMSDAY
IS HERE!

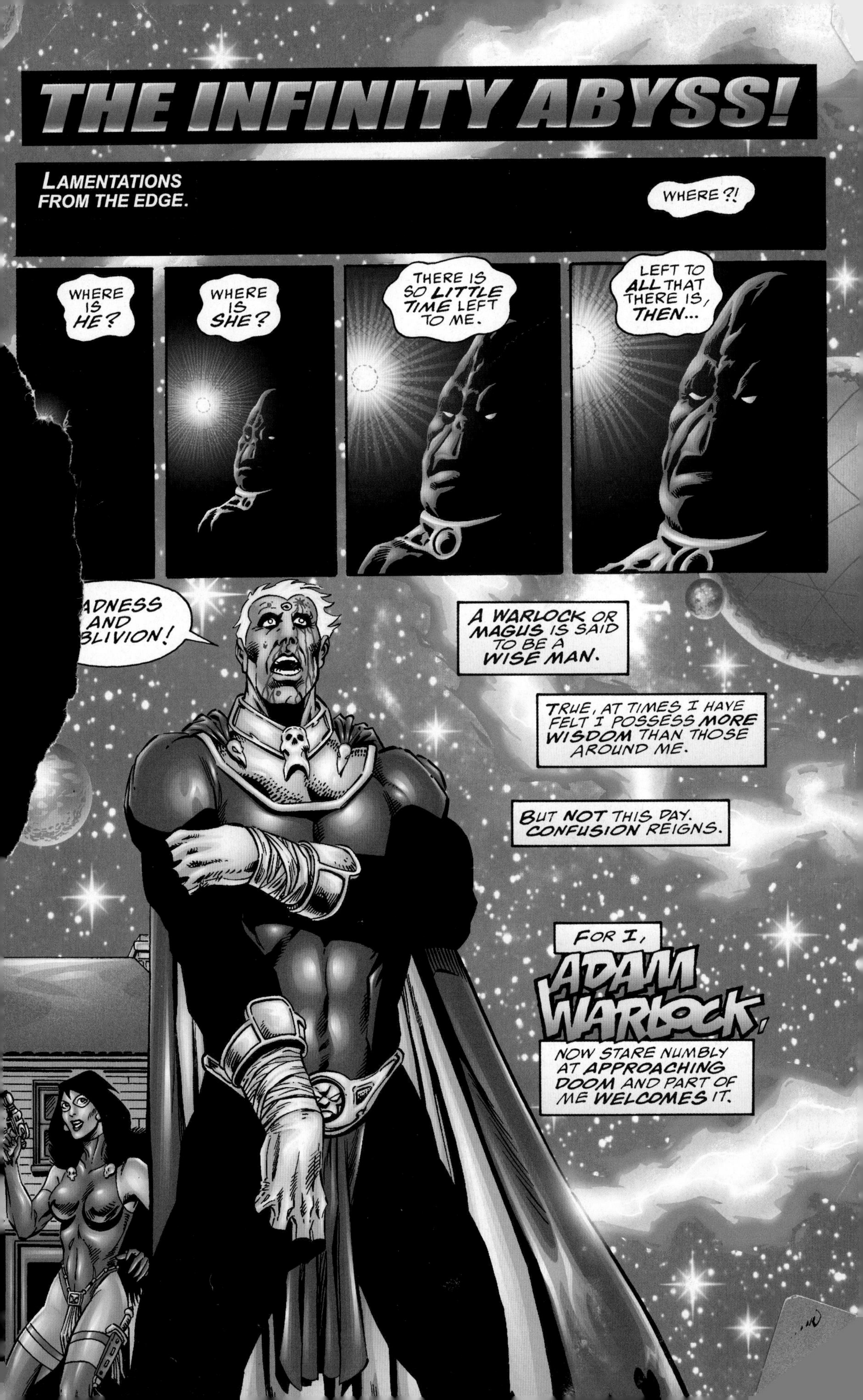

THE INFINITY ABYSS!
LAMENTATIONS FROM THE EDGE.
WHERE ?!
WHERE IS HE?
WHERE IS SHE?
THERE IS SO LITTLE TIME LEFT TO ME.
LEFT TO ALL THAT THERE IS, THEN...
ADNESS AND BLIVION!
A WARLOCK OR MAGUS IS SAID TO BE A WISE MAN.
TRUE, AT TIMES I HAVE FELT I POSSESS MORE WISDOM THAN THOSE AROUND ME.
BUT NOT THIS DAY. CONFUSION REIGNS.
FOR I,
ADAM WARLOCK,
NOW STARE NUMBLY AT APPROACHING DOOM AND PART OF ME WELCOMES IT.

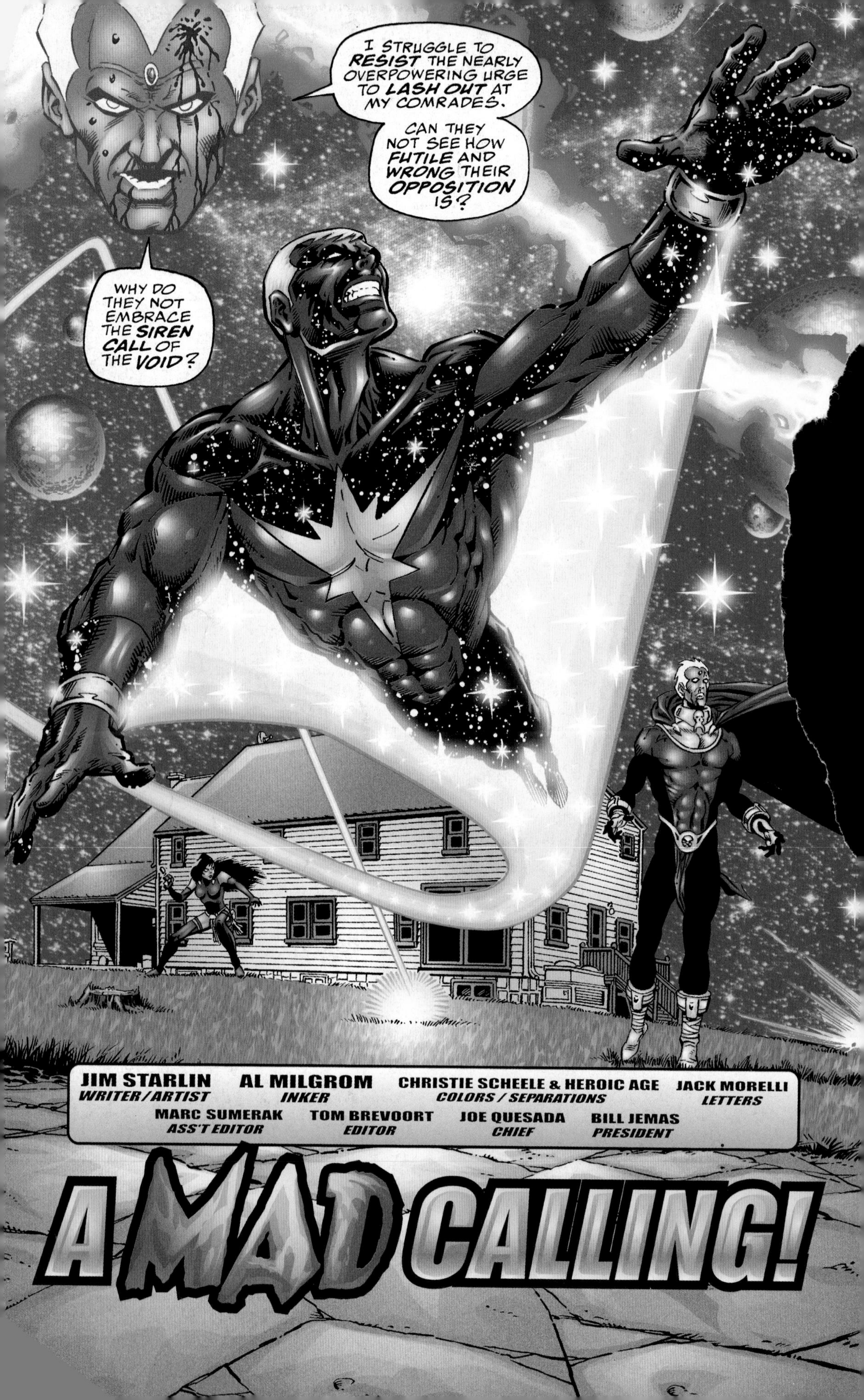
I STRUGGLE TO RESIST THE NEARLY OVERPOWERING URGE TO LASH OUT AT MY COMRADES.
CAN THEY NOT SEE HOW FUTILE AND WRONG THEIR OPPOSITION IS?
WHY DO THEY NOT EMBRACE THE SIREN CALL OF THE VOID?
JIM STARLIN WRITER/ARTIST
AL MILGROM INKER
CHRISTIE SCHEELE & HEROIC AGE COLORS / SEPARATIONS
JACK MORELLI LETTERS
MARC SUMERAK ASS'T EDITOR
TOM BREVOORT EDITOR
JOE QUESADA CHIEF
BILL JEMAS PRESIDENT
A MAD CALLING!

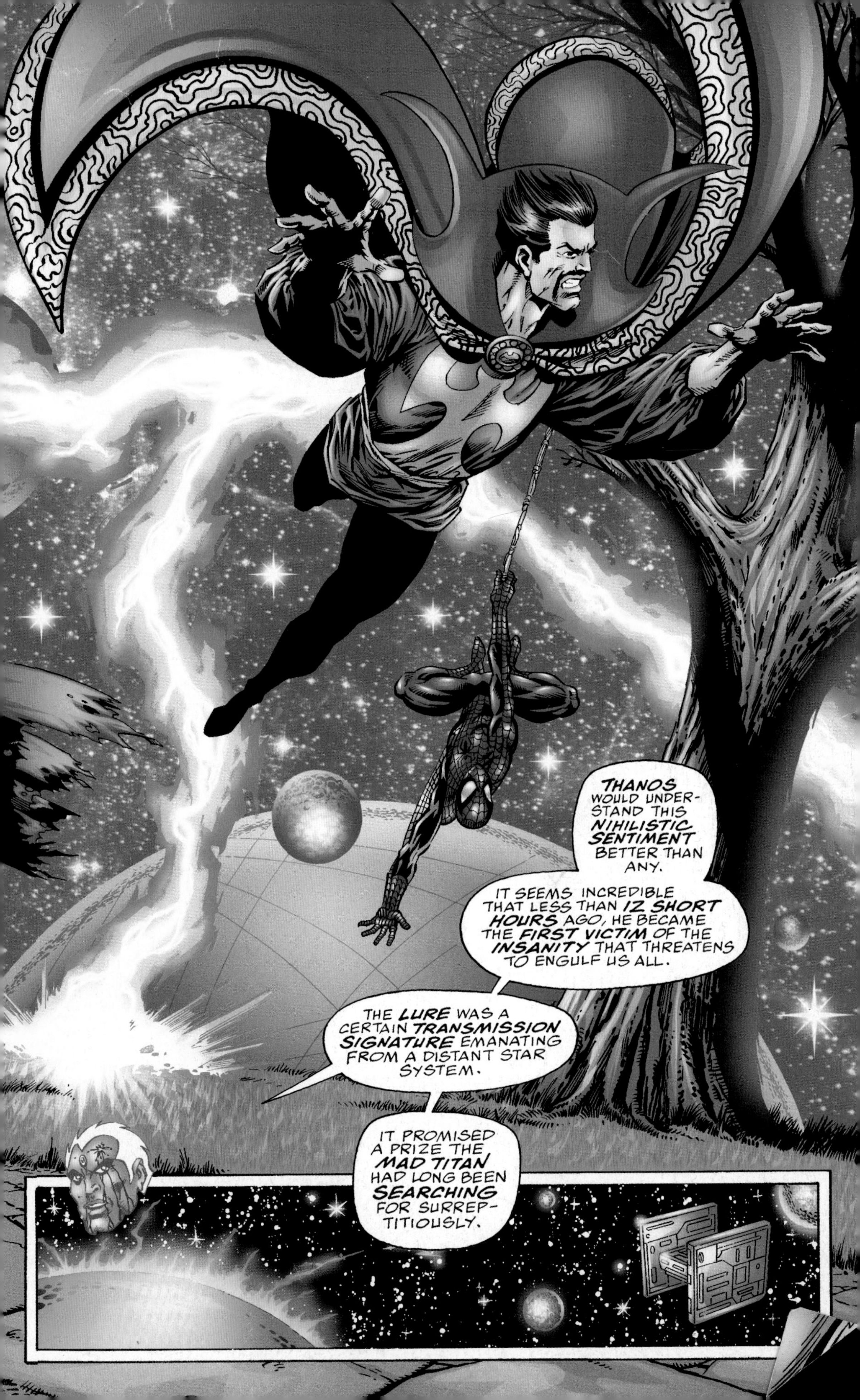
THANOS WOULD UNDERSTAND THIS NIHILISTIC SENTIMENT BETTER THAN ANY.
IT SEEMS INCREDIBLE THAT LESS THAN 12 SHORT HOURS AGO, HE BECAME THE FIRST VICTIM OF THE INSANITY THAT THREATENS TO ENGULF US ALL.
THE LURE WAS A CERTAIN TRANSMISSION SIGNATURE EMANATING FROM A DISTANT STAR SYSTEM.
IT PROMISED A PRIZE THE MAD TITAN HAD LONG BEEN SEARCHING FOR SURREPTITIOUSLY.

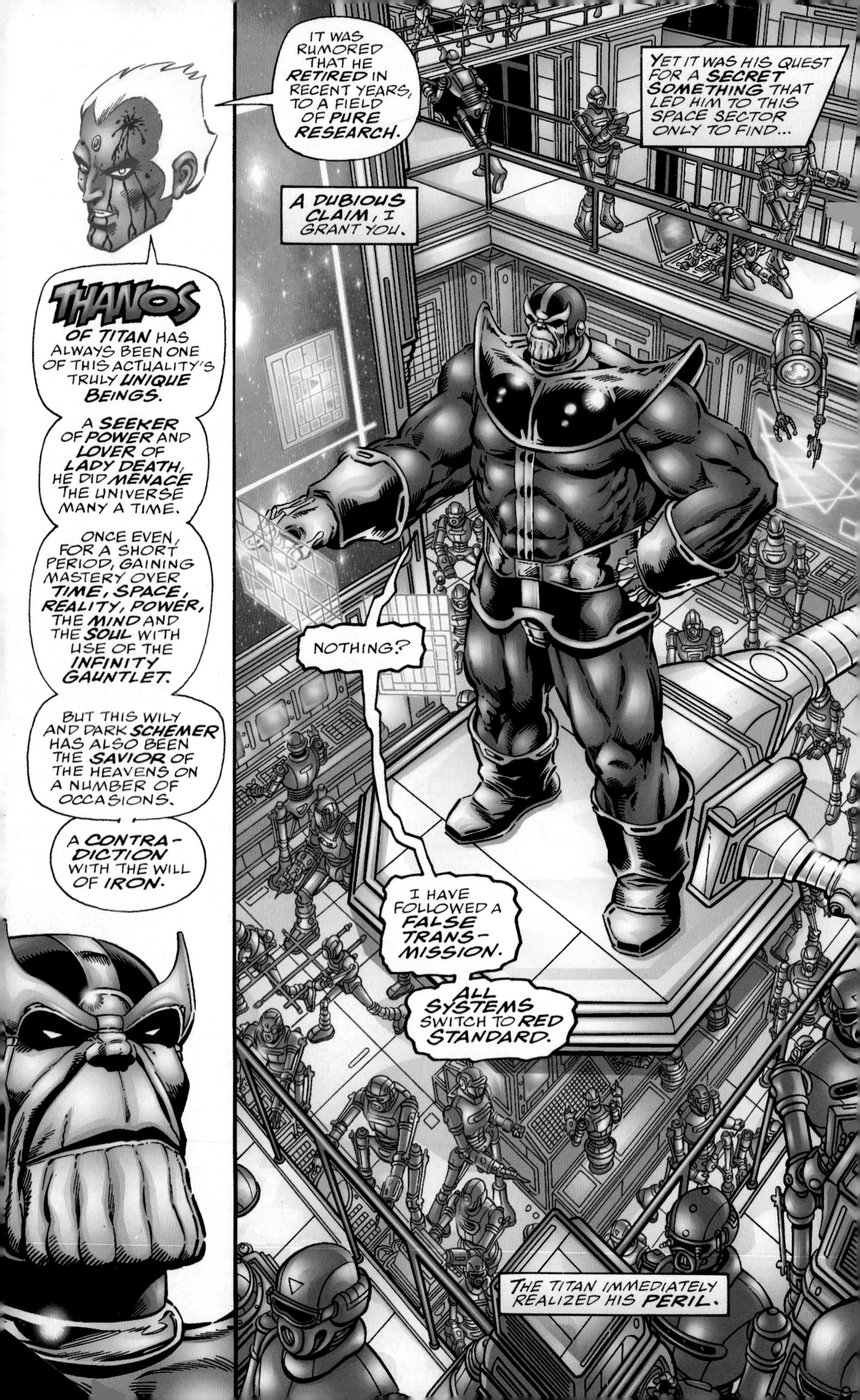

IT WAS RUMORED THAT HE RETIRED IN RECENT YEARS, TO A FIELD OF PURE RESEARCH.
YET IT WAS HIS QUEST FOR A SECRET SOMETHING THAT LED HIM TO THIS SPACE SECTOR ONLY TO FIND...
A DUBIOUS CLAIM, I GRANT YOU.
THANOS OF TITAN HAS ALWAYS BEEN ONE OF THIS ACTUALITY'S TRULY UNIQUE BEINGS.
A SEEKER OF POWER AND LOVER OF LADY DEATH, HE DID MENACE THE UNIVERSE MANY A TIME.
ONCE EVEN, FOR A SHORT PERIOD, GAINING MASTERY OVER TIME, SPACE, REALITY, POWER, THE MIND AND THE SOUL WITH USE OF THE INFINITY GAUNTLET.
BUT THIS WILY AND DARK SCHEMER HAS ALSO BEEN THE SAVIOR OF THE HEAVENS ON A NUMBER OF OCCASIONS.
A CONTRA-DICTION WITH THE WILL OF IRON.
NOTHING?
I HAVE FOLLOWED A FALSE TRANS-MISSION.
ALL SYSTEMS SWITCH TO RED STANDARD.
THE TITAN IMMEDIATELY REALIZED HIS PERIL.

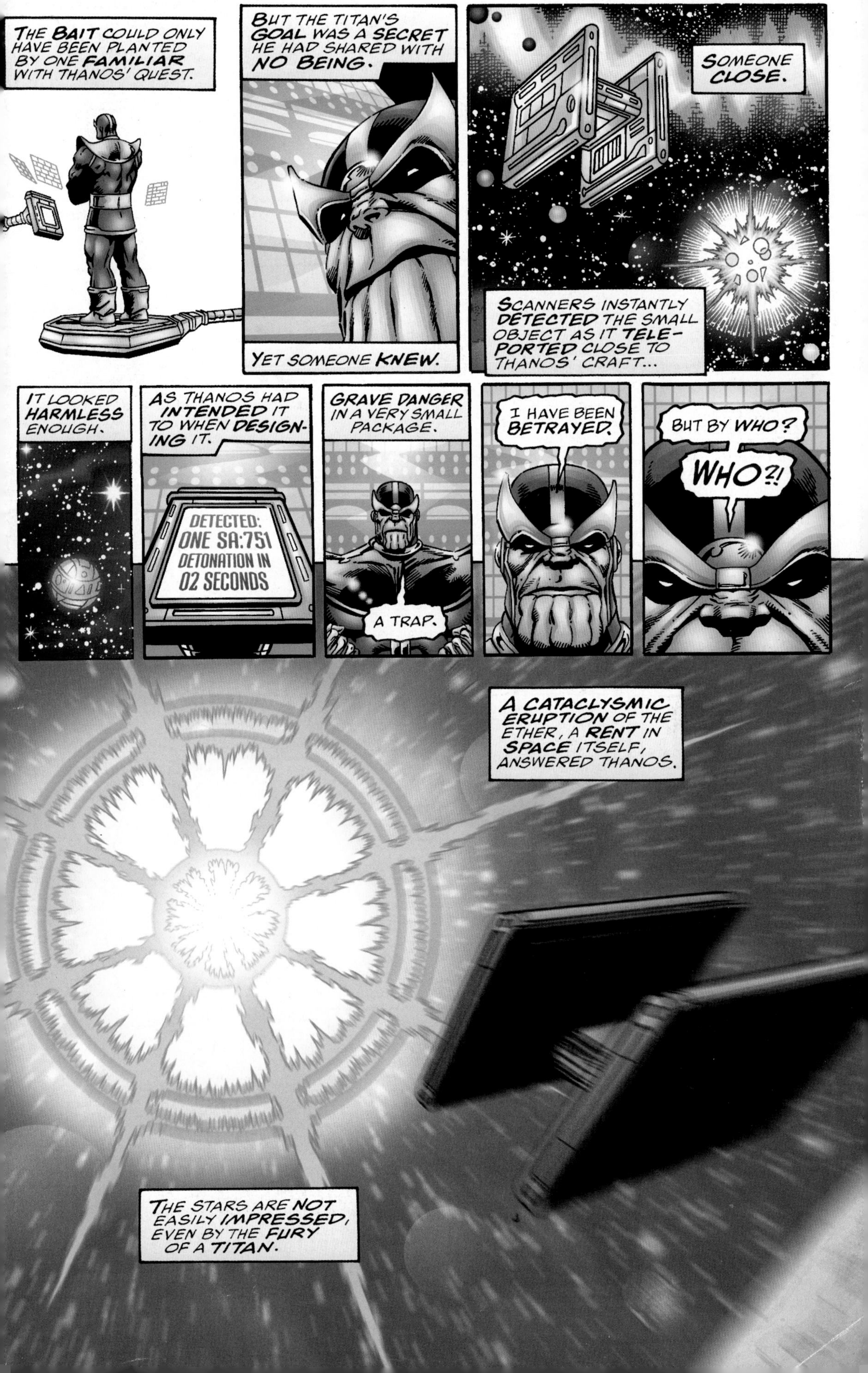
THE BAIT COULD ONLY HAVE BEEN PLANTED BY ONE FAMILIAR WITH THANOS' QUEST.
BUT THE TITAN'S GOAL WAS A SECRET HE HAD SHARED WITH NO BEING.
YET SOMEONE KNEW.
SOMEONE CLOSE.
SCANNERS INSTANTLY DETECTED THE SMALL OBJECT AS IT TELE-PORTED CLOSE TO THANOS' CRAFT...
IT LOOKED HARMLESS ENOUGH.
AS THANOS HAD INTENDED IT TO WHEN DESIGN-ING IT.
DETECTED: ONE SA:751 DETONATION IN 02 SECONDS
GRAVE DANGER IN A VERY SMALL PACKAGE.
A TRAP.
I HAVE BEEN BETRAYED.
BUT BY WHO?
WHO?!
A CATACLYSMIC ERUPTION OF THE ETHER, A RENT IN SPACE ITSELF, ANSWERED THANOS.
THE STARS ARE NOT EASILY IMPRESSED, EVEN BY THE FURY OF A TITAN.

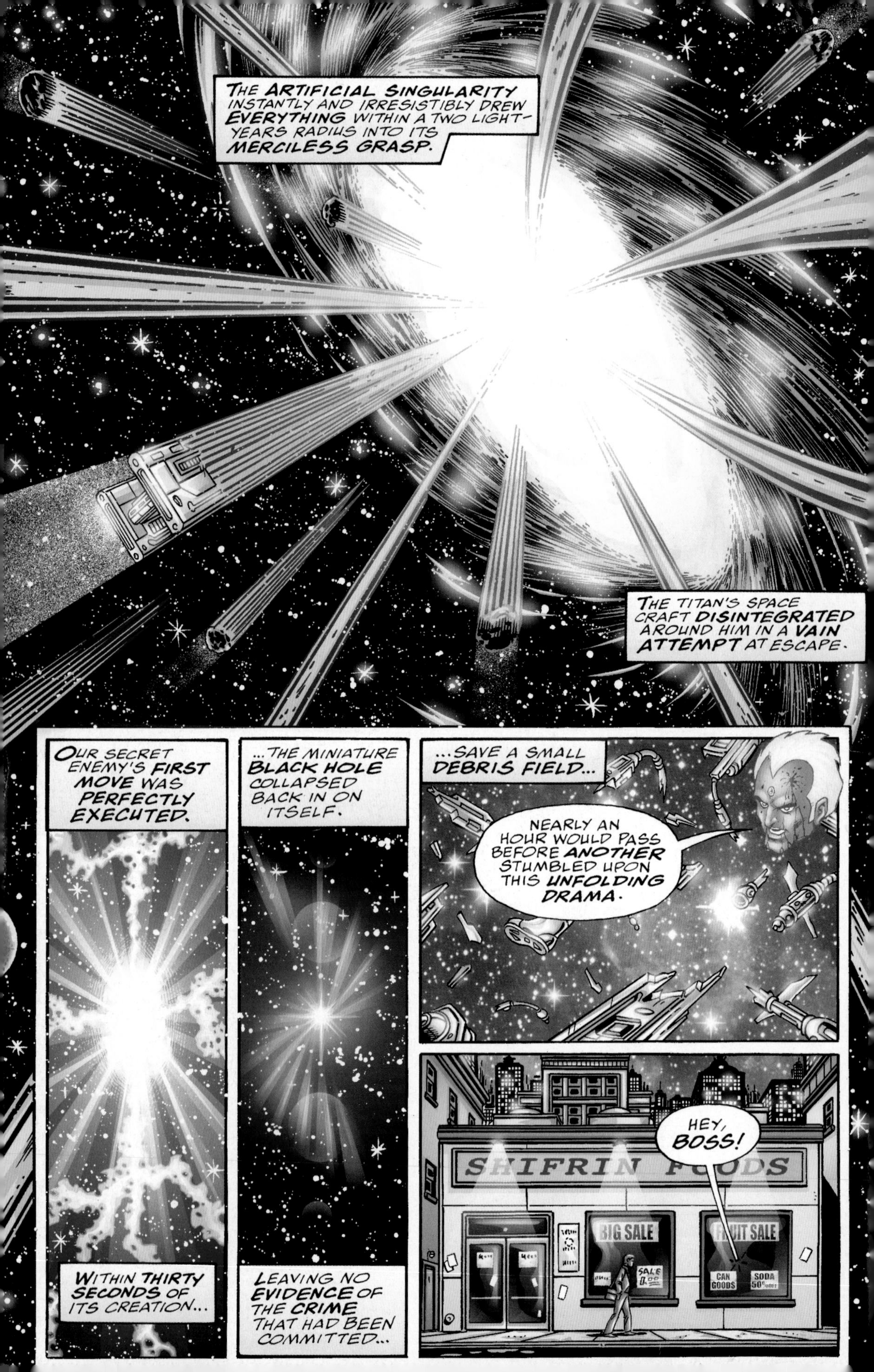
THE ARTIFICIAL SINGULARITY INSTANTLY AND IRRESISTIBLY DREW EVERYTHING WITHIN A TWO LIGHT-YEARS RADIUS INTO ITS MERCILESS GRASP.
THE TITAN'S SPACE CRAFT DISINTEGRATED AROUND HIM IN A VAIN ATTEMPT AT ESCAPE.
OUR SECRET ENEMY'S FIRST MOVE WAS PERFECTLY EXECUTED.
WITHIN THIRTY SECONDS OF ITS CREATION...
...THE MINIATURE BLACK HOLE COLLAPSED BACK IN ON ITSELF.
LEAVING NO EVIDENCE OF THE CRIME THAT HAD BEEN COMMITTED...
...SAVE A SMALL DEBRIS FIELD...
NEARLY AN HOUR WOULD PASS BEFORE ANOTHER STUMBLED UPON THIS UNFOLDING DRAMA.
SHIFRIN FOODS
BIG SALE
FRUIT SALE
CAN GOODS
SODA 50¢ OFF
HEY, BOSS!

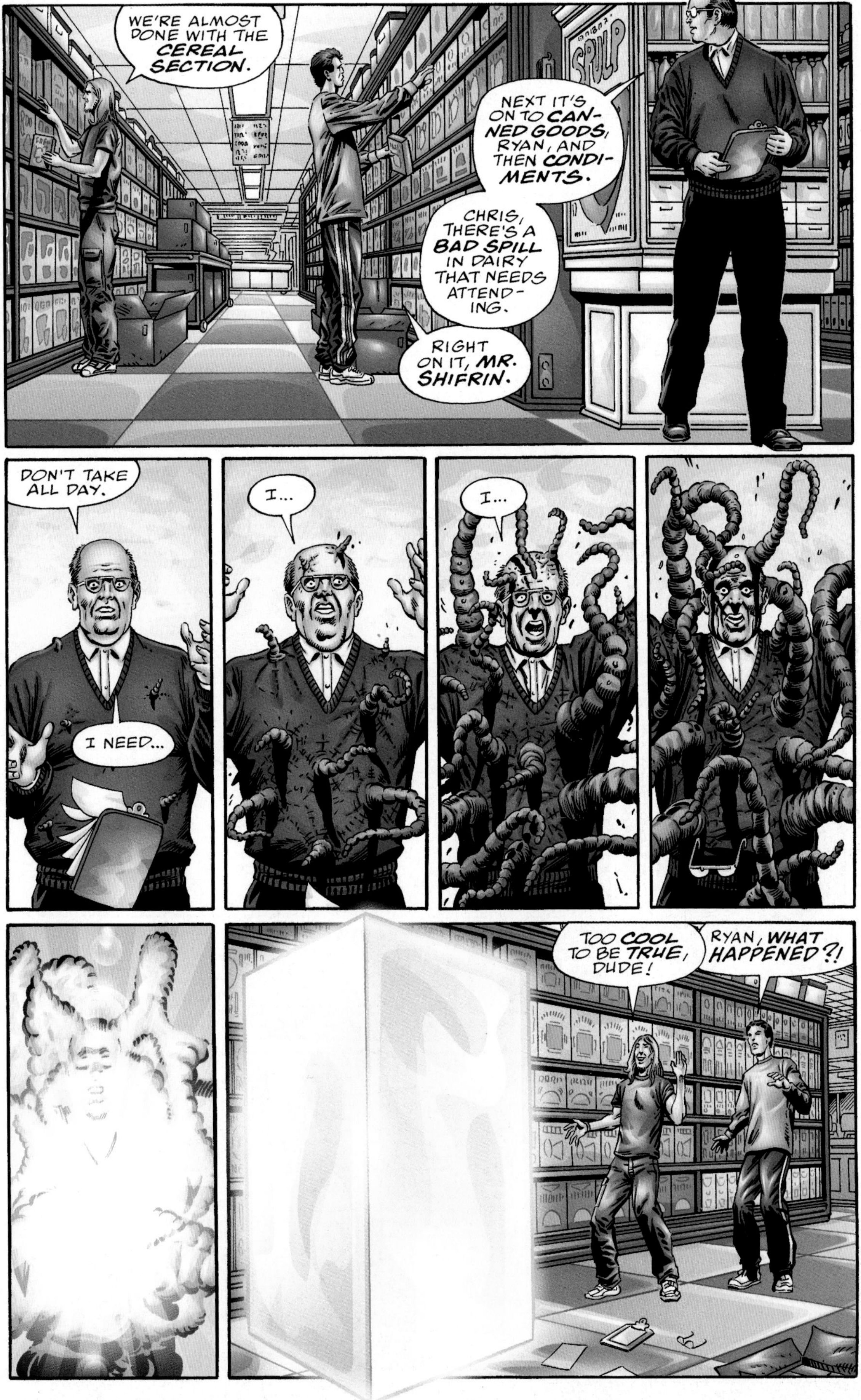
WE'RE ALMOST DONE WITH THE CEREAL SECTION.
NEXT IT'S ON TO CANNED GOODS, RYAN, AND THEN CONDIMENTS.
CHRIS, THERE'S A BAD SPILL IN DAIRY THAT NEEDS ATTENDING.
RIGHT ON IT, MR. SHIFRIN.
SPULP
DON'T TAKE ALL DAY.
I NEED...
I...
I...
TOO COOL TO BE TRUE, DUDE!
RYAN, WHAT HAPPENED?!

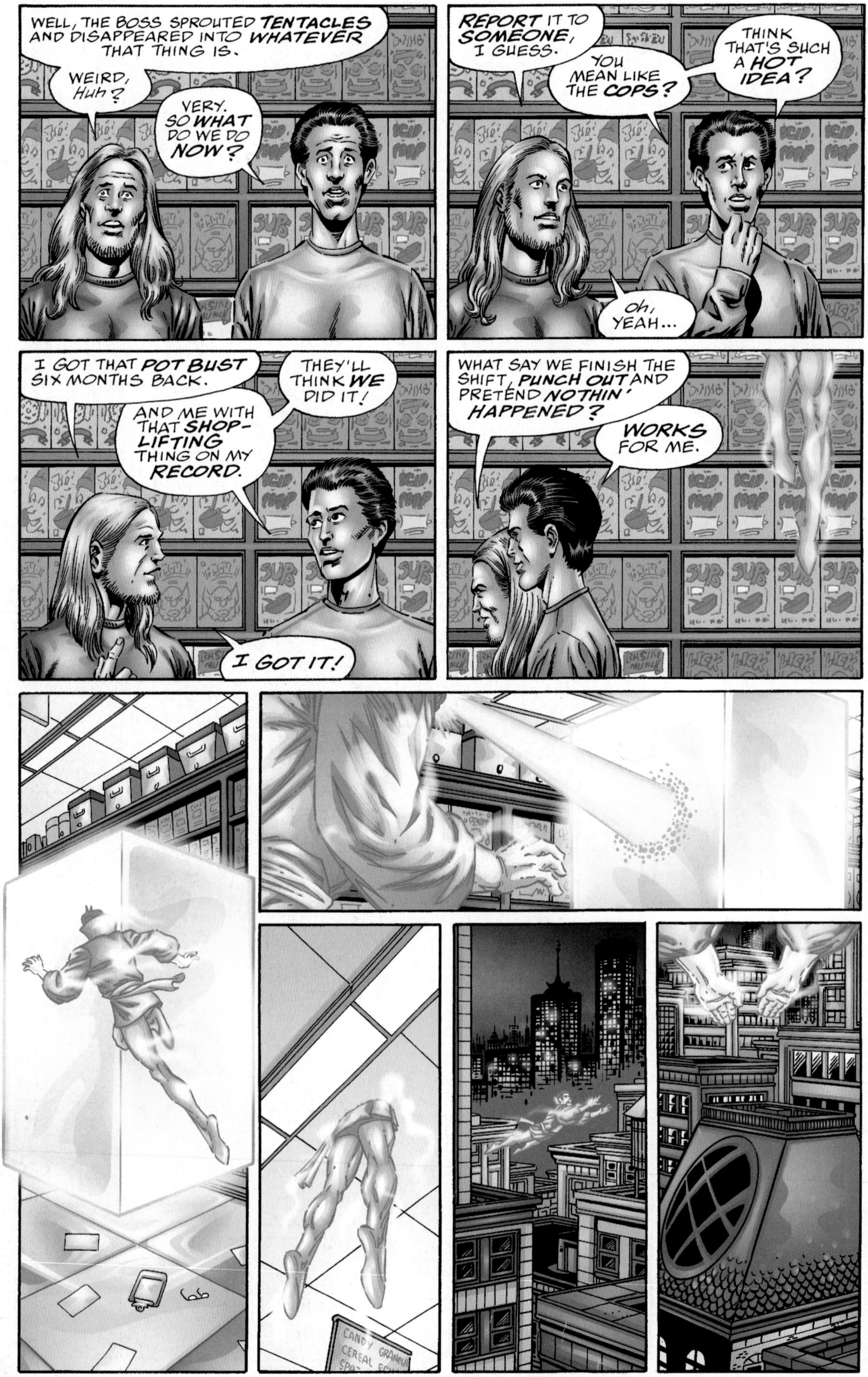
WELL, THE BOSS SPROUTED TENTACLES AND DISAPPEARED INTO WHATEVER THAT THING IS.
WEIRD, Huh?
VERY. SO WHAT DO WE DO NOW?
REPORT IT TO SOMEONE, I GUESS.
YOU MEAN LIKE THE COPS?
THINK THAT'S SUCH A HOT IDEA?
oh, YEAH...
I GOT THAT POT BUST SIX MONTHS BACK.
AND ME WITH THAT SHOP-LIFTING THING ON MY RECORD.
THEY'LL THINK WE DID IT!
I GOT IT!
WHAT SAY WE FINISH THE SHIFT, PUNCH OUT AND PRETEND NOTHIN' HAPPENED?
WORKS FOR ME.

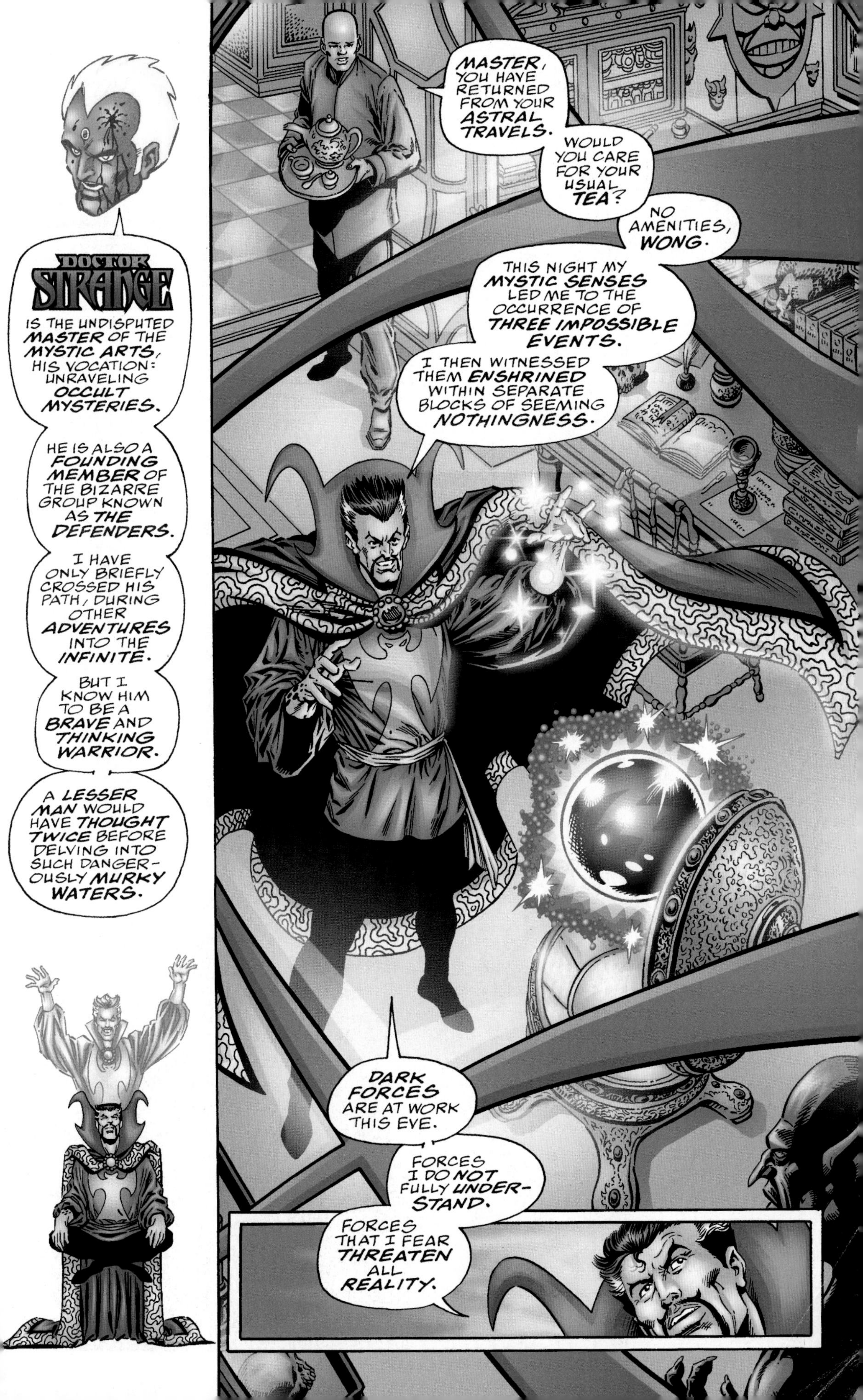
DOCTOR STRANGE
IS THE UNDISPUTED MASTER OF THE MYSTIC ARTS, HIS VOCATION: UNRAVELING OCCULT MYSTERIES.
HE IS ALSO A FOUNDING MEMBER OF THE BIZARRE GROUP KNOWN AS THE DEFENDERS.
I HAVE ONLY BRIEFLY CROSSED HIS PATH, DURING OTHER ADVENTURES INTO THE INFINITE.
BUT I KNOW HIM TO BE A BRAVE AND THINKING WARRIOR.
A LESSER MAN WOULD HAVE THOUGHT TWICE BEFORE DELVING INTO SUCH DANGER-OUSLY MURKY WATERS.
MASTER, YOU HAVE RETURNED FROM YOUR ASTRAL TRAVELS.
WOULD YOU CARE FOR YOUR USUAL TEA?
NO AMENITIES, WONG.
THIS NIGHT MY MYSTIC SENSES LED ME TO THE OCCURRENCE OF THREE IMPOSSIBLE EVENTS.
I THEN WITNESSED THEM ENSHRINED WITHIN SEPARATE BLOCKS OF SEEMING NOTHINGNESS.
DARK FORCES ARE AT WORK THIS EVE.
FORCES I DO NOT FULLY UNDER-STAND.
FORCES THAT I FEAR THREATEN ALL REALITY.

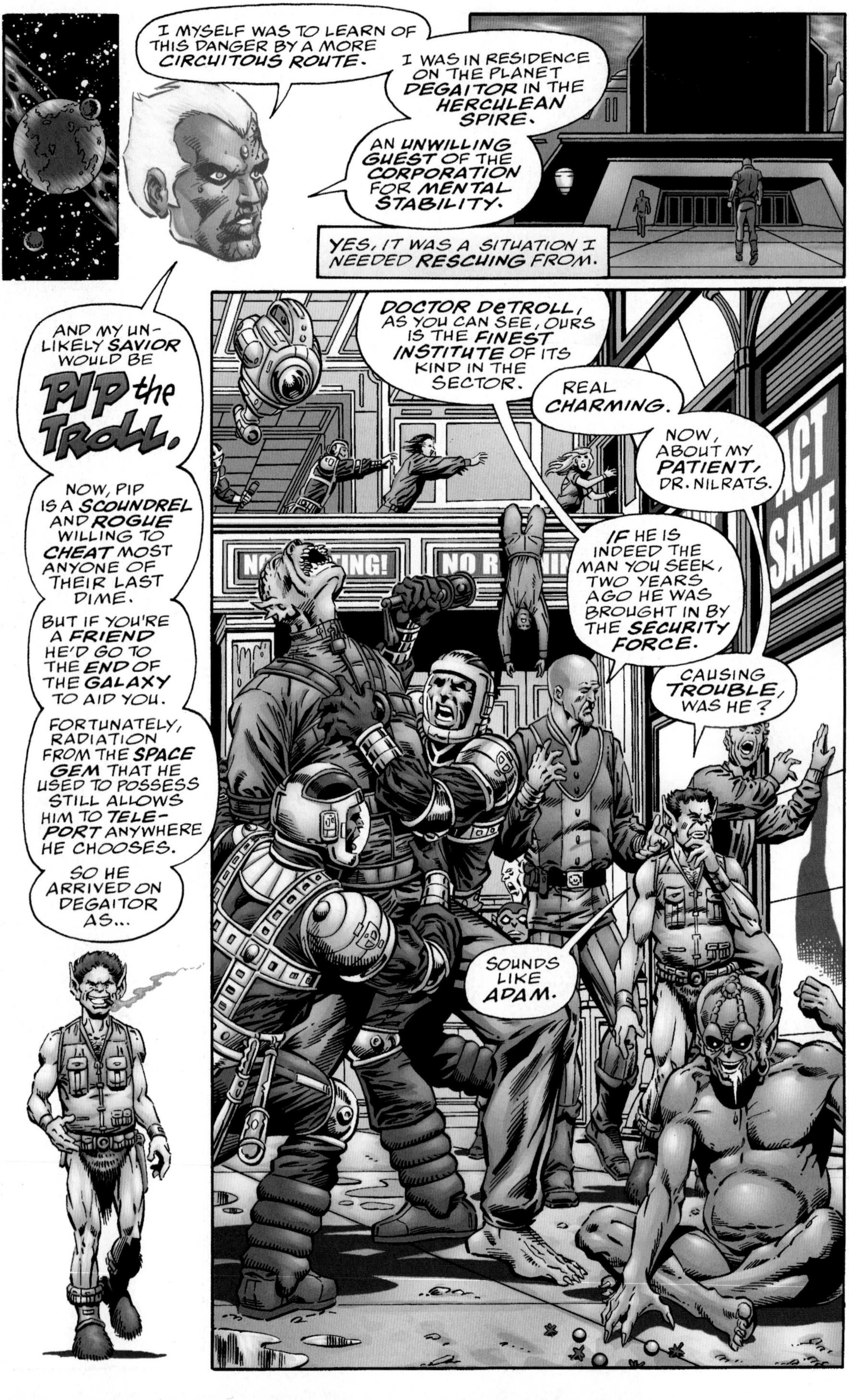
I MYSELF WAS TO LEARN OF THIS DANGER BY A MORE CIRCUITOUS ROUTE.
I WAS IN RESIDENCE ON THE PLANET DEGAITOR IN THE HERCULEAN SPIRE.
AN UNWILLING GUEST OF THE CORPORATION FOR MENTAL STABILITY.
YES, IT WAS A SITUATION I NEEDED RESCUING FROM.
AND MY UNLIKELY SAVIOR WOULD BE PIP the TROLL.
NOW, PIP IS A SCOUNDREL AND ROGUE WILLING TO CHEAT MOST ANYONE OF THEIR LAST DIME.
BUT IF YOU'RE A FRIEND HE'D GO TO THE END OF THE GALAXY TO AID YOU.
FORTUNATELY, RADIATION FROM THE SPACE GEM THAT HE USED TO POSSESS STILL ALLOWS HIM TO TELEPORT ANYWHERE HE CHOOSES.
SO HE ARRIVED ON DEGAITOR AS...
DOCTOR DETROLL, AS YOU CAN SEE, OURS IS THE FINEST INSTITUTE OF ITS KIND IN THE SECTOR.
REAL CHARMING.
NOW, ABOUT MY PATIENT, DR. NILRATS.
IF HE IS INDEED THE MAN YOU SEEK, TWO YEARS AGO HE WAS BROUGHT IN BY THE SECURITY FORCE.
CAUSING TROUBLE, WAS HE?
SOUNDS LIKE ADAM.

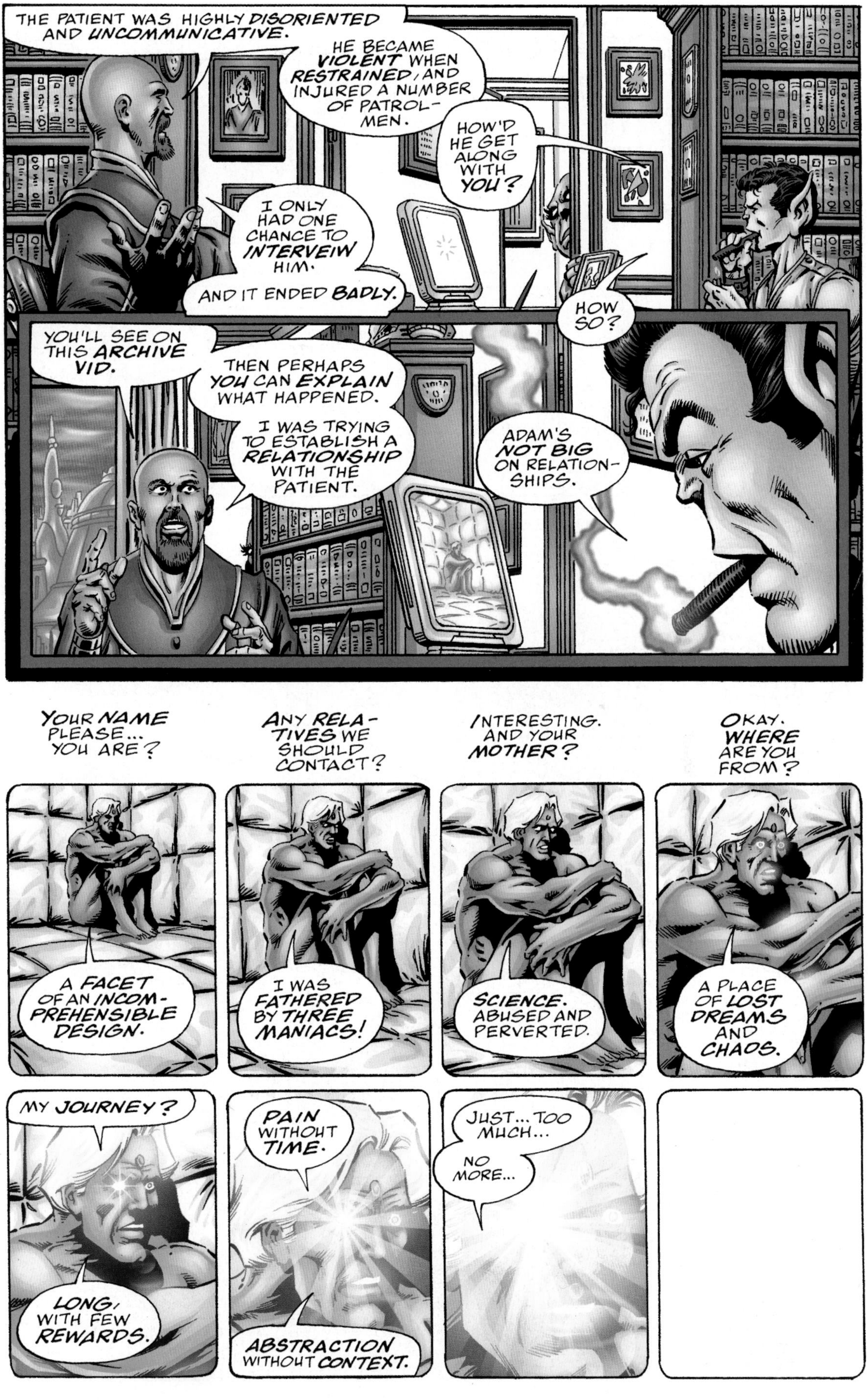
THE PATIENT WAS HIGHLY DISORIENTED AND UNCOMMUNICATIVE.
HE BECAME VIOLENT WHEN RESTRAINED, AND INJURED A NUMBER OF PATROLMEN.
HOW'D HE GET ALONG WITH YOU?
I ONLY HAD ONE CHANCE TO INTERVEIW HIM.
AND IT ENDED BADLY.
HOW SO?
YOU'LL SEE ON THIS ARCHIVE VID.
THEN PERHAPS YOU CAN EXPLAIN WHAT HAPPENED.
I WAS TRYING TO ESTABLISH A RELATIONSHIP WITH THE PATIENT.
ADAM'S NOT BIG ON RELATIONSHIPS.
YOUR NAME PLEASE... YOU ARE?
A FACET OF AN INCOMPREHENSIBLE DESIGN.
ANY RELATIVES WE SHOULD CONTACT?
I WAS FATHERED BY THREE MANIACS!
INTERESTING. AND YOUR MOTHER?
SCIENCE. ABUSED AND PERVERTED.
OKAY. WHERE ARE YOU FROM?
A PLACE OF LOST DREAMS AND CHAOS.
MY JOURNEY?
LONG, WITH FEW REWARDS.
PAIN WITHOUT TIME.
ABSTRACTION WITHOUT CONTEXT.
JUST... TOO MUCH...
NO MORE...

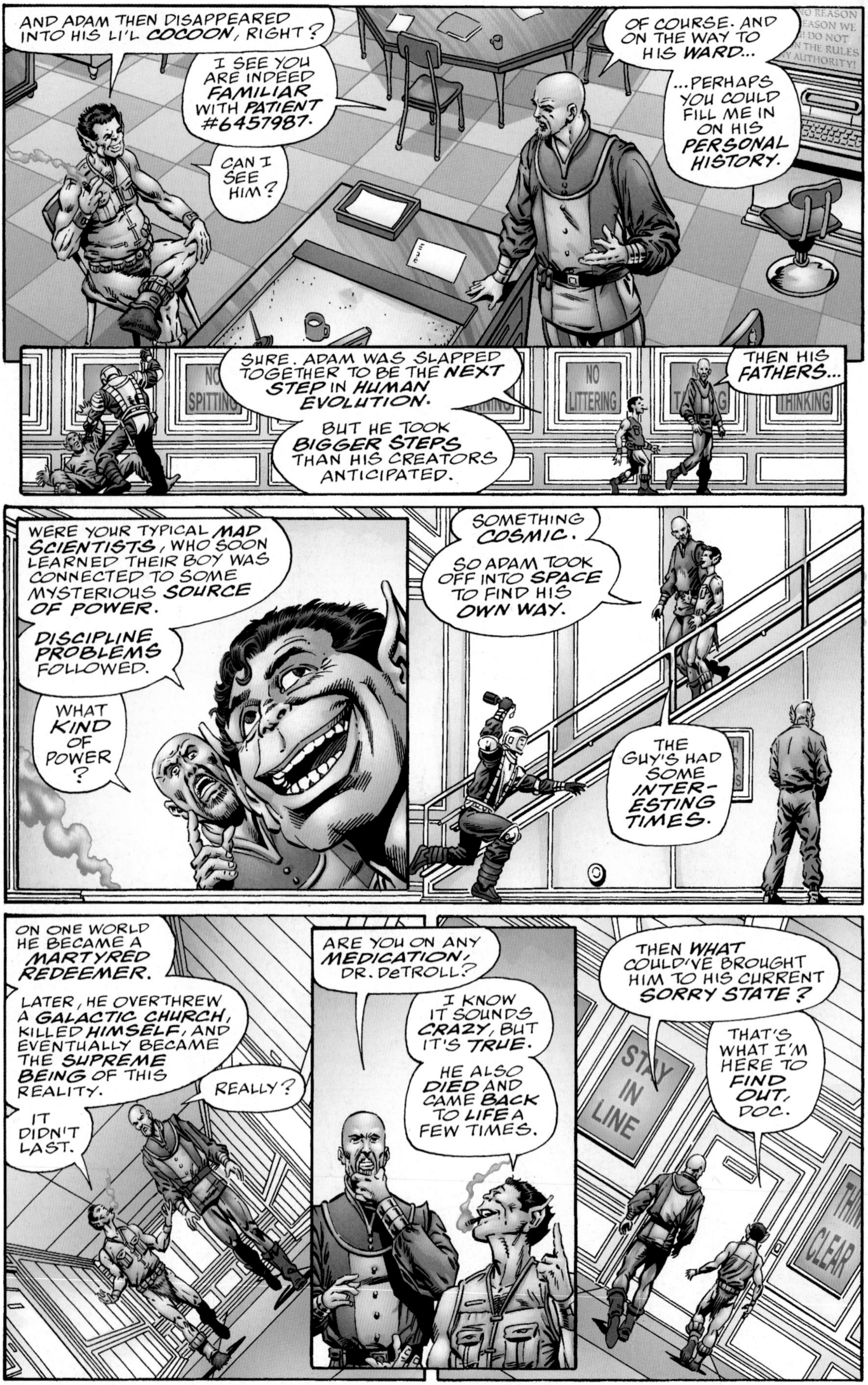

AND ADAM THEN DISAPPEARED INTO HIS LI'L COCOON, RIGHT?
I SEE YOU ARE INDEED FAMILIAR WITH PATIENT #6457987.
CAN I SEE HIM?
OF COURSE. AND ON THE WAY TO HIS WARD...
...PERHAPS YOU COULD FILL ME IN ON HIS PERSONAL HISTORY.
SURE. ADAM WAS SLAPPED TOGETHER TO BE THE NEXT STEP IN HUMAN EVOLUTION.
BUT HE TOOK BIGGER STEPS THAN HIS CREATORS ANTICIPATED.
NO LITTERING
THINKING
THEN HIS FATHERS...
WERE YOUR TYPICAL MAD SCIENTISTS, WHO SOON LEARNED THEIR BOY WAS CONNECTED TO SOME MYSTERIOUS SOURCE OF POWER.
DISCIPLINE PROBLEMS FOLLOWED.
WHAT KIND OF POWER?
SOMETHING COSMIC.
SO ADAM TOOK OFF INTO SPACE TO FIND HIS OWN WAY.
THE GUY'S HAD SOME INTERESTING TIMES.
ON ONE WORLD HE BECAME A MARTYRED REDEEMER.
LATER, HE OVERTHREW A GALACTIC CHURCH, KILLED HIMSELF, AND EVENTUALLY BECAME THE SUPREME BEING OF THIS REALITY.
REALLY?
IT DIDN'T LAST.
ARE YOU ON ANY MEDICATION, DR. DeTROLL?
I KNOW IT SOUNDS CRAZY, BUT IT'S TRUE.
HE ALSO DIED AND CAME BACK TO LIFE A FEW TIMES.
THEN WHAT COULD'VE BROUGHT HIM TO HIS CURRENT SORRY STATE?
THAT'S WHAT I'M HERE TO FIND OUT, DOC.
STAY IN LINE
CLEAR

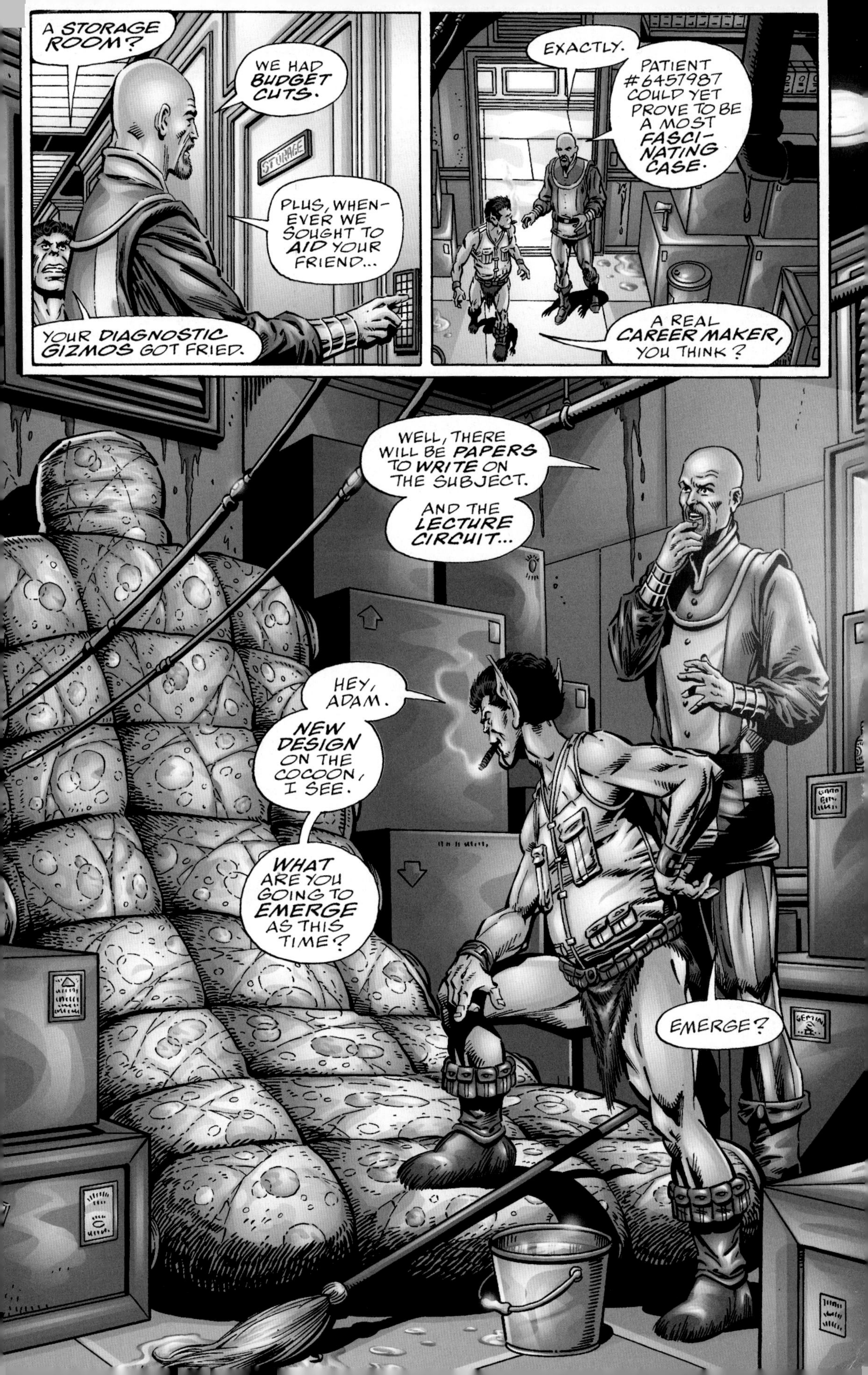
A STORAGE ROOM?
WE HAD BUDGET CUTS.
STORAGE
PLUS, WHENEVER WE SOUGHT TO AID YOUR FRIEND...
YOUR DIAGNOSTIC GIZMOS GOT FRIED.
EXACTLY.
PATIENT #6457987 COULD YET PROVE TO BE A MOST FASCINATING CASE.
A REAL CAREER MAKER, YOU THINK?
WELL, THERE WILL BE PAPERS TO WRITE ON THE SUBJECT.
AND THE LECTURE CIRCUIT...
HEY, ADAM.
NEW DESIGN ON THE COCOON, I SEE.
WHAT ARE YOU GOING TO EMERGE AS THIS TIME?
EMERGE?

HE'S GOING TO COME **OUT** OF THAT **THING**?

ALWAYS HAS BEFORE.

THEN WE MUST **HURRY!**

WE SHOULD RETURN HIM TO **GENERAL POPULATION** AND CALL A **NEWS CONFERENCE.**

SURE.

DO THAT.

THIS IS MY **TICKET** OUT OF-- **WHAT ?!?**

WHERE'D THEY GO?

MY PATIENT!

MY CAREER!

WHERE DID **WE** AND **DR. NILRATS'** DREAMS GO?

LIGHT YEARS AWAY, TO A **SPACE CRAFT** WAY BEYOND PIP'S MEANS.

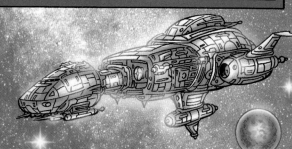

THE **PACKAGE** IS DELIVERED AND ON THE **EXAMINING TABLE.**

WERE THERE ANY DIFFI-CULTIES?

NOTHING I COULDN'T HANDLE.

THE **DOC** TRIED TO GET **TOUGH** WITH ME.

THEN THERE WERE THOSE **SIX SECURITY GUARDS.**

NO, MAKE THAT **EIGHT.**

THEY NEVER KNEW WHAT **HIT** THEM!

YOU SHOULD HAVE **SEEN** ME!

I WAS--

HEY!!

THAT **STOGIE** COST ME **GOOD MONEY!**

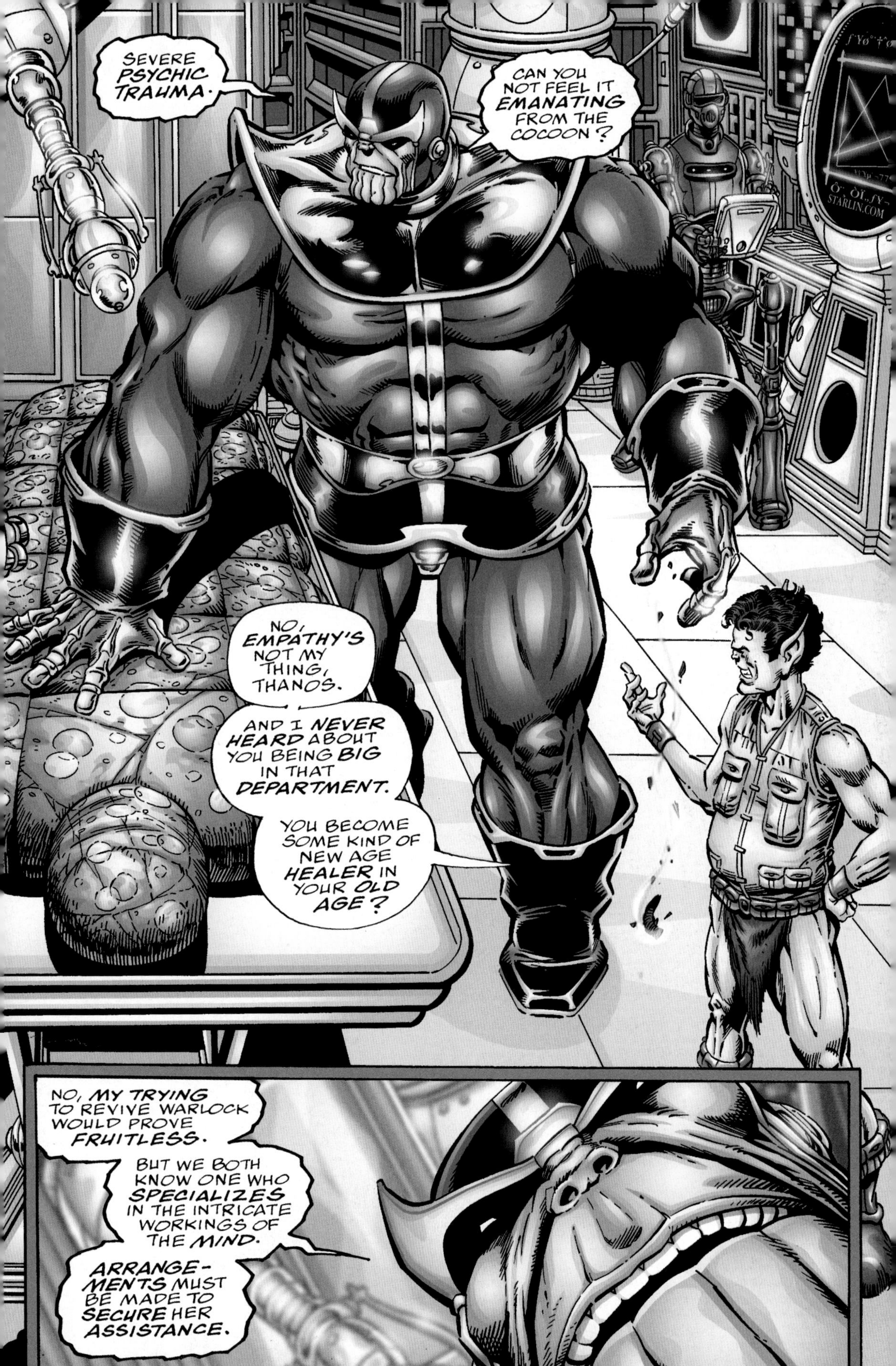
SEVERE PSYCHIC TRAUMA.
CAN YOU NOT FEEL IT EMANATING FROM THE COCOON?
STARLIN.COM
NO, EMPATHY'S NOT MY THING, THANOS.
AND I NEVER HEARD ABOUT YOU BEING BIG IN THAT DEPARTMENT.
YOU BECOME SOME KIND OF NEW AGE HEALER IN YOUR OLD AGE?
NO, MY TRYING TO REVIVE WARLOCK WOULD PROVE FRUITLESS.
BUT WE BOTH KNOW ONE WHO SPECIALIZES IN THE INTRICATE WORKINGS OF THE MIND.
ARRANGE-MENTS MUST BE MADE TO SECURE HER ASSISTANCE.

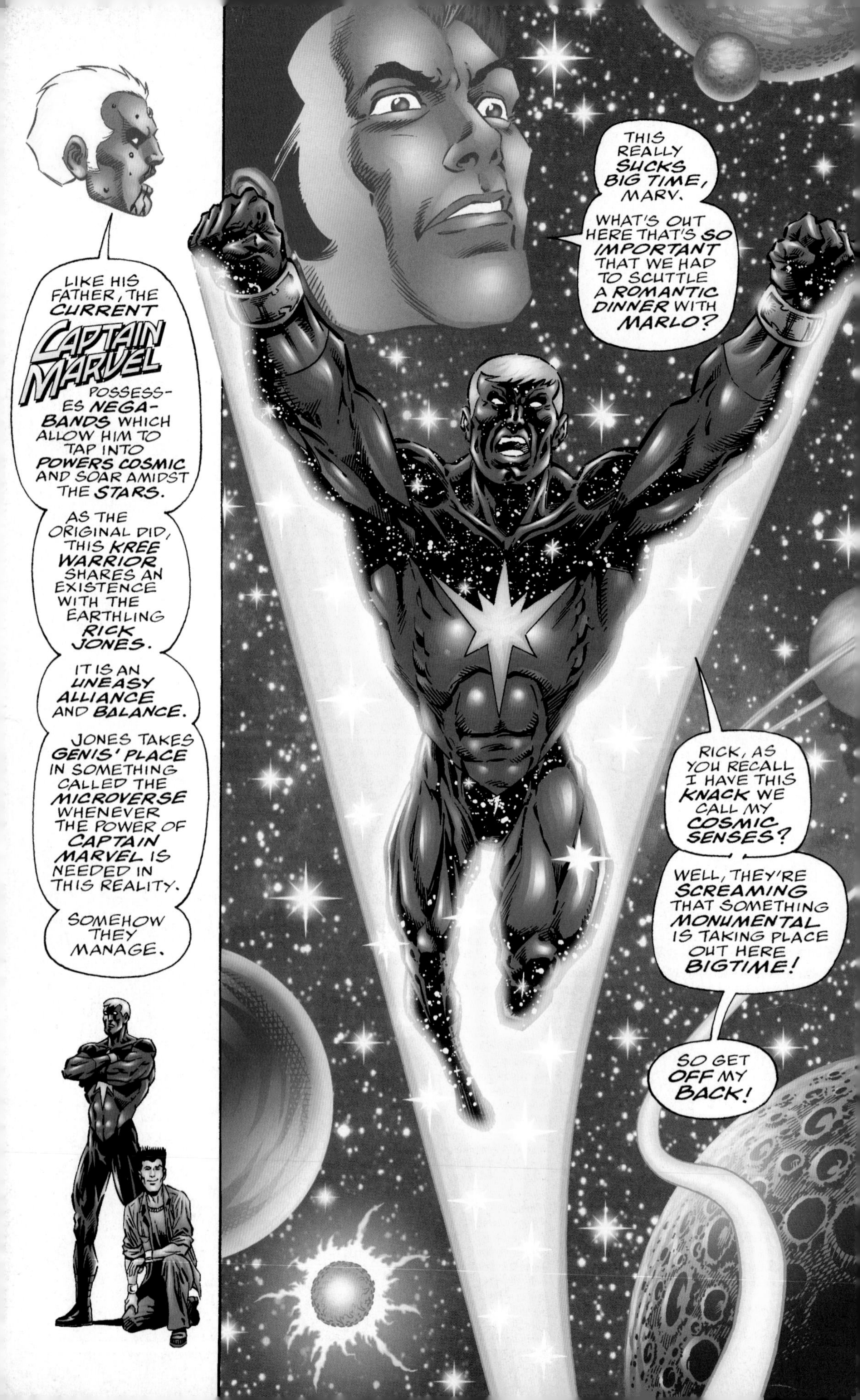
LIKE HIS FATHER, THE CURRENT CAPTAIN MARVEL POSSESS-ES NEGA-BANDS WHICH ALLOW HIM TO TAP INTO POWERS COSMIC AND SOAR AMIDST THE STARS.
AS THE ORIGINAL DID, THIS KREE WARRIOR SHARES AN EXISTENCE WITH THE EARTHLING RICK JONES.
IT IS AN UNEASY ALLIANCE AND BALANCE.
JONES TAKES GENIS' PLACE IN SOMETHING CALLED THE MICROVERSE WHENEVER THE POWER OF CAPTAIN MARVEL IS NEEDED IN THIS REALITY.
SOMEHOW THEY MANAGE.
THIS REALLY SUCKS BIG TIME, MARV.
WHAT'S OUT HERE THAT'S SO IMPORTANT THAT WE HAD TO SCUTTLE A ROMANTIC DINNER WITH MARLO?
RICK, AS YOU RECALL I HAVE THIS KNACK WE CALL MY COSMIC SENSES?
WELL, THEY'RE SCREAMING THAT SOMETHING MONUMENTAL IS TAKING PLACE OUT HERE BIGTIME!
SO GET OFF MY BACK!

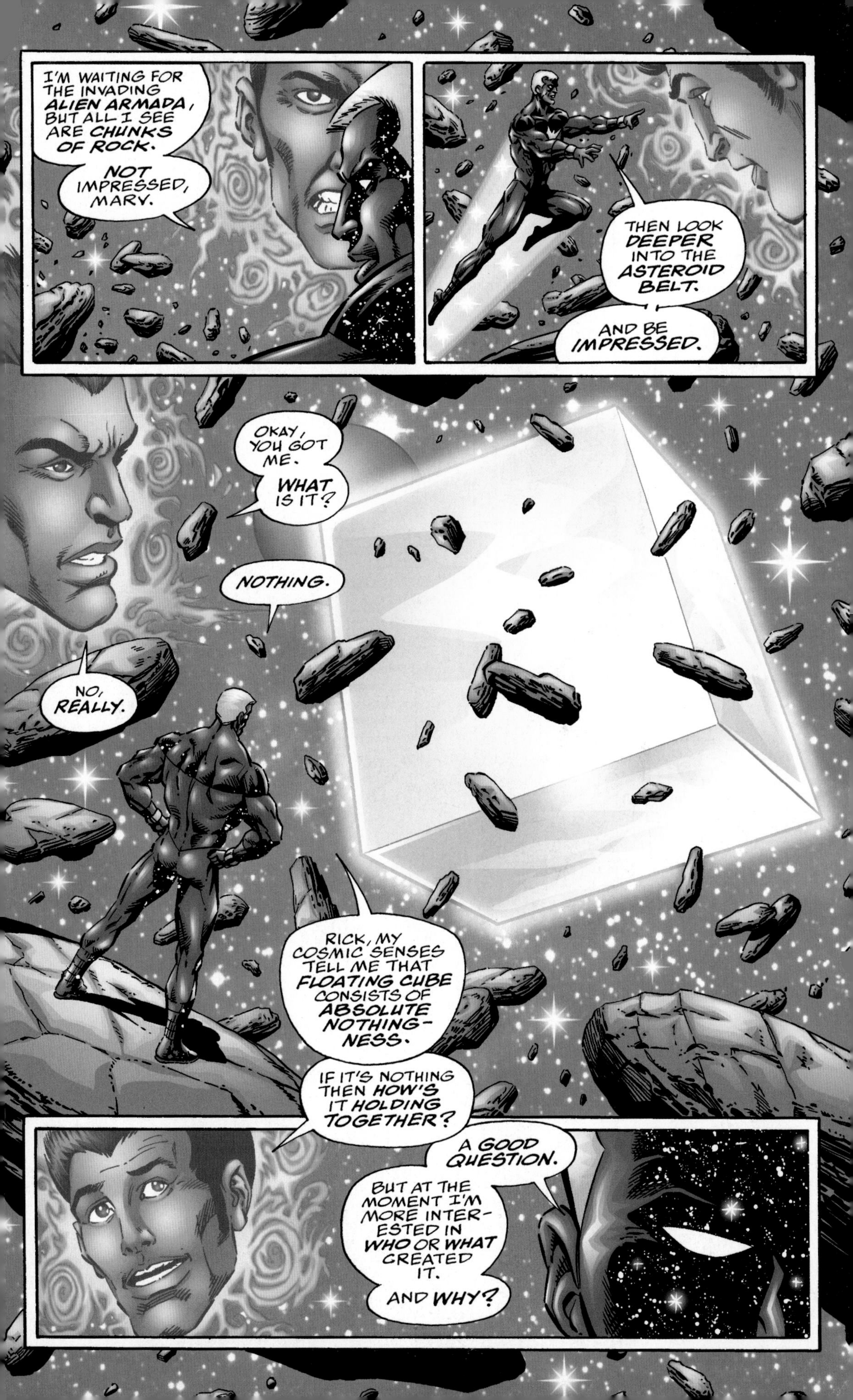
I'M WAITING FOR THE INVADING ALIEN ARMADA, BUT ALL I SEE ARE CHUNKS OF ROCK.
NOT IMPRESSED, MARV.
THEN LOOK DEEPER INTO THE ASTEROID BELT.
AND BE IMPRESSED.
OKAY, YOU GOT ME.
WHAT IS IT?
NOTHING.
NO, REALLY.
RICK, MY COSMIC SENSES TELL ME THAT FLOATING CUBE CONSISTS OF ABSOLUTE NOTHING-NESS.
IF IT'S NOTHING THEN HOW'S IT HOLDING TOGETHER?
A GOOD QUESTION.
BUT AT THE MOMENT I'M MORE INTER-ESTED IN WHO OR WHAT CREATED IT.
AND WHY?

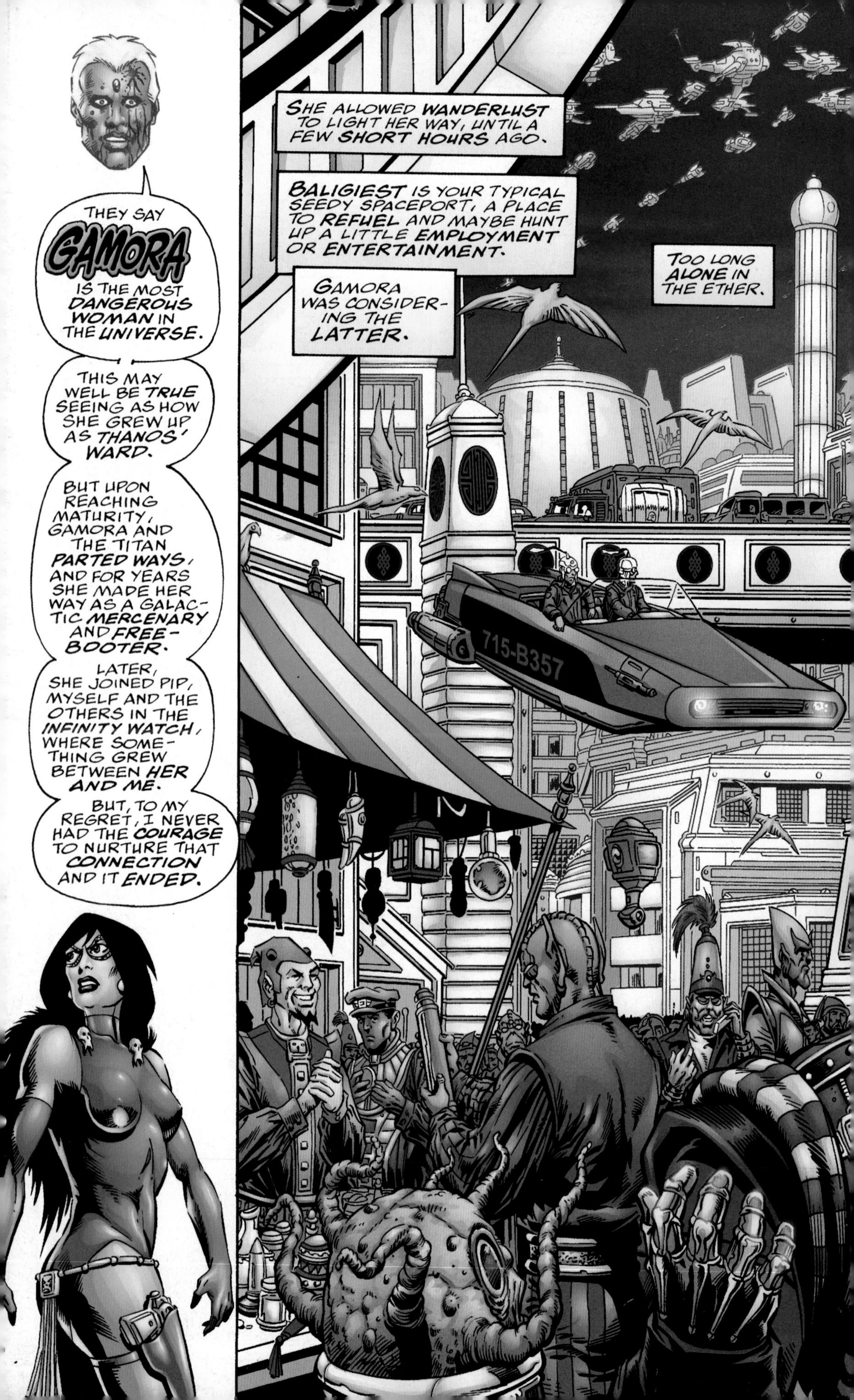

THEY SAY GAMORA IS THE MOST DANGEROUS WOMAN IN THE UNIVERSE.
THIS MAY WELL BE TRUE SEEING AS HOW SHE GREW UP AS THANOS' WARD.
BUT UPON REACHING MATURITY, GAMORA AND THE TITAN PARTED WAYS, AND FOR YEARS SHE MADE HER WAY AS A GALACTIC MERCENARY AND FREE-BOOTER.
LATER, SHE JOINED PIP, MYSELF AND THE OTHERS IN THE INFINITY WATCH, WHERE SOMETHING GREW BETWEEN HER AND ME.
BUT, TO MY REGRET, I NEVER HAD THE COURAGE TO NURTURE THAT CONNECTION AND IT ENDED.
SHE ALLOWED WANDERLUST TO LIGHT HER WAY, UNTIL A FEW SHORT HOURS AGO.
BALIGIEST IS YOUR TYPICAL SEEDY SPACEPORT, A PLACE TO REFUEL AND MAYBE HUNT UP A LITTLE EMPLOYMENT OR ENTERTAINMENT.
GAMORA WAS CONSIDERING THE LATTER.
TOO LONG ALONE IN THE ETHER.
715-B357

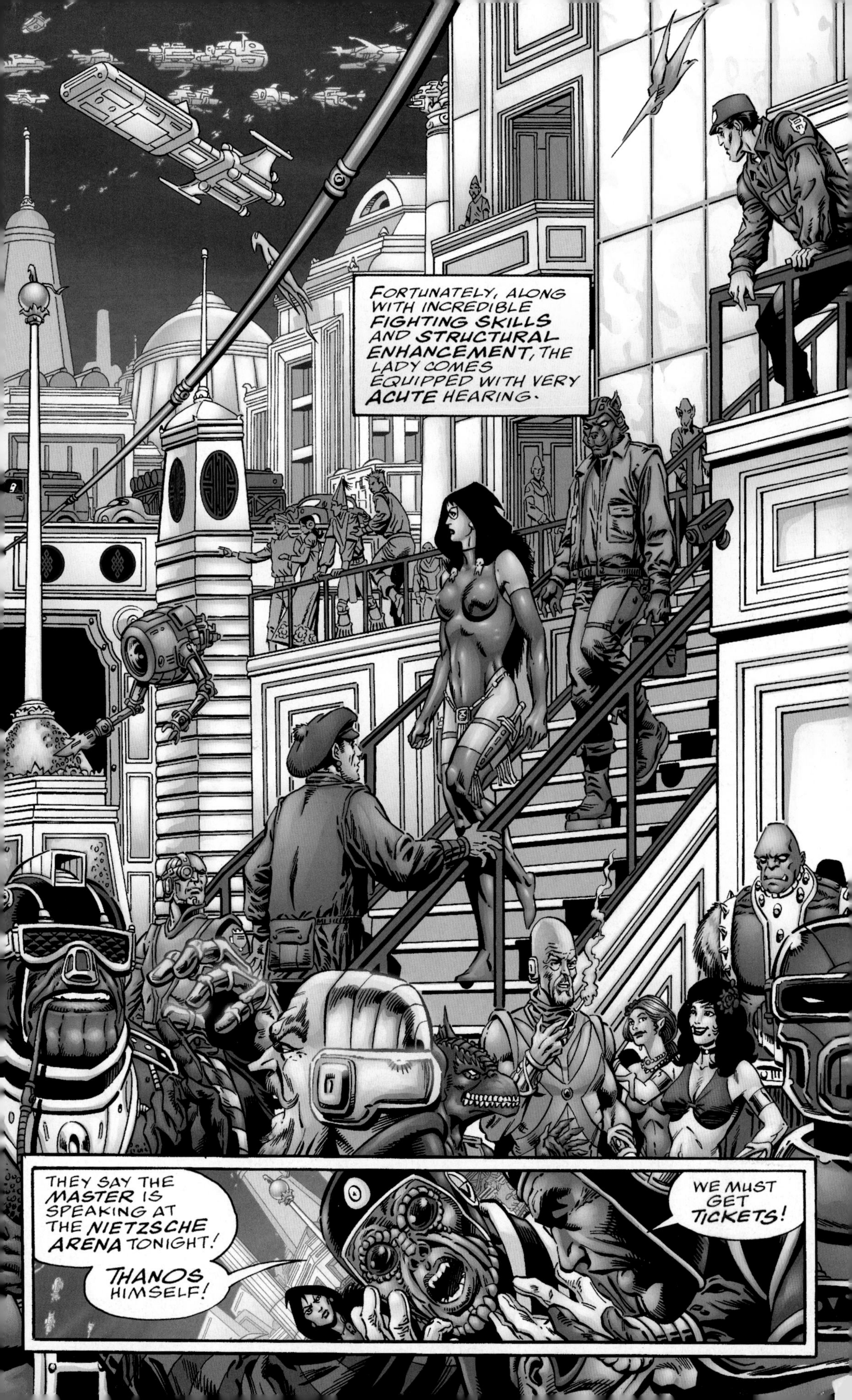
FORTUNATELY, ALONG WITH INCREDIBLE FIGHTING SKILLS AND STRUCTURAL ENHANCEMENT, THE LADY COMES EQUIPPED WITH VERY ACUTE HEARING.
THEY SAY THE MASTER IS SPEAKING AT THE NIETZSCHE ARENA TONIGHT!
THANOS HIMSELF!
WE MUST GET TICKETS!

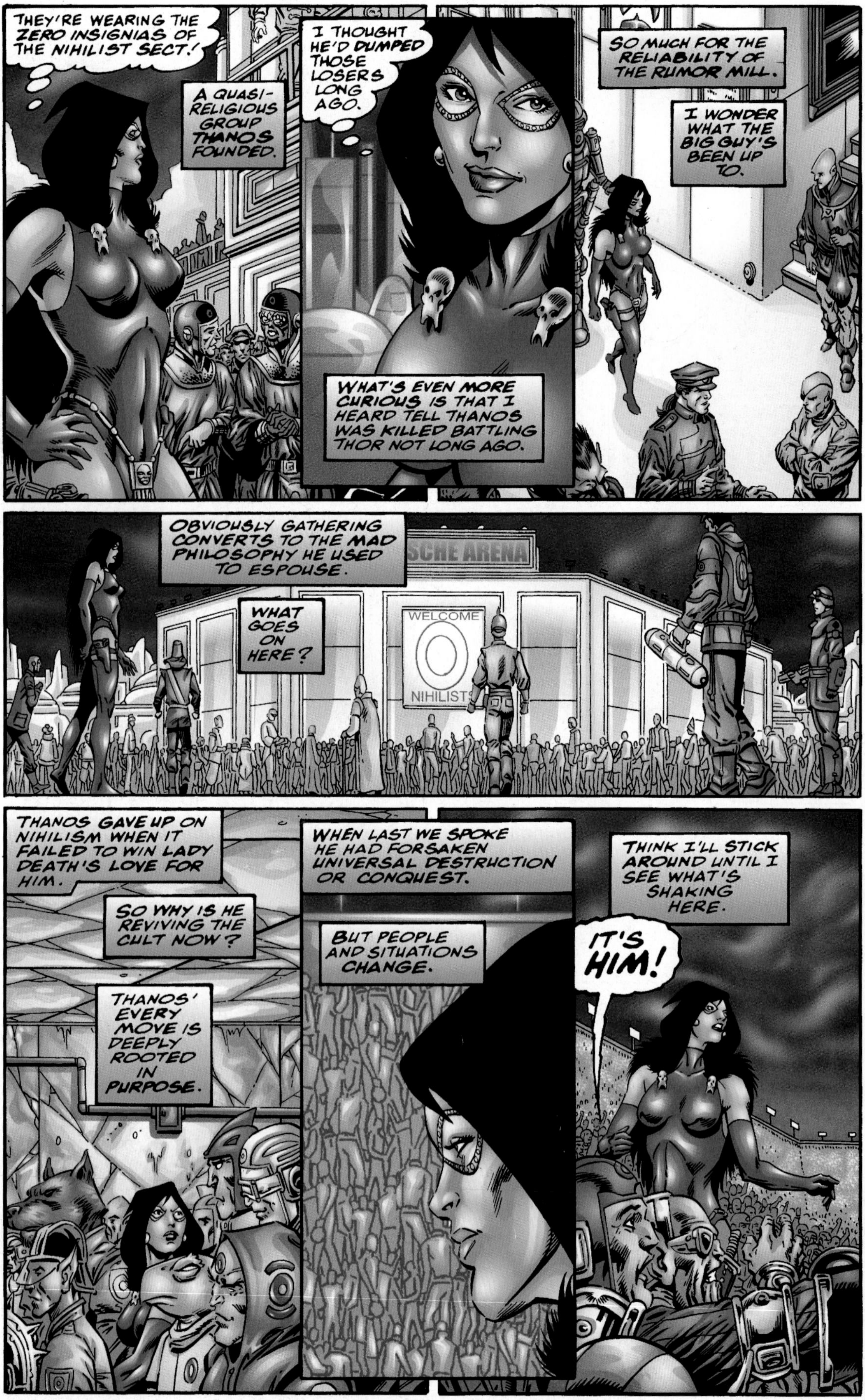
THEY'RE WEARING THE ZERO INSIGNIAS OF THE NIHILIST SECT!
A QUASI-RELIGIOUS GROUP THANOS FOUNDED.
I THOUGHT HE'D DUMPED THOSE LOSERS LONG AGO.
WHAT'S EVEN MORE CURIOUS IS THAT I HEARD TELL THANOS WAS KILLED BATTLING THOR NOT LONG AGO.
SO MUCH FOR THE RELIABILITY OF THE RUMOR MILL.
I WONDER WHAT THE BIG GUY'S BEEN UP TO.
OBVIOUSLY GATHERING CONVERTS TO THE MAD PHILOSOPHY HE USED TO ESPOUSE.
SCHE ARENA
WHAT GOES ON HERE?
WELCOME
NIHILISTS
THANOS GAVE UP ON NIHILISM WHEN IT FAILED TO WIN LADY DEATH'S LOVE FOR HIM.
SO WHY IS HE REVIVING THE CULT NOW?
THANOS' EVERY MOVE IS DEEPLY ROOTED IN PURPOSE.
WHEN LAST WE SPOKE HE HAD FORSAKEN UNIVERSAL DESTRUCTION OR CONQUEST.
BUT PEOPLE AND SITUATIONS CHANGE.
THINK I'LL STICK AROUND UNTIL I SEE WHAT'S SHAKING HERE.
IT'S HIM!

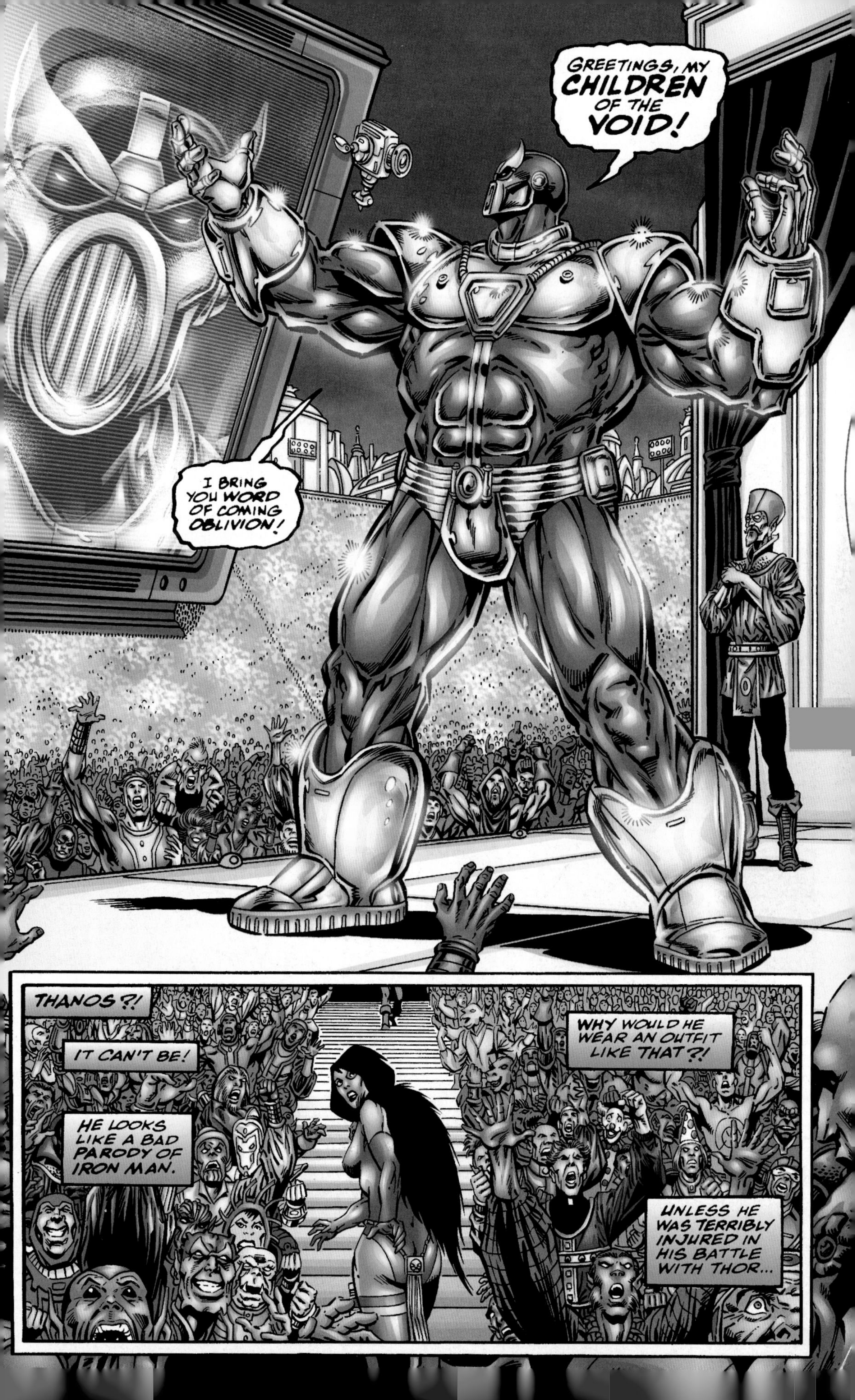

GREETINGS, MY CHILDREN OF THE VOID!
I BRING YOU WORD OF COMING OBLIVION!
THANOS ?!
IT CAN'T BE!
HE LOOKS LIKE A BAD PARODY OF IRON MAN.
WHY WOULD HE WEAR AN OUTFIT LIKE THAT ?!
UNLESS HE WAS TERRIBLY INJURED IN HIS BATTLE WITH THOR...

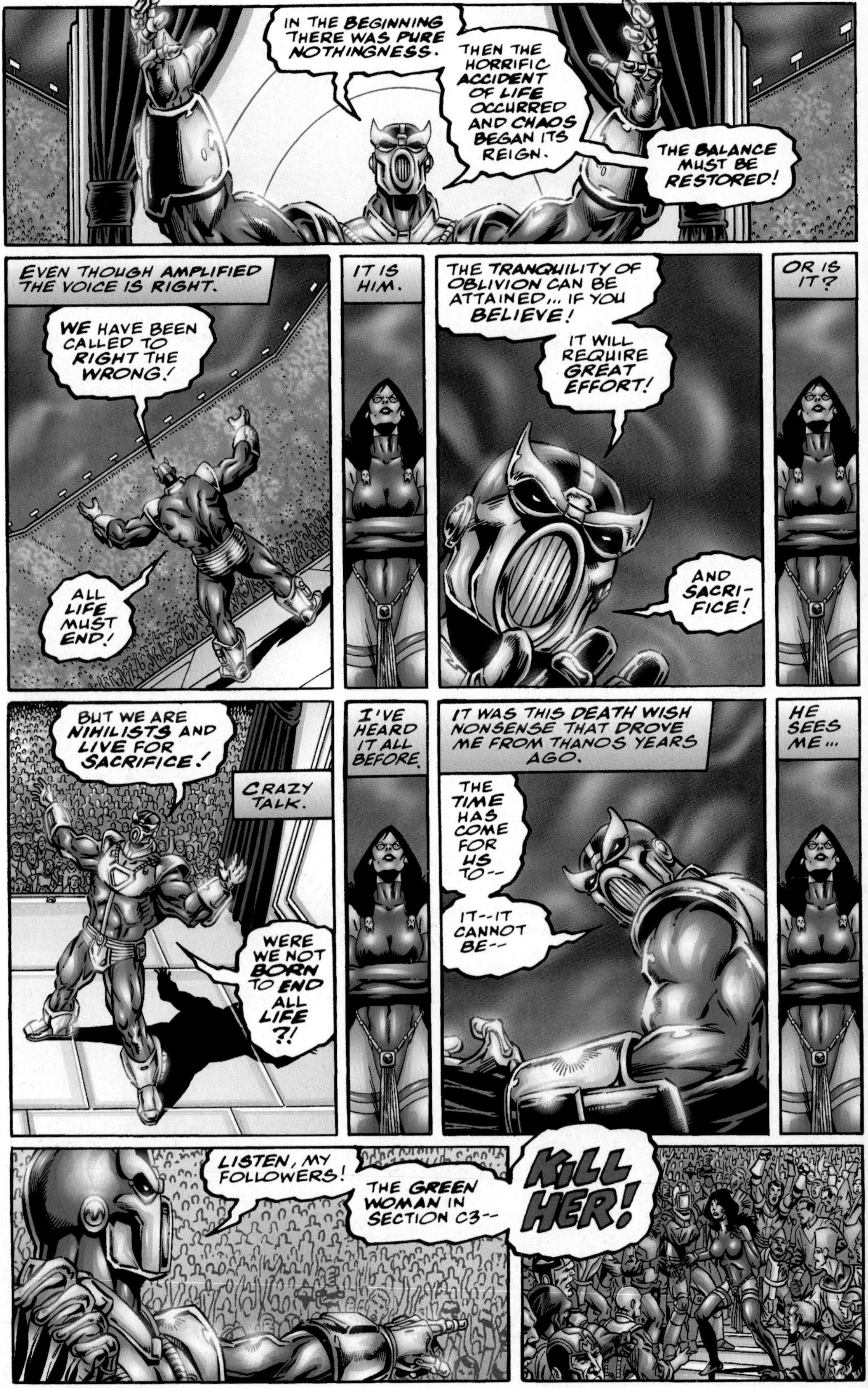
IN THE BEGINNING THERE WAS PURE NOTHINGNESS.
THEN THE HORRIFIC ACCIDENT OF LIFE OCCURRED AND CHAOS BEGAN ITS REIGN.
THE BALANCE MUST BE RESTORED!
EVEN THOUGH AMPLIFIED THE VOICE IS RIGHT.
WE HAVE BEEN CALLED TO RIGHT THE WRONG!
ALL LIFE MUST END!
IT IS HIM.
THE TRANQUILITY OF OBLIVION CAN BE ATTAINED... IF YOU BELIEVE!
IT WILL REQUIRE GREAT EFFORT!
AND SACRIFICE!
OR IS IT?
BUT WE ARE NIHILISTS AND LIVE FOR SACRIFICE!
CRAZY TALK.
WERE WE NOT BORN TO END ALL LIFE?!
I'VE HEARD IT ALL BEFORE.
IT WAS THIS DEATH WISH NONSENSE THAT DROVE ME FROM THANOS YEARS AGO.
THE TIME HAS COME FOR US TO--
IT--IT CANNOT BE--
HE SEES ME...
LISTEN, MY FOLLOWERS!
THE GREEN WOMAN IN SECTION C3--
KILL HER!

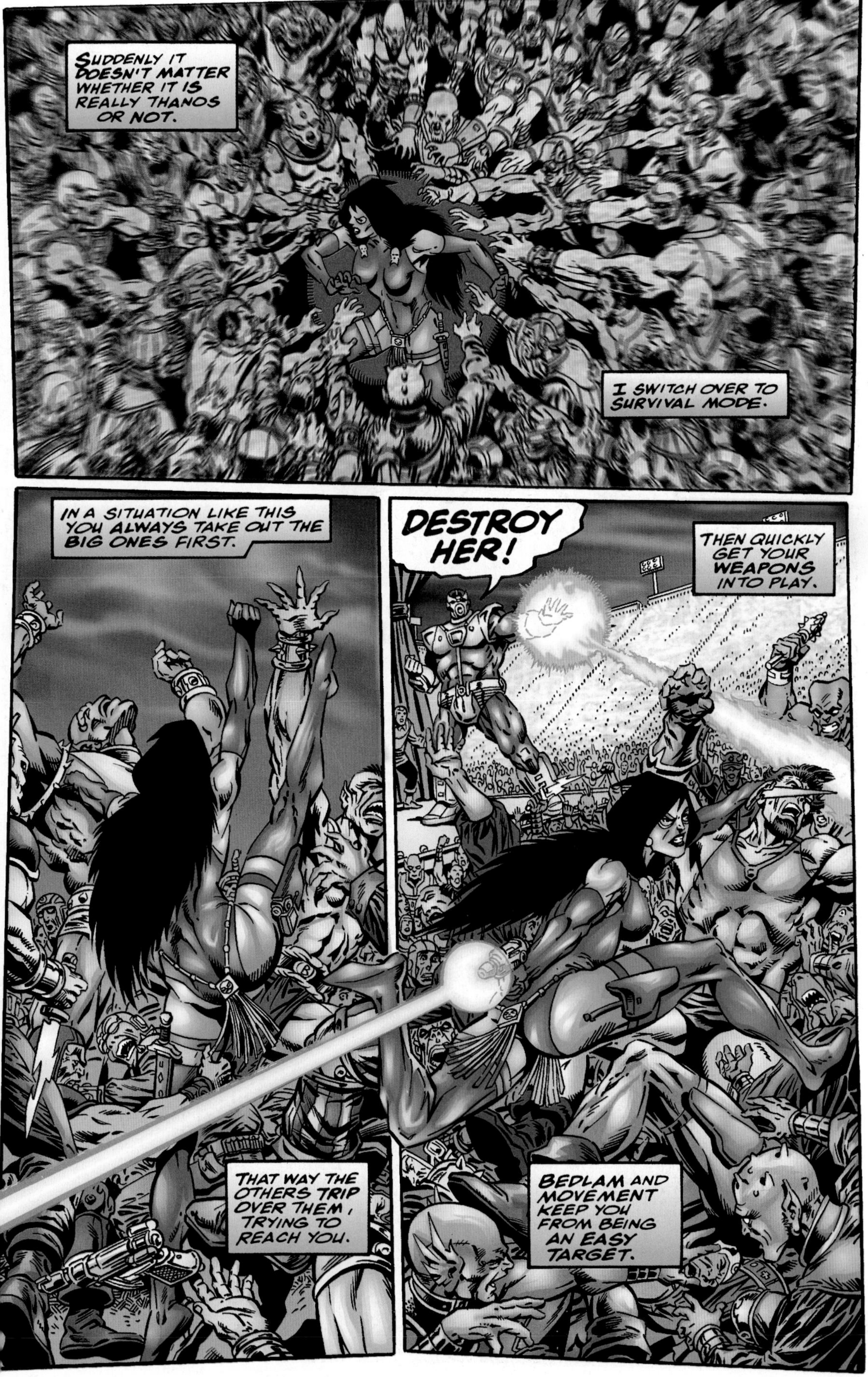
SUDDENLY IT DOESN'T MATTER WHETHER IT IS REALLY THANOS OR NOT.
I SWITCH OVER TO SURVIVAL MODE.
IN A SITUATION LIKE THIS YOU ALWAYS TAKE OUT THE BIG ONES FIRST.
THAT WAY THE OTHERS TRIP OVER THEM, TRYING TO REACH YOU.
DESTROY HER!
THEN QUICKLY GET YOUR WEAPONS INTO PLAY.
BEDLAM AND MOVEMENT KEEP YOU FROM BEING AN EASY TARGET.

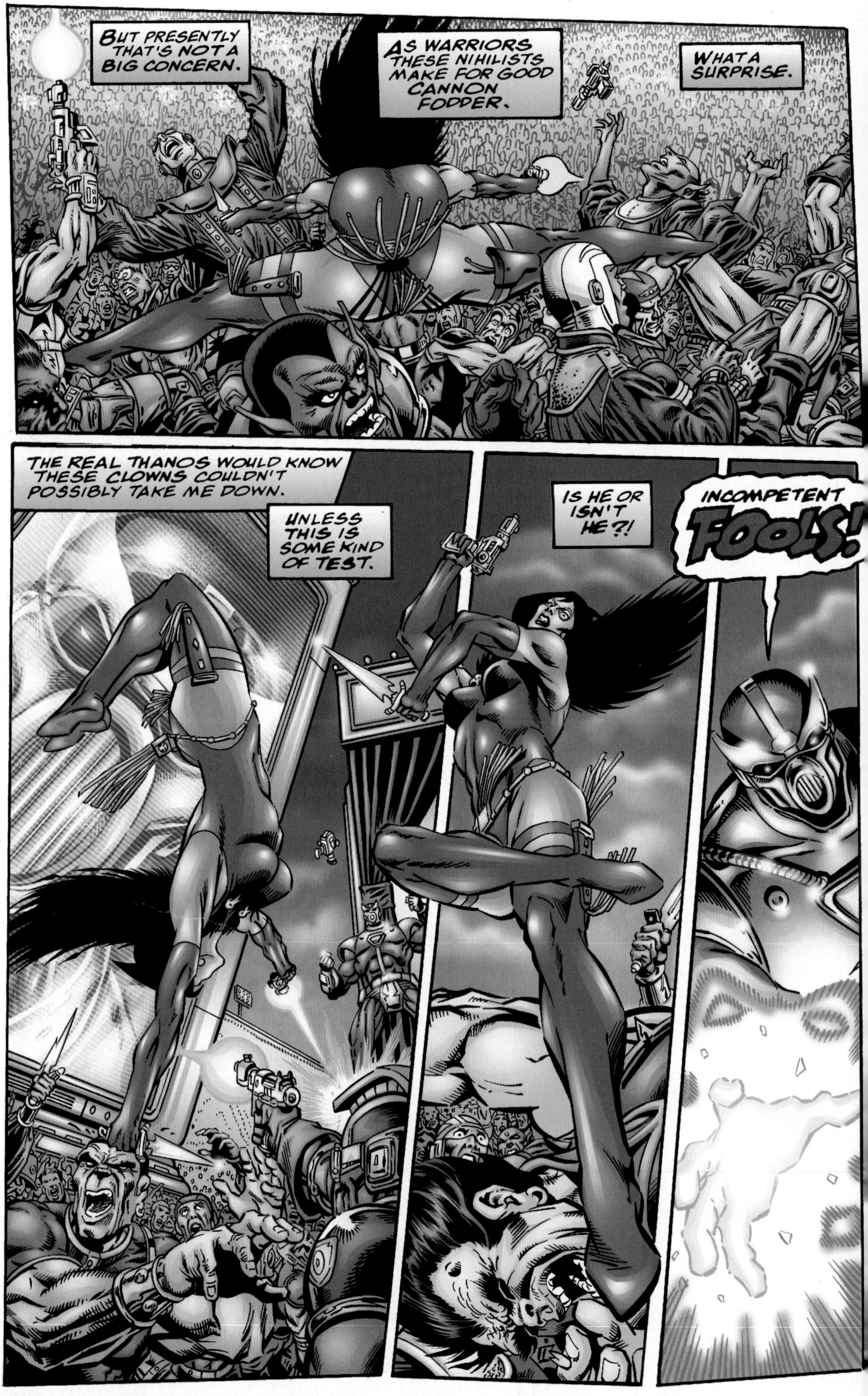

BUT PRESENTLY THAT'S NOT A BIG CONCERN.
AS WARRIORS THESE NIHILISTS MAKE FOR GOOD CANNON FODDER.
WHAT A SURPRISE.
THE REAL THANOS WOULD KNOW THESE CLOWNS COULDN'T POSSIBLY TAKE ME DOWN.
UNLESS THIS IS SOME KIND OF TEST.
IS HE OR ISN'T HE?!
INCOMPETENT FOOLS!

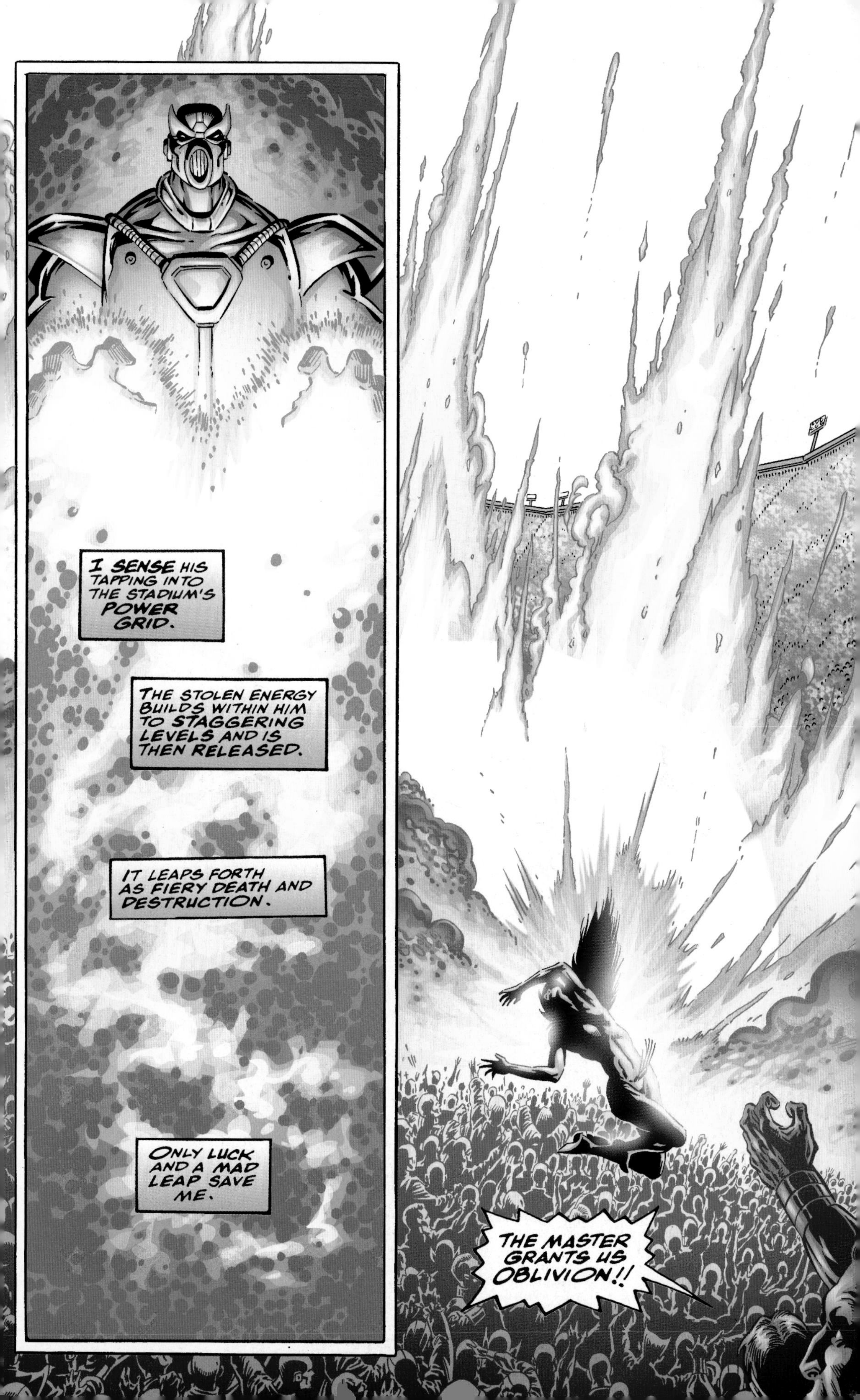

I SENSE HIS TAPPING INTO THE STADIUM'S POWER GRID.
THE STOLEN ENERGY BUILDS WITHIN HIM TO STAGGERING LEVELS AND IS THEN RELEASED.
IT LEAPS FORTH AS FIERY DEATH AND DESTRUCTION.
ONLY LUCK AND A MAD LEAP SAVE ME.
THE MASTER GRANTS US OBLIVION!!

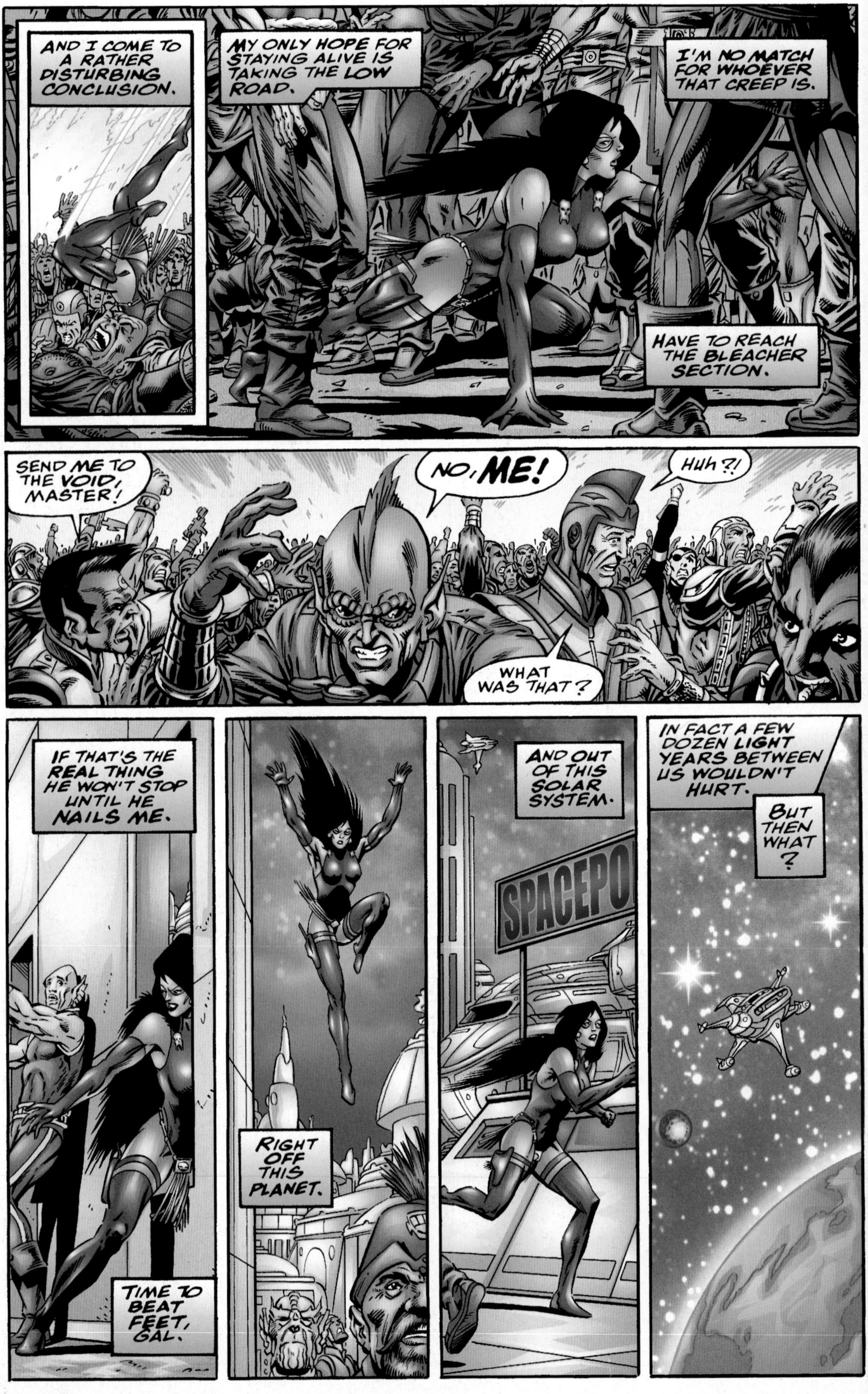
AND I COME TO A RATHER DISTURBING CONCLUSION.
MY ONLY HOPE FOR STAYING ALIVE IS TAKING THE LOW ROAD.
I'M NO MATCH FOR WHOEVER THAT CREEP IS.
HAVE TO REACH THE BLEACHER SECTION.
SEND ME TO THE VOID, MASTER!
NO, ME!
Huh ?!
WHAT WAS THAT ?
IF THAT'S THE REAL THING HE WON'T STOP UNTIL HE NAILS ME.
TIME TO BEAT FEET, GAL.
RIGHT OFF THIS PLANET.
AND OUT OF THIS SOLAR SYSTEM.
SPACEPO
IN FACT A FEW DOZEN LIGHT YEARS BETWEEN US WOULDN'T HURT.
BUT THEN WHAT ?

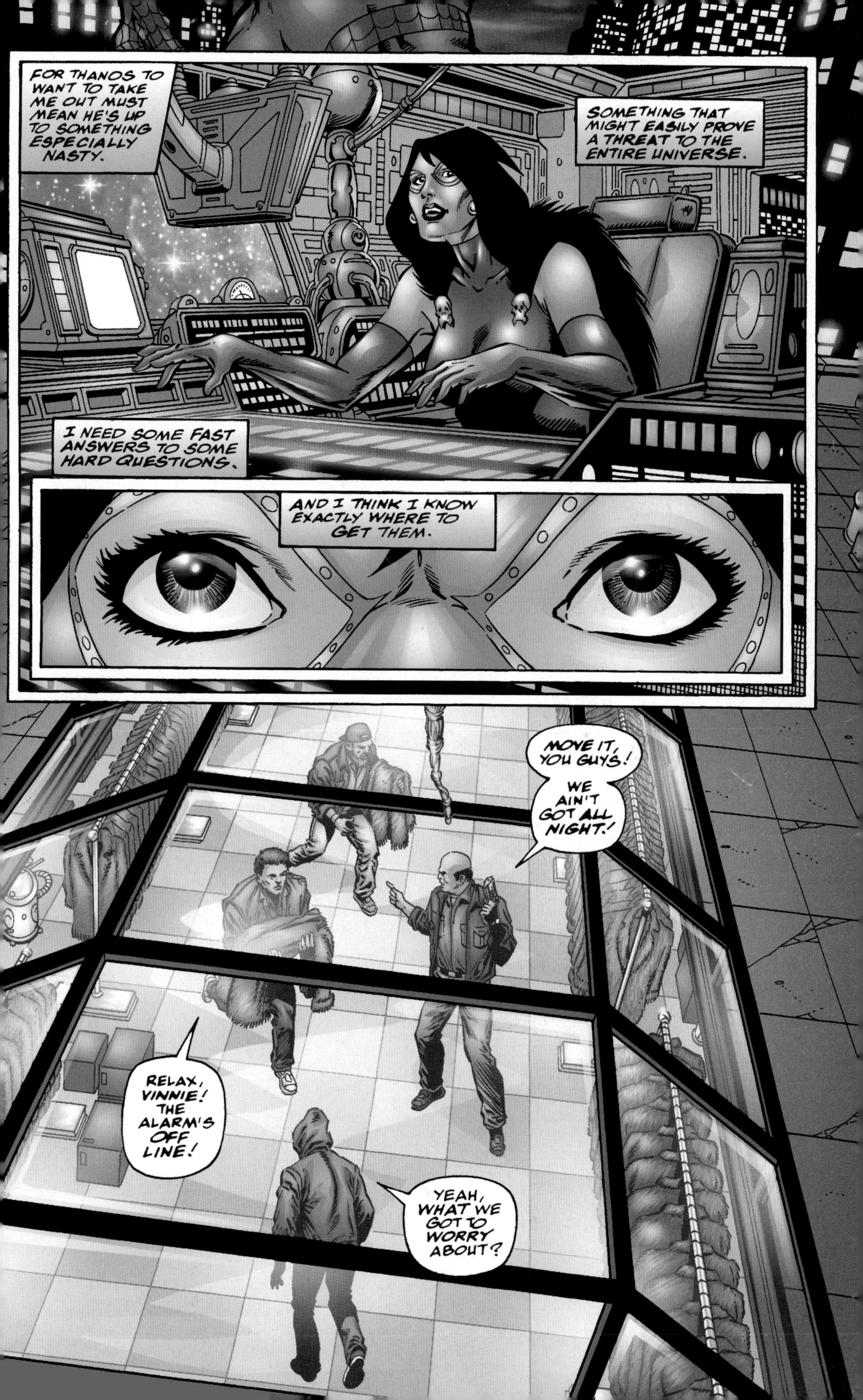
FOR THANOS TO WANT TO TAKE ME OUT MUST MEAN HE'S UP TO SOMETHING ESPECIALLY NASTY.
SOMETHING THAT MIGHT EASILY PROVE A THREAT TO THE ENTIRE UNIVERSE.
I NEED SOME FAST ANSWERS TO SOME HARD QUESTIONS.
AND I THINK I KNOW EXACTLY WHERE TO GET THEM.
MOVE IT, YOU GUYS! WE AIN'T GOT ALL NIGHT!
RELAX, VINNIE! THE ALARM'S OFF LINE!
YEAH, WHAT WE GOT TO WORRY ABOUT?

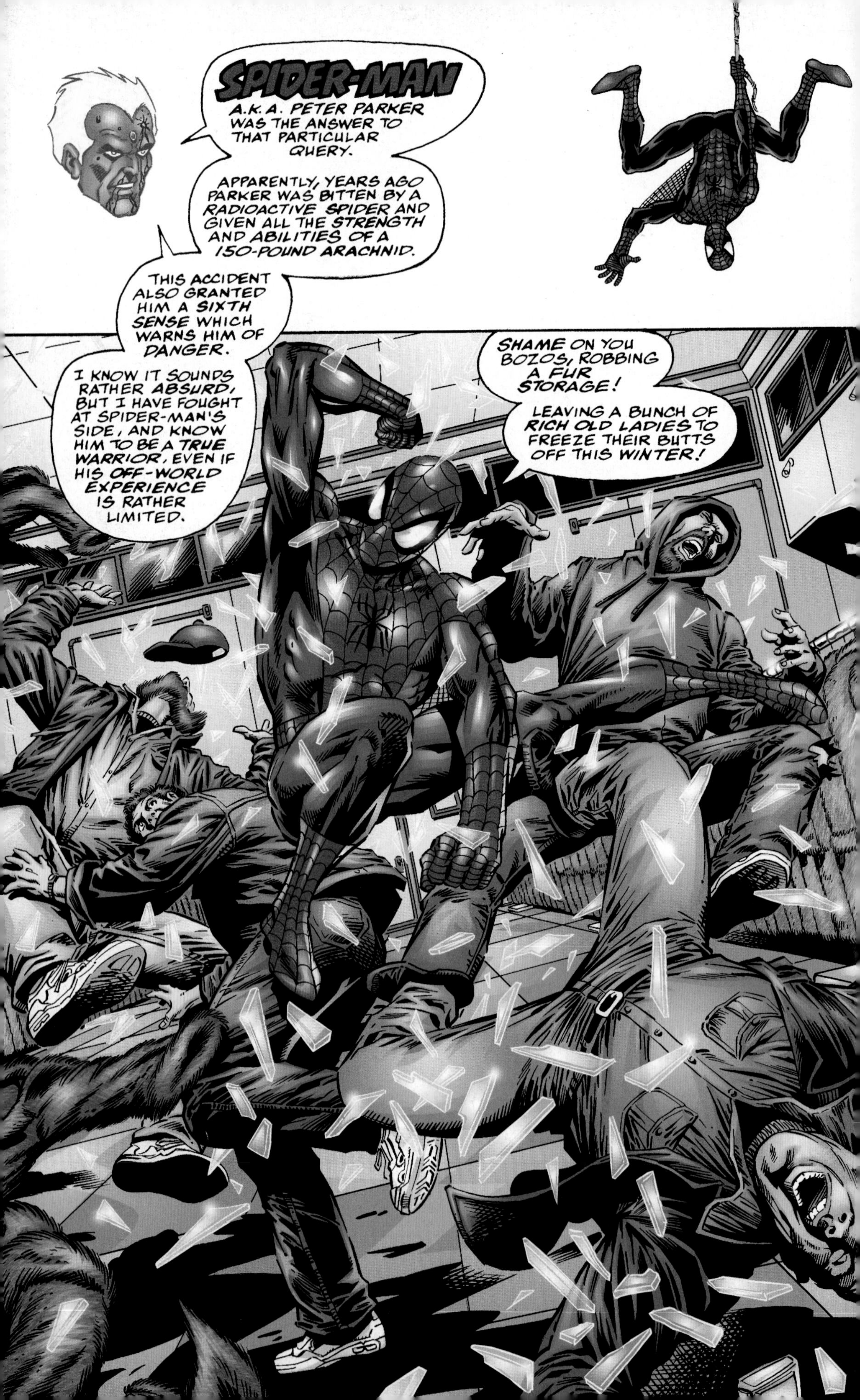
SPIDER-MAN
A.K.A. PETER PARKER WAS THE ANSWER TO THAT PARTICULAR QUERY.
APPARENTLY, YEARS AGO PARKER WAS BITTEN BY A *RADIOACTIVE SPIDER* AND GIVEN ALL THE *STRENGTH* AND *ABILITIES* OF A *150-POUND ARACHNID.*
THIS ACCIDENT ALSO GRANTED HIM A *SIXTH SENSE* WHICH WARNS HIM OF *DANGER.*
I KNOW IT SOUNDS RATHER *ABSURD,* BUT I HAVE FOUGHT AT SPIDER-MAN'S SIDE, AND KNOW HIM TO BE A *TRUE WARRIOR,* EVEN IF HIS *OFF-WORLD EXPERIENCE* IS RATHER LIMITED.
SHAME ON YOU BOZOS, ROBBING A *FUR STORAGE!*
LEAVING A BUNCH OF *RICH OLD LADIES* TO FREEZE THEIR BUTTS OFF THIS *WINTER!*

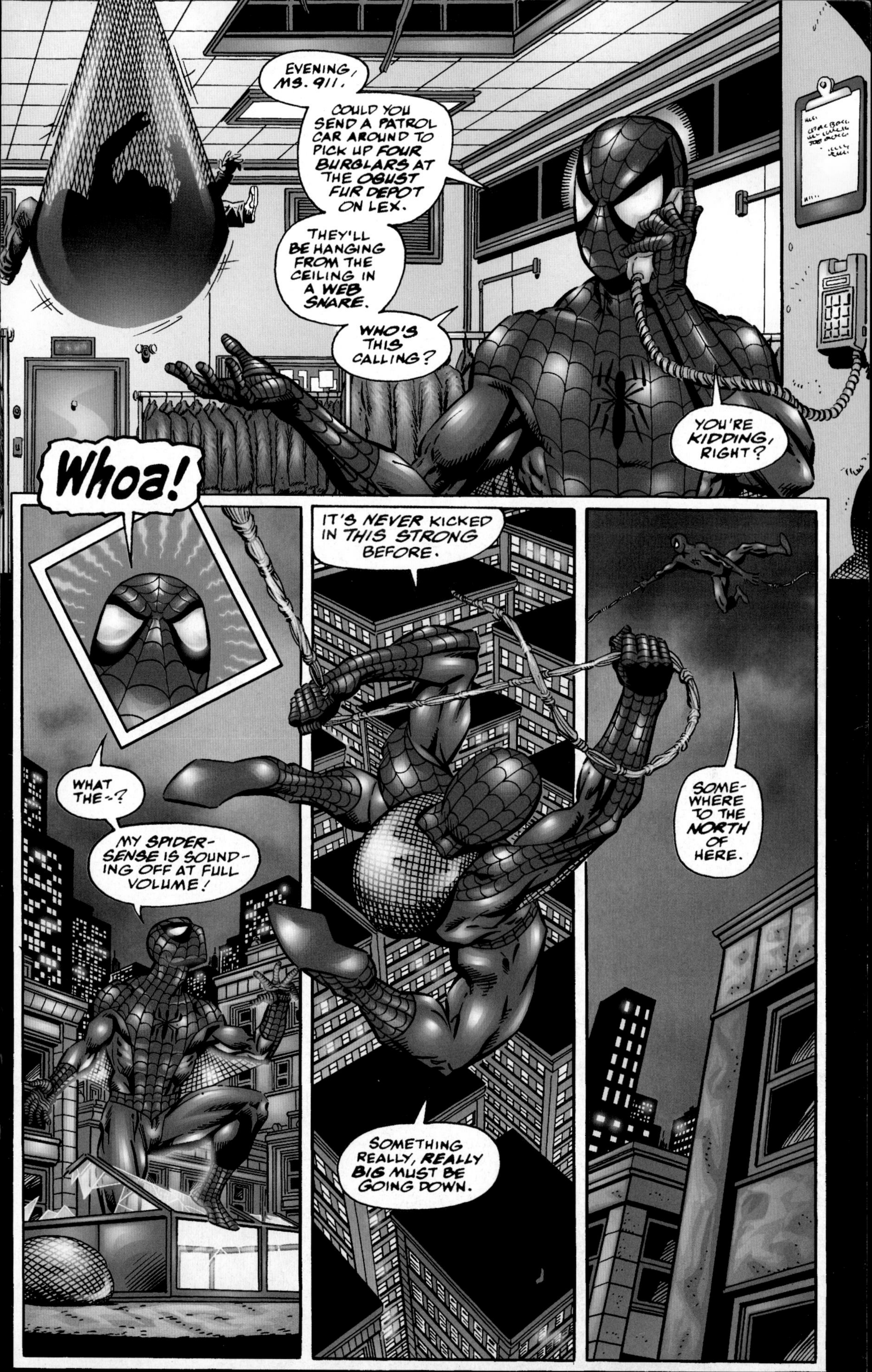
EVENING, MS. 911.
COULD YOU SEND A PATROL CAR AROUND TO PICK UP FOUR BURGLARS AT THE OGUST FUR DEPOT ON LEX.
THEY'LL BE HANGING FROM THE CEILING IN A WEB SNARE.
WHO'S THIS CALLING?
YOU'RE KIDDING, RIGHT?
Whoa!
WHAT THE--?
MY SPIDER-SENSE IS SOUNDING OFF AT FULL VOLUME!
IT'S NEVER KICKED IN THIS STRONG BEFORE.
SOMETHING REALLY, REALLY BIG MUST BE GOING DOWN.
SOMEWHERE TO THE NORTH OF HERE.

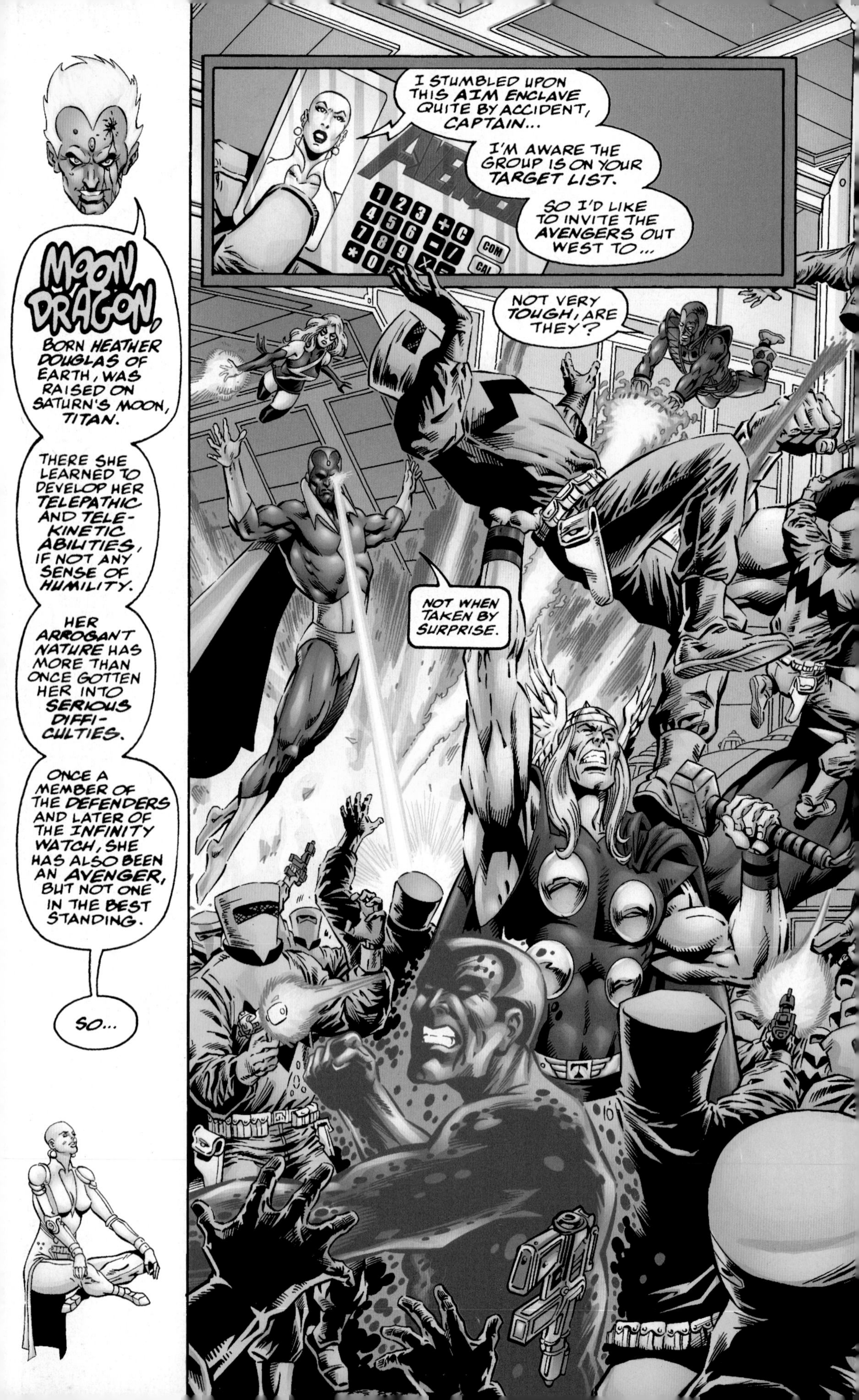
MOON DRAGON,
BORN HEATHER DOUGLAS OF EARTH, WAS RAISED ON SATURN'S MOON, TITAN.
THERE SHE LEARNED TO DEVELOP HER TELEPATHIC AND TELE-KINETIC ABILITIES, IF NOT ANY SENSE OF HUMILITY.
HER ARROGANT NATURE HAS MORE THAN ONCE GOTTEN HER INTO SERIOUS DIFFI-CULTIES.
ONCE A MEMBER OF THE DEFENDERS AND LATER OF THE INFINITY WATCH, SHE HAS ALSO BEEN AN AVENGER, BUT NOT ONE IN THE BEST STANDING.
SO...
I STUMBLED UPON THIS AIM ENCLAVE QUITE BY ACCIDENT, CAPTAIN...
I'M AWARE THE GROUP IS ON YOUR TARGET LIST.
SO I'D LIKE TO INVITE THE AVENGERS OUT WEST TO...
NOT VERY TOUGH, ARE THEY?
NOT WHEN TAKEN BY SURPRISE.

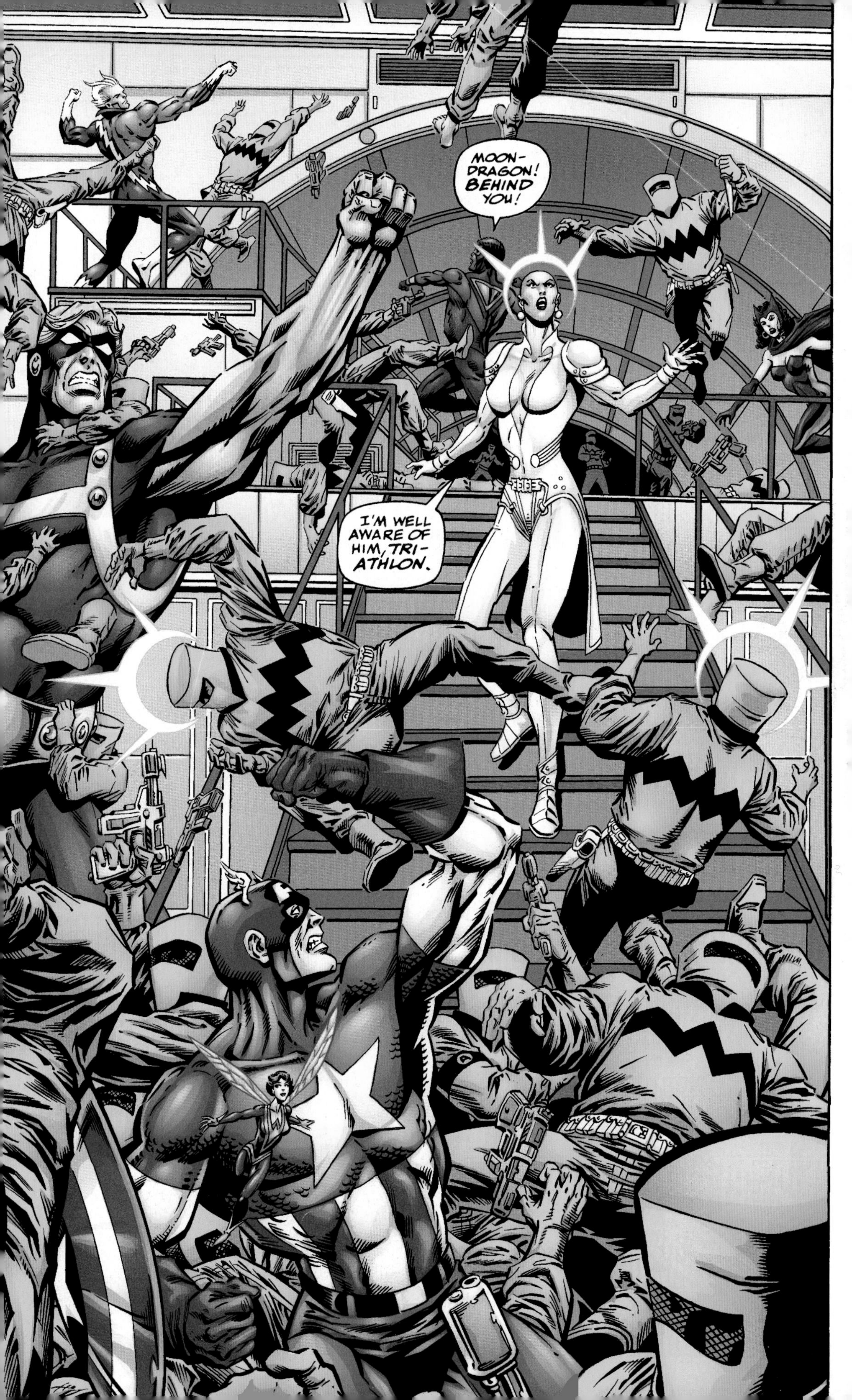
MOON-DRAGON! BEHIND YOU!
I'M WELL AWARE OF HIM, TRI-ATHLON.

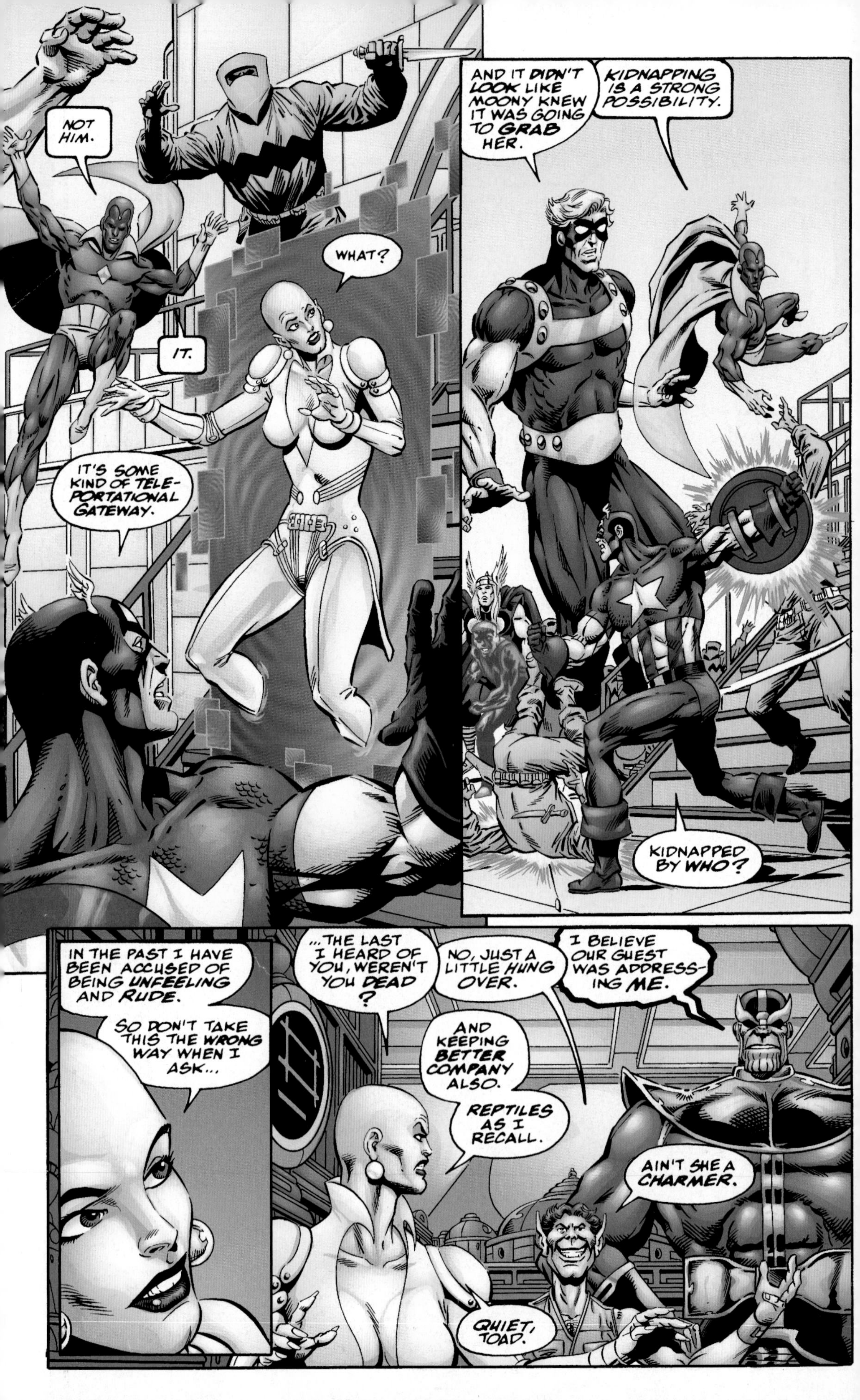
NOT HIM.
WHAT?
IT.
IT'S SOME KIND OF TELE-PORTATIONAL GATEWAY.
AND IT DIDN'T LOOK LIKE MOONY KNEW IT WAS GOING TO GRAB HER.
KIDNAPPING IS A STRONG POSSIBILITY.
KIDNAPPED BY WHO?
IN THE PAST I HAVE BEEN ACCUSED OF BEING UNFEELING AND RUDE.
SO DON'T TAKE THIS THE WRONG WAY WHEN I ASK...
...THE LAST I HEARD OF YOU, WEREN'T YOU DEAD?
NO, JUST A LITTLE HUNG OVER.
AND KEEPING BETTER COMPANY ALSO.
REPTILES AS I RECALL.
I BELIEVE OUR GUEST WAS ADDRESS-ING ME.
AIN'T SHE A CHARMER.
QUIET, TOAD.

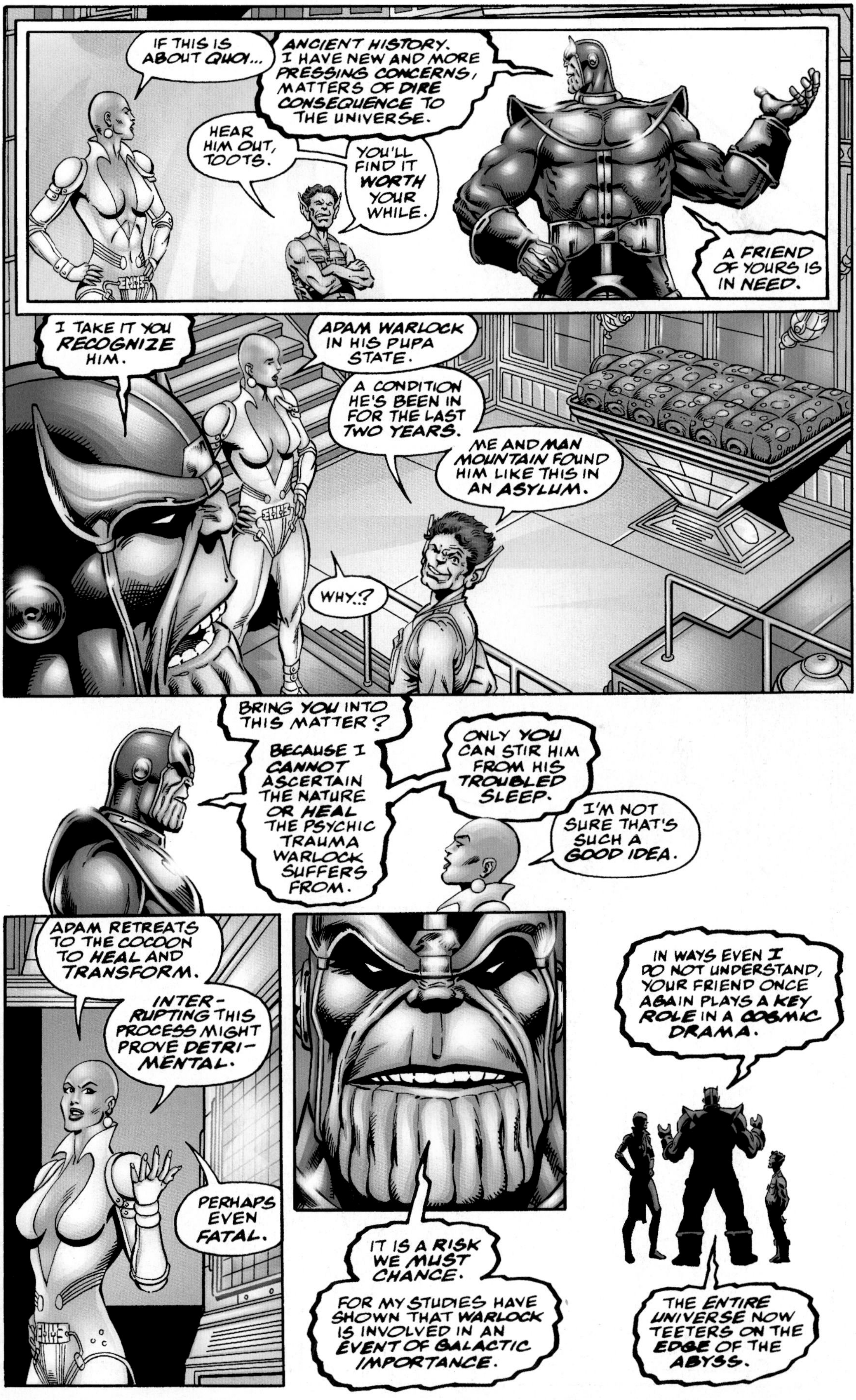
IF THIS IS ABOUT QUOI...
ANCIENT HISTORY. I HAVE NEW AND MORE PRESSING CONCERNS, MATTERS OF DIRE CONSEQUENCE TO THE UNIVERSE.
HEAR HIM OUT, TOOTS.
YOU'LL FIND IT WORTH YOUR WHILE.
A FRIEND OF YOURS IS IN NEED.
I TAKE IT YOU RECOGNIZE HIM.
ADAM WARLOCK IN HIS PUPA STATE.
A CONDITION HE'S BEEN IN FOR THE LAST TWO YEARS.
ME AND MAN MOUNTAIN FOUND HIM LIKE THIS IN AN ASYLUM.
WHY..?
BRING YOU INTO THIS MATTER?
BECAUSE I CANNOT ASCERTAIN THE NATURE OR HEAL THE PSYCHIC TRAUMA WARLOCK SUFFERS FROM.
ONLY YOU CAN STIR HIM FROM HIS TROUBLED SLEEP.
I'M NOT SURE THAT'S SUCH A GOOD IDEA.
ADAM RETREATS TO THE COCOON TO HEAL AND TRANSFORM.
INTER-RUPTING THIS PROCESS MIGHT PROVE DETRI-MENTAL.
PERHAPS EVEN FATAL.
IT IS A RISK WE MUST CHANCE.
FOR MY STUDIES HAVE SHOWN THAT WARLOCK IS INVOLVED IN AN EVENT OF GALACTIC IMPORTANCE.
IN WAYS EVEN I DO NOT UNDERSTAND, YOUR FRIEND ONCE AGAIN PLAYS A KEY ROLE IN A COSMIC DRAMA.
THE ENTIRE UNIVERSE NOW TEETERS ON THE EDGE OF THE ABYSS.

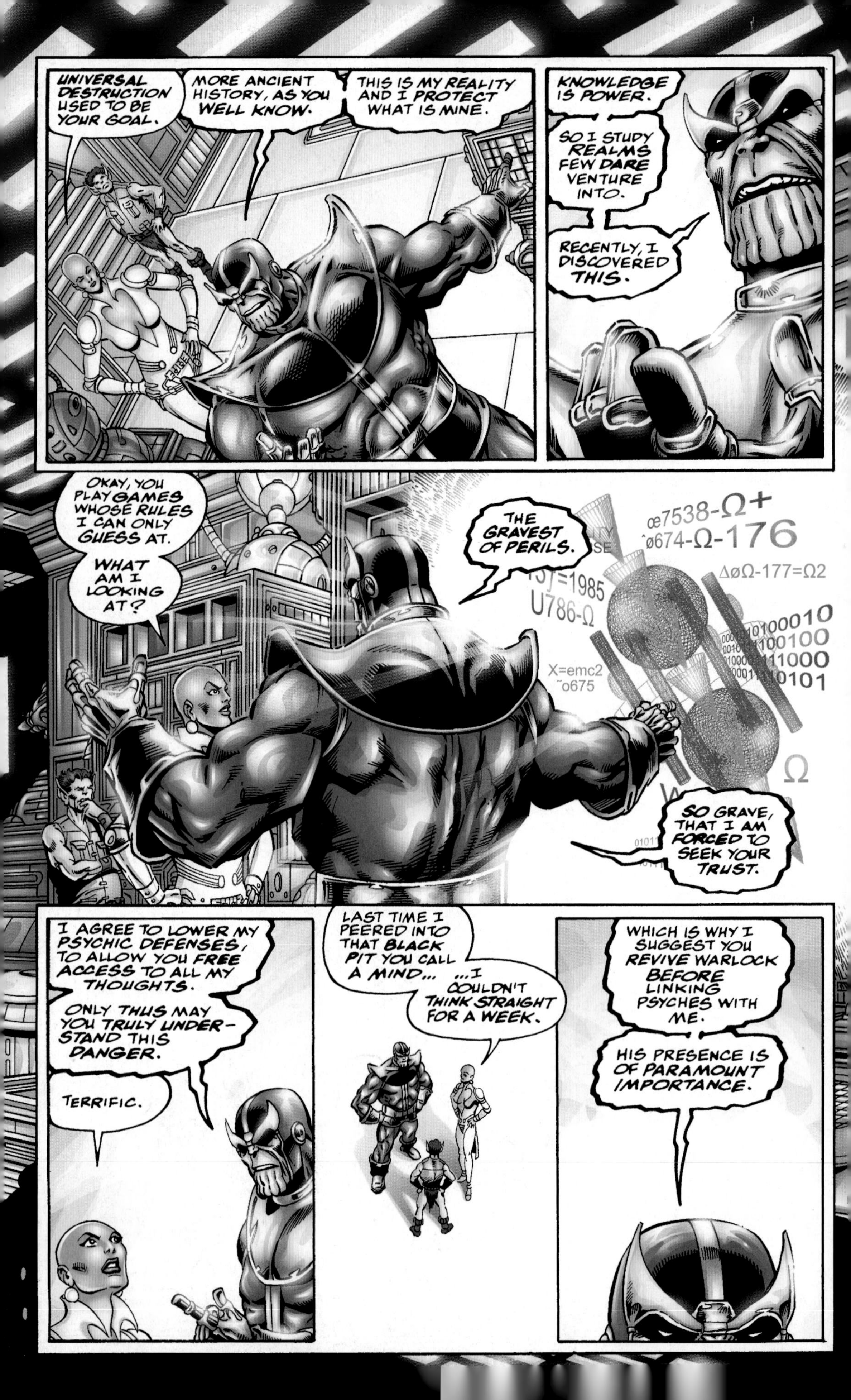
UNIVERSAL DESTRUCTION USED TO BE YOUR GOAL.
MORE ANCIENT HISTORY, AS YOU WELL KNOW.
THIS IS MY REALITY AND I PROTECT WHAT IS MINE.
KNOWLEDGE IS POWER.
SO I STUDY REALMS FEW DARE VENTURE INTO.
RECENTLY, I DISCOVERED THIS.
OKAY, YOU PLAY GAMES WHOSE RULES I CAN ONLY GUESS AT.
WHAT AM I LOOKING AT?
THE GRAVEST OF PERILS.
œ7538-Ω+
ˆø674-Ω-176
ΔøΩ-177=Ω2
U786-Ω
X=emc2
˜o675
SO GRAVE, THAT I AM FORCED TO SEEK YOUR TRUST.
I AGREE TO LOWER MY PSYCHIC DEFENSES, TO ALLOW YOU FREE ACCESS TO ALL MY THOUGHTS.
ONLY THUS MAY YOU TRULY UNDER-STAND THIS DANGER.
TERRIFIC.
LAST TIME I PEERED INTO THAT BLACK PIT YOU CALL A MIND...
...I COULDN'T THINK STRAIGHT FOR A WEEK.
WHICH IS WHY I SUGGEST YOU REVIVE WARLOCK BEFORE LINKING PSYCHES WITH ME.
HIS PRESENCE IS OF PARAMOUNT IMPORTANCE.

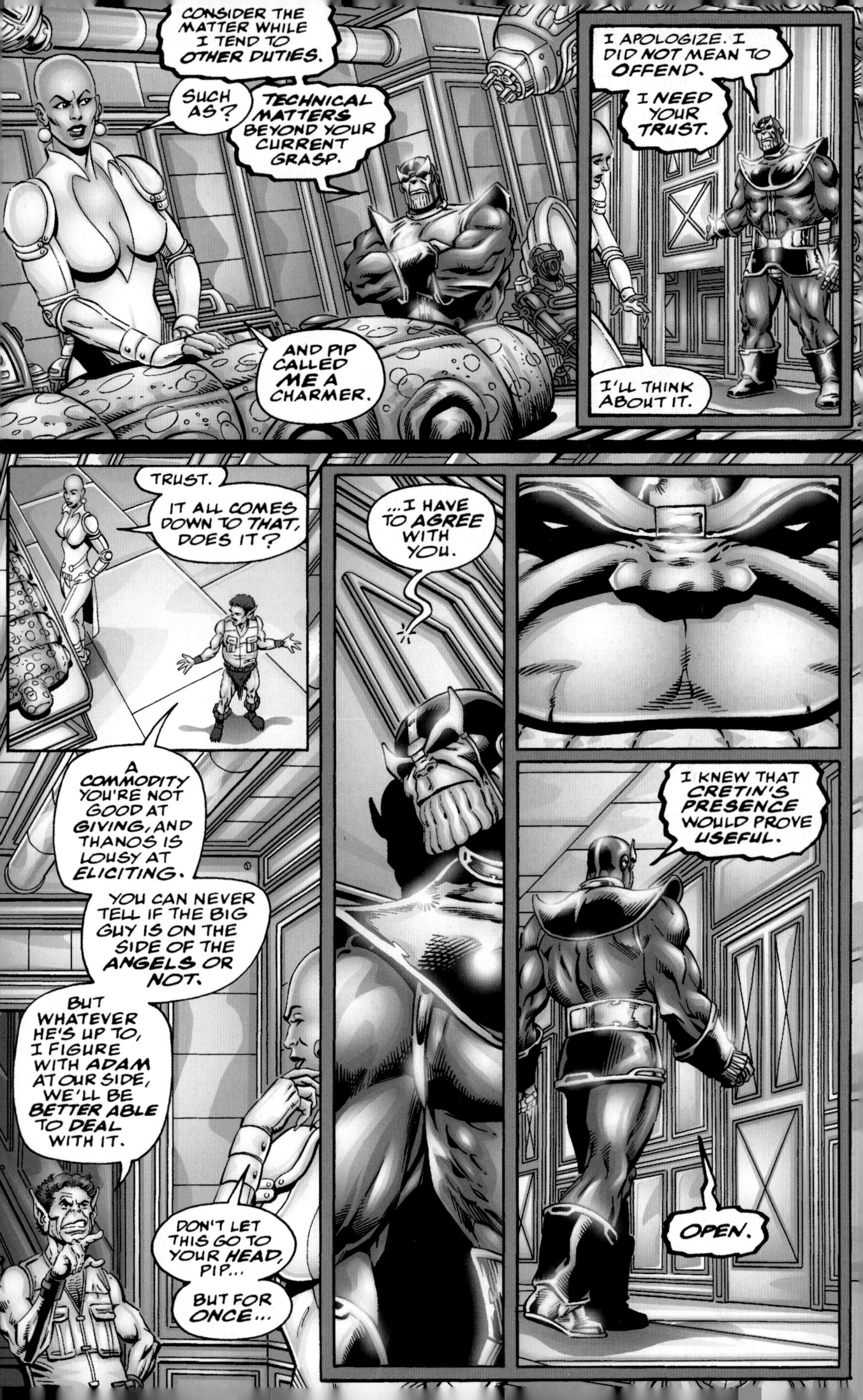
CONSIDER THE MATTER WHILE I TEND TO OTHER DUTIES.
SUCH AS?
TECHNICAL MATTERS BEYOND YOUR CURRENT GRASP.
AND PIP CALLED ME A CHARMER.
I APOLOGIZE. I DID NOT MEAN TO OFFEND.
I NEED YOUR TRUST.
I'LL THINK ABOUT IT.
TRUST.
IT ALL COMES DOWN TO THAT, DOES IT?
A COMMODITY YOU'RE NOT GOOD AT GIVING, AND THANOS IS LOUSY AT ELICITING.
YOU CAN NEVER TELL IF THE BIG GUY IS ON THE SIDE OF THE ANGELS OR NOT.
BUT WHATEVER HE'S UP TO, I FIGURE WITH ADAM AT OUR SIDE, WE'LL BE BETTER ABLE TO DEAL WITH IT.
DON'T LET THIS GO TO YOUR HEAD, PIP...
BUT FOR ONCE...
...I HAVE TO AGREE WITH YOU.
I KNEW THAT CRETIN'S PRESENCE WOULD PROVE USEFUL.
OPEN.

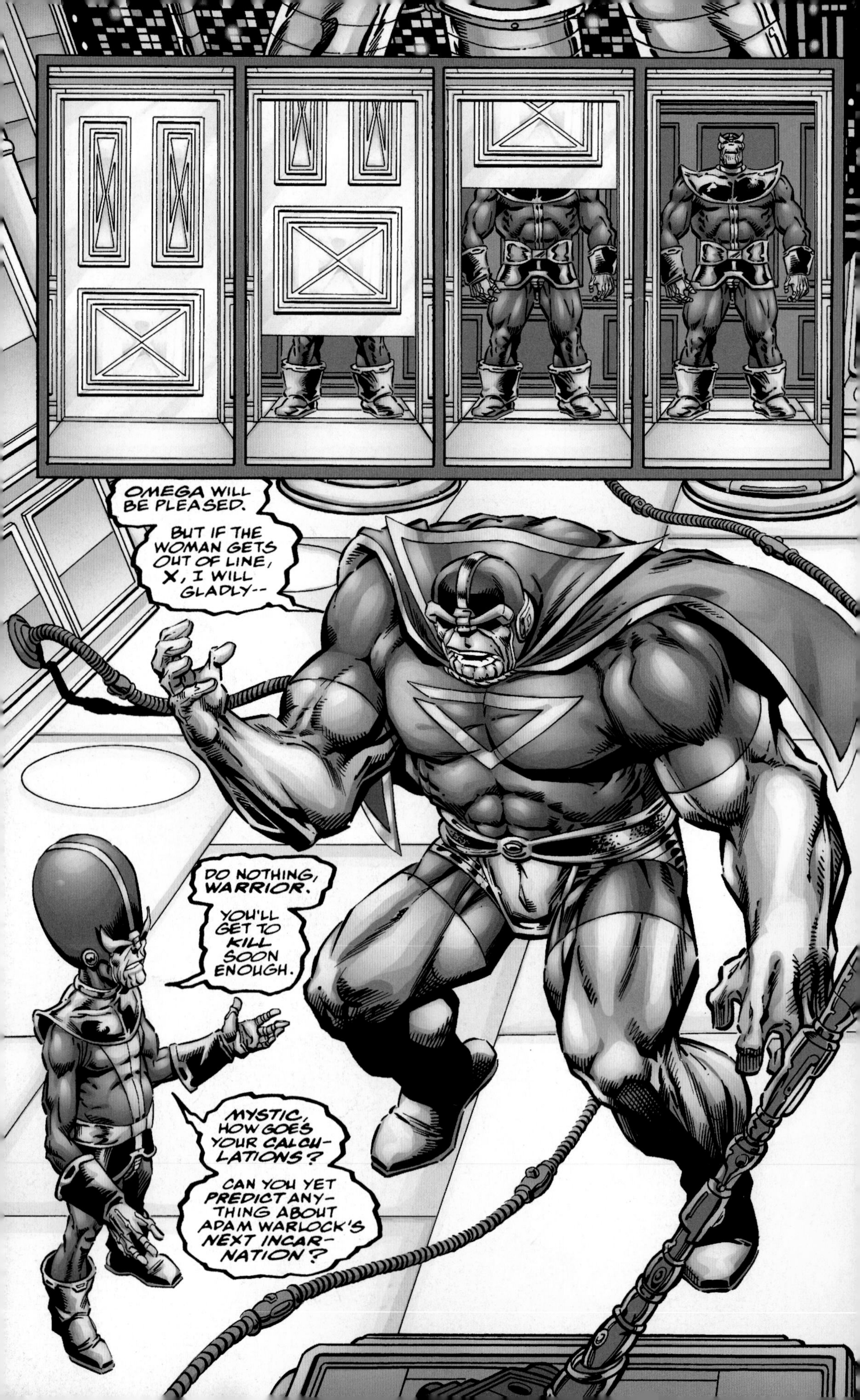
OMEGA WILL BE PLEASED.
BUT IF THE WOMAN GETS OUT OF LINE, X, I WILL GLADLY--
DO NOTHING, WARRIOR.
YOU'LL GET TO KILL SOON ENOUGH.
MYSTIC, HOW GOES YOUR CALCULATIONS?
CAN YOU YET PREDICT ANYTHING ABOUT ADAM WARLOCK'S NEXT INCARNATION?

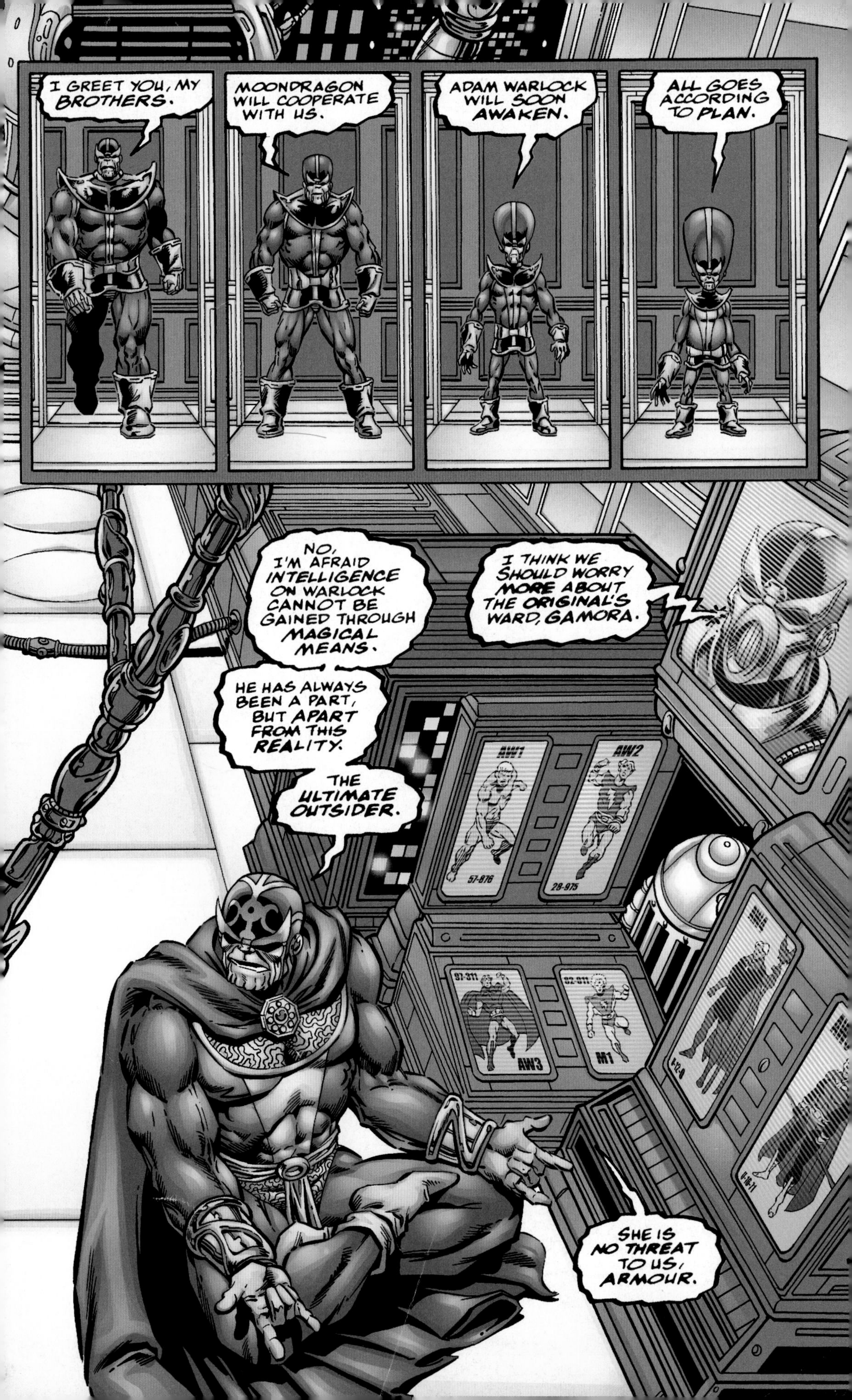

I GREET YOU, MY BROTHERS.
MOONDRAGON WILL COOPERATE WITH US.
ADAM WARLOCK WILL SOON AWAKEN.
ALL GOES ACCORDING TO PLAN.
NO, I'M AFRAID INTELLIGENCE ON WARLOCK CANNOT BE GAINED THROUGH MAGICAL MEANS.
I THINK WE SHOULD WORRY MORE ABOUT THE ORIGINAL'S WARD, GAMORA.
HE HAS ALWAYS BEEN A PART, BUT APART FROM THIS REALITY.
THE ULTIMATE OUTSIDER.
AW1
AW2
57-876
28-975
AW3
M1
SHE IS NO THREAT TO US, ARMOUR.

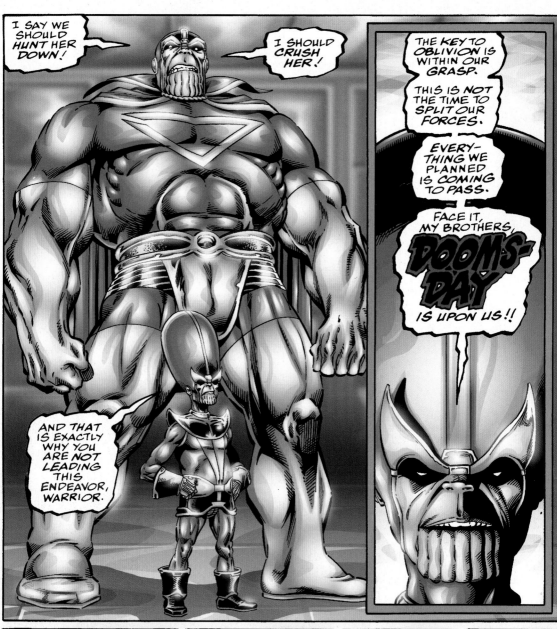

I SAY WE SHOULD **HUNT** HER **DOWN**!

I SHOULD **CRUSH** HER!

THE KEY TO OBLIVION IS WITHIN OUR GRASP.

THIS IS **NOT** THE TIME TO **SPLIT** OUR FORCES.

EVERY-THING WE PLANNED IS **COMING** TO PASS.

FACE IT, MY BROTHERS, **DOOMS-DAY** IS UPON US!!

AND THAT IS EXACTLY WHY YOU ARE **NOT** LEADING THIS ENDEAVOR, WARRIOR.

TIME DRAWS SO SHORT.

THE FORCES OF DARK-NESS GROW SO STRONG.

HAVE I FAILED?!

IF I HAVE, THEN ALL THE UNI-VERSE ...

...WILL **PAY** FOR MY SHORTCOMINGS.

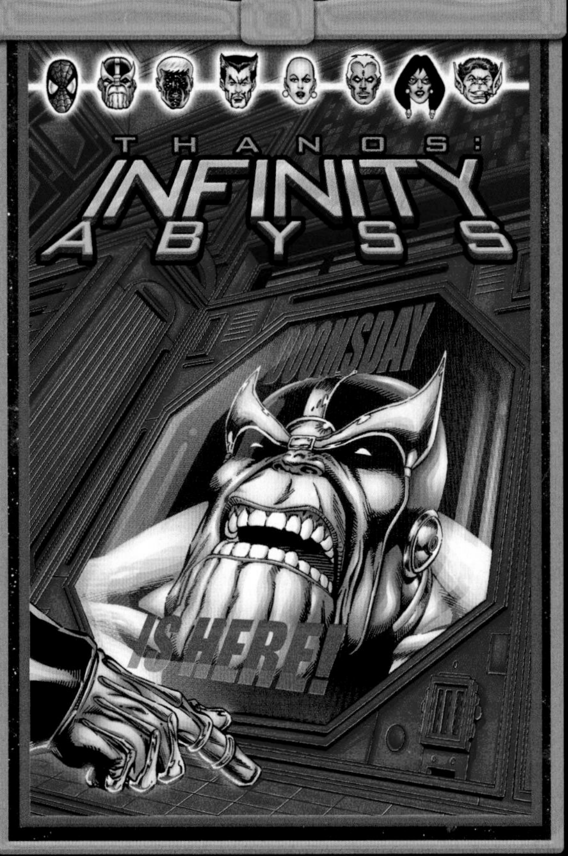
THANOS:
INFINITY
ABYSS
DOOMSDAY
IS HERE!

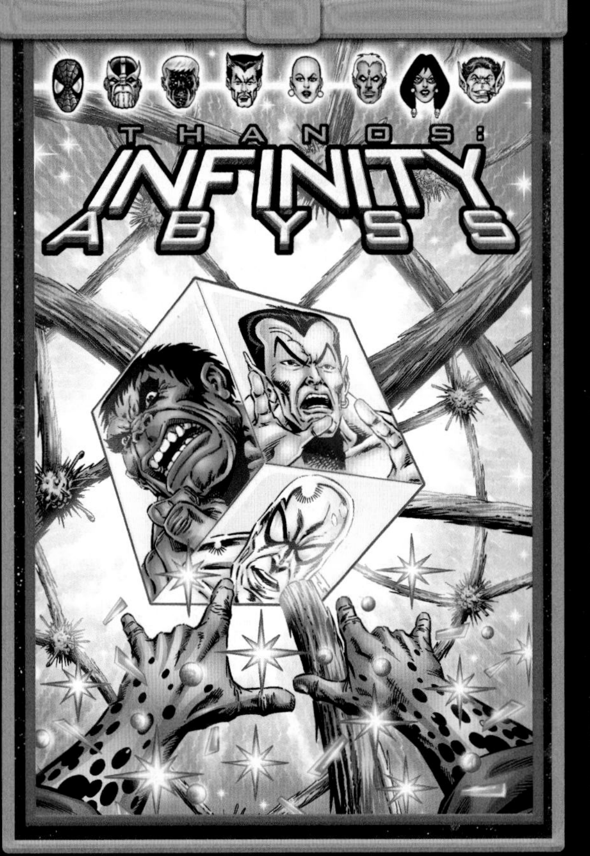
THANOS:
INFINITY
ABYSS

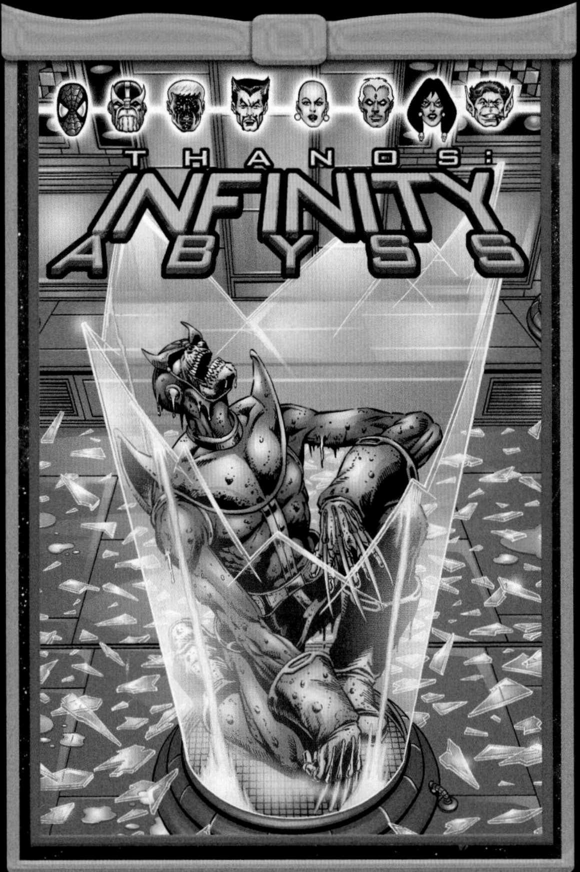
THANOS:
INFINITY
ABYSS

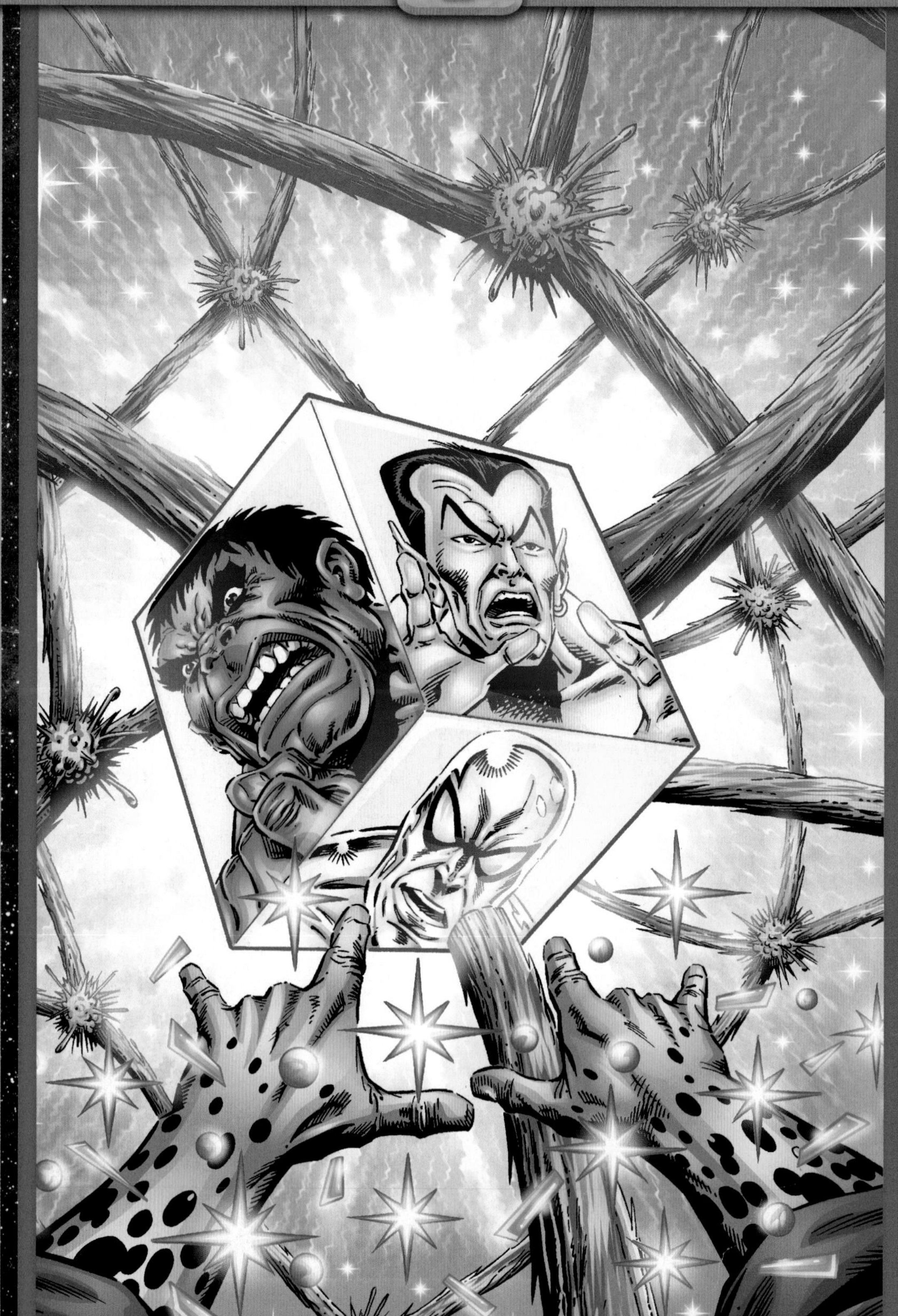

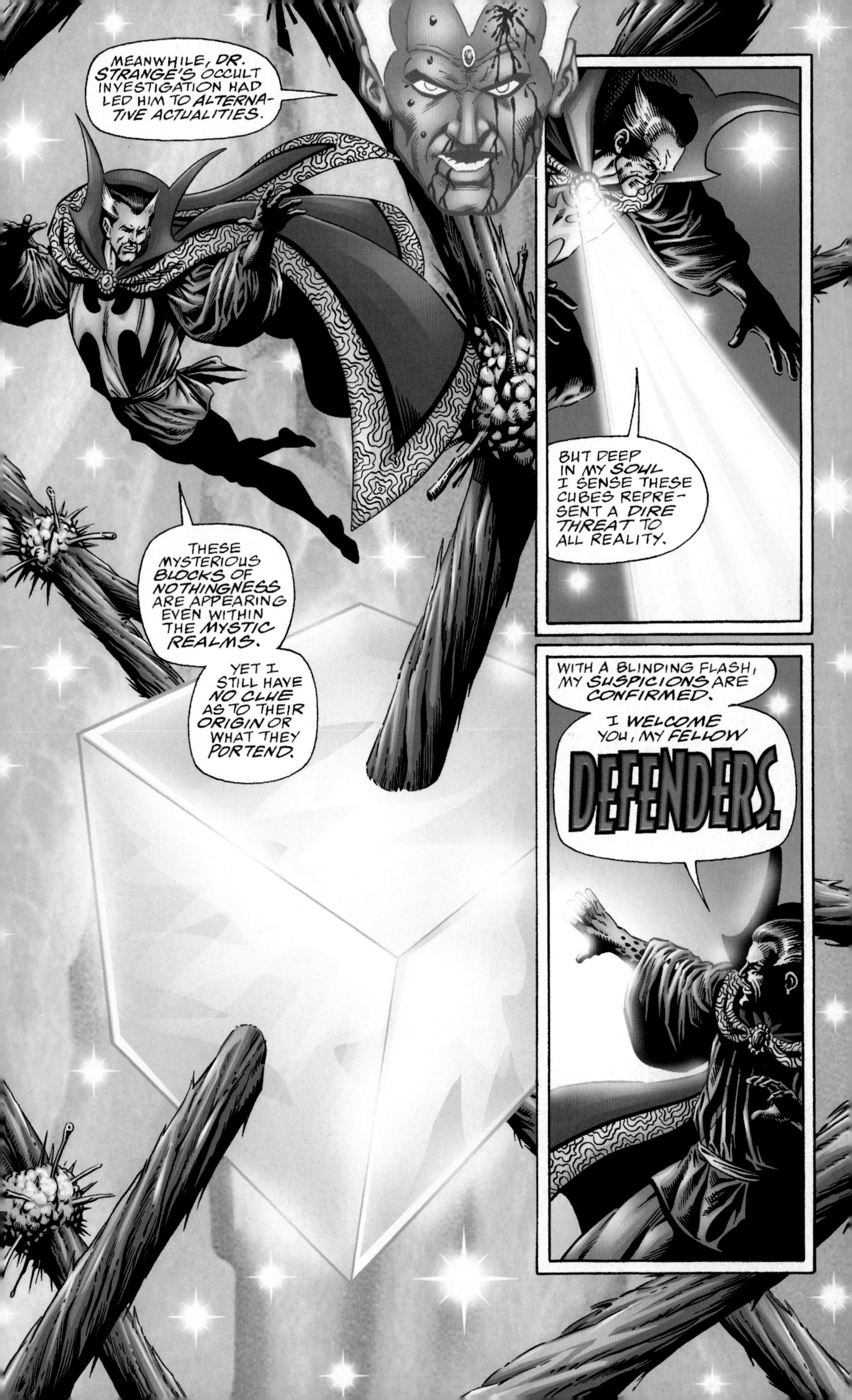
MEANWHILE, DR. STRANGE'S OCCULT INVESTIGATION HAD LED HIM TO ALTERNATIVE ACTUALITIES.
THESE MYSTERIOUS BLOCKS OF NOTHINGNESS ARE APPEARING EVEN WITHIN THE MYSTIC REALMS.
YET I STILL HAVE NO CLUE AS TO THEIR ORIGIN OR WHAT THEY PORTEND.
BUT DEEP IN MY SOUL I SENSE THESE CUBES REPRESENT A DIRE THREAT TO ALL REALITY.
WITH A BLINDING FLASH, MY SUSPICIONS ARE CONFIRMED.
I WELCOME YOU, MY FELLOW
DEFENDERS.

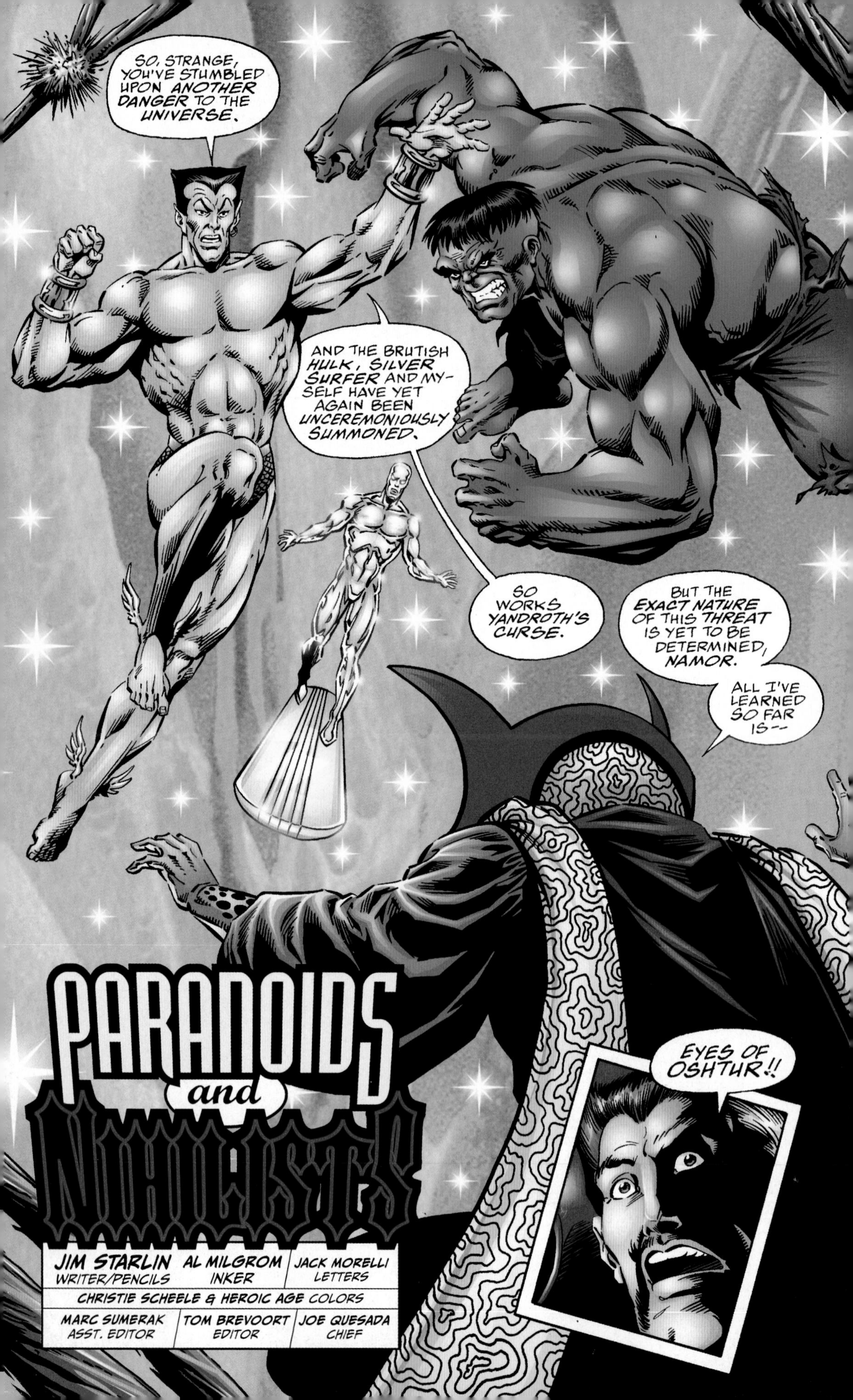
SO, STRANGE, YOU'VE STUMBLED UPON ANOTHER DANGER TO THE UNIVERSE.
AND THE BRUTISH HULK, SILVER SURFER AND MY-SELF HAVE YET AGAIN BEEN UNCEREMONIOUSLY SUMMONED.
SO WORKS YANDROTH'S CURSE.
BUT THE EXACT NATURE OF THIS THREAT IS YET TO BE DETERMINED, NAMOR.
ALL I'VE LEARNED SO FAR IS--
EYES OF OSHTUR!!
PARANOIDS and NIHILISTS
JIM STARLIN WRITER/PENCILS
AL MILGROM INKER
JACK MORELLI LETTERS
CHRISTIE SCHEELE & HEROIC AGE COLORS
MARC SUMERAK ASST. EDITOR
TOM BREVOORT EDITOR
JOE QUESADA CHIEF

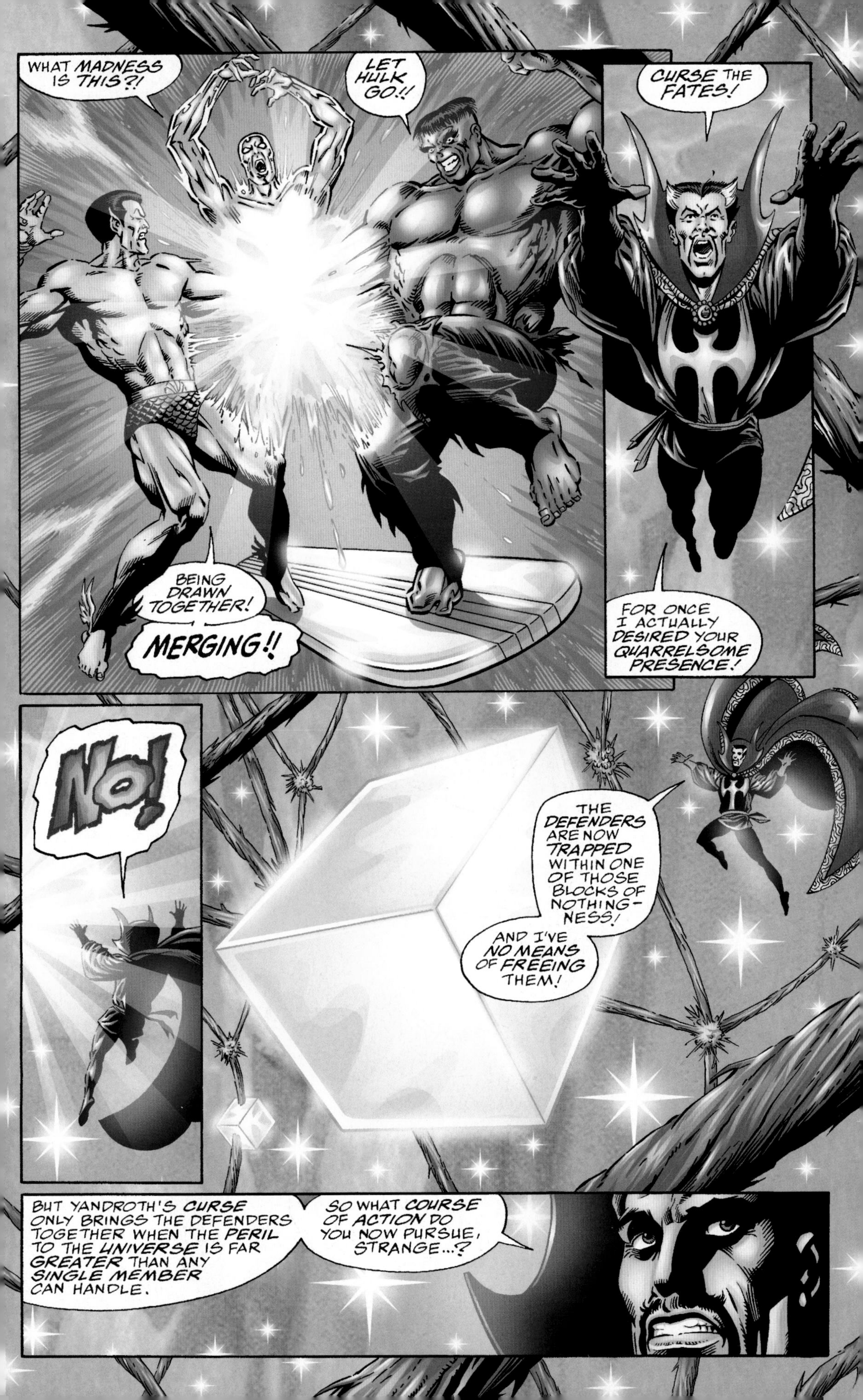
WHAT MADNESS IS THIS?!
LET HULK GO!!
CURSE THE FATES!
BEING DRAWN TOGETHER!
MERGING!!
FOR ONCE I ACTUALLY DESIRED YOUR QUARRELSOME PRESENCE!
NO!
THE DEFENDERS ARE NOW TRAPPED WITHIN ONE OF THOSE BLOCKS OF NOTHING-NESS!
AND I'VE NO MEANS OF FREEING THEM!
BUT YANDROTH'S CURSE ONLY BRINGS THE DEFENDERS TOGETHER WHEN THE PERIL TO THE UNIVERSE IS FAR GREATER THAN ANY SINGLE MEMBER CAN HANDLE.
SO WHAT COURSE OF ACTION DO YOU NOW PURSUE, STRANGE...?

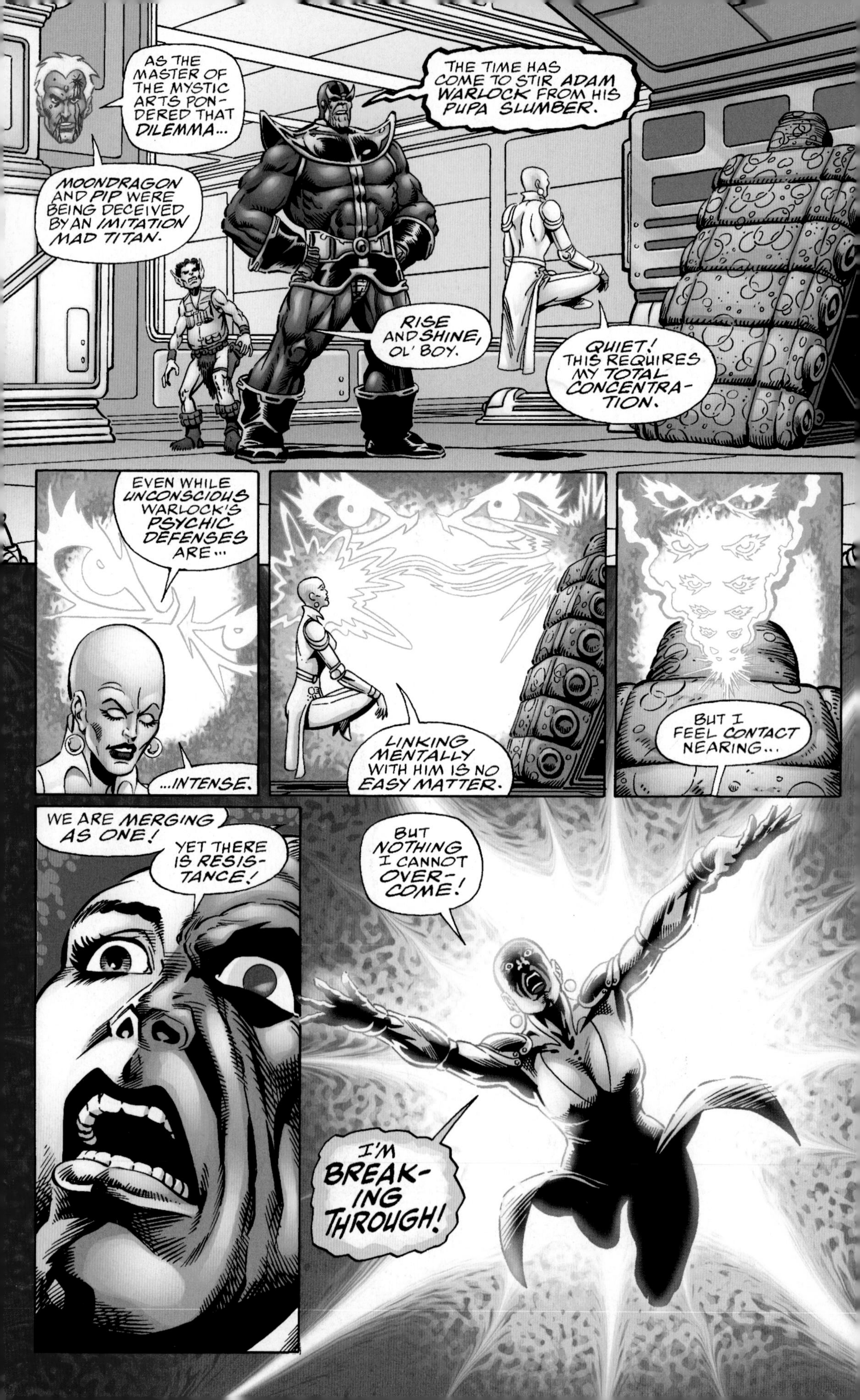
AS THE MASTER OF THE MYSTIC ARTS PONDERED THAT DILEMMA...
MOONDRAGON AND PIP WERE BEING DECEIVED BY AN IMITATION MAD TITAN.
THE TIME HAS COME TO STIR ADAM WARLOCK FROM HIS PUPA SLUMBER.
RISE AND SHINE, OL' BOY.
QUIET! THIS REQUIRES MY TOTAL CONCENTRATION.
EVEN WHILE UNCONSCIOUS WARLOCK'S PSYCHIC DEFENSES ARE...
...INTENSE.
LINKING MENTALLY WITH HIM IS NO EASY MATTER.
BUT I FEEL CONTACT NEARING...
WE ARE MERGING AS ONE!
YET THERE IS RESISTANCE!
BUT NOTHING I CANNOT OVERCOME!
I'M BREAKING THROUGH!

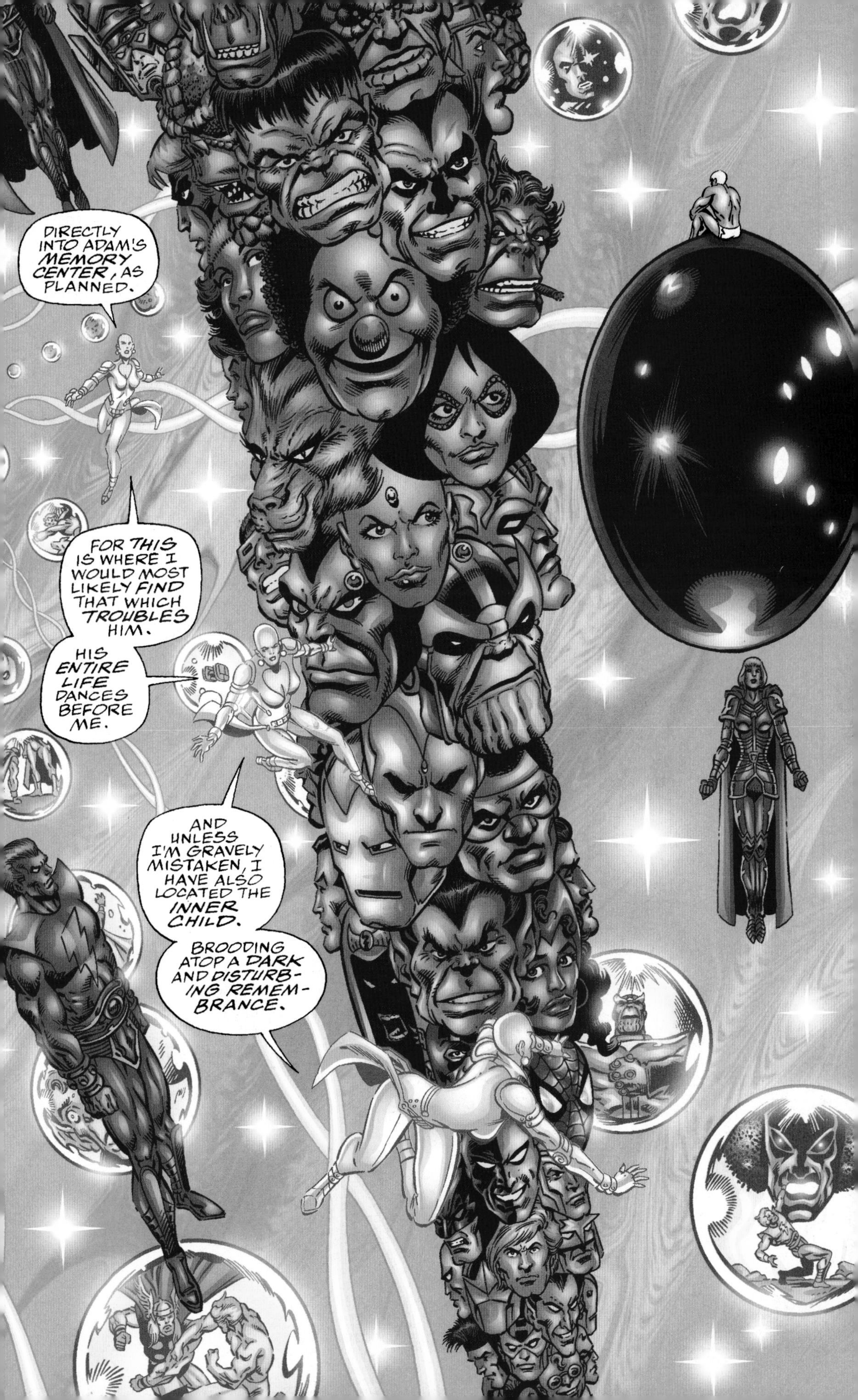
DIRECTLY INTO ADAM'S MEMORY CENTER, AS PLANNED.
FOR THIS IS WHERE I WOULD MOST LIKELY FIND THAT WHICH TROUBLES HIM.
HIS ENTIRE LIFE DANCES BEFORE ME.
AND UNLESS I'M GRAVELY MISTAKEN, I HAVE ALSO LOCATED THE INNER CHILD.
BROODING ATOP A DARK AND DISTURB-ING REMEM-BRANCE.

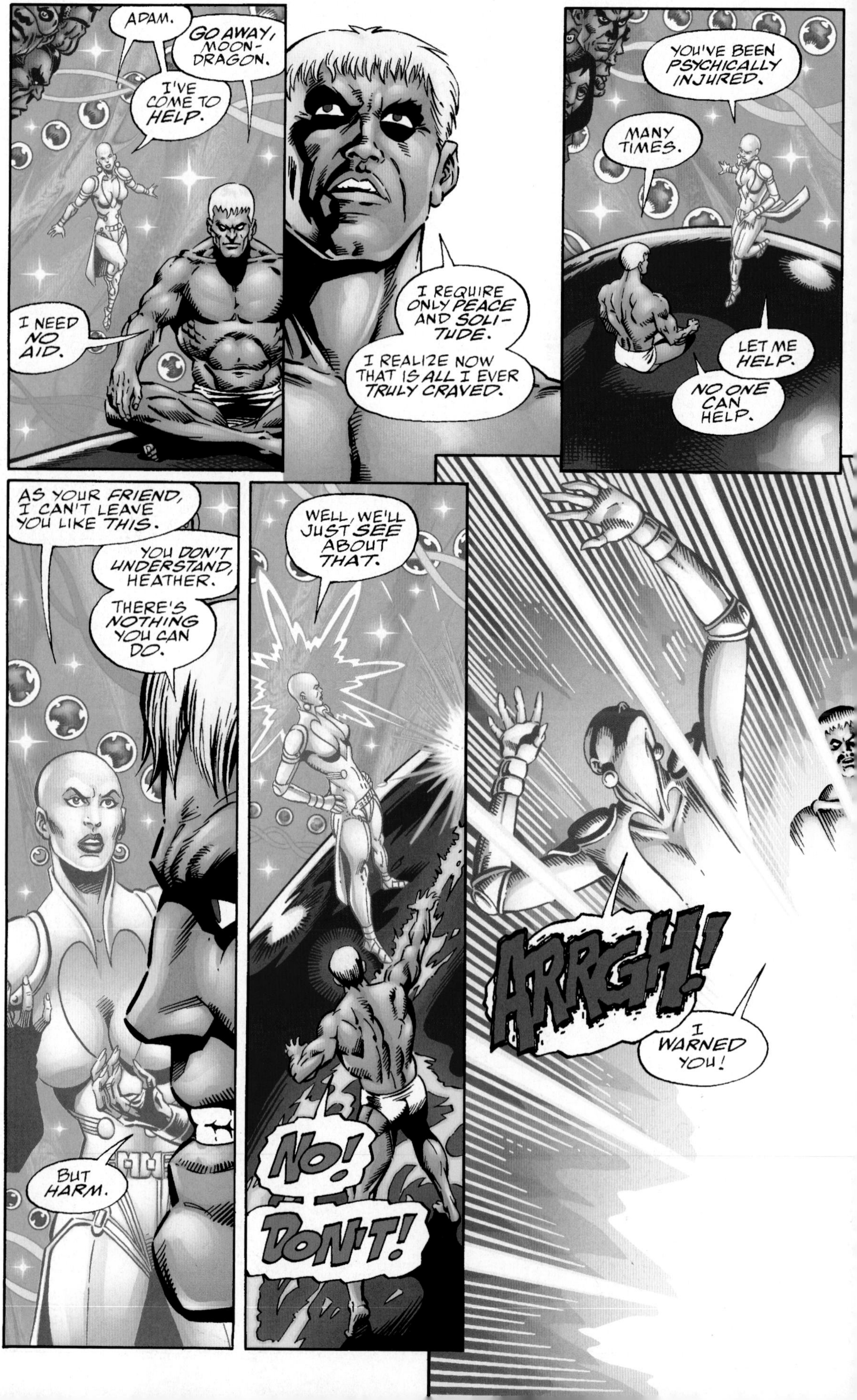

ADAM.
GO AWAY, MOON-DRAGON.
I'VE COME TO HELP.
I NEED NO AID.
I REQUIRE ONLY PEACE AND SOLI-TUDE.
I REALIZE NOW THAT IS ALL I EVER TRULY CRAVED.
YOU'VE BEEN PSYCHICALLY INJURED.
MANY TIMES.
LET ME HELP.
NO ONE CAN HELP.
AS YOUR FRIEND, I CAN'T LEAVE YOU LIKE THIS.
YOU DON'T UNDERSTAND, HEATHER.
THERE'S NOTHING YOU CAN DO.
BUT HARM.
WELL, WE'LL JUST SEE ABOUT THAT.
NO! DON'T!
ARRGH!
I WARNED YOU!

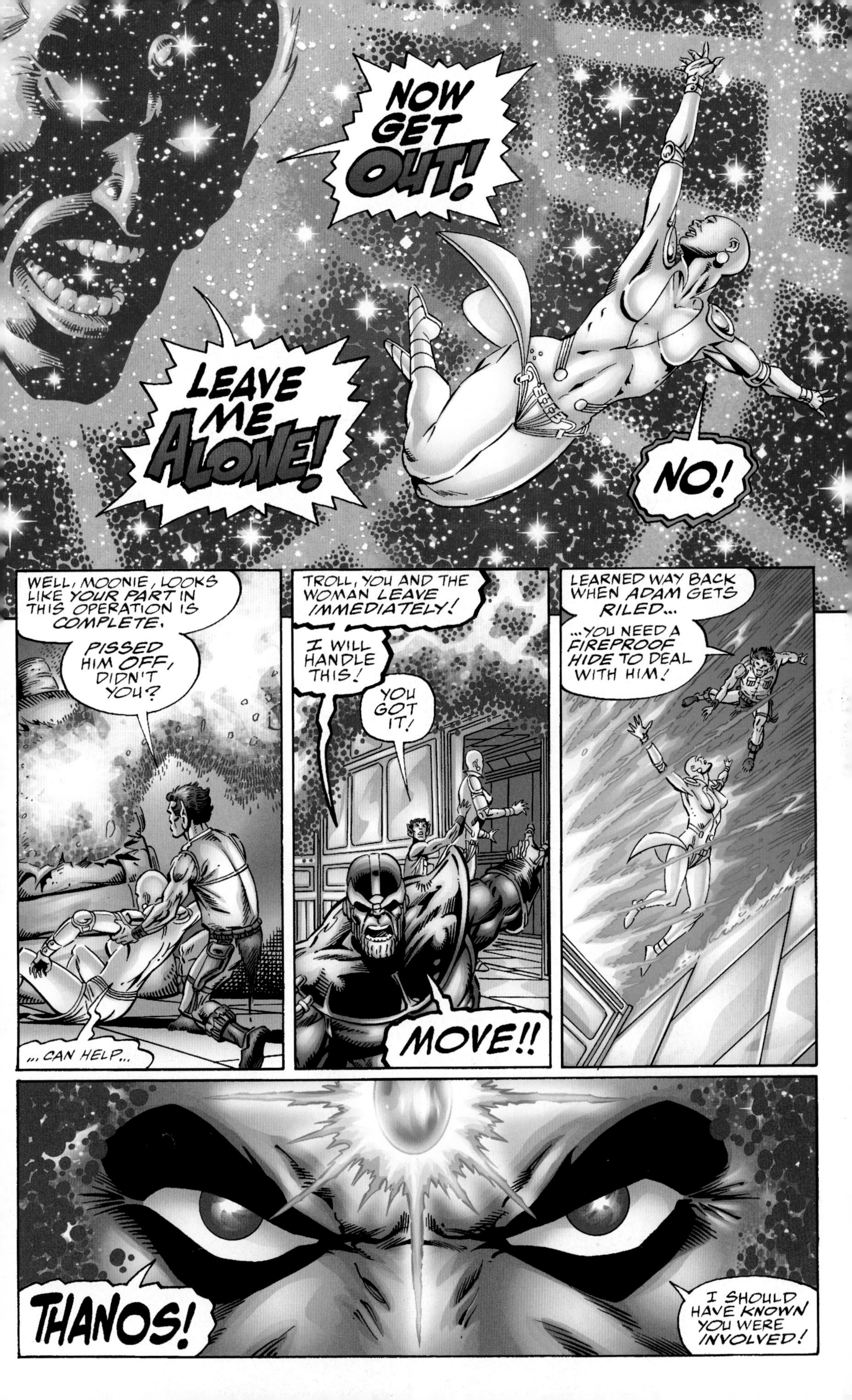
NOW GET OUT!
LEAVE ME ALONE!
NO!
WELL, MOONIE, LOOKS LIKE YOUR PART IN THIS OPERATION IS COMPLETE.
PISSED HIM OFF, DIDN'T YOU?
...CAN HELP...
TROLL, YOU AND THE WOMAN LEAVE IMMEDIATELY!
I WILL HANDLE THIS!
YOU GOT IT!
MOVE!!
LEARNED WAY BACK WHEN ADAM GETS RILED...
...YOU NEED A FIREPROOF HIDE TO DEAL WITH HIM!
THANOS!
I SHOULD HAVE KNOWN YOU WERE INVOLVED!

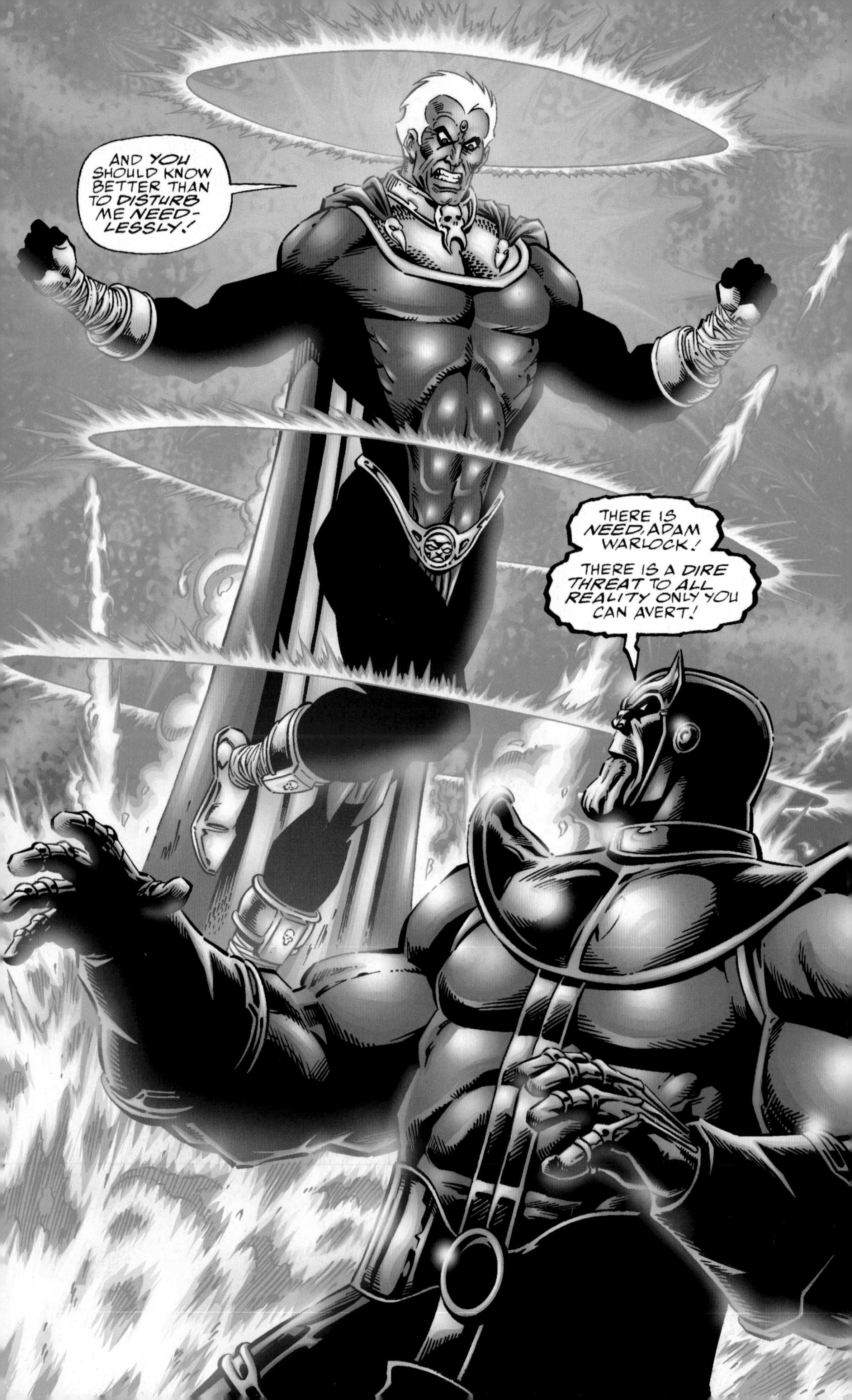
AND YOU SHOULD KNOW BETTER THAN TO DISTURB ME NEED-LESSLY!
THERE IS NEED, ADAM WARLOCK!
THERE IS A DIRE THREAT TO ALL REALITY ONLY YOU CAN AVERT!

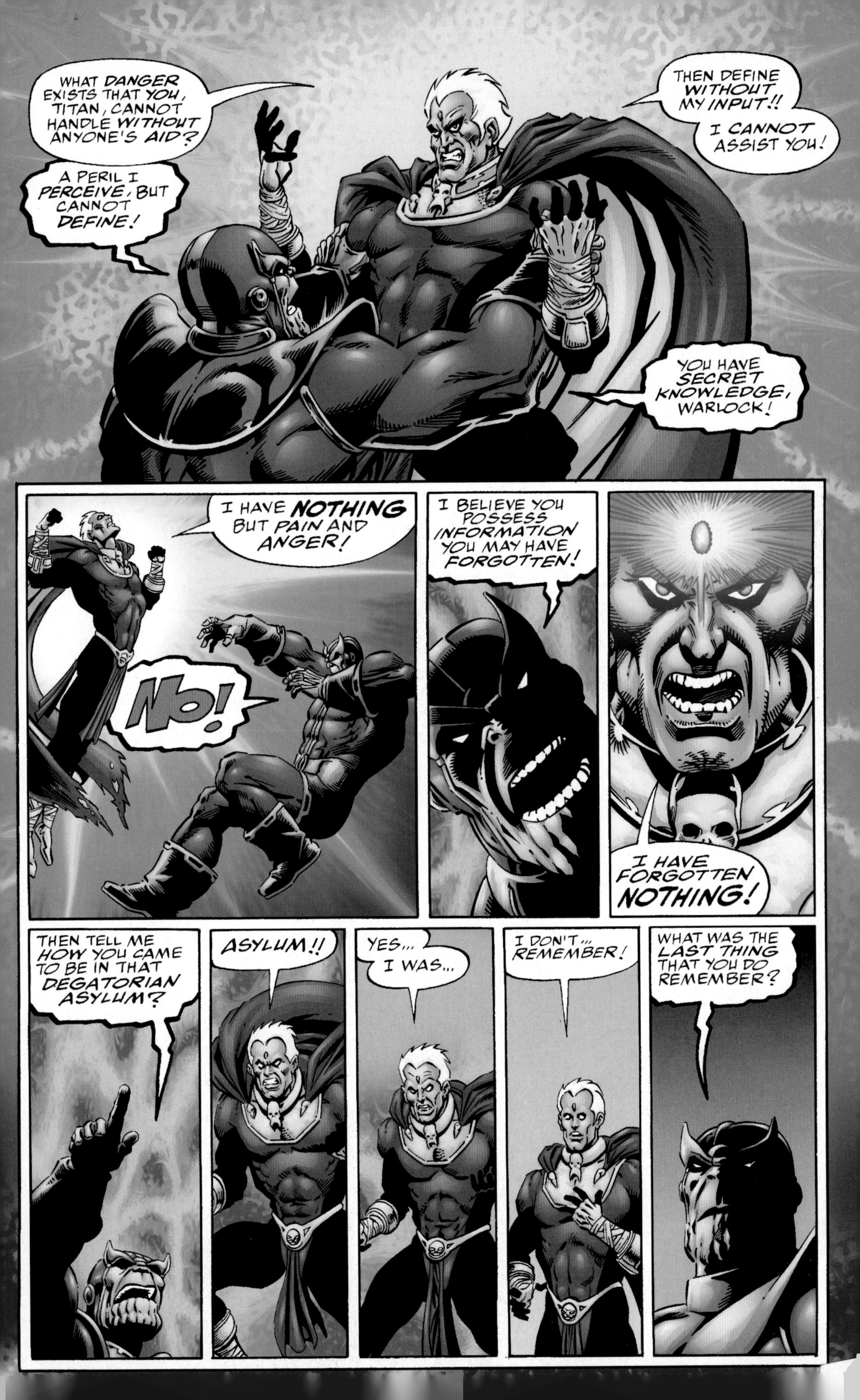

WHAT DANGER EXISTS THAT YOU, TITAN, CANNOT HANDLE WITHOUT ANYONE'S AID?
A PERIL I PERCEIVE, BUT CANNOT DEFINE!
THEN DEFINE WITHOUT MY INPUT!!
I CANNOT ASSIST YOU!
YOU HAVE SECRET KNOWLEDGE, WARLOCK!
I HAVE NOTHING BUT PAIN AND ANGER!
NO!
I BELIEVE YOU POSSESS INFORMATION YOU MAY HAVE FORGOTTEN!
I HAVE FORGOTTEN NOTHING!
THEN TELL ME HOW YOU CAME TO BE IN THAT DEGATORIAN ASYLUM?
ASYLUM!!
YES... I WAS...
I DON'T... REMEMBER!
WHAT WAS THE LAST THING THAT YOU DO REMEMBER?

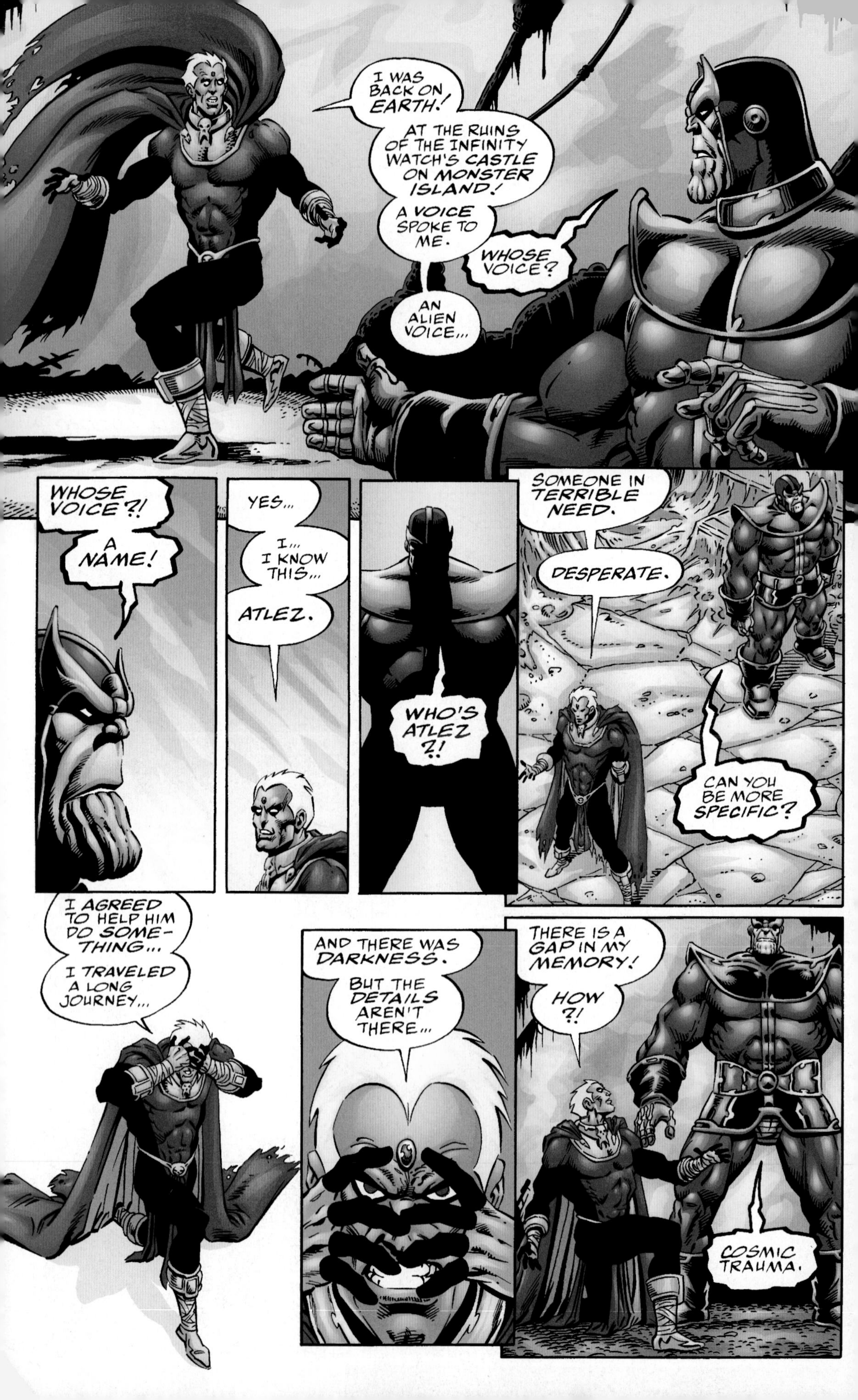
I WAS BACK ON EARTH!
AT THE RUINS OF THE INFINITY WATCH'S CASTLE ON MONSTER ISLAND!
A VOICE SPOKE TO ME.
WHOSE VOICE?
AN ALIEN VOICE...
WHOSE VOICE?!
A NAME!
YES...
I... I KNOW THIS...
ATLEZ.
WHO'S ATLEZ ?!
SOMEONE IN TERRIBLE NEED.
DESPERATE.
CAN YOU BE MORE SPECIFIC?
I AGREED TO HELP HIM DO SOME-THING...
I TRAVELED A LONG JOURNEY...
AND THERE WAS DARKNESS.
BUT THE DETAILS AREN'T THERE...
THERE IS A GAP IN MY MEMORY!
HOW ?!
COSMIC TRAUMA.

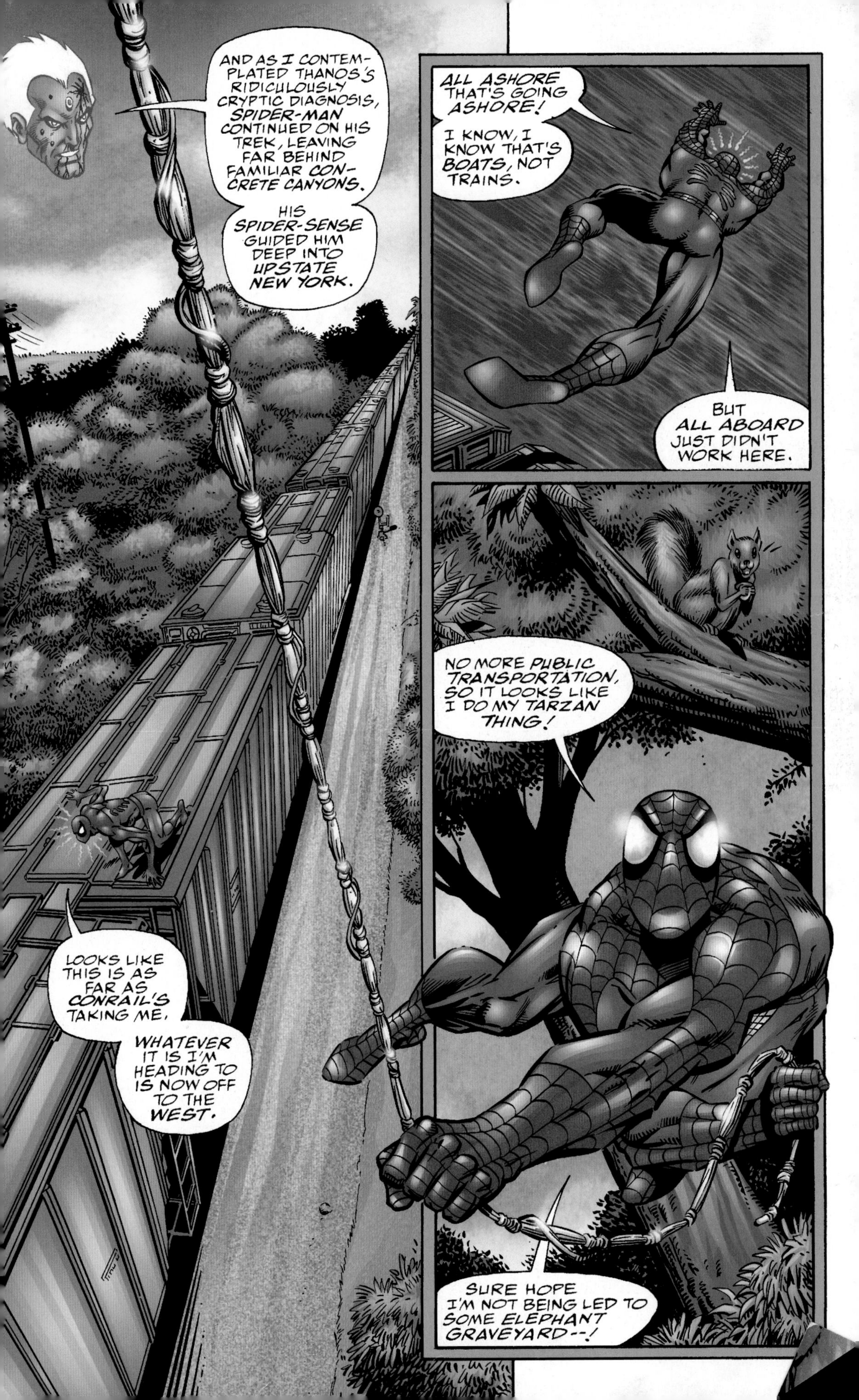
AND AS I CONTEMPLATED THANOS'S RIDICULOUSLY CRYPTIC DIAGNOSIS, SPIDER-MAN CONTINUED ON HIS TREK, LEAVING FAR BEHIND FAMILIAR CONCRETE CANYONS.
HIS SPIDER-SENSE GUIDED HIM DEEP INTO UPSTATE NEW YORK.
LOOKS LIKE THIS IS AS FAR AS CONRAIL'S TAKING ME.
WHATEVER IT IS I'M HEADING TO IS NOW OFF TO THE WEST.
ALL ASHORE THAT'S GOING ASHORE!
I KNOW, I KNOW THAT'S BOATS, NOT TRAINS.
BUT ALL ABOARD JUST DIDN'T WORK HERE.
NO MORE PUBLIC TRANSPORTATION, SO IT LOOKS LIKE I DO MY TARZAN THING!
SURE HOPE I'M NOT BEING LED TO SOME ELEPHANT GRAVEYARD--!

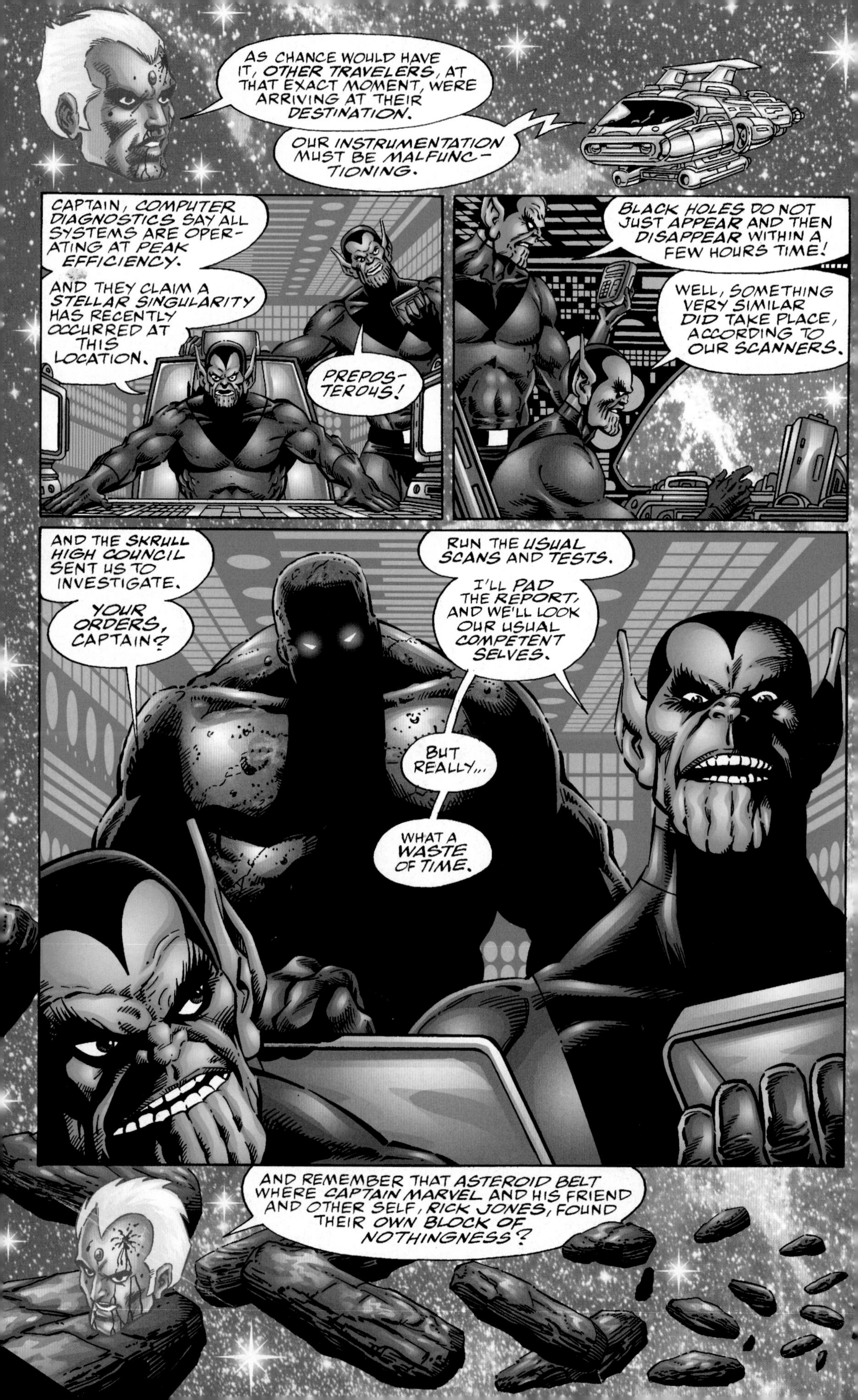
AS CHANCE WOULD HAVE IT, OTHER TRAVELERS, AT THAT EXACT MOMENT, WERE ARRIVING AT THEIR DESTINATION.
OUR INSTRUMENTATION MUST BE MALFUNC-TIONING.
CAPTAIN, COMPUTER DIAGNOSTICS SAY ALL SYSTEMS ARE OPER-ATING AT PEAK EFFICIENCY.
AND THEY CLAIM A STELLAR SINGULARITY HAS RECENTLY OCCURRED AT THIS LOCATION.
PREPOS-TEROUS!
BLACK HOLES DO NOT JUST APPEAR AND THEN DISAPPEAR WITHIN A FEW HOURS TIME!
WELL, SOMETHING VERY SIMILAR DID TAKE PLACE, ACCORDING TO OUR SCANNERS.
AND THE SKRULL HIGH COUNCIL SENT US TO INVESTIGATE.
YOUR ORDERS, CAPTAIN?
RUN THE USUAL SCANS AND TESTS.
I'LL PAD THE REPORT, AND WE'LL LOOK OUR USUAL COMPETENT SELVES.
BUT REALLY...
WHAT A WASTE OF TIME.
AND REMEMBER THAT ASTEROID BELT WHERE CAPTAIN MARVEL AND HIS FRIEND AND OTHER SELF, RICK JONES, FOUND THEIR OWN BLOCK OF NOTHINGNESS?

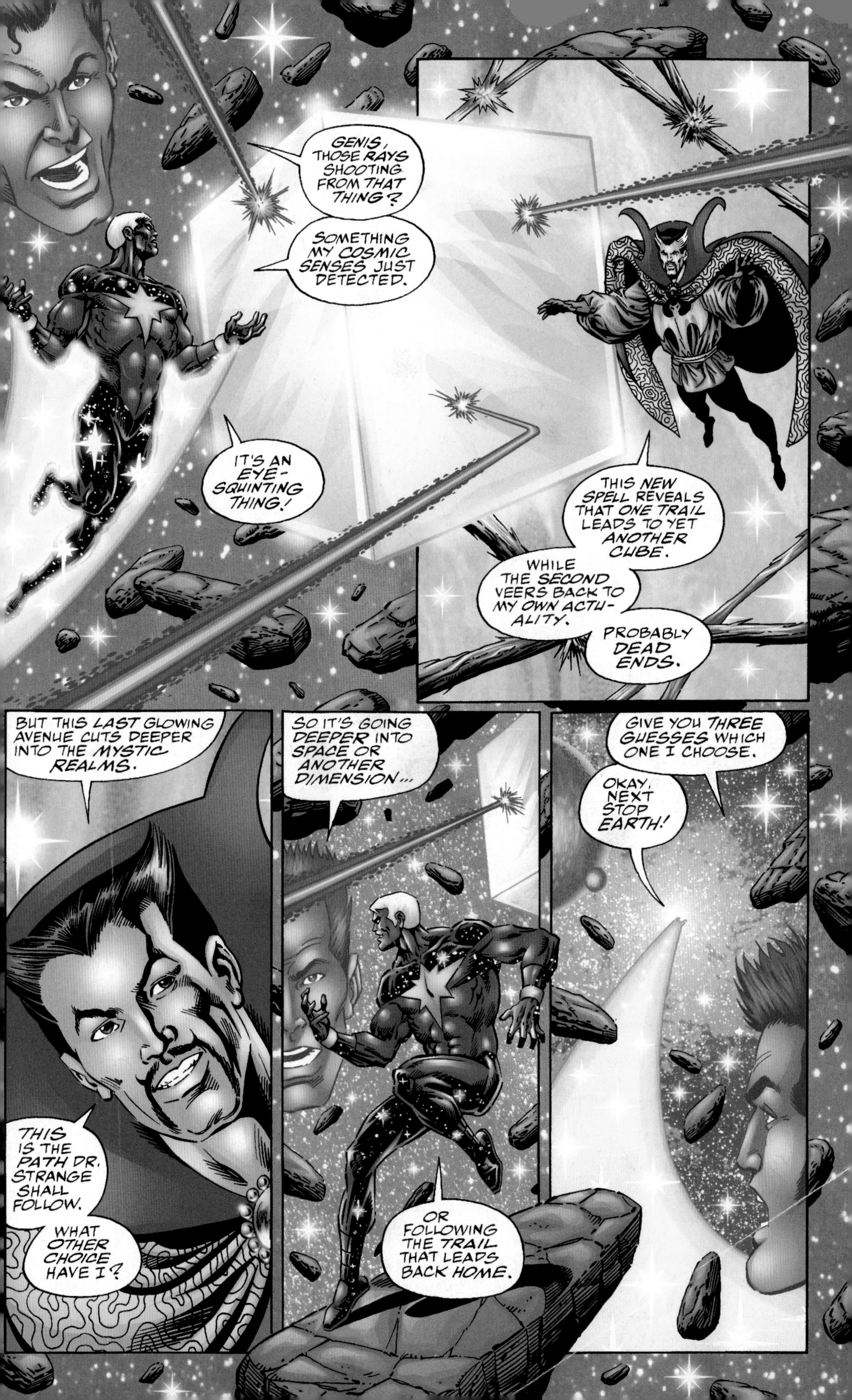
GENIS, THOSE RAYS SHOOTING FROM THAT THING?
SOMETHING MY COSMIC SENSES JUST DETECTED.
IT'S AN EYE-SQUINTING THING!
THIS NEW SPELL REVEALS THAT ONE TRAIL LEADS TO YET ANOTHER CUBE.
WHILE THE SECOND VEERS BACK TO MY OWN ACTUALITY.
PROBABLY DEAD ENDS.
BUT THIS LAST GLOWING AVENUE CUTS DEEPER INTO THE MYSTIC REALMS.
THIS IS THE PATH DR. STRANGE SHALL FOLLOW.
WHAT OTHER CHOICE HAVE I?
SO IT'S GOING DEEPER INTO SPACE OR ANOTHER DIMENSION...
OR FOLLOWING THE TRAIL THAT LEADS BACK HOME.
GIVE YOU THREE GUESSES WHICH ONE I CHOOSE.
OKAY. NEXT STOP EARTH!

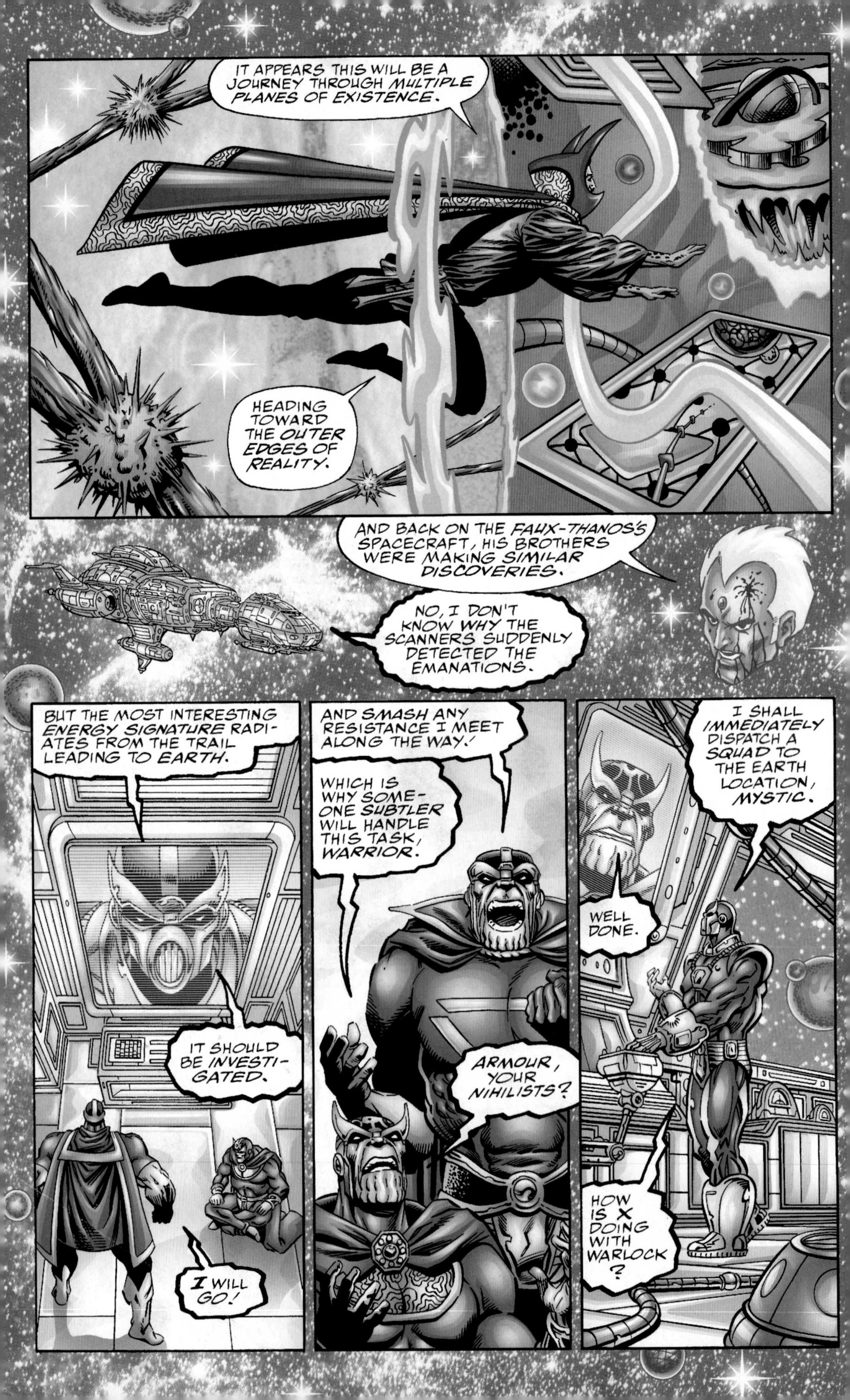
IT APPEARS THIS WILL BE A JOURNEY THROUGH MULTIPLE PLANES OF EXISTENCE.
HEADING TOWARD THE OUTER EDGES OF REALITY.
AND BACK ON THE FAUX-THANOS'S SPACECRAFT, HIS BROTHERS WERE MAKING SIMILAR DISCOVERIES.
NO, I DON'T KNOW WHY THE SCANNERS SUDDENLY DETECTED THE EMANATIONS.
BUT THE MOST INTERESTING ENERGY SIGNATURE RADIATES FROM THE TRAIL LEADING TO EARTH.
IT SHOULD BE INVESTIGATED.
I WILL GO!
AND SMASH ANY RESISTANCE I MEET ALONG THE WAY!
WHICH IS WHY SOMEONE SUBTLER WILL HANDLE THIS TASK, WARRIOR.
ARMOUR, YOUR NIHILISTS?
I SHALL IMMEDIATELY DISPATCH A SQUAD TO THE EARTH LOCATION, MYSTIC.
WELL DONE.
HOW IS X DOING WITH WARLOCK?

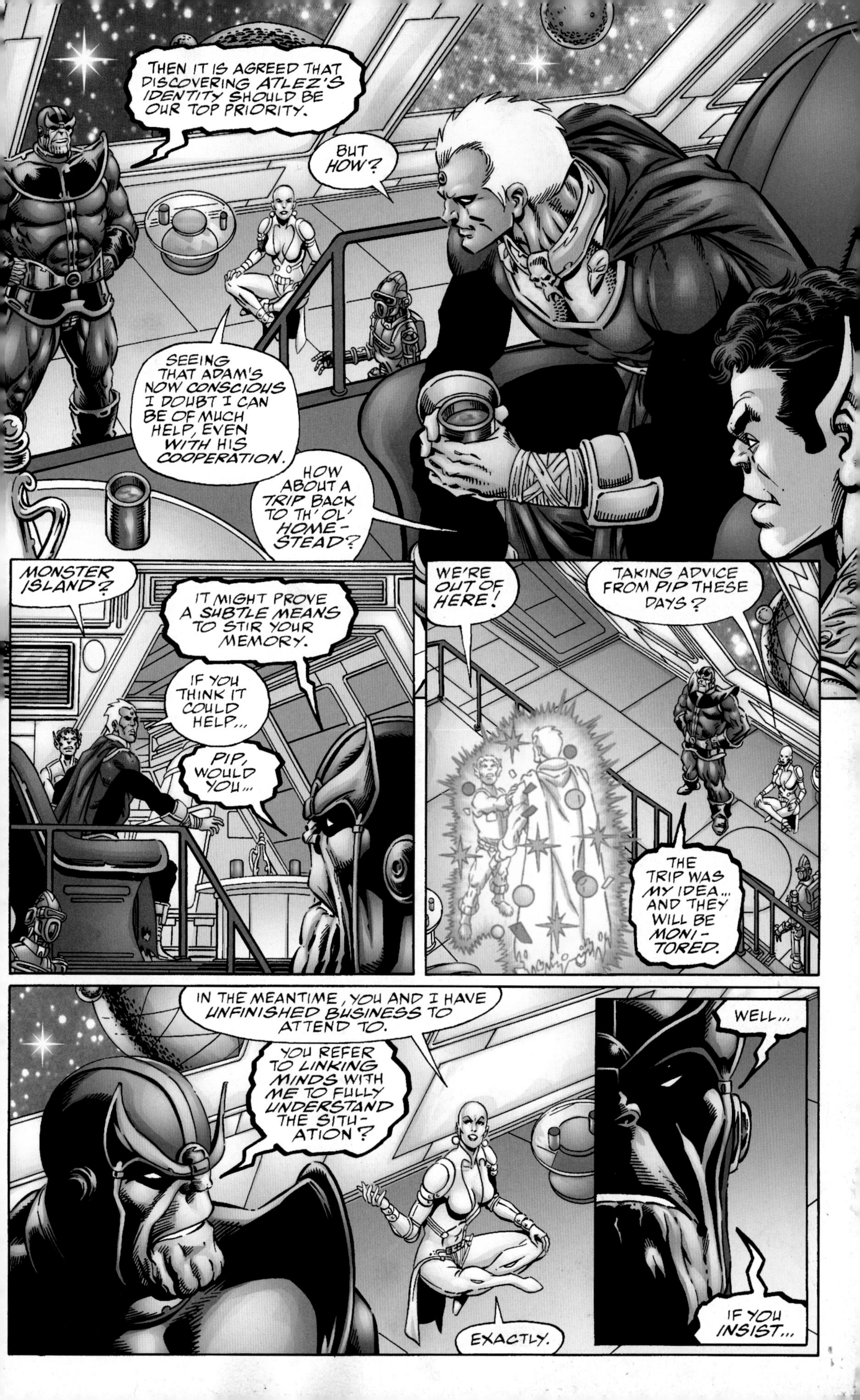
THEN IT IS AGREED THAT DISCOVERING ATLEZ'S IDENTITY SHOULD BE OUR TOP PRIORITY.
BUT HOW?
SEEING THAT ADAM'S NOW CONSCIOUS I DOUBT I CAN BE OF MUCH HELP, EVEN WITH HIS COOPERATION.
HOW ABOUT A TRIP BACK TO TH' OL' HOME-STEAD?
MONSTER ISLAND?
IT MIGHT PROVE A SUBTLE MEANS TO STIR YOUR MEMORY.
IF YOU THINK IT COULD HELP...
PIP, WOULD YOU...
WE'RE OUT OF HERE!
TAKING ADVICE FROM PIP THESE DAYS?
THE TRIP WAS MY IDEA... AND THEY WILL BE MONI-TORED.
IN THE MEANTIME, YOU AND I HAVE UNFINISHED BUSINESS TO ATTEND TO.
YOU REFER TO LINKING MINDS WITH ME TO FULLY UNDERSTAND THE SITU-ATION?
EXACTLY.
WELL...
IF YOU INSIST...

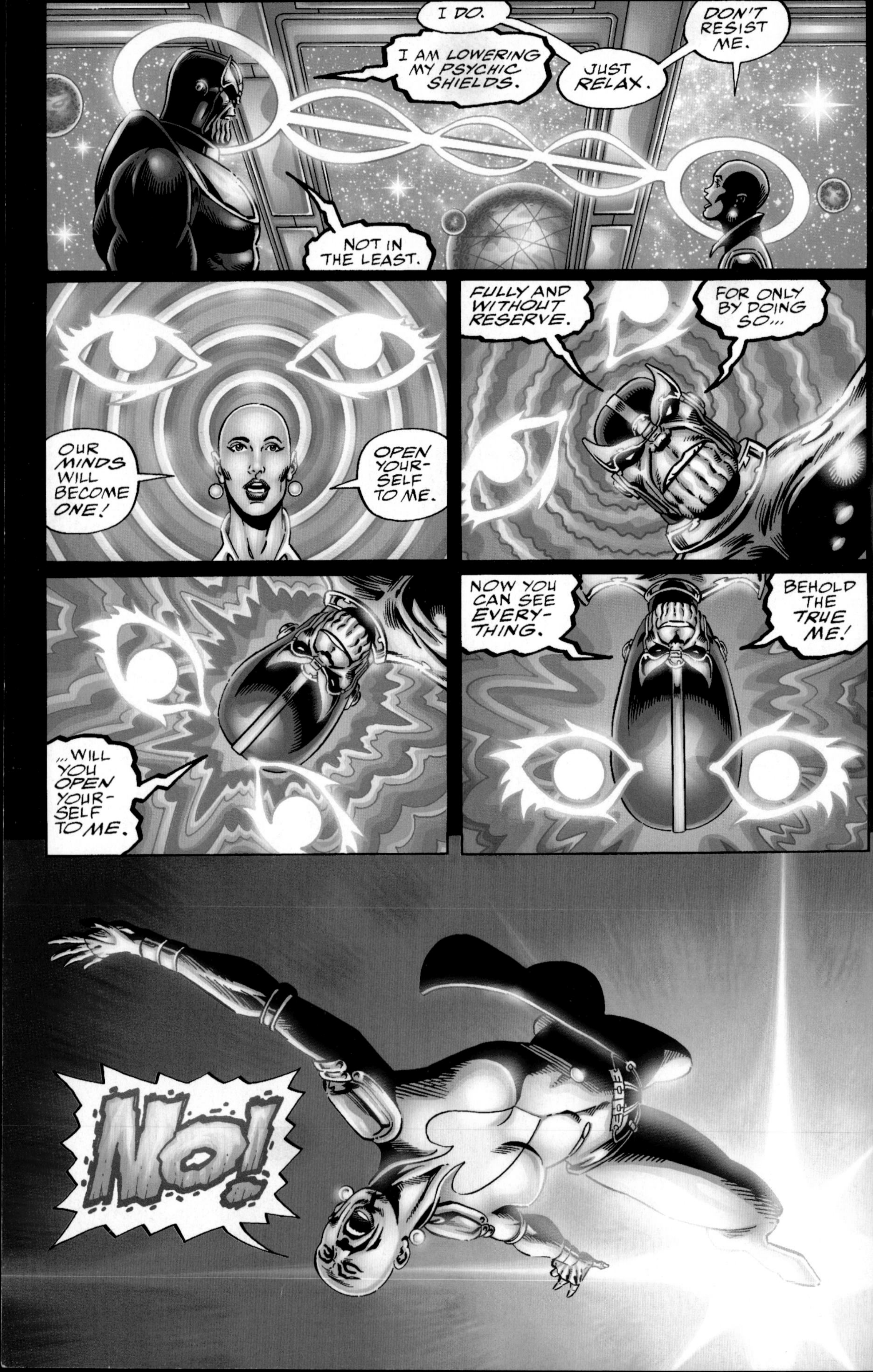
I DO.
I AM LOWERING MY PSYCHIC SHIELDS.
JUST RELAX.
DON'T RESIST ME.
NOT IN THE LEAST.
OUR MINDS WILL BECOME ONE!
OPEN YOURSELF TO ME.
FULLY AND WITHOUT RESERVE.
FOR ONLY BY DOING SO...
...WILL YOU OPEN YOURSELF TO ME.
NOW YOU CAN SEE EVERYTHING.
BEHOLD THE TRUE ME!
NO!

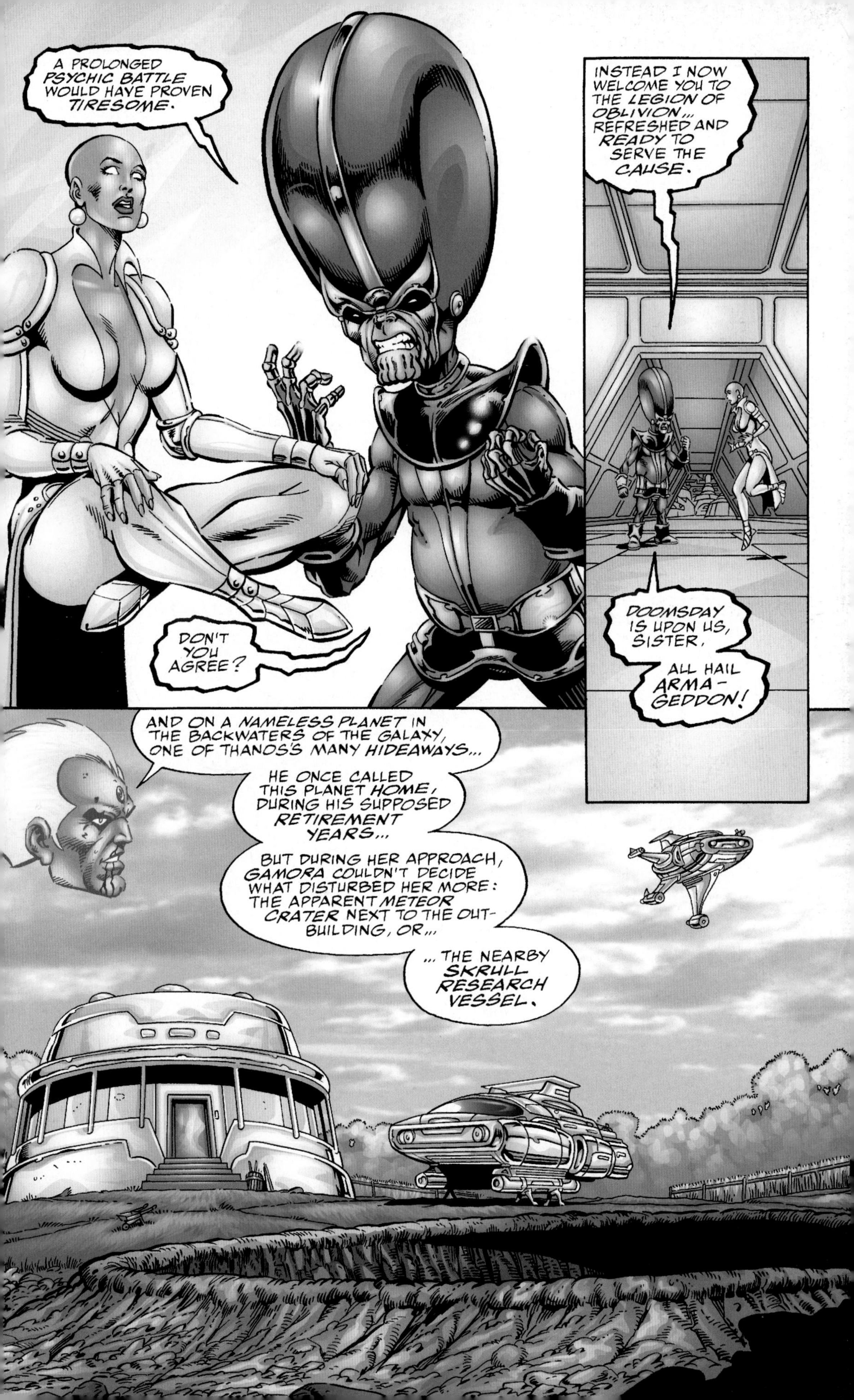
A PROLONGED PSYCHIC BATTLE WOULD HAVE PROVEN TIRESOME.
DON'T YOU AGREE?
INSTEAD I NOW WELCOME YOU TO THE LEGION OF OBLIVION... REFRESHED AND READY TO SERVE THE CAUSE.
DOOMSDAY IS UPON US, SISTER.
ALL HAIL ARMAGEDDON!
AND ON A NAMELESS PLANET IN THE BACKWATERS OF THE GALAXY, ONE OF THANOS'S MANY HIDEAWAYS...
HE ONCE CALLED THIS PLANET HOME, DURING HIS SUPPOSED RETIREMENT YEARS...
BUT DURING HER APPROACH, GAMORA COULDN'T DECIDE WHAT DISTURBED HER MORE: THE APPARENT METEOR CRATER NEXT TO THE OUT-BUILDING, OR...
... THE NEARBY SKRULL RESEARCH VESSEL.

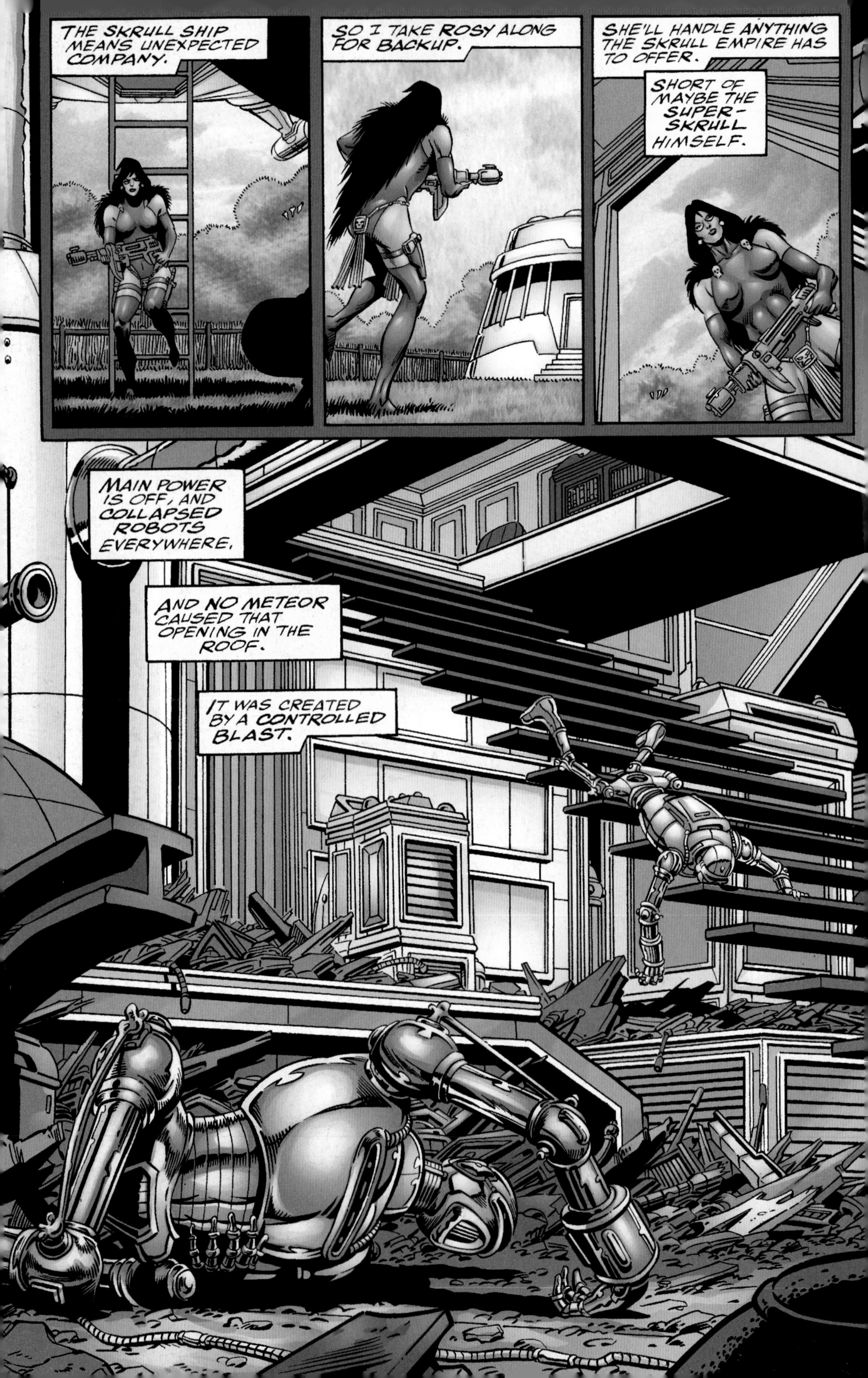
THE SKRULL SHIP MEANS UNEXPECTED COMPANY.
SO I TAKE ROSY ALONG FOR BACKUP.
SHE'LL HANDLE ANYTHING THE SKRULL EMPIRE HAS TO OFFER.
SHORT OF MAYBE THE SUPER-SKRULL HIMSELF.
MAIN POWER IS OFF, AND COLLAPSED ROBOTS EVERYWHERE.
AND NO METEOR CAUSED THAT OPENING IN THE ROOF.
IT WAS CREATED BY A CONTROLLED BLAST.

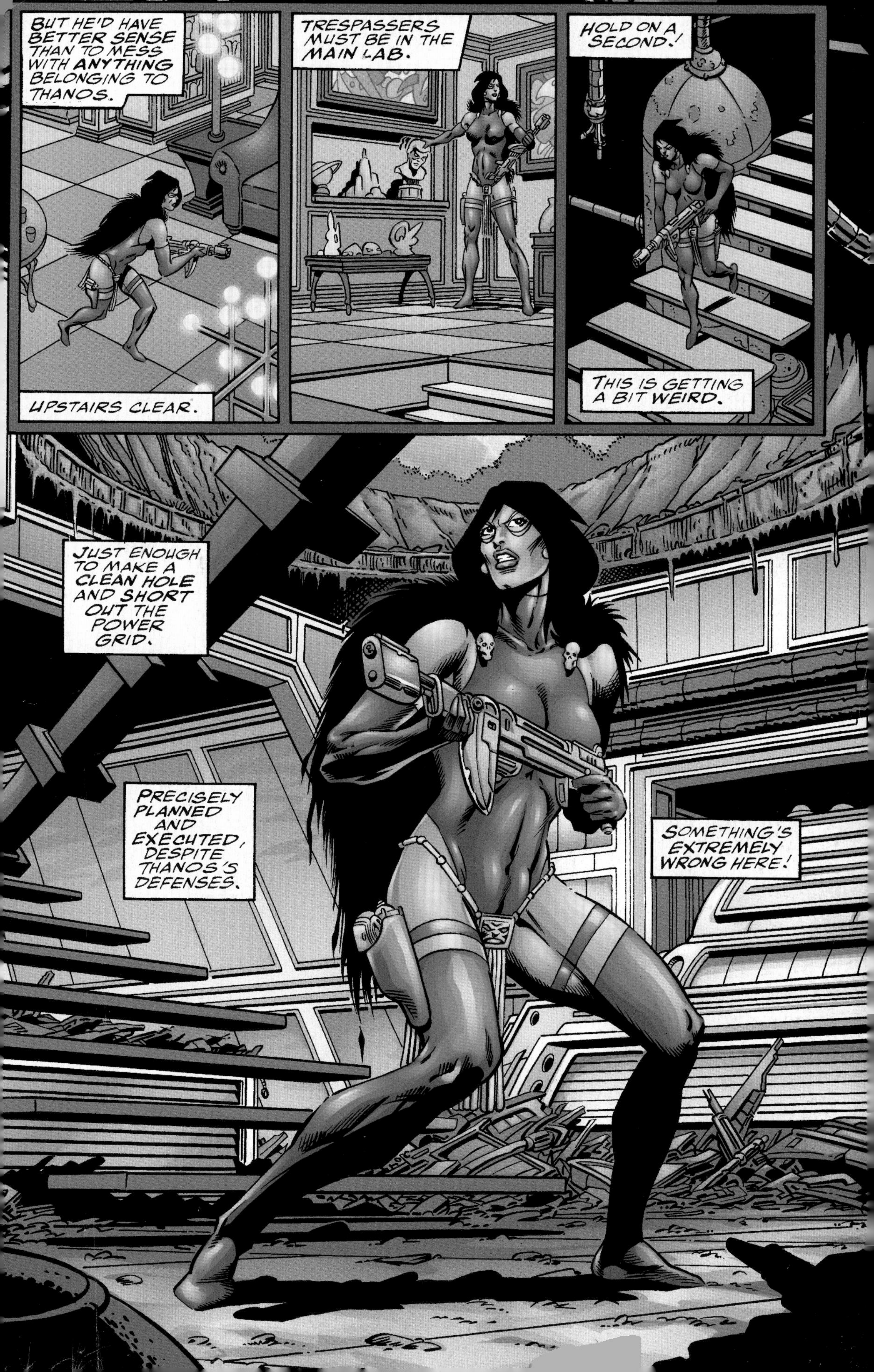
BUT HE'D HAVE BETTER SENSE THAN TO MESS WITH ANYTHING BELONGING TO THANOS.
UPSTAIRS CLEAR.
TRESPASSERS MUST BE IN THE MAIN LAB.
HOLD ON A SECOND!
THIS IS GETTING A BIT WEIRD.
JUST ENOUGH TO MAKE A CLEAN HOLE AND SHORT OUT THE POWER GRID.
PRECISELY PLANNED AND EXECUTED, DESPITE THANOS'S DEFENSES.
SOMETHING'S EXTREMELY WRONG HERE!

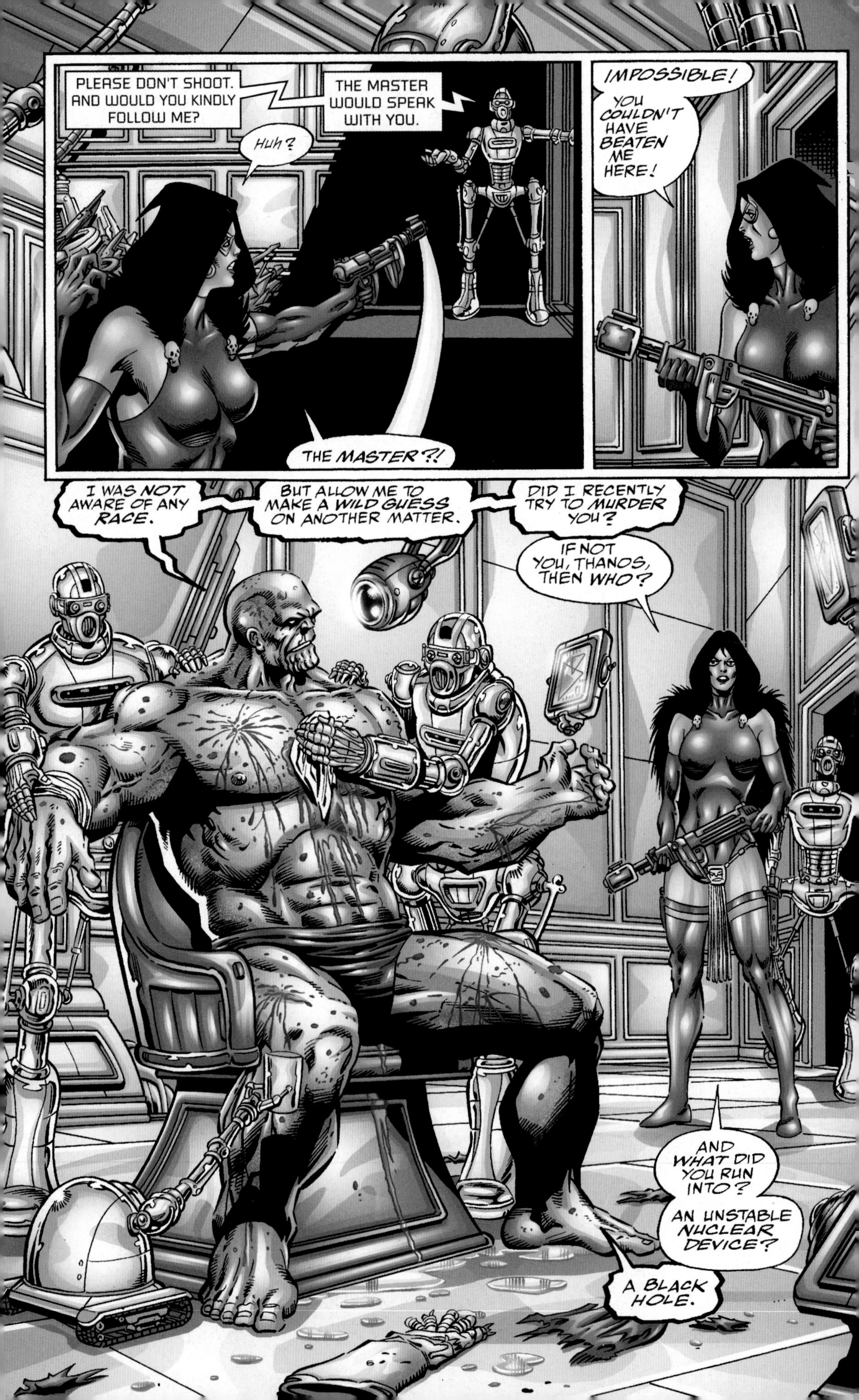
PLEASE DON'T SHOOT. AND WOULD YOU KINDLY FOLLOW ME?
THE MASTER WOULD SPEAK WITH YOU.
Huh?
THE MASTER?!
IMPOSSIBLE!
YOU COULDN'T HAVE BEATEN ME HERE!
I WAS NOT AWARE OF ANY RACE.
BUT ALLOW ME TO MAKE A WILD GUESS ON ANOTHER MATTER.
DID I RECENTLY TRY TO MURDER YOU?
IF NOT YOU, THANOS, THEN WHO?
AND WHAT DID YOU RUN INTO?
AN UNSTABLE NUCLEAR DEVICE?
A BLACK HOLE.

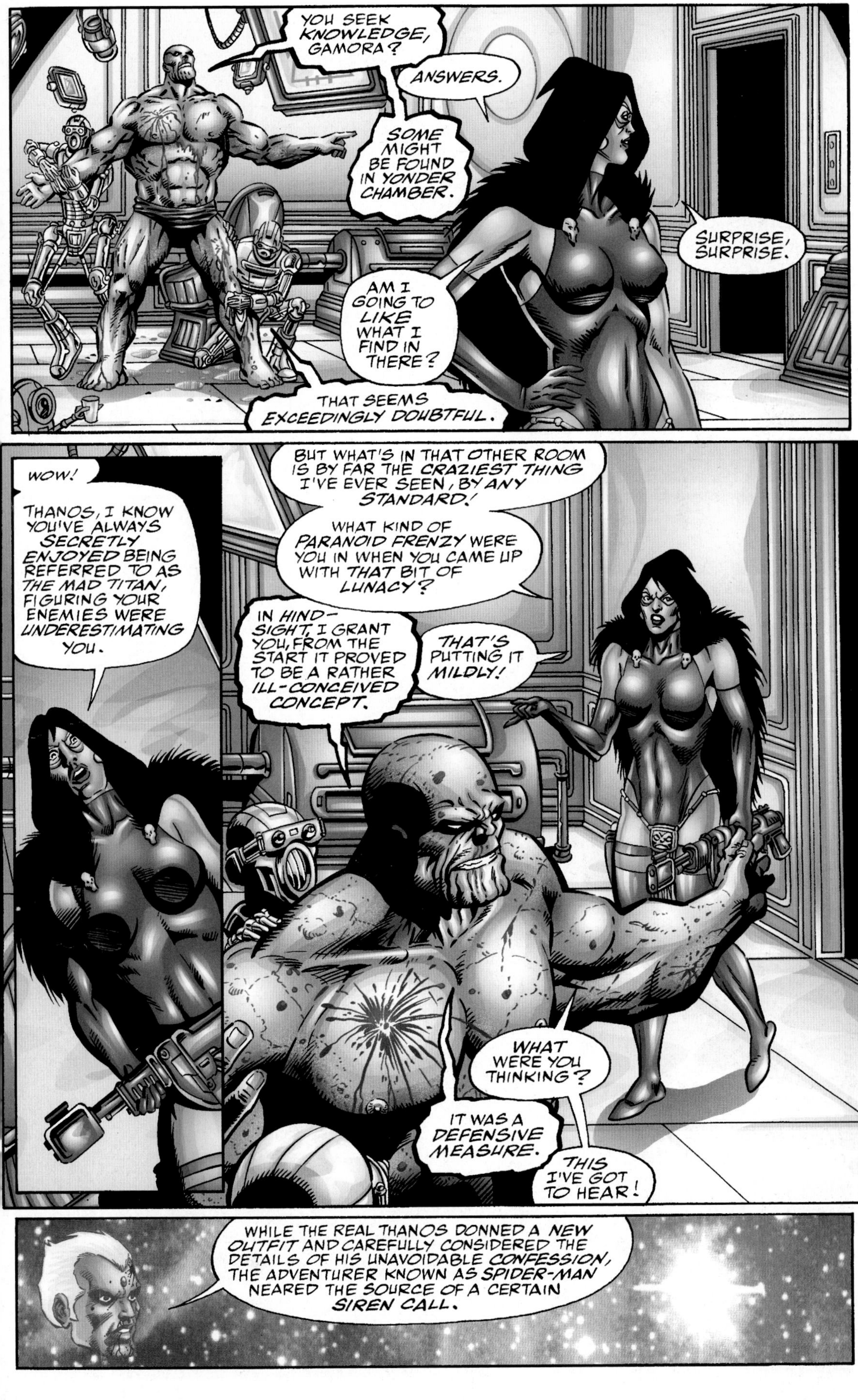
YOU SEEK KNOWLEDGE, GAMORA?
ANSWERS.
SOME MIGHT BE FOUND IN YONDER CHAMBER.
SURPRISE, SURPRISE.
AM I GOING TO LIKE WHAT I FIND IN THERE?
THAT SEEMS EXCEEDINGLY DOUBTFUL.
WOW!
THANOS, I KNOW YOU'VE ALWAYS SECRETLY ENJOYED BEING REFERRED TO AS THE MAD TITAN, FIGURING YOUR ENEMIES WERE UNDERESTIMATING YOU.
BUT WHAT'S IN THAT OTHER ROOM IS BY FAR THE CRAZIEST THING I'VE EVER SEEN, BY ANY STANDARD!
WHAT KIND OF PARANOID FRENZY WERE YOU IN WHEN YOU CAME UP WITH THAT BIT OF LUNACY?
IN HIND-SIGHT, I GRANT YOU, FROM THE START IT PROVED TO BE A RATHER ILL-CONCEIVED CONCEPT.
THAT'S PUTTING IT MILDLY!
WHAT WERE YOU THINKING?
IT WAS A DEFENSIVE MEASURE.
THIS I'VE GOT TO HEAR!
WHILE THE REAL THANOS DONNED A NEW OUTFIT AND CAREFULLY CONSIDERED THE DETAILS OF HIS UNAVOIDABLE CONFESSION, THE ADVENTURER KNOWN AS SPIDER-MAN NEARED THE SOURCE OF A CERTAIN SIREN CALL.

THIS HAS GOT TO BE THE PLACE!

THE WAY MY SPIDER-SENSE IS WAILING, I'VE GOT TO BE ALMOST ON TOP OF WHATEVER'S STIMU-LATING IT.

THAT CLEARING AHEAD...

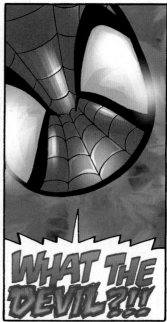

WHAT THE DEVIL?!!...

I WAS EXPECTING MEPHISTO, OR MAYBE GALACTUS, OR AT LEAST A KREE INVASION FORCE.

INSTEAD I GET A NORMAN ROCKWELL FARMHOUSE!

WHAT'S GOING DOWN HERE?

DARK AND POWERFUL FORCES RUN UNCHECKED.

THERE ARE STILL SO MANY OBSTACLES TO OVERCOME.

DID I PICK THE PROPER PLAYERS?

HAVE I DOOMED THE SUCCESSOR??

WILL THE PIECES OF THE PUZZLE FALL INTO PLACE QUICKLY ENOUGH?

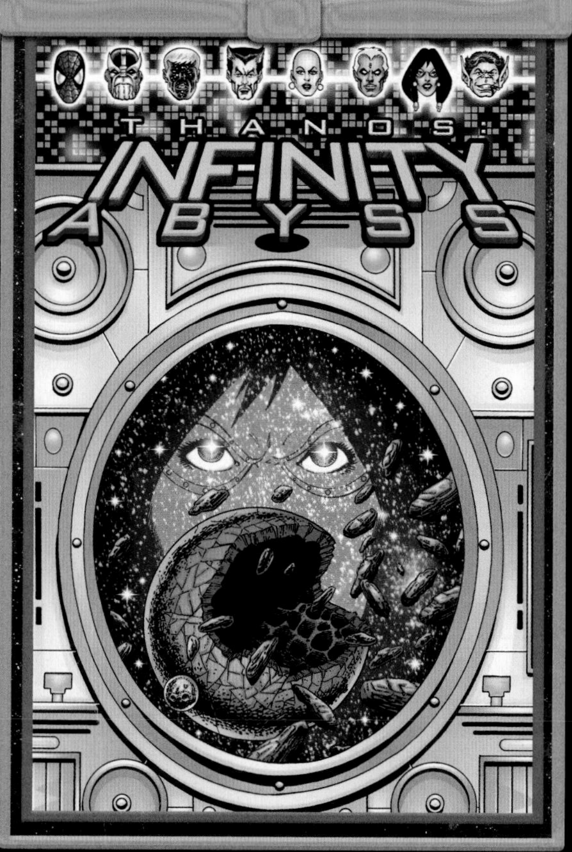
THANOS:
INFINITY
ABYSS
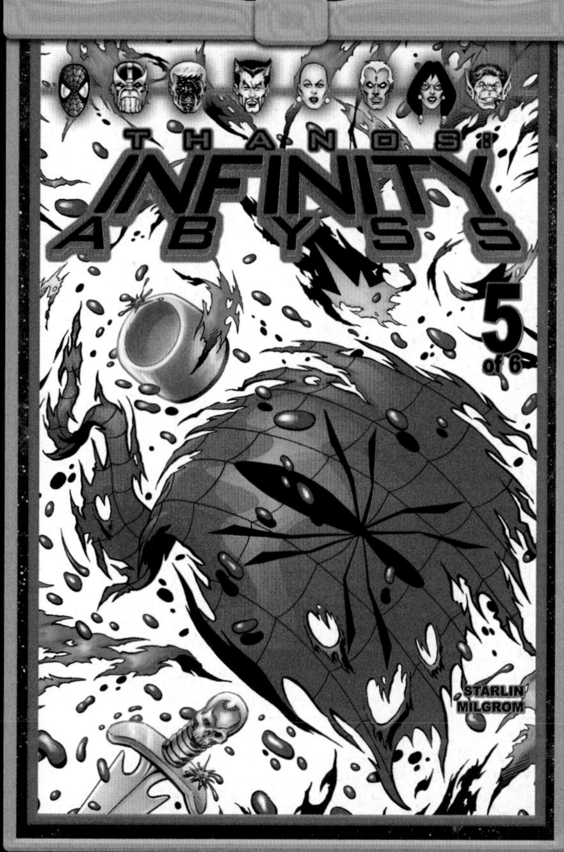
THANOS:
INFINITY
ABYSS
5
of 6
STARLIN
MILGROM
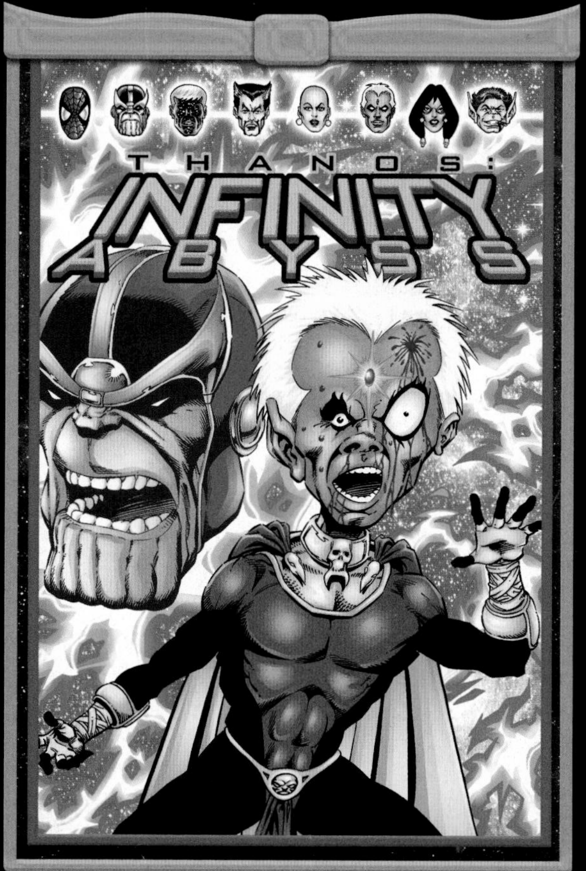
THANOS:
INFINITY
ABYSS

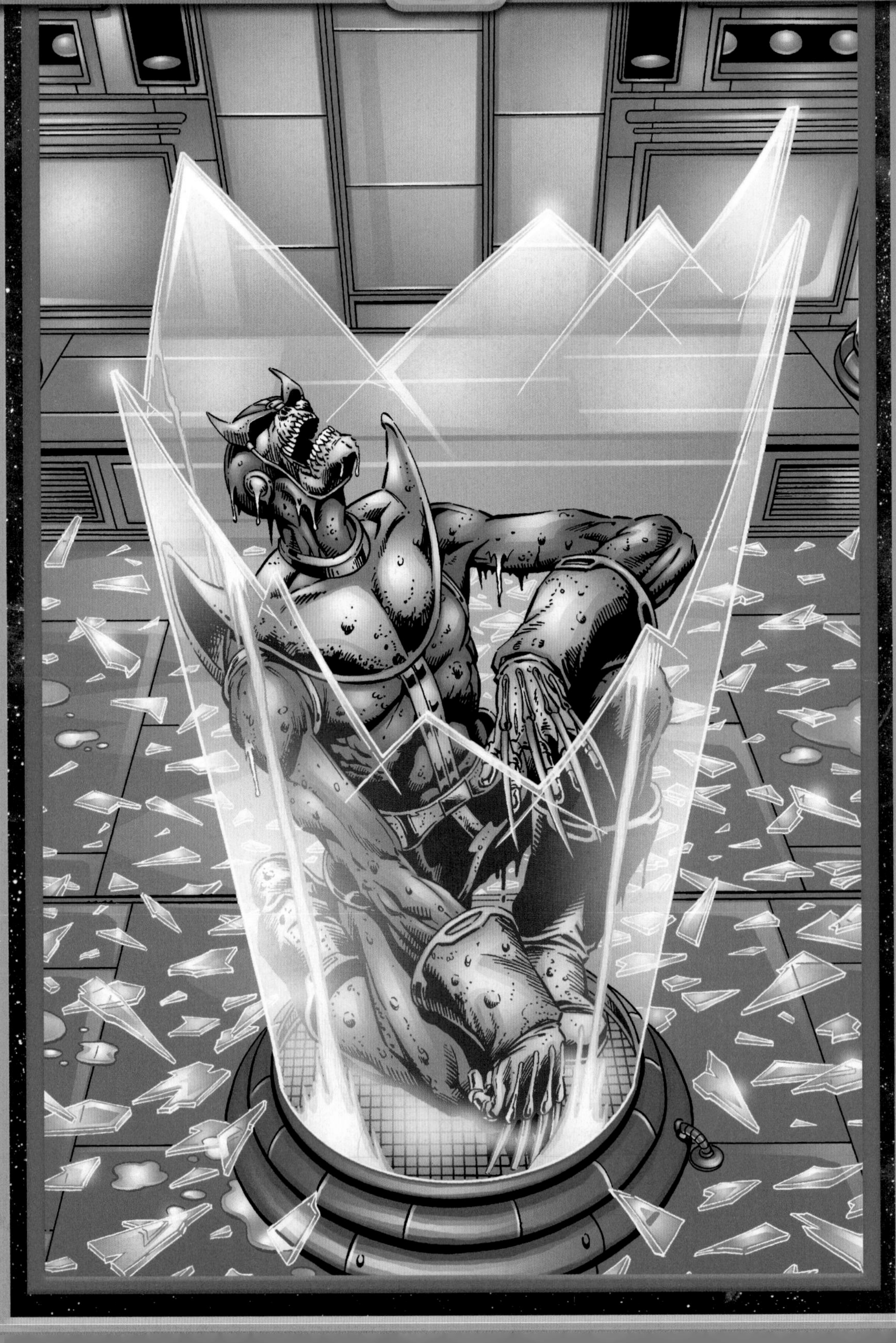

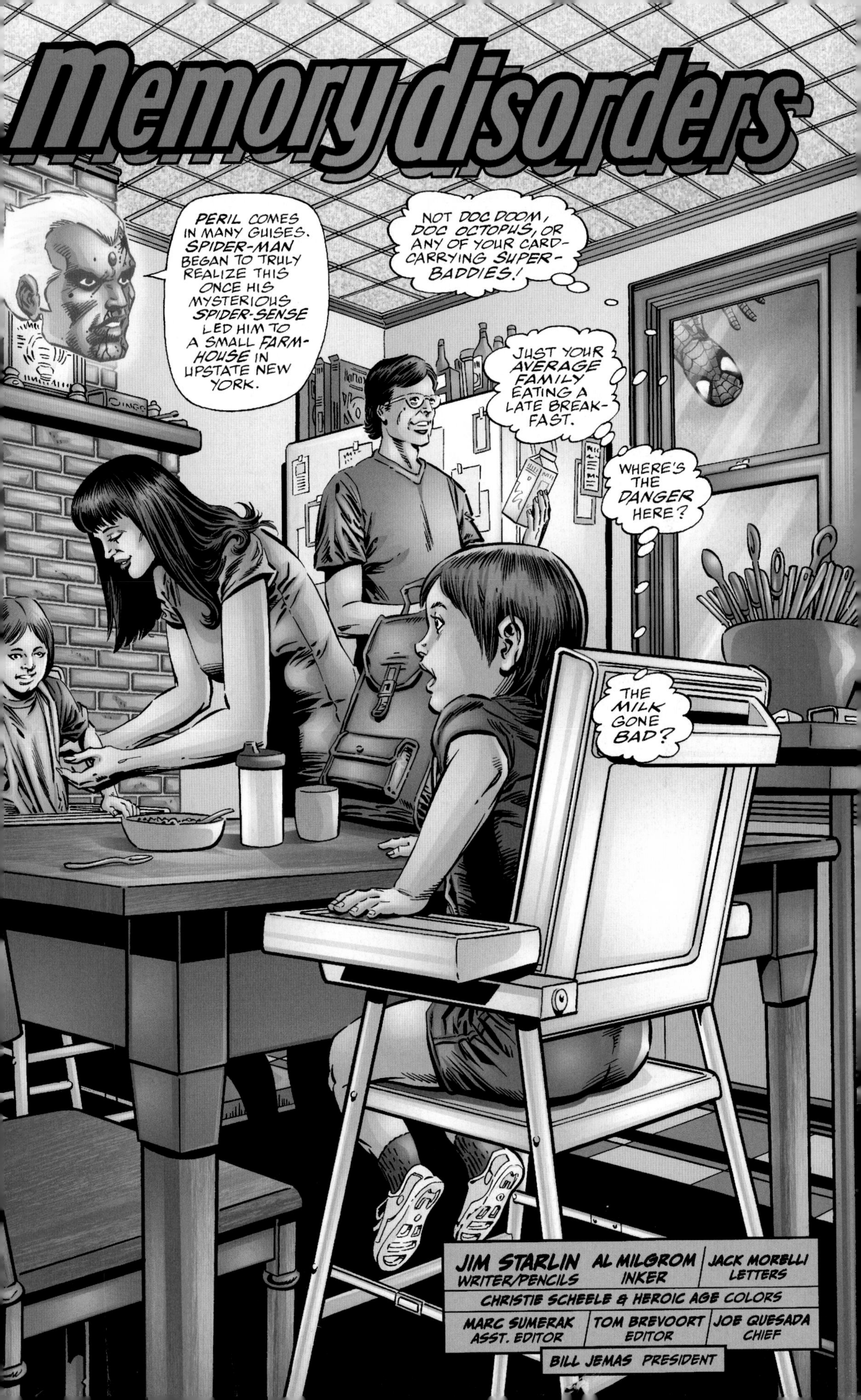
Memory disorders
PERIL COMES IN MANY GUISES. SPIDER-MAN BEGAN TO TRULY REALIZE THIS ONCE HIS MYSTERIOUS SPIDER-SENSE LED HIM TO A SMALL FARM-HOUSE IN UPSTATE NEW YORK.
NOT DOC DOOM, DOC OCTOPUS, OR ANY OF YOUR CARD-CARRYING SUPER-BADDIES!
JUST YOUR AVERAGE FAMILY EATING A LATE BREAK-FAST.
WHERE'S THE DANGER HERE?
THE MILK GONE BAD?
JIM STARLIN WRITER/PENCILS
AL MILGROM INKER
JACK MORELLI LETTERS
CHRISTIE SCHEELE & HEROIC AGE COLORS
MARC SUMERAK ASST. EDITOR
TOM BREVOORT EDITOR
JOE QUESADA CHIEF
BILL JEMAS PRESIDENT

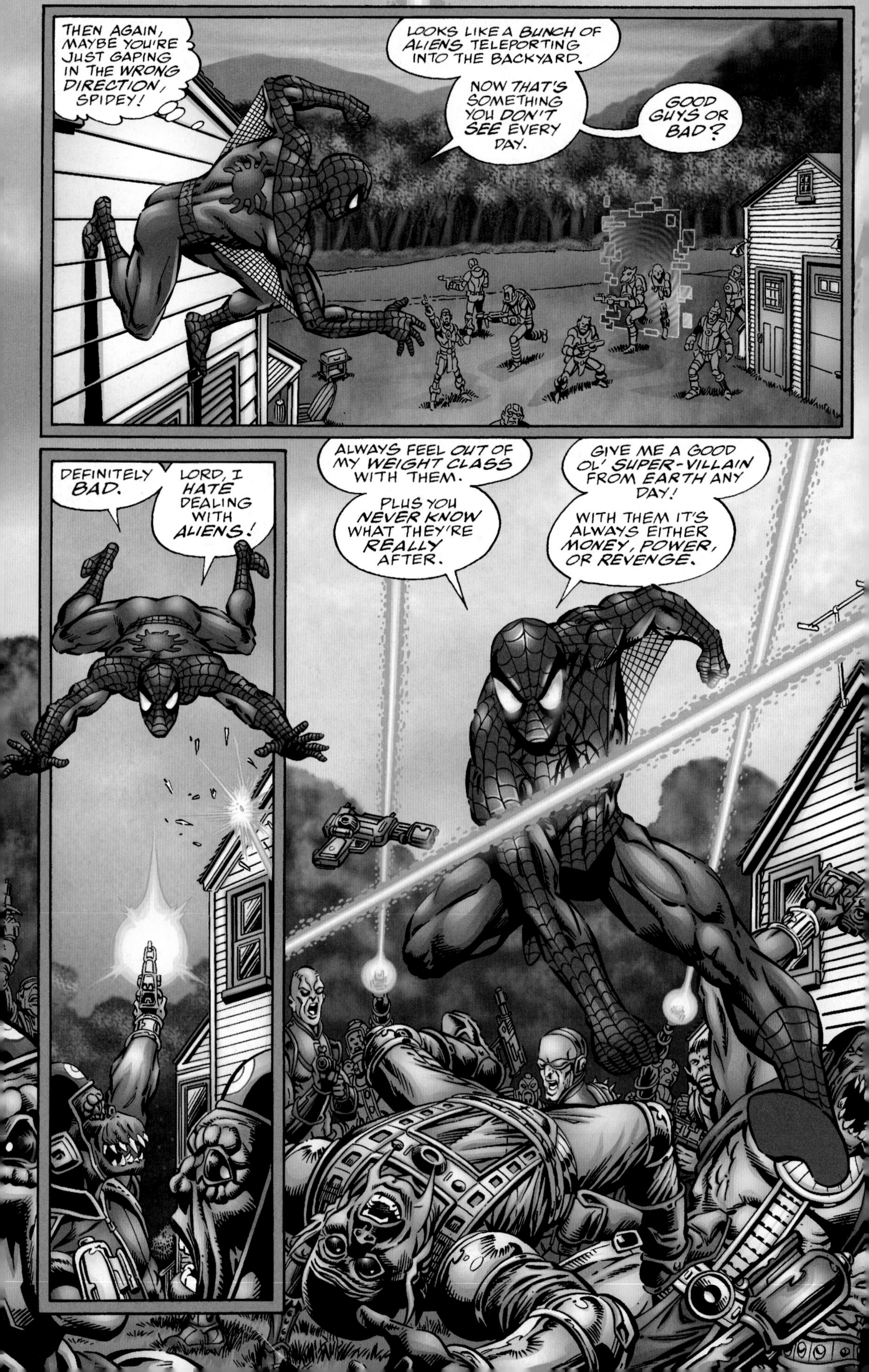
THEN AGAIN, MAYBE YOU'RE JUST GAPING IN THE WRONG DIRECTION, SPIDEY!
LOOKS LIKE A BUNCH OF ALIENS TELEPORTING INTO THE BACKYARD.
NOW THAT'S SOMETHING YOU DON'T SEE EVERY DAY.
GOOD GUYS OR BAD?
DEFINITELY BAD.
LORD, I HATE DEALING WITH ALIENS!
ALWAYS FEEL OUT OF MY WEIGHT CLASS WITH THEM.
PLUS YOU NEVER KNOW WHAT THEY'RE REALLY AFTER.
GIVE ME A GOOD OL' SUPER-VILLAIN FROM EARTH ANY DAY!
WITH THEM IT'S ALWAYS EITHER MONEY, POWER, OR REVENGE.

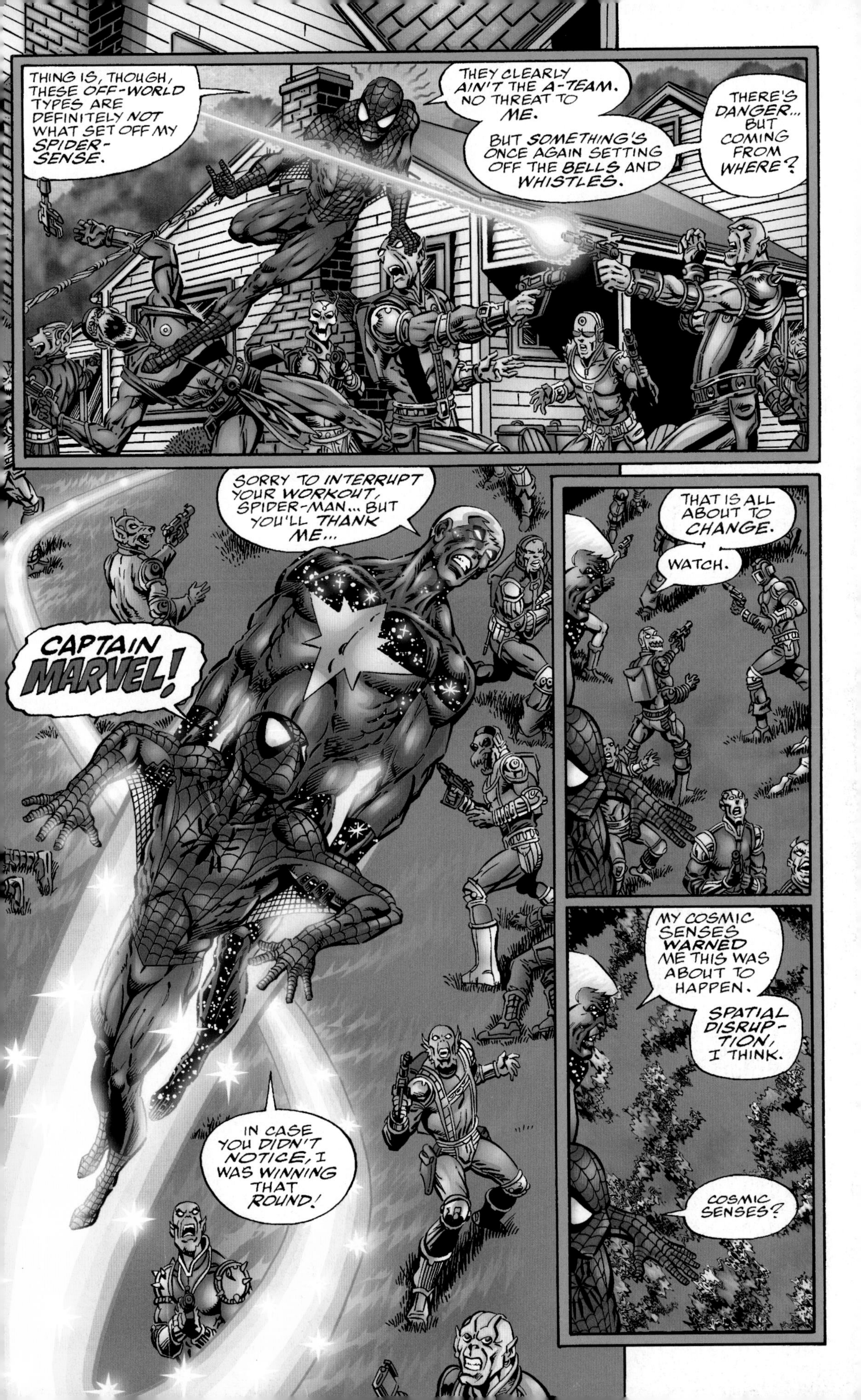
THING IS, THOUGH, THESE OFF-WORLD TYPES ARE DEFINITELY NOT WHAT SET OFF MY SPIDER-SENSE.
THEY CLEARLY AIN'T THE A-TEAM. NO THREAT TO ME.
BUT SOMETHING'S ONCE AGAIN SETTING OFF THE BELLS AND WHISTLES.
THERE'S DANGER... BUT COMING FROM WHERE?
SORRY TO INTERRUPT YOUR WORKOUT, SPIDER-MAN... BUT YOU'LL THANK ME...
CAPTAIN MARVEL!
IN CASE YOU DIDN'T NOTICE, I WAS WINNING THAT ROUND!
THAT IS ALL ABOUT TO CHANGE.
WATCH.
MY COSMIC SENSES WARNED ME THIS WAS ABOUT TO HAPPEN.
SPATIAL DISRUPTION, I THINK.
COSMIC SENSES?

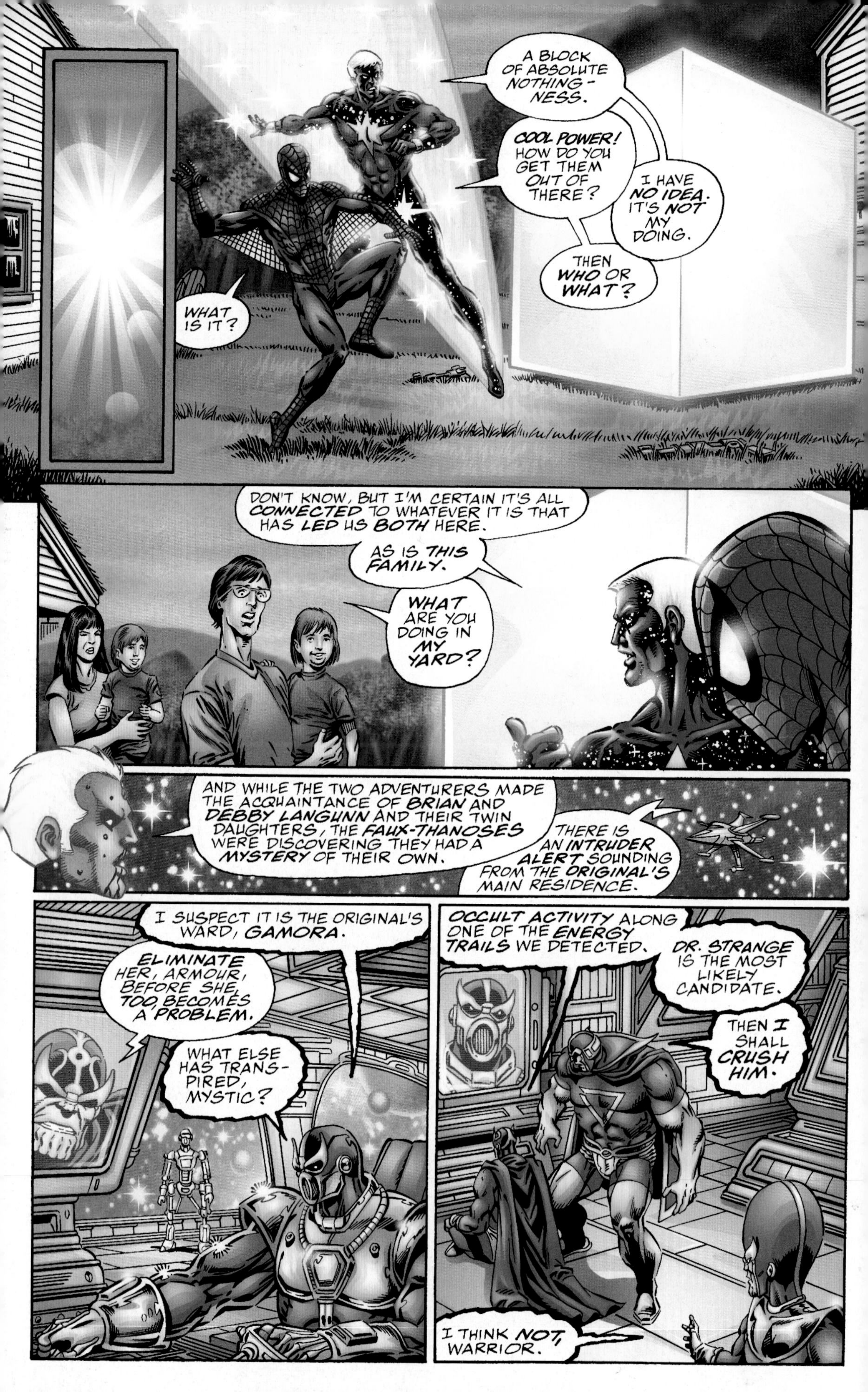
A BLOCK OF ABSOLUTE NOTHING-NESS.
COOL POWER! HOW DO YOU GET THEM OUT OF THERE?
I HAVE NO IDEA. IT'S NOT MY DOING.
THEN WHO OR WHAT?
WHAT IS IT?
DON'T KNOW, BUT I'M CERTAIN IT'S ALL CONNECTED TO WHATEVER IT IS THAT HAS LED US BOTH HERE.
AS IS THIS FAMILY.
WHAT ARE YOU DOING IN MY YARD?
AND WHILE THE TWO ADVENTURERS MADE THE ACQUAINTANCE OF BRIAN AND DEBBY LANGUNN AND THEIR TWIN DAUGHTERS, THE FAUX-THANOSES WERE DISCOVERING THEY HAD A MYSTERY OF THEIR OWN.
THERE IS AN INTRUDER ALERT SOUNDING FROM THE ORIGINAL'S MAIN RESIDENCE.
I SUSPECT IT IS THE ORIGINAL'S WARD, GAMORA.
ELIMINATE HER, ARMOUR, BEFORE SHE, TOO, BECOMES A PROBLEM.
WHAT ELSE HAS TRANS-PIRED, MYSTIC?
OCCULT ACTIVITY ALONG ONE OF THE ENERGY TRAILS WE DETECTED.
DR. STRANGE IS THE MOST LIKELY CANDIDATE.
THEN I SHALL CRUSH HIM.
I THINK NOT, WARRIOR.

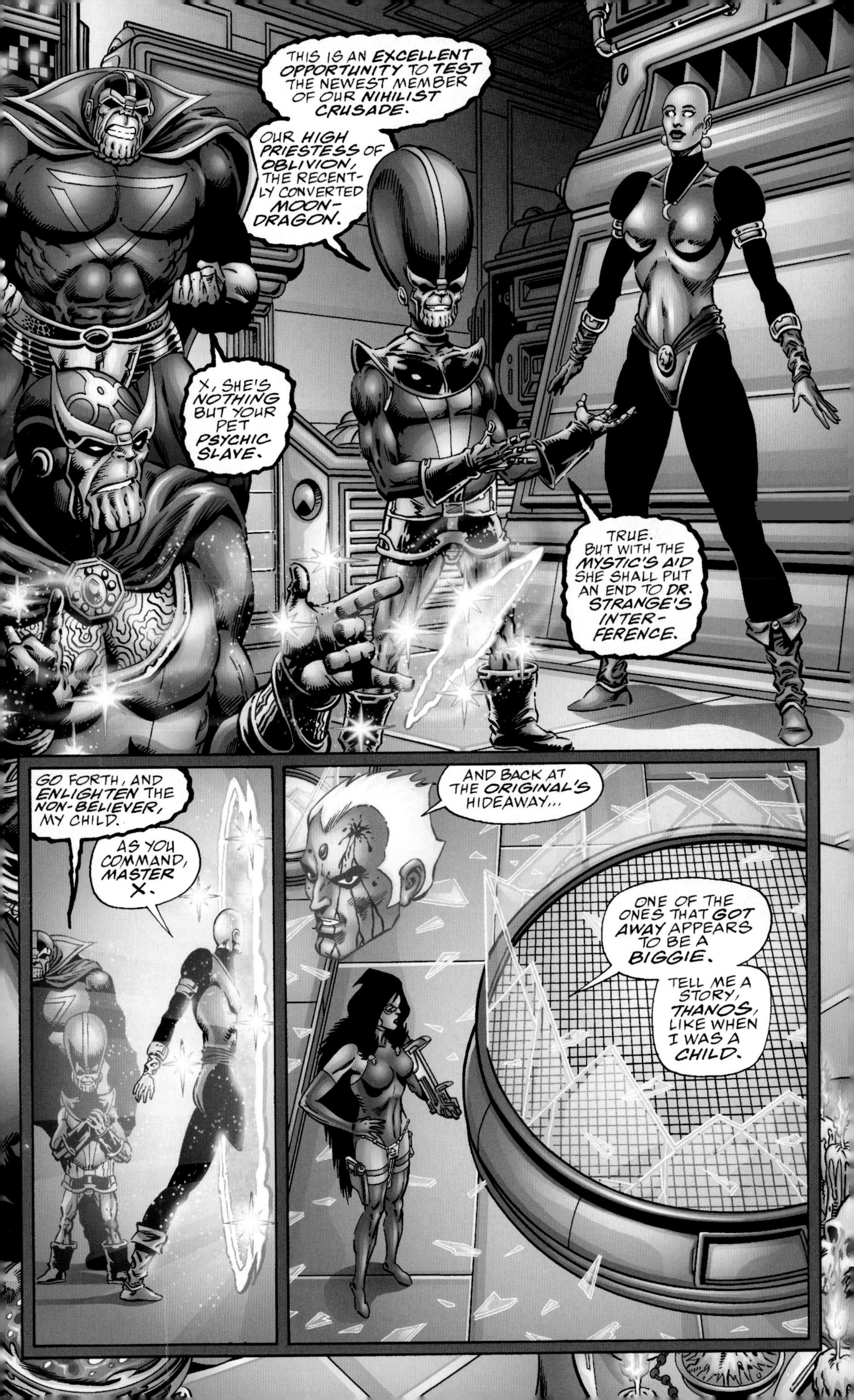
THIS IS AN EXCELLENT OPPORTUNITY TO TEST THE NEWEST MEMBER OF OUR NIHILIST CRUSADE.
OUR HIGH PRIESTESS OF OBLIVION, THE RECENTLY CONVERTED MOONDRAGON.
X, SHE'S NOTHING BUT YOUR PET PSYCHIC SLAVE.
TRUE. BUT WITH THE MYSTIC'S AID SHE SHALL PUT AN END TO DR. STRANGE'S INTERFERENCE.
GO FORTH, AND ENLIGHTEN THE NON-BELIEVER, MY CHILD.
AS YOU COMMAND, MASTER X.
AND BACK AT THE ORIGINAL'S HIDEAWAY...
ONE OF THE ONES THAT GOT AWAY APPEARS TO BE A BIGGIE.
TELL ME A STORY, THANOS, LIKE WHEN I WAS A CHILD.

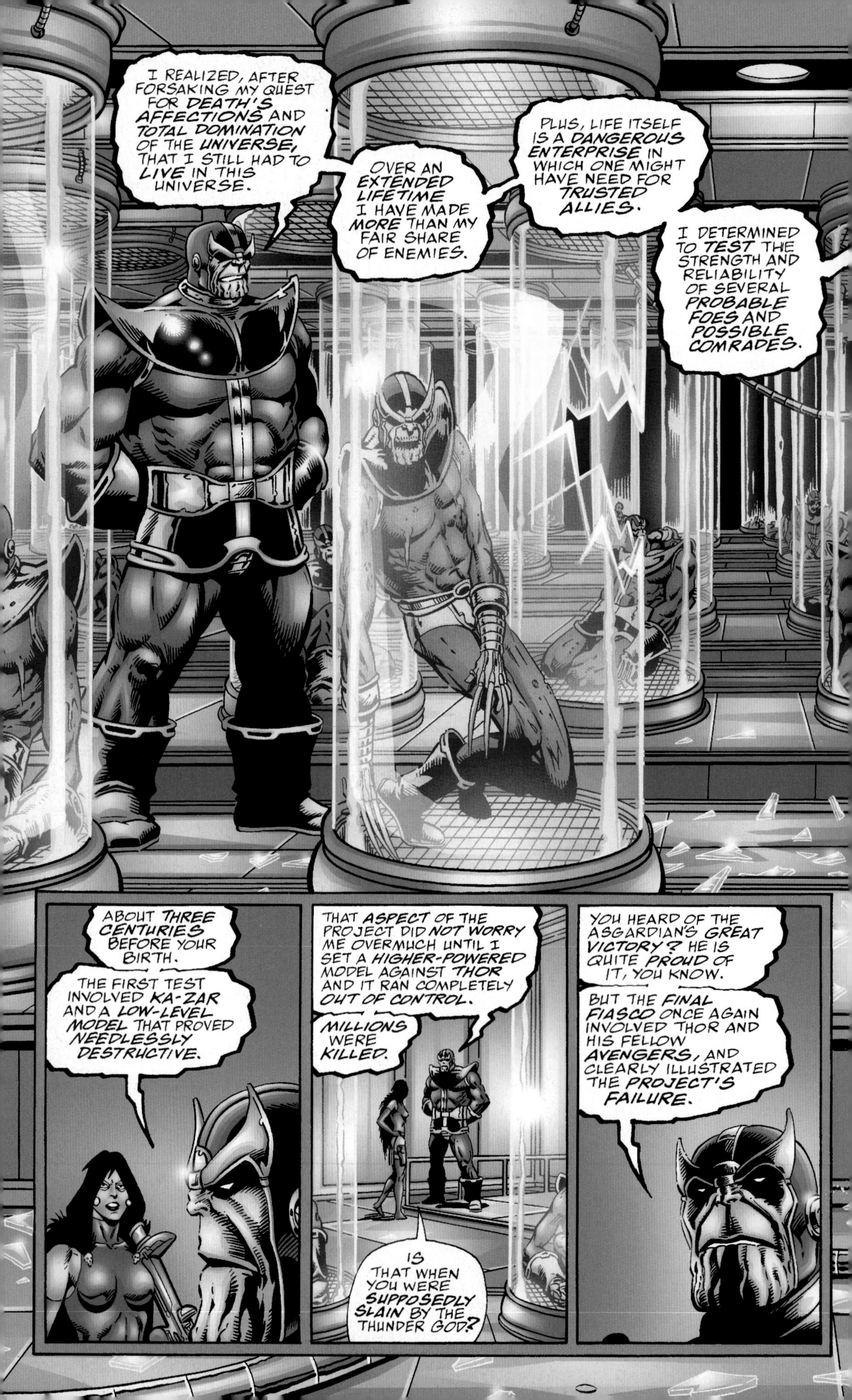
I REALIZED, AFTER FORSAKING MY QUEST FOR DEATH'S AFFECTIONS AND TOTAL DOMINATION OF THE UNIVERSE, THAT I STILL HAD TO LIVE IN THIS UNIVERSE.
OVER AN EXTENDED LIFETIME I HAVE MADE MORE THAN MY FAIR SHARE OF ENEMIES.
PLUS, LIFE ITSELF IS A DANGEROUS ENTERPRISE IN WHICH ONE MIGHT HAVE NEED FOR TRUSTED ALLIES.
I DETERMINED TO TEST THE STRENGTH AND RELIABILITY OF SEVERAL PROBABLE FOES AND POSSIBLE COMRADES.
ABOUT THREE CENTURIES BEFORE YOUR BIRTH.
THE FIRST TEST INVOLVED KA-ZAR AND A LOW-LEVEL MODEL THAT PROVED NEEDLESSLY DESTRUCTIVE.
THAT ASPECT OF THE PROJECT DID NOT WORRY ME OVERMUCH UNTIL I SET A HIGHER-POWERED MODEL AGAINST THOR AND IT RAN COMPLETELY OUT OF CONTROL.
MILLIONS WERE KILLED.
IS THAT WHEN YOU WERE SUPPOSEDLY SLAIN BY THE THUNDER GOD?
YOU HEARD OF THE ASGARDIAN'S GREAT VICTORY? HE IS QUITE PROUD OF IT, YOU KNOW.
BUT THE FINAL FIASCO ONCE AGAIN INVOLVED THOR AND HIS FELLOW AVENGERS, AND CLEARLY ILLUSTRATED THE PROJECT'S FAILURE.

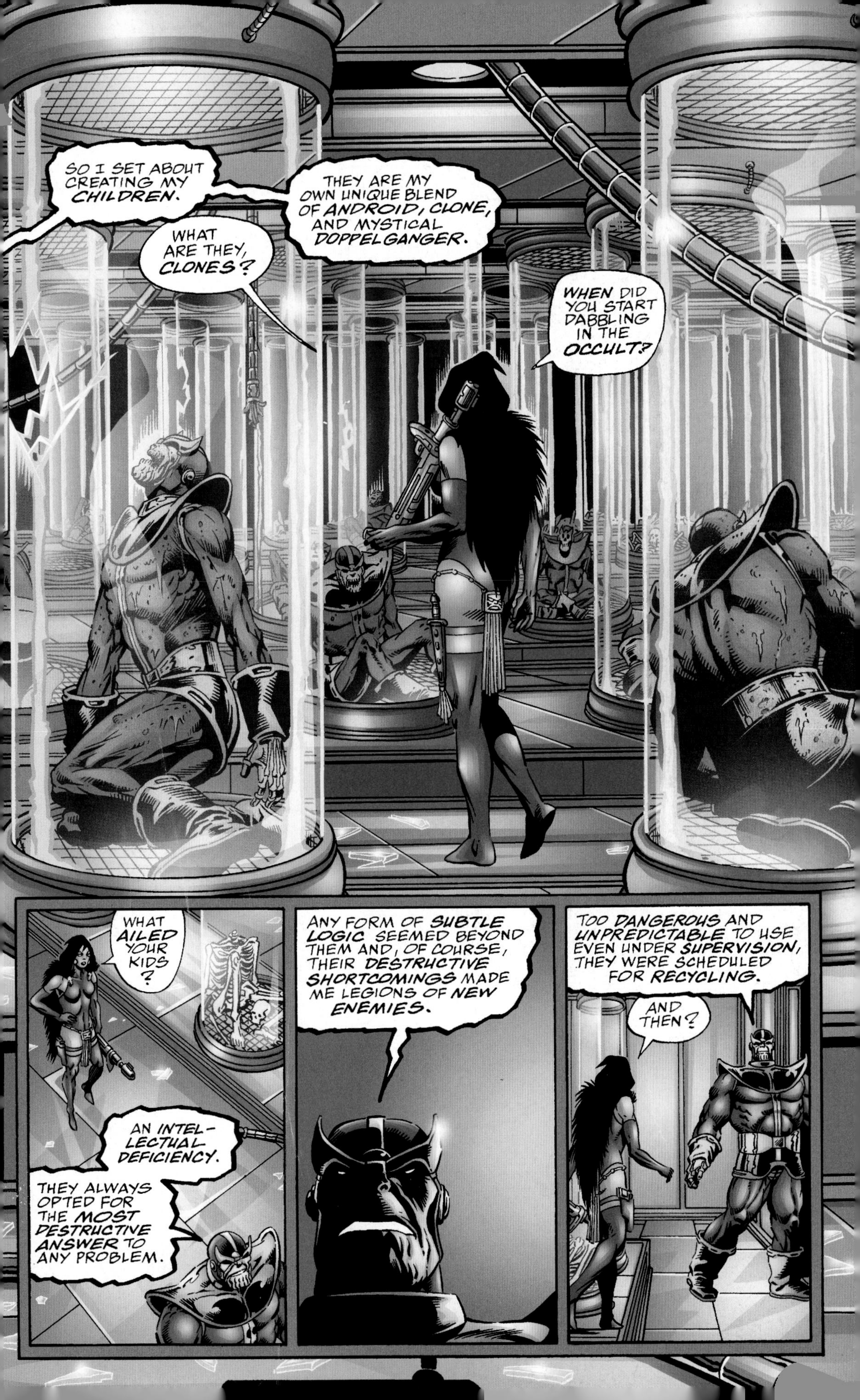
SO I SET ABOUT CREATING MY CHILDREN.
WHAT ARE THEY, CLONES?
THEY ARE MY OWN UNIQUE BLEND OF ANDROID, CLONE, AND MYSTICAL DOPPELGANGER.
WHEN DID YOU START DABBLING IN THE OCCULT?
WHAT AILED YOUR KIDS?
AN INTELLECTUAL DEFICIENCY.
THEY ALWAYS OPTED FOR THE MOST DESTRUCTIVE ANSWER TO ANY PROBLEM.
ANY FORM OF SUBTLE LOGIC SEEMED BEYOND THEM AND, OF COURSE, THEIR DESTRUCTIVE SHORTCOMINGS MADE ME LEGIONS OF NEW ENEMIES.
TOO DANGEROUS AND UNPREDICTABLE TO USE EVEN UNDER SUPERVISION, THEY WERE SCHEDULED FOR RECYCLING.
AND THEN?

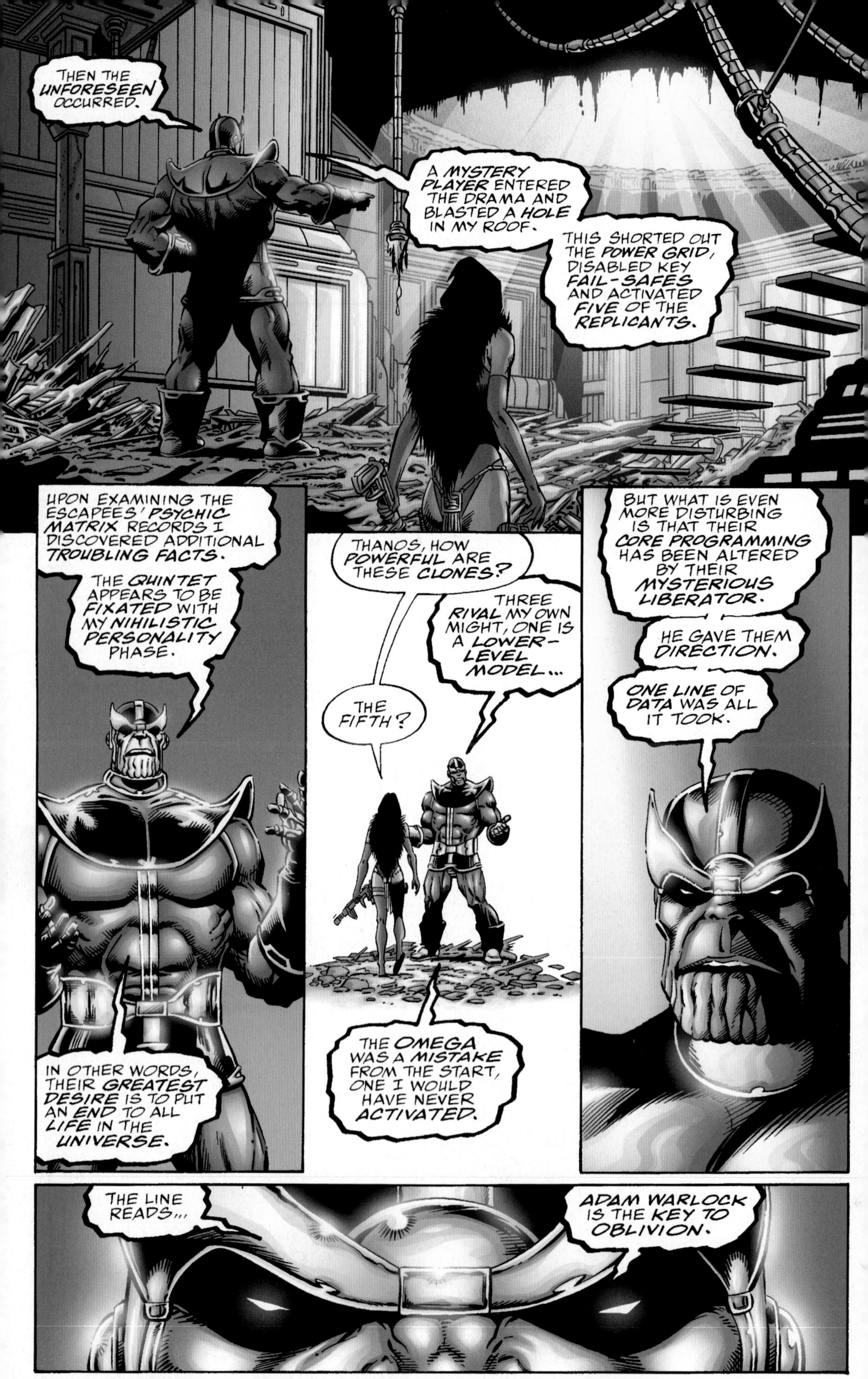
THEN THE UNFORESEEN OCCURRED.
A MYSTERY PLAYER ENTERED THE DRAMA AND BLASTED A HOLE IN MY ROOF.
THIS SHORTED OUT THE POWER GRID, DISABLED KEY FAIL-SAFES AND ACTIVATED FIVE OF THE REPLICANTS.
UPON EXAMINING THE ESCAPEES' PSYCHIC MATRIX RECORDS I DISCOVERED ADDITIONAL TROUBLING FACTS.
THE QUINTET APPEARS TO BE FIXATED WITH MY NIHILISTIC PERSONALITY PHASE.
IN OTHER WORDS, THEIR GREATEST DESIRE IS TO PUT AN END TO ALL LIFE IN THE UNIVERSE.
THANOS, HOW POWERFUL ARE THESE CLONES?
THREE RIVAL MY OWN MIGHT, ONE IS A LOWER-LEVEL MODEL...
THE FIFTH?
THE OMEGA WAS A MISTAKE FROM THE START, ONE I WOULD HAVE NEVER ACTIVATED.
BUT WHAT IS EVEN MORE DISTURBING IS THAT THEIR CORE PROGRAMMING HAS BEEN ALTERED BY THEIR MYSTERIOUS LIBERATOR.
HE GAVE THEM DIRECTION.
ONE LINE OF DATA WAS ALL IT TOOK.
THE LINE READS...
ADAM WARLOCK IS THE KEY TO OBLIVION.

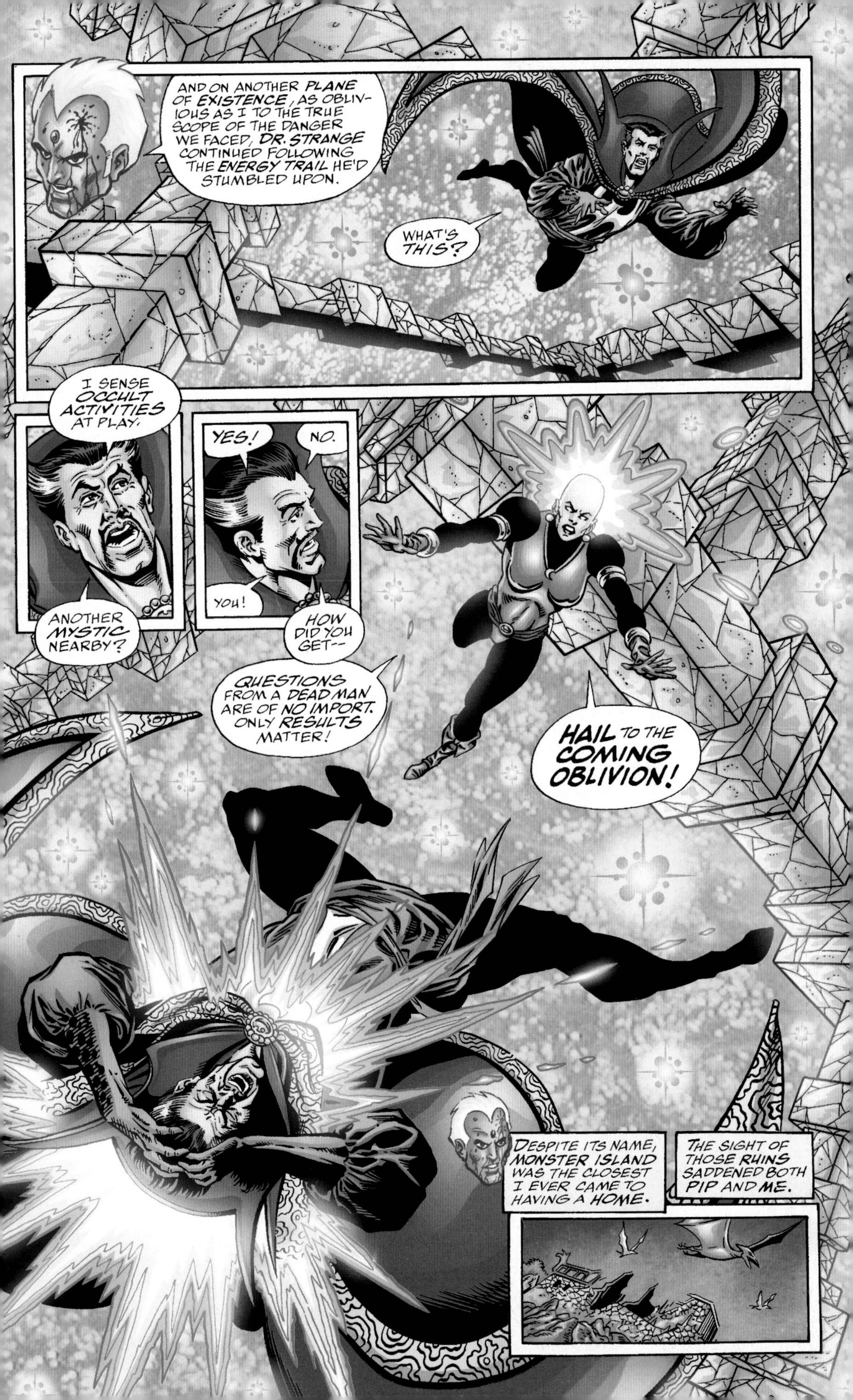
AND ON ANOTHER PLANE OF EXISTENCE, AS OBLIVIOUS AS I TO THE TRUE SCOPE OF THE DANGER WE FACED, DR. STRANGE CONTINUED FOLLOWING THE ENERGY TRAIL HE'D STUMBLED UPON.
WHAT'S THIS?
I SENSE OCCULT ACTIVITIES AT PLAY.
ANOTHER MYSTIC NEARBY?
YES!
NO.
YOU!
HOW DID YOU GET--
QUESTIONS FROM A DEAD MAN ARE OF NO IMPORT. ONLY RESULTS MATTER!
HAIL TO THE COMING OBLIVION!
DESPITE ITS NAME, MONSTER ISLAND WAS THE CLOSEST I EVER CAME TO HAVING A HOME.
THE SIGHT OF THOSE RUINS SADDENED BOTH PIP AND ME.

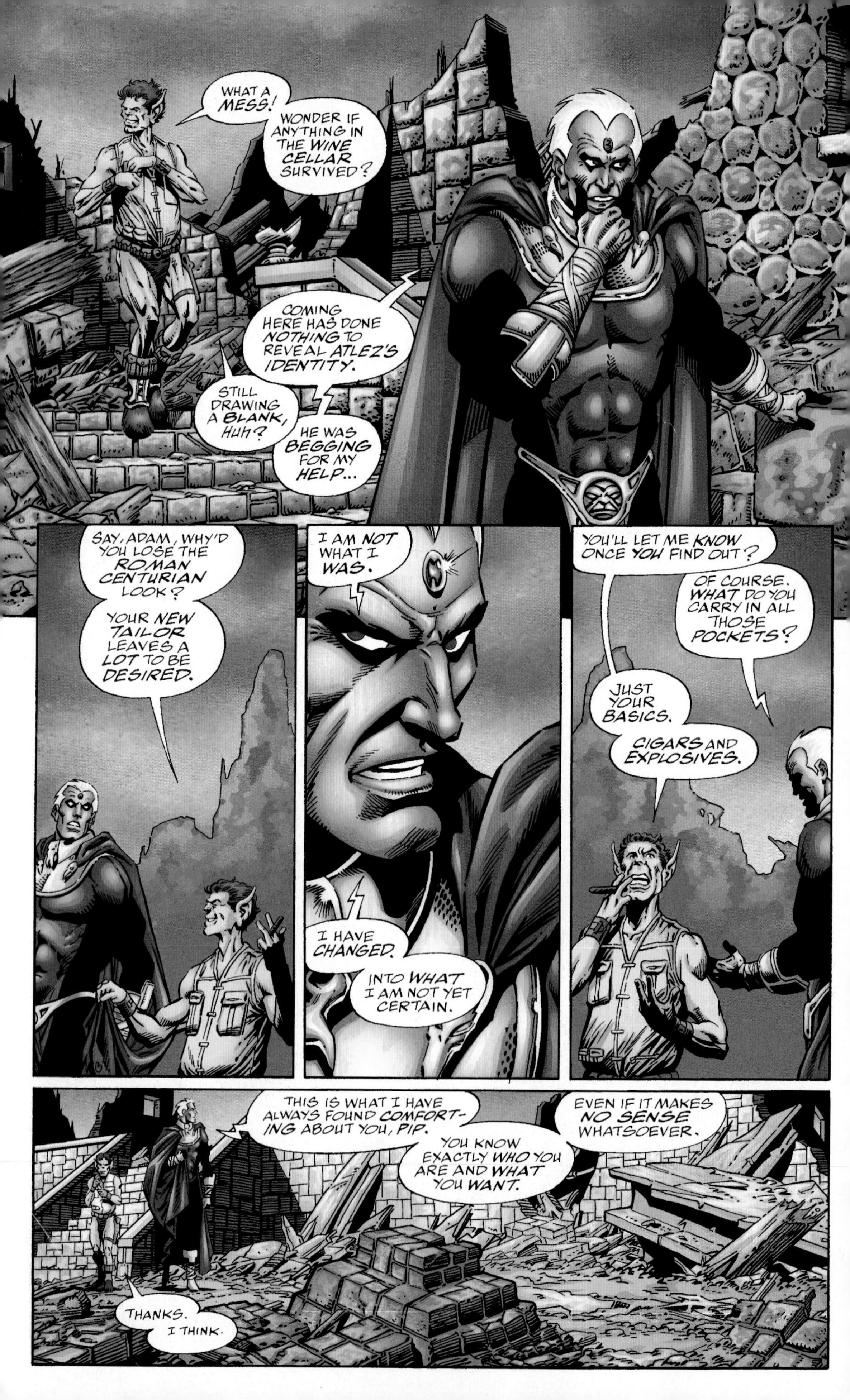
WHAT A MESS!
WONDER IF ANYTHING IN THE WINE CELLAR SURVIVED?
COMING HERE HAS DONE NOTHING TO REVEAL ATLEZ'S IDENTITY.
STILL DRAWING A BLANK, HUH?
HE WAS BEGGING FOR MY HELP...
SAY, ADAM, WHY'D YOU LOSE THE ROMAN CENTURIAN LOOK?
YOUR NEW TAILOR LEAVES A LOT TO BE DESIRED.
I AM NOT WHAT I WAS.
I HAVE CHANGED.
INTO WHAT I AM NOT YET CERTAIN.
YOU'LL LET ME KNOW ONCE YOU FIND OUT?
OF COURSE. WHAT DO YOU CARRY IN ALL THOSE POCKETS?
JUST YOUR BASICS.
CIGARS AND EXPLOSIVES.
THIS IS WHAT I HAVE ALWAYS FOUND COMFORTING ABOUT YOU, PIP.
YOU KNOW EXACTLY WHO YOU ARE AND WHAT YOU WANT.
EVEN IF IT MAKES NO SENSE WHATSOEVER.
THANKS. I THINK.

YOU JUST HAVE TO KNOW HOW TO *ENJOY* LIFE.

YOUR *GIFT,* NOT MINE.

I WAS *BORN* IN, LIVED MY *ENTIRE* EXISTENCE IN, AND SEVERAL TIMES *DIED* AMIDST *CONFLICT.*

WITHOUT EVER TRULY KNOWING *WHY.*

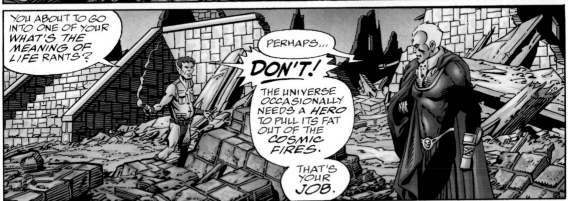

YOU ABOUT TO GO INTO ONE OF YOUR *WHAT'S THE MEANING OF LIFE* RANTS?

PERHAPS...

DON'T!

THE UNIVERSE OCCASIONALLY NEEDS A *HERO* TO PULL ITS FAT OUT OF THE *COSMIC FIRES.*

THAT'S YOUR *JOB.*

SO *DEATH* AND *RESURRECTION* ARE ALL I HAVE TO LOOK FORWARD TO?

MAYBE IF YOU TRIED TO LIGHTEN UP A BIT.

A *LAUGHING ETERNAL WARRIOR?* I FIND THAT HARD TO VISUALIZE.

ALL RIGHT, THEN *ANSWER* ME THIS: WHEN *ATLEZ* CALLED TO YOU...

...WAS HE *FAR AWAY* OR *NEARBY*?

I HADN'T THOUGHT OF THAT.

FAR AWAY.

BEYOND INFINITY.

BEYOND...

OF COURSE!

ETERNITY!

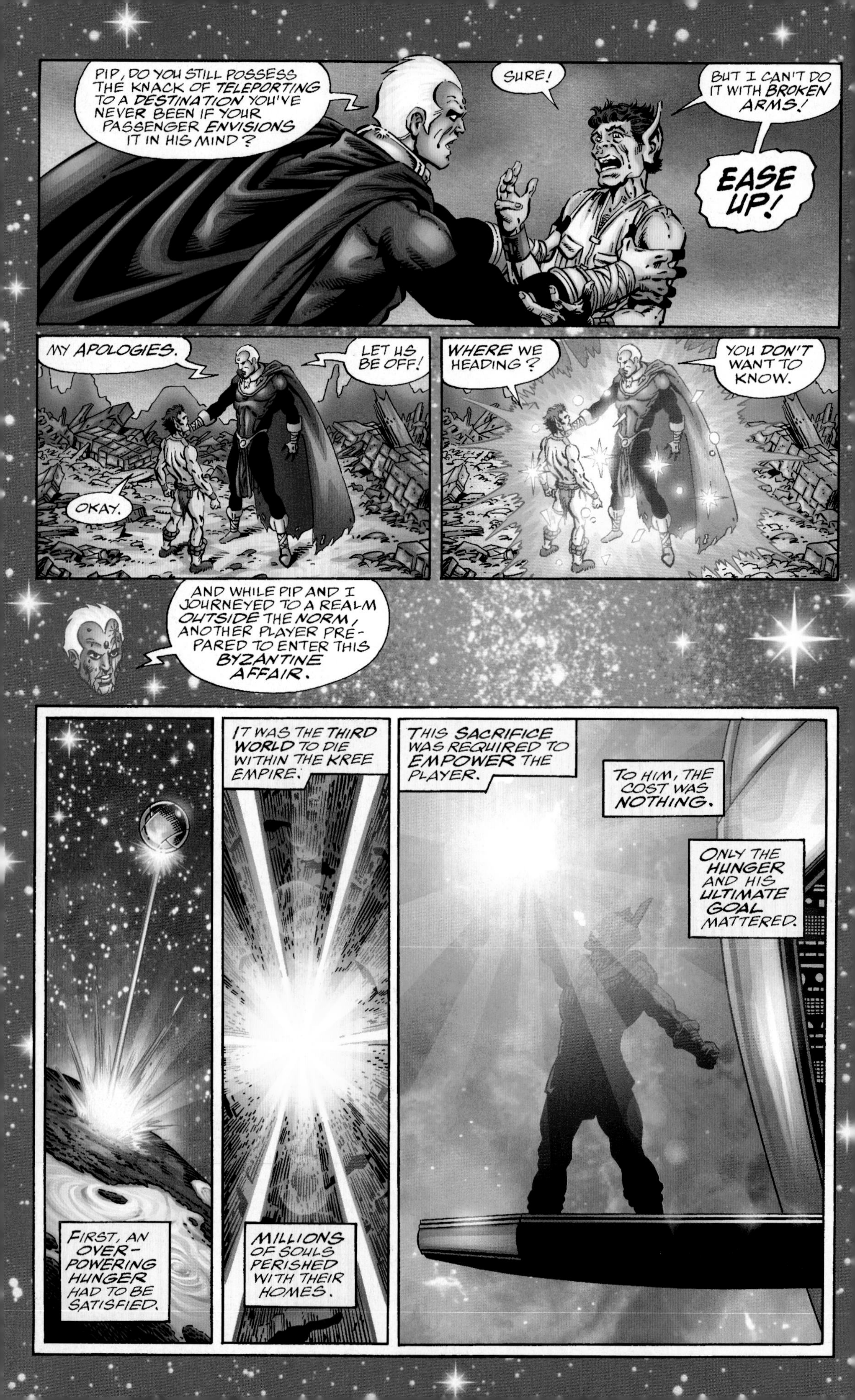

PIP, DO YOU STILL POSSESS THE KNACK OF TELEPORTING TO A DESTINATION YOU'VE NEVER BEEN IF YOUR PASSENGER ENVISIONS IT IN HIS MIND?
SURE!
BUT I CAN'T DO IT WITH BROKEN ARMS!
EASE UP!
MY APOLOGIES.
LET US BE OFF!
OKAY.
WHERE WE HEADING?
YOU DON'T WANT TO KNOW.
AND WHILE PIP AND I JOURNEYED TO A REALM OUTSIDE THE NORM, ANOTHER PLAYER PRE-PARED TO ENTER THIS BYZANTINE AFFAIR.
FIRST, AN OVER-POWERING HUNGER HAD TO BE SATISFIED.
IT WAS THE THIRD WORLD TO DIE WITHIN THE KREE EMPIRE.
MILLIONS OF SOULS PERISHED WITH THEIR HOMES.
THIS SACRIFICE WAS REQUIRED TO EMPOWER THE PLAYER.
TO HIM, THE COST WAS NOTHING.
ONLY THE HUNGER AND HIS ULTIMATE GOAL MATTERED.

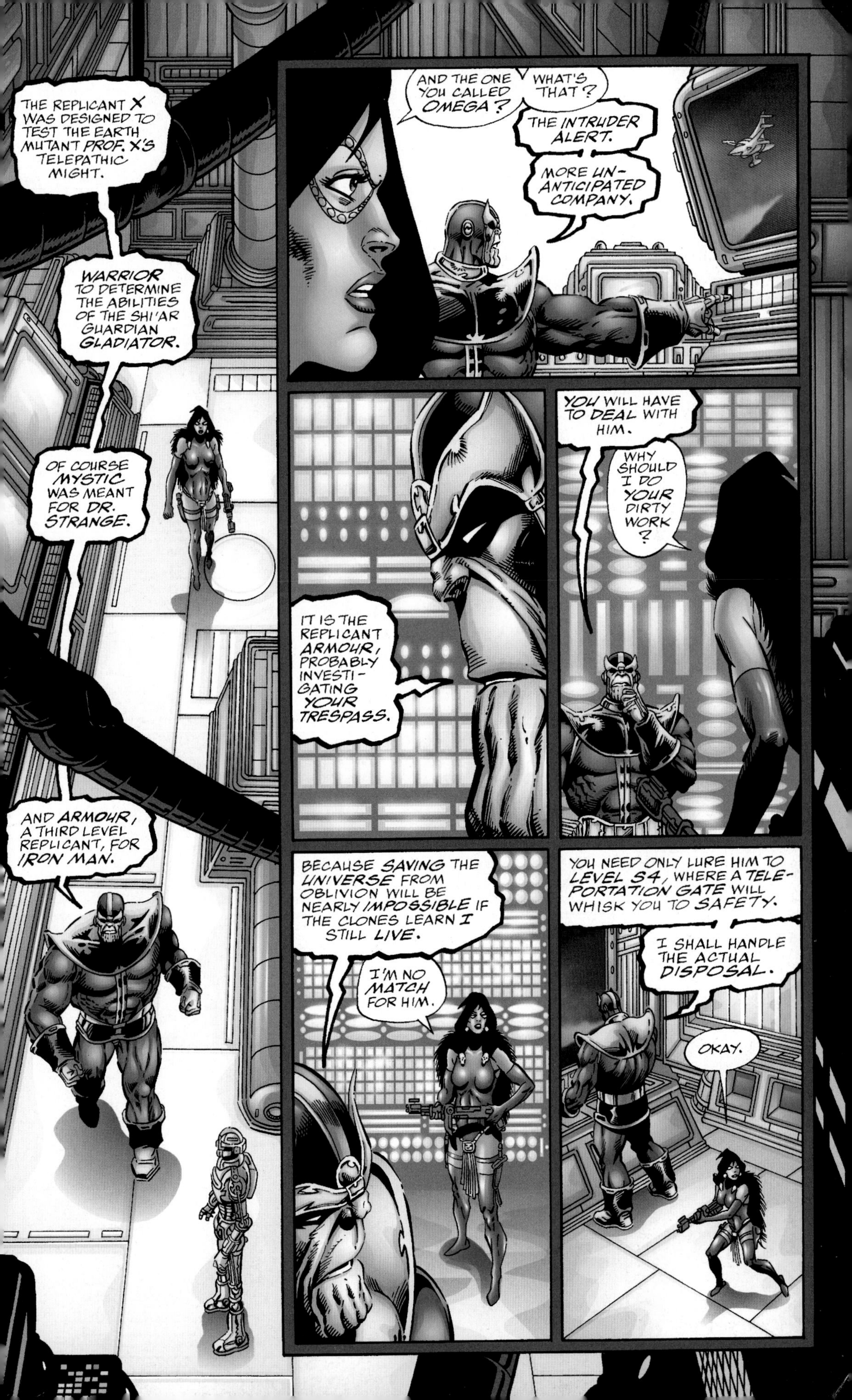

THE REPLICANT X WAS DESIGNED TO TEST THE EARTH MUTANT PROF. X'S TELEPATHIC MIGHT.
WARRIOR TO DETERMINE THE ABILITIES OF THE SHI'AR GUARDIAN GLADIATOR.
OF COURSE MYSTIC WAS MEANT FOR DR. STRANGE.
AND ARMOUR, A THIRD LEVEL REPLICANT, FOR IRON MAN.
AND THE ONE YOU CALLED OMEGA?
WHAT'S THAT?
THE INTRUDER ALERT.
MORE UN-ANTICIPATED COMPANY.
IT IS THE REPLICANT ARMOUR, PROBABLY INVESTI-GATING YOUR TRESPASS.
YOU WILL HAVE TO DEAL WITH HIM.
WHY SHOULD I DO YOUR DIRTY WORK?
BECAUSE SAVING THE UNIVERSE FROM OBLIVION WILL BE NEARLY IMPOSSIBLE IF THE CLONES LEARN I STILL LIVE.
I'M NO MATCH FOR HIM.
YOU NEED ONLY LURE HIM TO LEVEL S4, WHERE A TELE-PORTATION GATE WILL WHISK YOU TO SAFETY.
I SHALL HANDLE THE ACTUAL DISPOSAL.
OKAY.

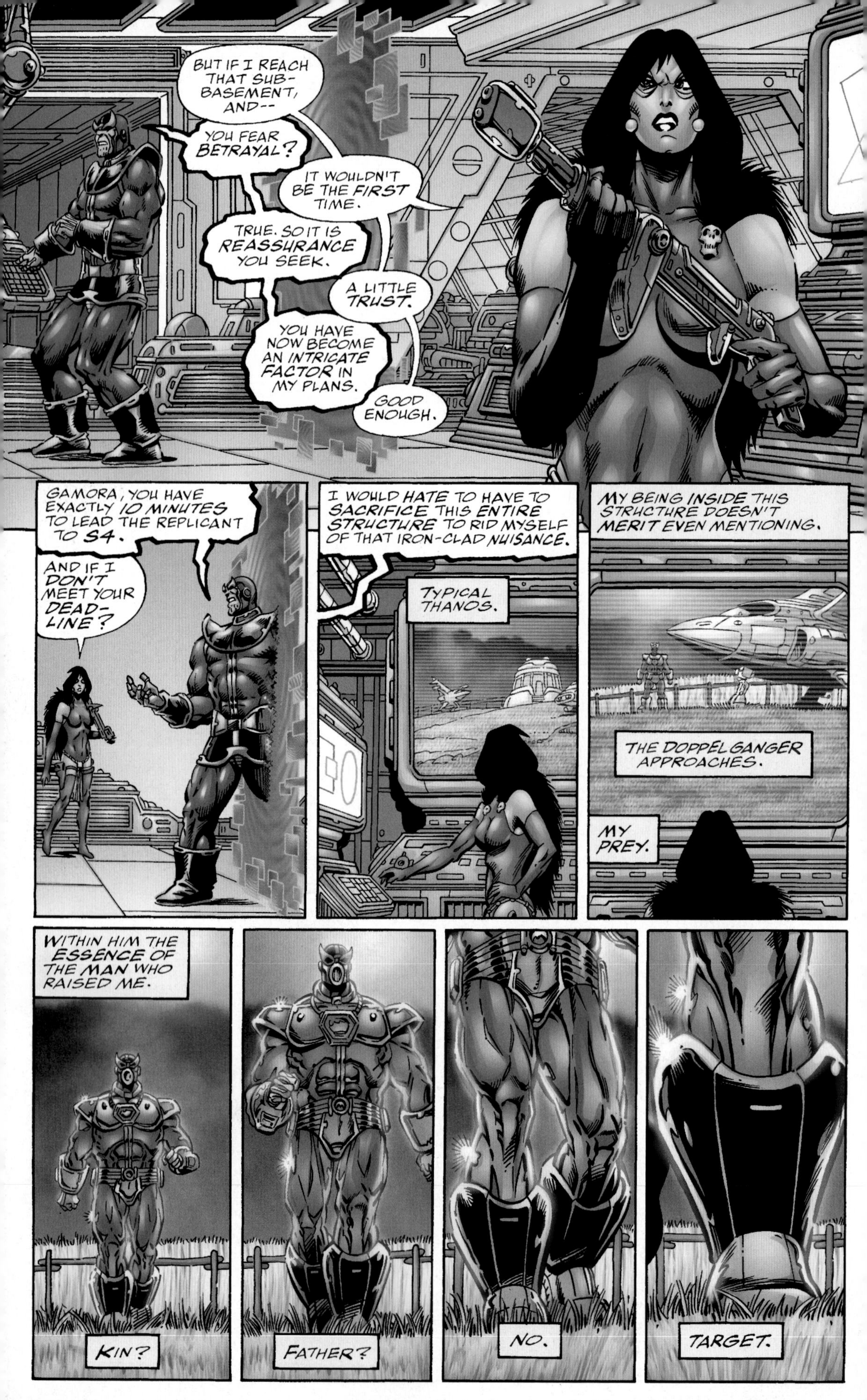
BUT IF I REACH THAT SUB-BASEMENT, AND--
YOU FEAR BETRAYAL?
IT WOULDN'T BE THE FIRST TIME.
TRUE. SO IT IS REASSURANCE YOU SEEK.
A LITTLE TRUST.
YOU HAVE NOW BECOME AN INTRICATE FACTOR IN MY PLANS.
GOOD ENOUGH.
GAMORA, YOU HAVE EXACTLY 10 MINUTES TO LEAD THE REPLICANT TO S4.
AND IF I DON'T MEET YOUR DEAD-LINE?
I WOULD HATE TO HAVE TO SACRIFICE THIS ENTIRE STRUCTURE TO RID MYSELF OF THAT IRON-CLAD NUISANCE.
TYPICAL THANOS.
MY BEING INSIDE THIS STRUCTURE DOESN'T MERIT EVEN MENTIONING.
THE DOPPELGANGER APPROACHES.
MY PREY.
WITHIN HIM THE ESSENCE OF THE MAN WHO RAISED ME.
KIN?
FATHER?
NO.
TARGET.

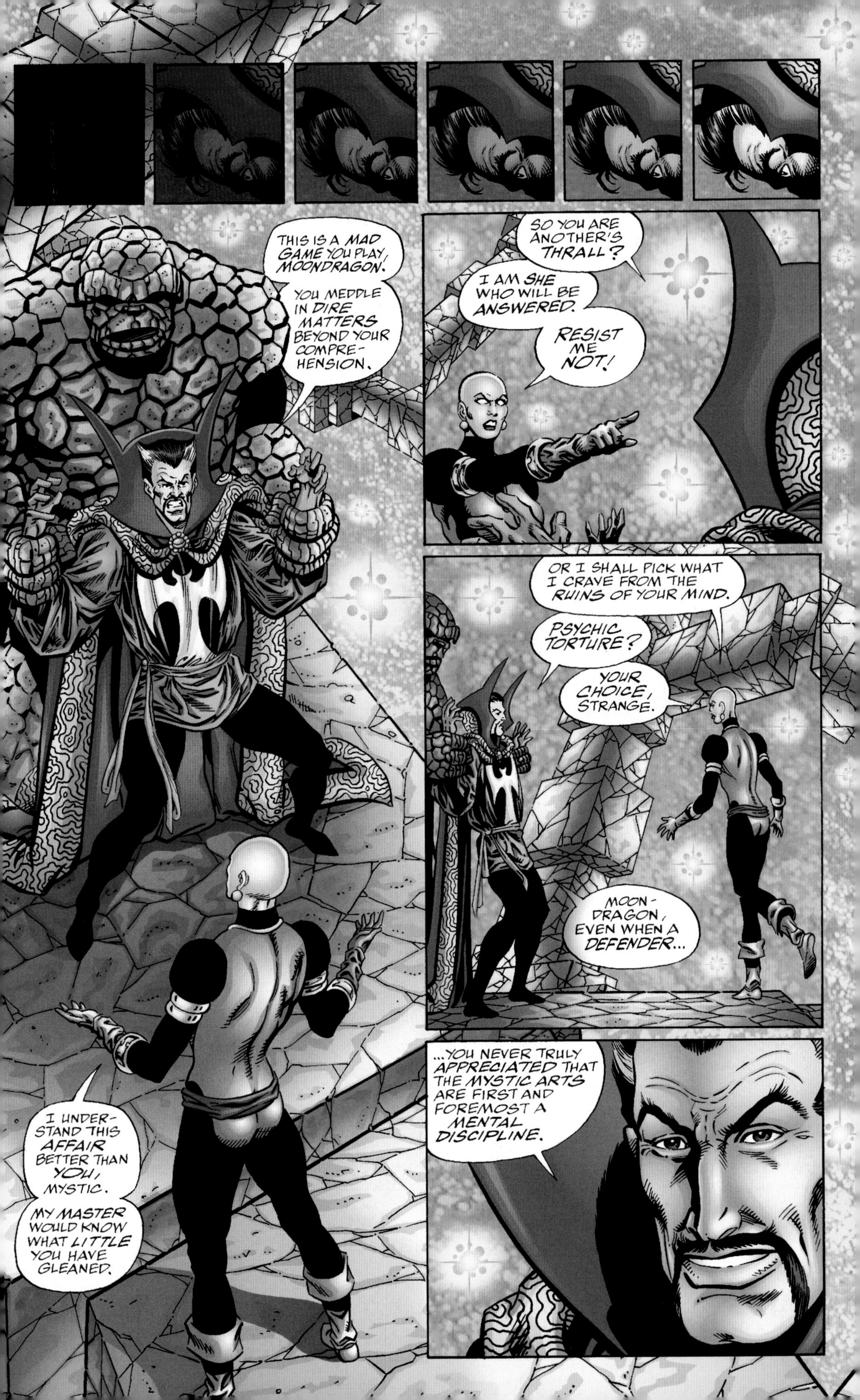

THIS IS A MAD GAME YOU PLAY, MOONDRAGON.
YOU MEDDLE IN DIRE MATTERS BEYOND YOUR COMPRE-HENSION.
I UNDER-STAND THIS AFFAIR BETTER THAN YOU, MYSTIC.
MY MASTER WOULD KNOW WHAT LITTLE YOU HAVE GLEANED.
SO YOU ARE ANOTHER'S THRALL?
I AM SHE WHO WILL BE ANSWERED.
RESIST ME NOT!
OR I SHALL PICK WHAT I CRAVE FROM THE RUINS OF YOUR MIND.
PSYCHIC TORTURE?
YOUR CHOICE, STRANGE.
MOON-DRAGON, EVEN WHEN A DEFENDER...
...YOU NEVER TRULY APPRECIATED THAT THE MYSTIC ARTS ARE FIRST AND FOREMOST A MENTAL DISCIPLINE.

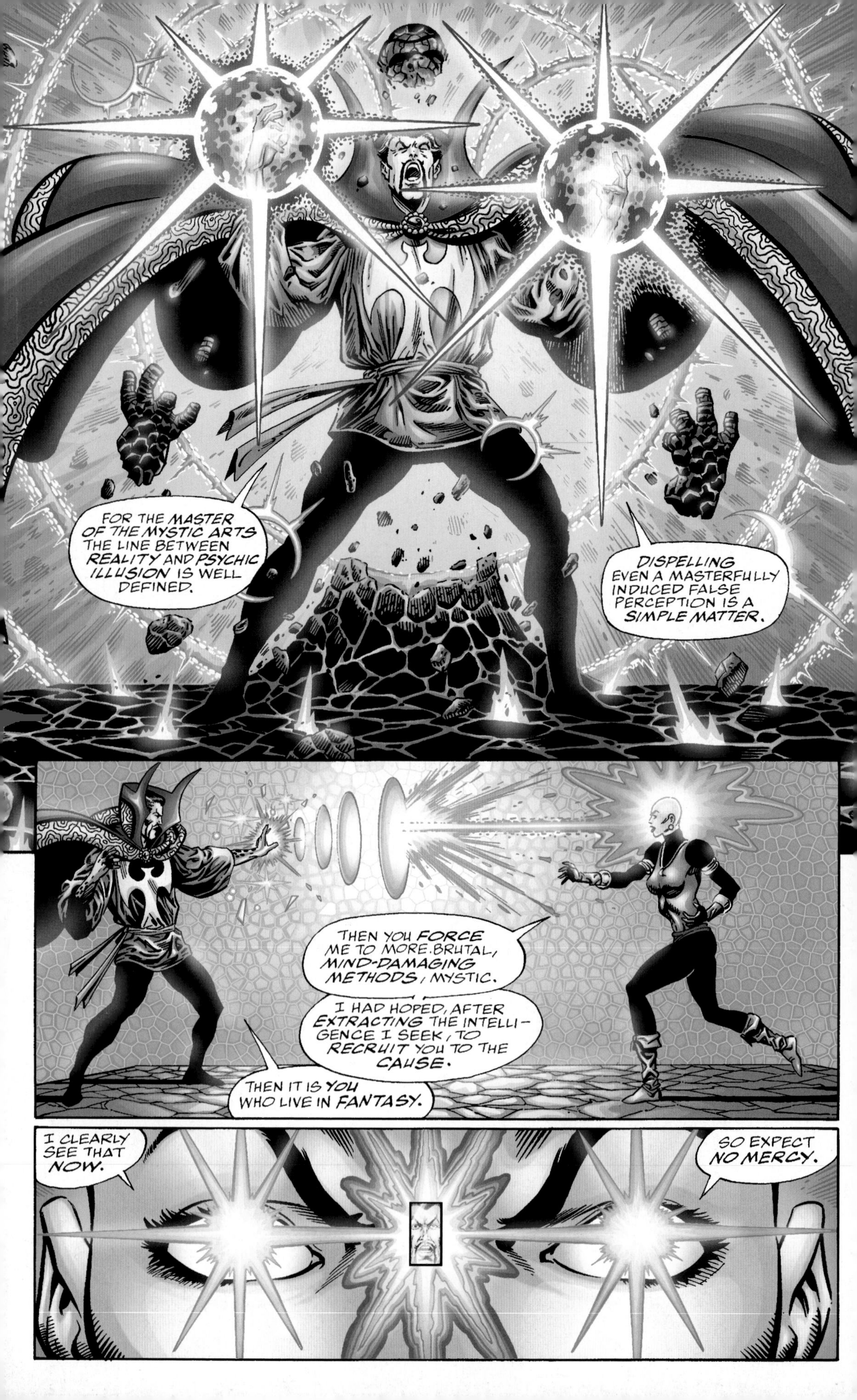
FOR THE MASTER OF THE MYSTIC ARTS THE LINE BETWEEN REALITY AND PSYCHIC ILLUSION IS WELL DEFINED.
DISPELLING EVEN A MASTERFULLY INDUCED FALSE PERCEPTION IS A SIMPLE MATTER.
THEN YOU FORCE ME TO MORE BRUTAL, MIND-DAMAGING METHODS, MYSTIC.
I HAD HOPED, AFTER EXTRACTING THE INTELLIGENCE I SEEK, TO RECRUIT YOU TO THE CAUSE.
THEN IT IS YOU WHO LIVE IN FANTASY.
I CLEARLY SEE THAT NOW.
SO EXPECT NO MERCY.

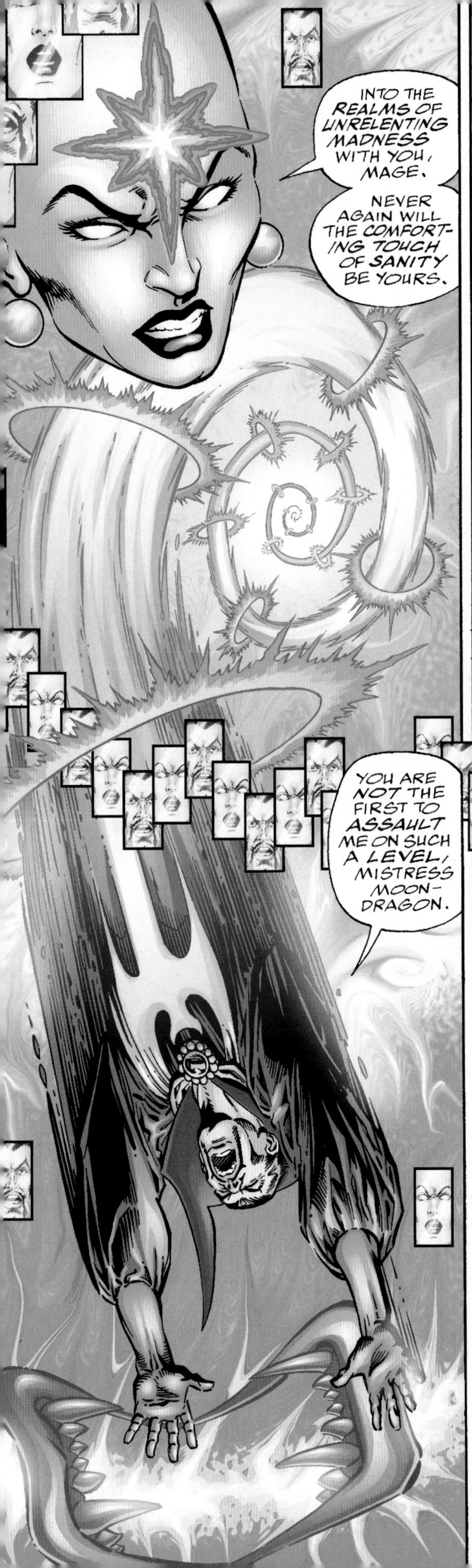
INTO THE REALMS OF UNRELENTING MADNESS WITH YOU, MAGE.
NEVER AGAIN WILL THE COMFORTING TOUCH OF SANITY BE YOURS.
YOU ARE NOT THE FIRST TO ASSAULT ME ON SUCH A LEVEL, MISTRESS MOON-DRAGON.

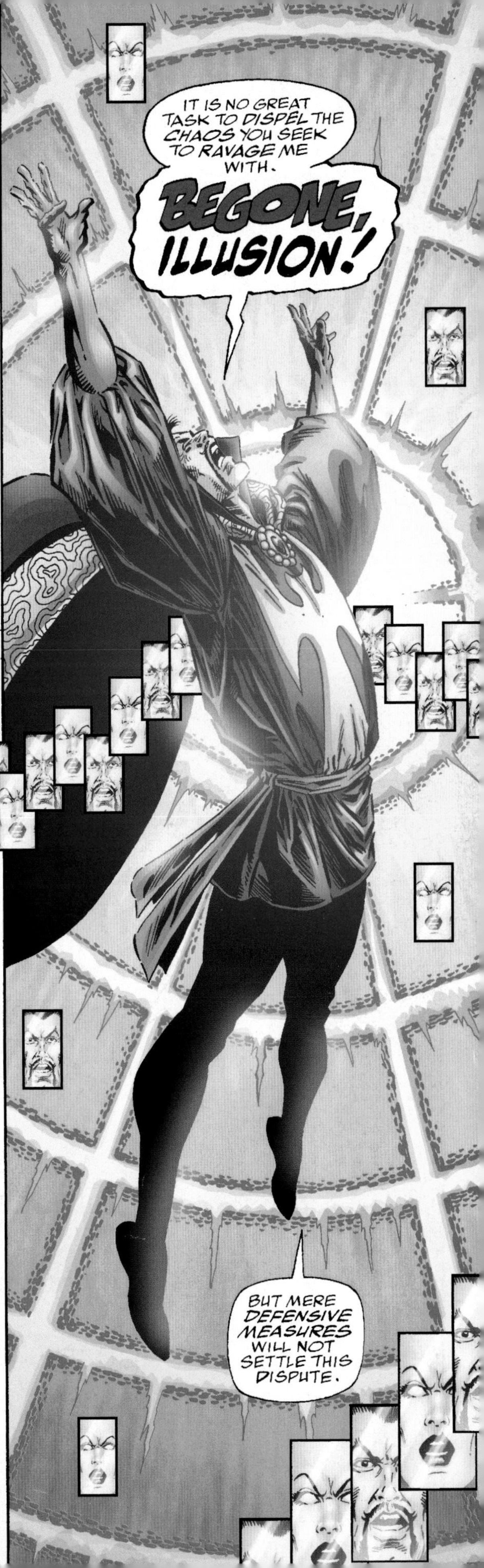
IT IS NO GREAT TASK TO DISPEL THE CHAOS YOU SEEK TO RAVAGE ME WITH.
BEGONE, ILLUSION!
BUT MERE DEFENSIVE MEASURES WILL NOT SETTLE THIS DISPUTE.

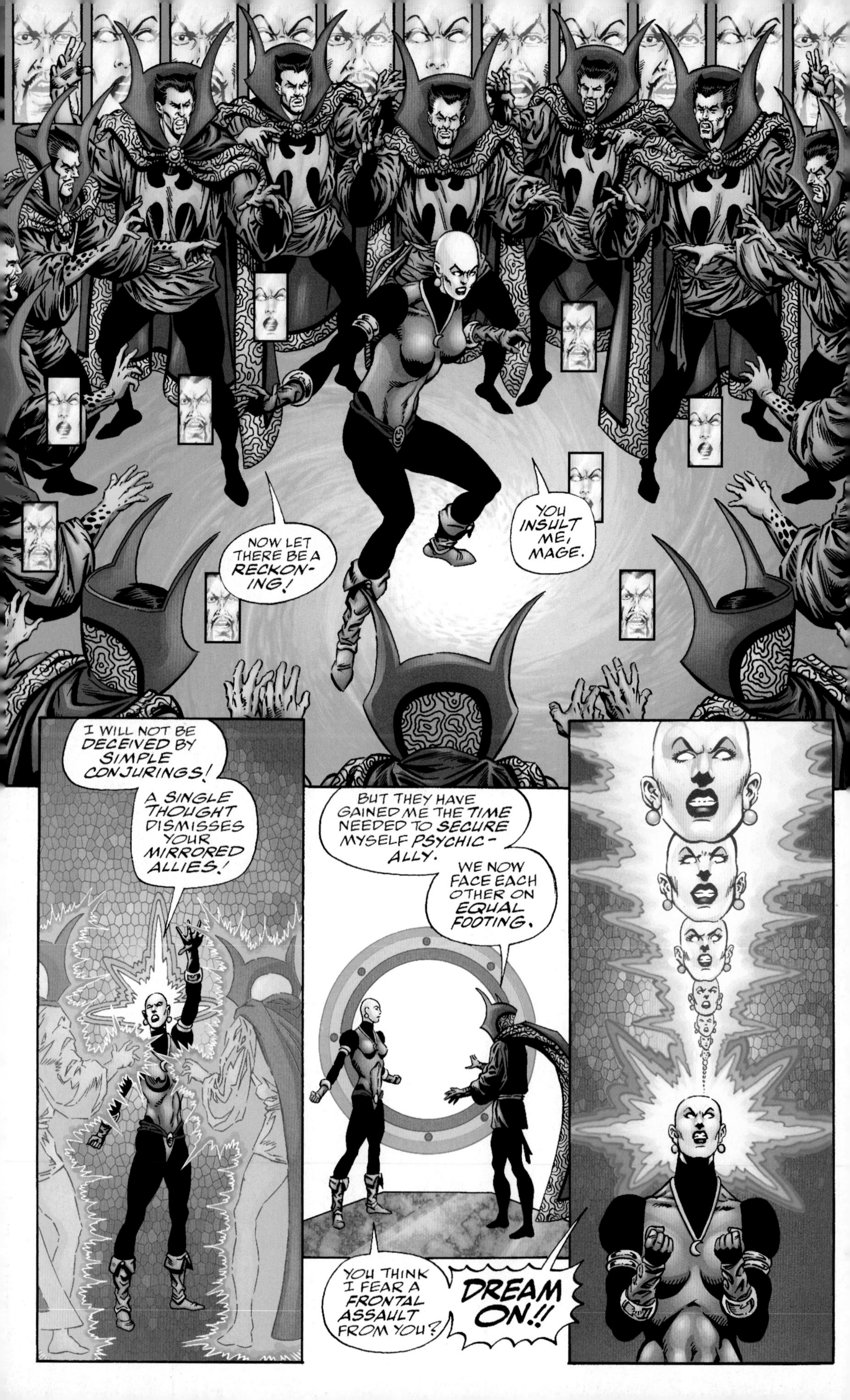
NOW LET THERE BE A RECKONING!
YOU INSULT ME, MAGE.
I WILL NOT BE DECEIVED BY SIMPLE CONJURINGS!
A SINGLE THOUGHT DISMISSES YOUR MIRRORED ALLIES!
BUT THEY HAVE GAINED ME THE TIME NEEDED TO SECURE MYSELF PSYCHIC-ALLY.
WE NOW FACE EACH OTHER ON EQUAL FOOTING.
YOU THINK I FEAR A FRONTAL ASSAULT FROM YOU?
DREAM ON!!

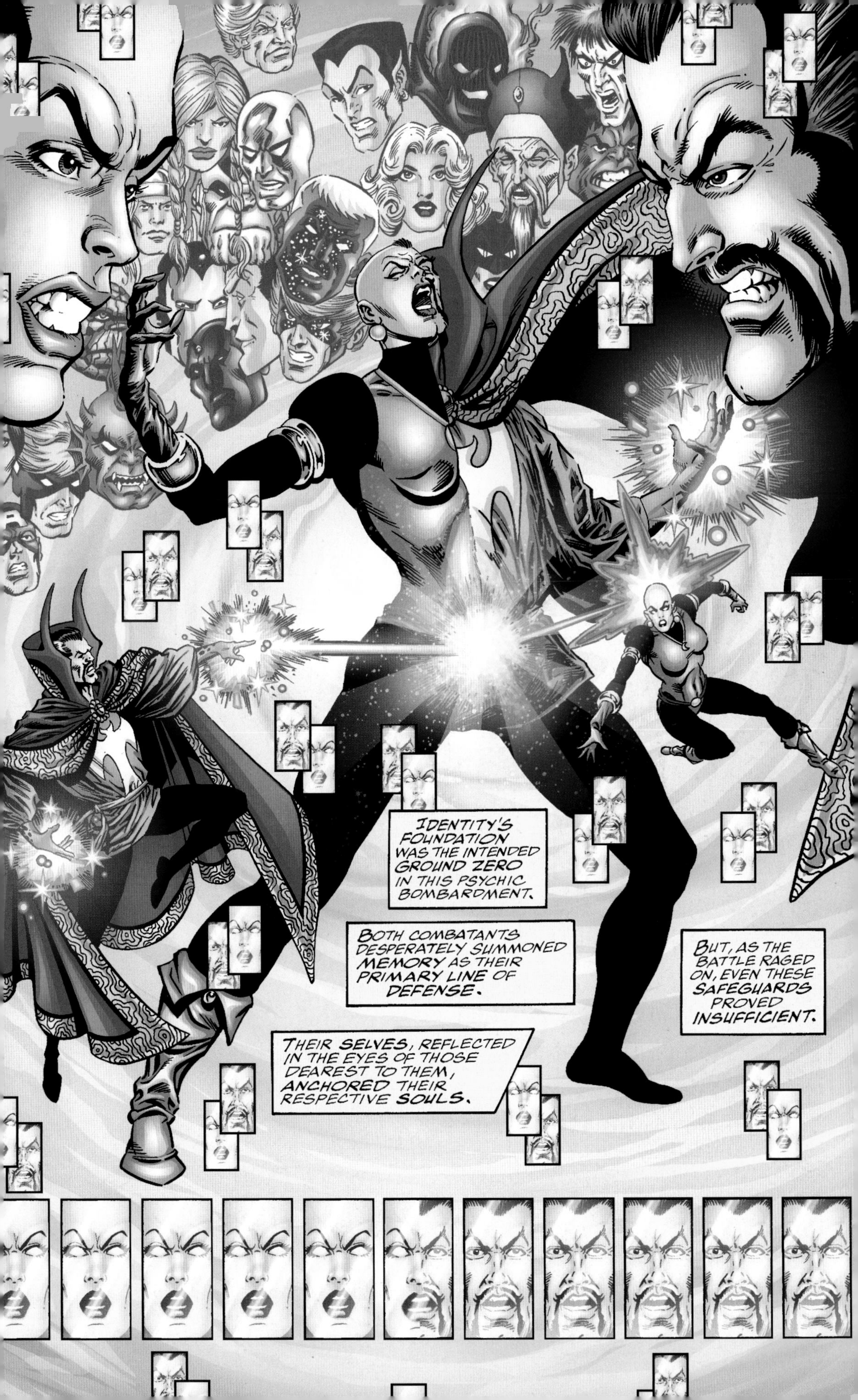
IDENTITY'S FOUNDATION WAS THE INTENDED GROUND ZERO IN THIS PSYCHIC BOMBARDMENT.
BOTH COMBATANTS DESPERATELY SUMMONED MEMORY AS THEIR PRIMARY LINE OF DEFENSE.
THEIR SELVES, REFLECTED IN THE EYES OF THOSE DEAREST TO THEM, ANCHORED THEIR RESPECTIVE SOULS.
BUT, AS THE BATTLE RAGED ON, EVEN THESE SAFEGUARDS PROVED INSUFFICIENT.

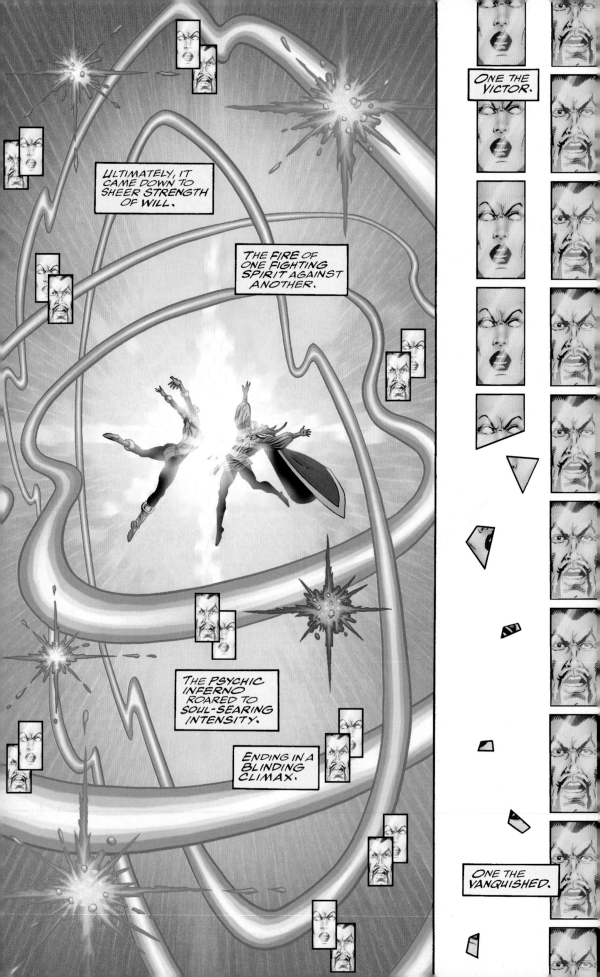

ULTIMATELY, IT CAME DOWN TO SHEER STRENGTH OF WILL.

THE FIRE OF ONE FIGHTING SPIRIT AGAINST ANOTHER.

THE PSYCHIC INFERNO ROARED TO SOUL-SEARING INTENSITY.

ENDING IN A BLINDING CLIMAX.

ONE THE VICTOR.

ONE THE VANQUISHED.

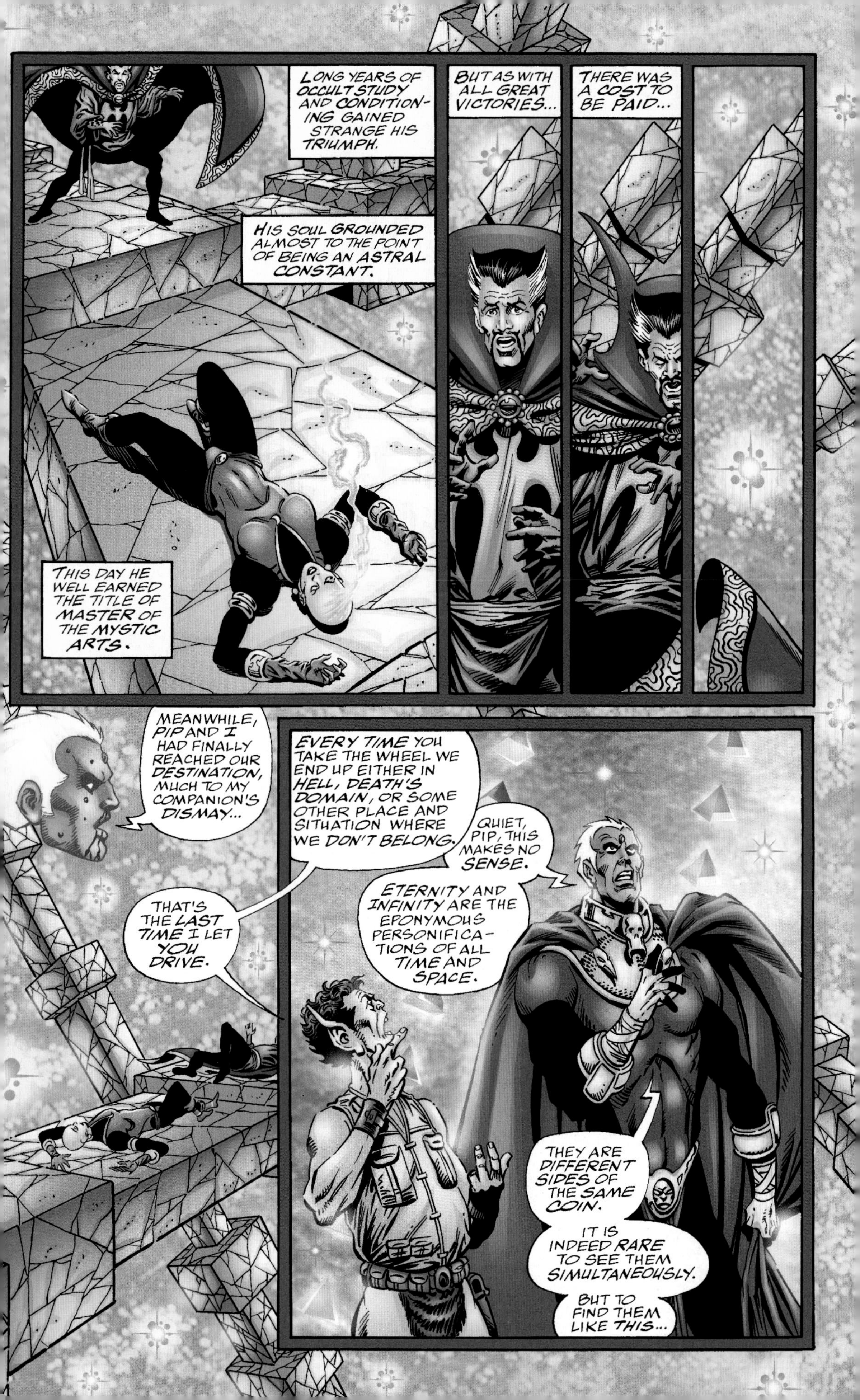

LONG YEARS OF OCCULT STUDY AND CONDITIONING GAINED STRANGE HIS TRIUMPH.
HIS SOUL GROUNDED ALMOST TO THE POINT OF BEING AN ASTRAL CONSTANT.
THIS DAY HE WELL EARNED THE TITLE OF MASTER OF THE MYSTIC ARTS.
BUT AS WITH ALL GREAT VICTORIES...
THERE WAS A COST TO BE PAID...
MEANWHILE, PIP AND I HAD FINALLY REACHED OUR DESTINATION, MUCH TO MY COMPANION'S DISMAY...
EVERY TIME YOU TAKE THE WHEEL WE END UP EITHER IN HELL, DEATH'S DOMAIN, OR SOME OTHER PLACE AND SITUATION WHERE WE DON'T BELONG.
THAT'S THE LAST TIME I LET YOU DRIVE.
QUIET, PIP, THIS MAKES NO SENSE.
ETERNITY AND INFINITY ARE THE EPONYMOUS PERSONIFICATIONS OF ALL TIME AND SPACE.
THEY ARE DIFFERENT SIDES OF THE SAME COIN.
IT IS INDEED RARE TO SEE THEM SIMULTANEOUSLY.
BUT TO FIND THEM LIKE THIS...

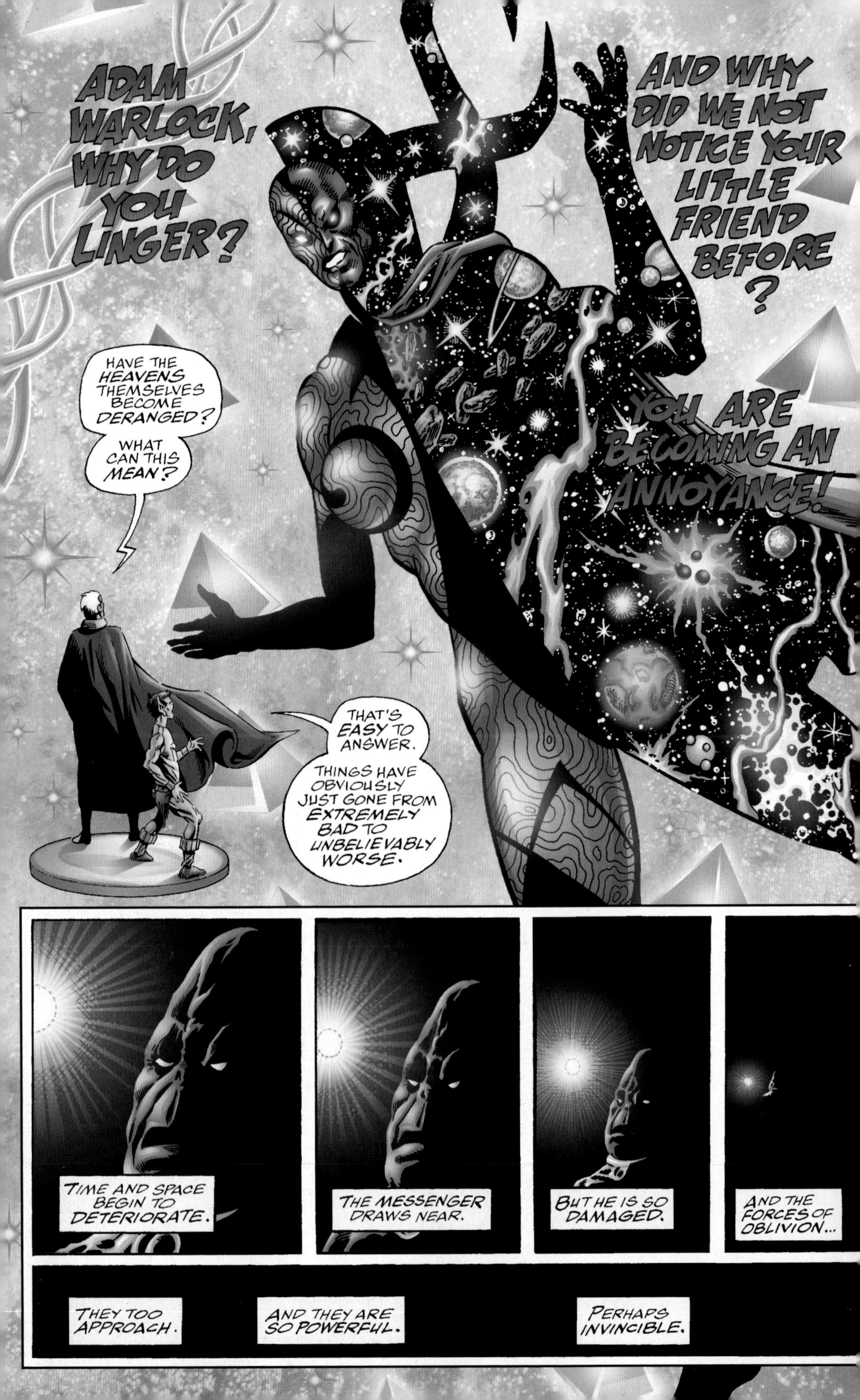
ADAM WARLOCK, WHY DO YOU LINGER?
AND WHY DID WE NOT NOTICE YOUR LITTLE FRIEND BEFORE?
HAVE THE HEAVENS THEMSELVES BECOME DERANGED?
WHAT CAN THIS MEAN?
YOU ARE BECOMING AN ANNOYANCE!
THAT'S EASY TO ANSWER.
THINGS HAVE OBVIOUSLY JUST GONE FROM EXTREMELY BAD TO UNBELIEVABLY WORSE.
TIME AND SPACE BEGIN TO DETERIORATE.
THE MESSENGER DRAWS NEAR.
BUT HE IS SO DAMAGED.
AND THE FORCES OF OBLIVION...
THEY TOO APPROACH.
AND THEY ARE SO POWERFUL.
PERHAPS INVINCIBLE.

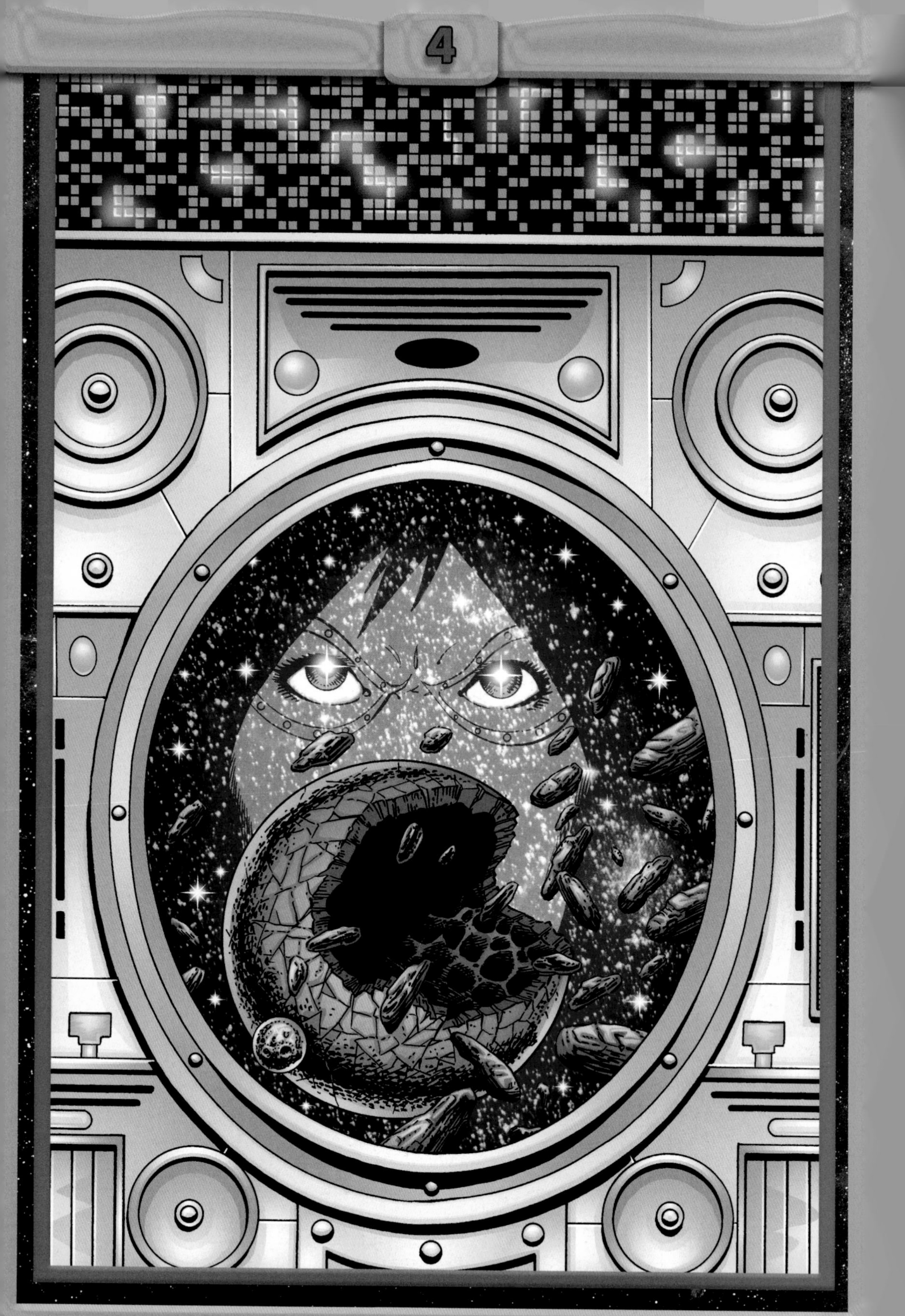
4

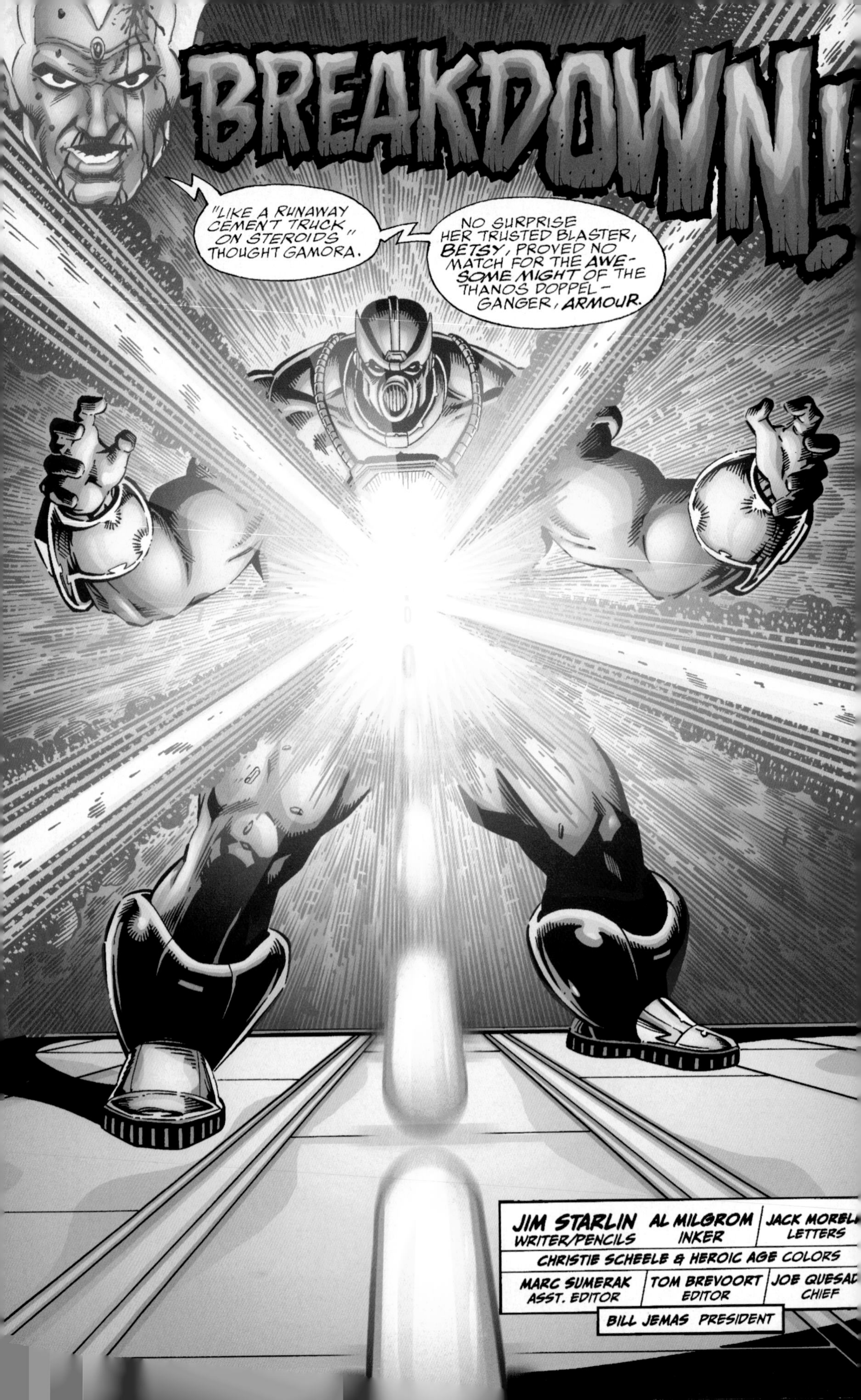
BREAKDOWN!
"LIKE A RUNAWAY CEMENT TRUCK ON STEROIDS" THOUGHT GAMORA.
NO SURPRISE HER TRUSTED BLASTER, BETSY, PROVED NO MATCH FOR THE AWESOME MIGHT OF THE THANOS DOPPELGANGER, ARMOUR.
JIM STARLIN WRITER/PENCILS
AL MILGROM INKER
JACK MOREL LETTERS
CHRISTIE SCHEELE & HEROIC AGE COLORS
MARC SUMERAK ASST. EDITOR
TOM BREVOORT EDITOR
JOE QUESA CHIEF
BILL JEMAS PRESIDENT

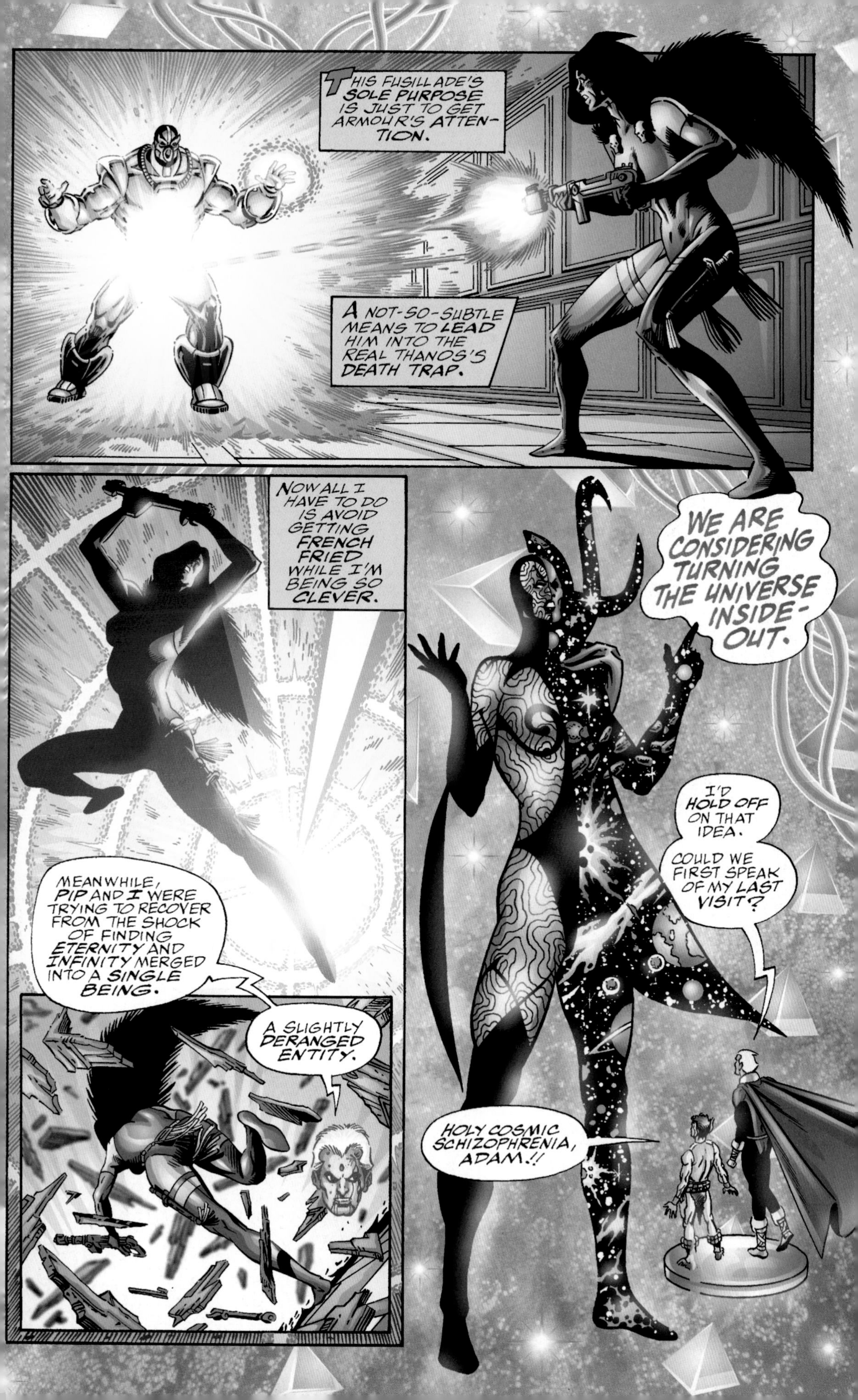
THIS FUSILLADE'S SOLE PURPOSE IS JUST TO GET ARMOUR'S ATTENTION.
A NOT-SO-SUBTLE MEANS TO LEAD HIM INTO THE REAL THANOS'S DEATH TRAP.
NOW ALL I HAVE TO DO IS AVOID GETTING FRENCH FRIED WHILE I'M BEING SO CLEVER.
WE ARE CONSIDERING TURNING THE UNIVERSE INSIDE-OUT.
I'D HOLD OFF ON THAT IDEA.
COULD WE FIRST SPEAK OF MY LAST VISIT?
MEANWHILE, PIP AND I WERE TRYING TO RECOVER FROM THE SHOCK OF FINDING ETERNITY AND INFINITY MERGED INTO A SINGLE BEING.
A SLIGHTLY DERANGED ENTITY.
HOLY COSMIC SCHIZOPHRENIA, ADAM.!!

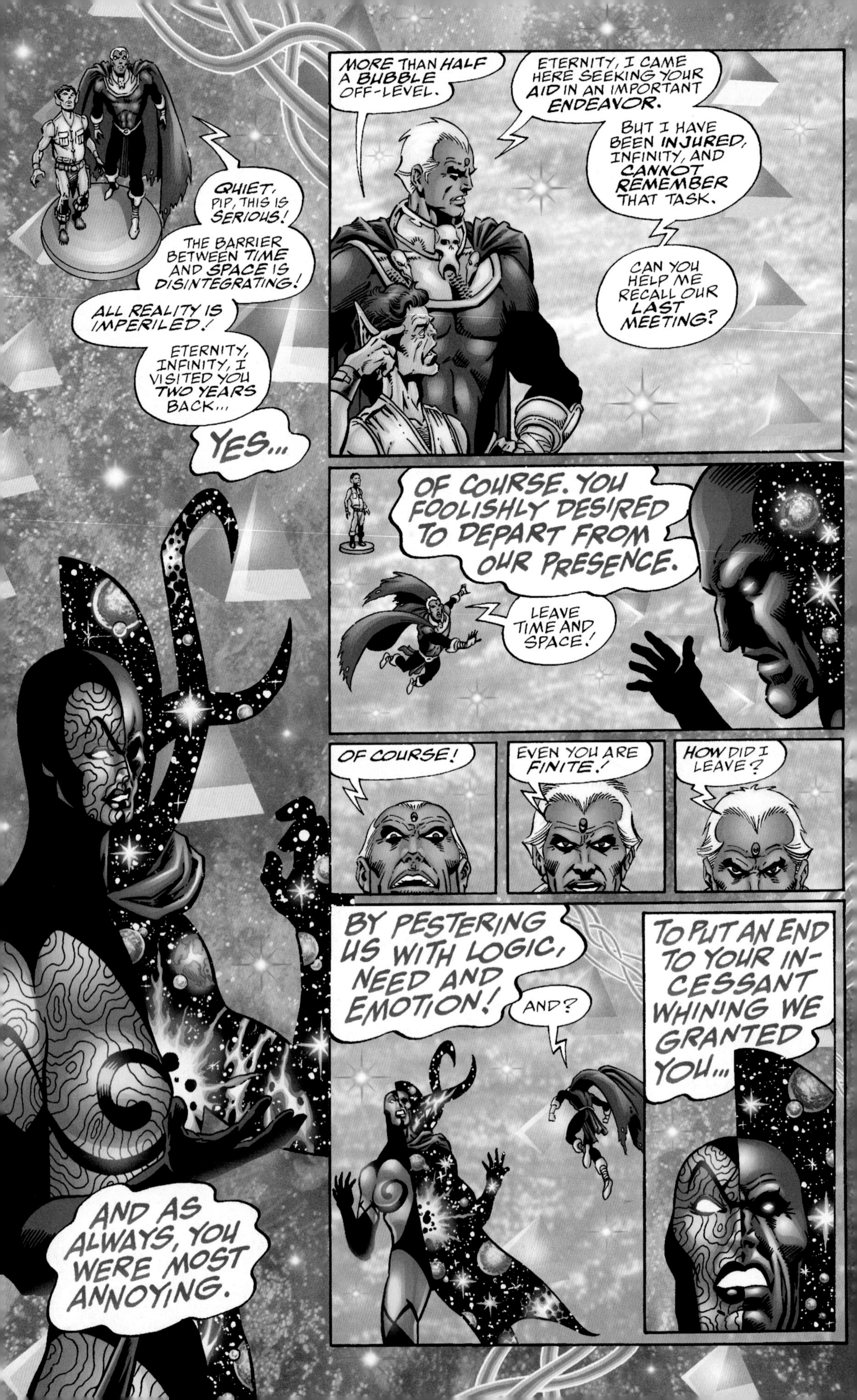
QUIET, PIP, THIS IS SERIOUS!
THE BARRIER BETWEEN TIME AND SPACE IS DISINTEGRATING!
ALL REALITY IS IMPERILED!
ETERNITY, INFINITY, I VISITED YOU TWO YEARS BACK...
YES...
MORE THAN HALF A BUBBLE OFF-LEVEL.
ETERNITY, I CAME HERE SEEKING YOUR AID IN AN IMPORTANT ENDEAVOR.
BUT I HAVE BEEN INJURED, INFINITY, AND CANNOT REMEMBER THAT TASK.
CAN YOU HELP ME RECALL OUR LAST MEETING?
OF COURSE. YOU FOOLISHLY DESIRED TO DEPART FROM OUR PRESENCE.
LEAVE TIME AND SPACE!
OF COURSE!
EVEN YOU ARE FINITE!
HOW DID I LEAVE?
AND AS ALWAYS, YOU WERE MOST ANNOYING.
BY PESTERING US WITH LOGIC, NEED AND EMOTION!
AND?
TO PUT AN END TO YOUR INCESSANT WHINING WE GRANTED YOU...

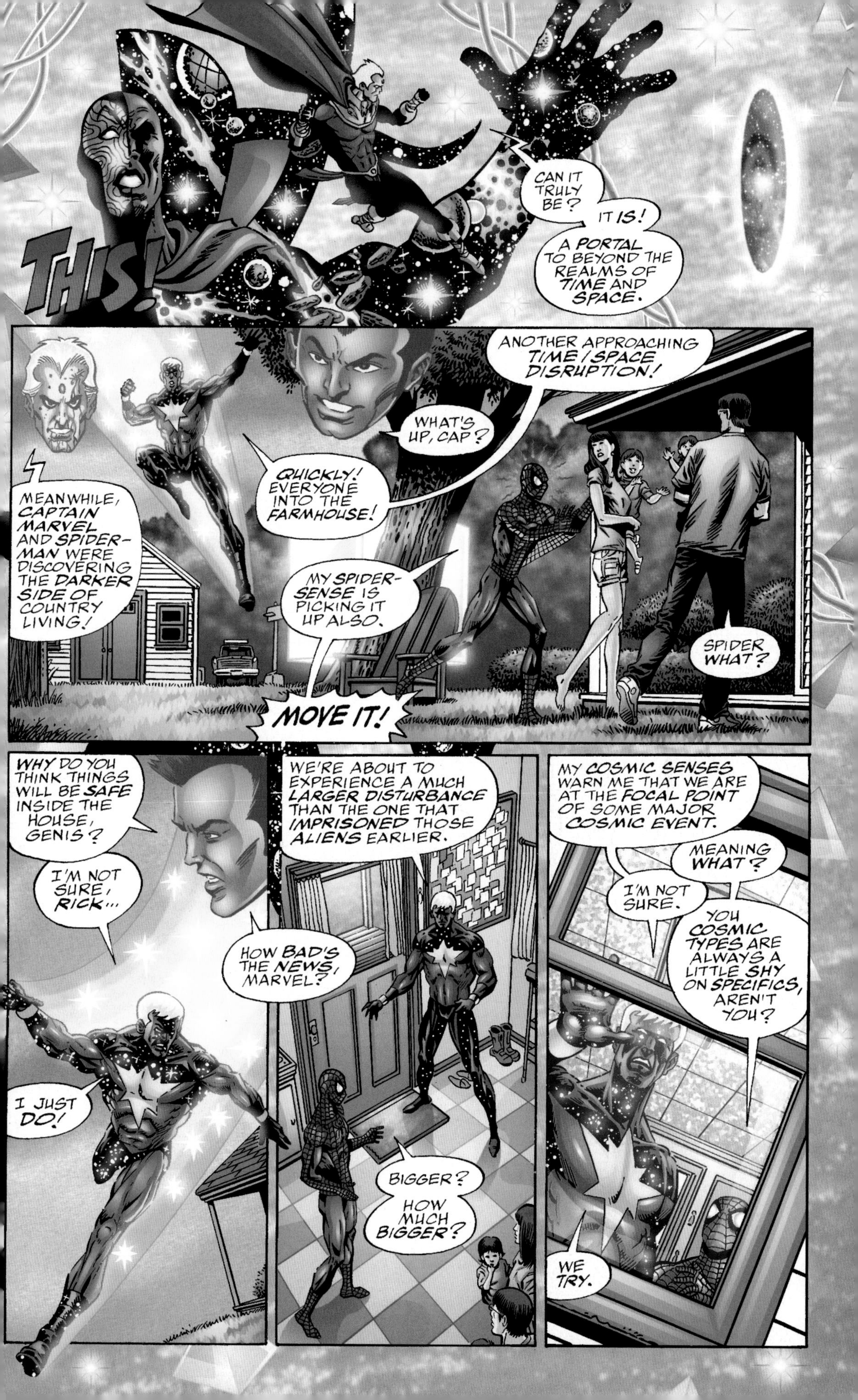
THIS!
CAN IT TRULY BE?
IT IS!
A PORTAL TO BEYOND THE REALMS OF TIME AND SPACE.
MEANWHILE, CAPTAIN MARVEL AND SPIDER-MAN WERE DISCOVERING THE DARKER SIDE OF COUNTRY LIVING!
ANOTHER APPROACHING TIME/SPACE DISRUPTION!
WHAT'S UP, CAP?
QUICKLY! EVERYONE INTO THE FARMHOUSE!
MY SPIDER-SENSE IS PICKING IT UP ALSO.
SPIDER WHAT?
MOVE IT!
WHY DO YOU THINK THINGS WILL BE SAFE INSIDE THE HOUSE, GENIS?
I'M NOT SURE, RICK...
I JUST DO!
WE'RE ABOUT TO EXPERIENCE A MUCH LARGER DISTURBANCE THAN THE ONE THAT IMPRISONED THOSE ALIENS EARLIER.
HOW BAD'S THE NEWS, MARVEL?
BIGGER?
HOW MUCH BIGGER?
MY COSMIC SENSES WARN ME THAT WE ARE AT THE FOCAL POINT OF SOME MAJOR COSMIC EVENT.
MEANING WHAT?
I'M NOT SURE.
YOU COSMIC TYPES ARE ALWAYS A LITTLE SHY ON SPECIFICS, AREN'T YOU?
WE TRY.

YOU MIGHT BE GETTING A *BAD READING* THIS TIME.

LOOKS PRETTY *PEACEFUL* OUT THERE TO ME.

WAIT A MINUTE!

THOUGHT IT WAS JUST *FOG* AT FIRST!

IT'S *NOT!*

EVERYTHING'S *FADING AWAY* TO *NOTHINGNESS!*

WE'RE GOING TO BE...

IT PASSED US BY!

EVERYTHING ELSE HAS *DISAPPEARED* BUT *US!*

HOW?!

WHY?!

IT APPEARS THAT WE HAVE BEEN *PROTECTED* FROM THIS *PLAGUE* OF *NOTHINGNESS.*

BY *WHAT?*

ONCE AGAIN, I *CANNOT SAY.*

MY *COSMIC SENSES* ARE HAVING DIFFICULTY *FOCUSING* ON THE *ENERGIES* AT PLAY.

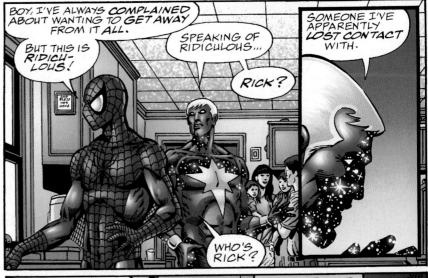

BOY, I'VE ALWAYS *COMPLAINED* ABOUT WANTING TO *GET AWAY* FROM IT ALL.

BUT THIS IS *RIDICULOUS!*

SPEAKING OF RIDICULOUS...

RICK?

WHO'S *RICK?*

SOMEONE I'VE APPARENTLY *LOST CONTACT* WITH.

AND WHILE WE'RE ON THE SUBJECT OF *LOST CONTACT...*

I CAN'T HAVE DITCHED HIM.

I WAS KEEPING MY SPEED DOWN AND HE WAS RIGHT BEHIND ME.

WHERE?!

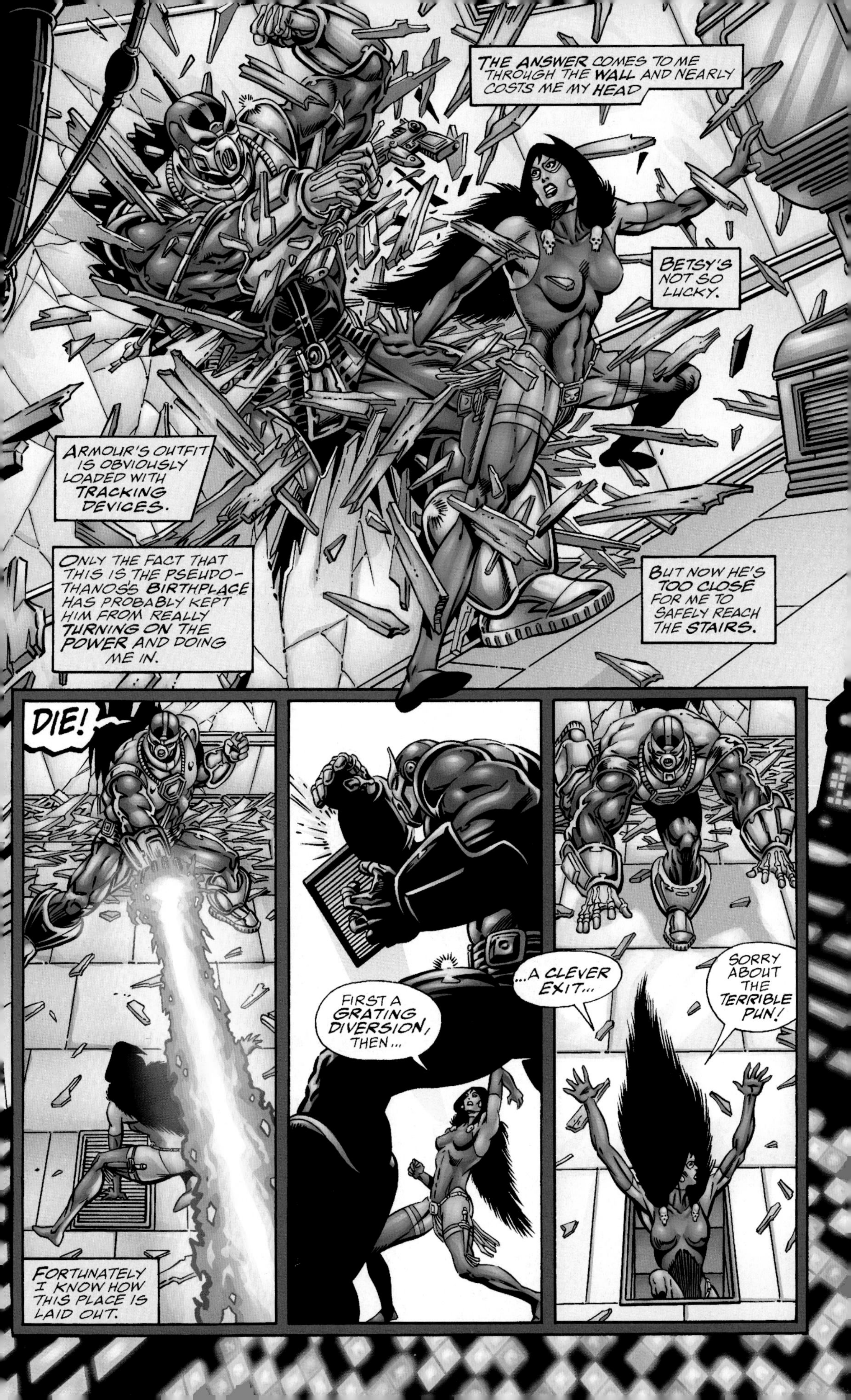
THE ANSWER COMES TO ME THROUGH THE WALL AND NEARLY COSTS ME MY HEAD
BETSY'S NOT SO LUCKY.
ARMOUR'S OUTFIT IS OBVIOUSLY LOADED WITH TRACKING DEVICES.
ONLY THE FACT THAT THIS IS THE PSEUDO-THANOS'S BIRTHPLACE HAS PROBABLY KEPT HIM FROM REALLY TURNING ON THE POWER AND DOING ME IN.
BUT NOW HE'S TOO CLOSE FOR ME TO SAFELY REACH THE STAIRS.
DIE!
FORTUNATELY I KNOW HOW THIS PLACE IS LAID OUT.
FIRST A GRATING DIVERSION, THEN...
...A CLEVER EXIT...
SORRY ABOUT THE TERRIBLE PUN!

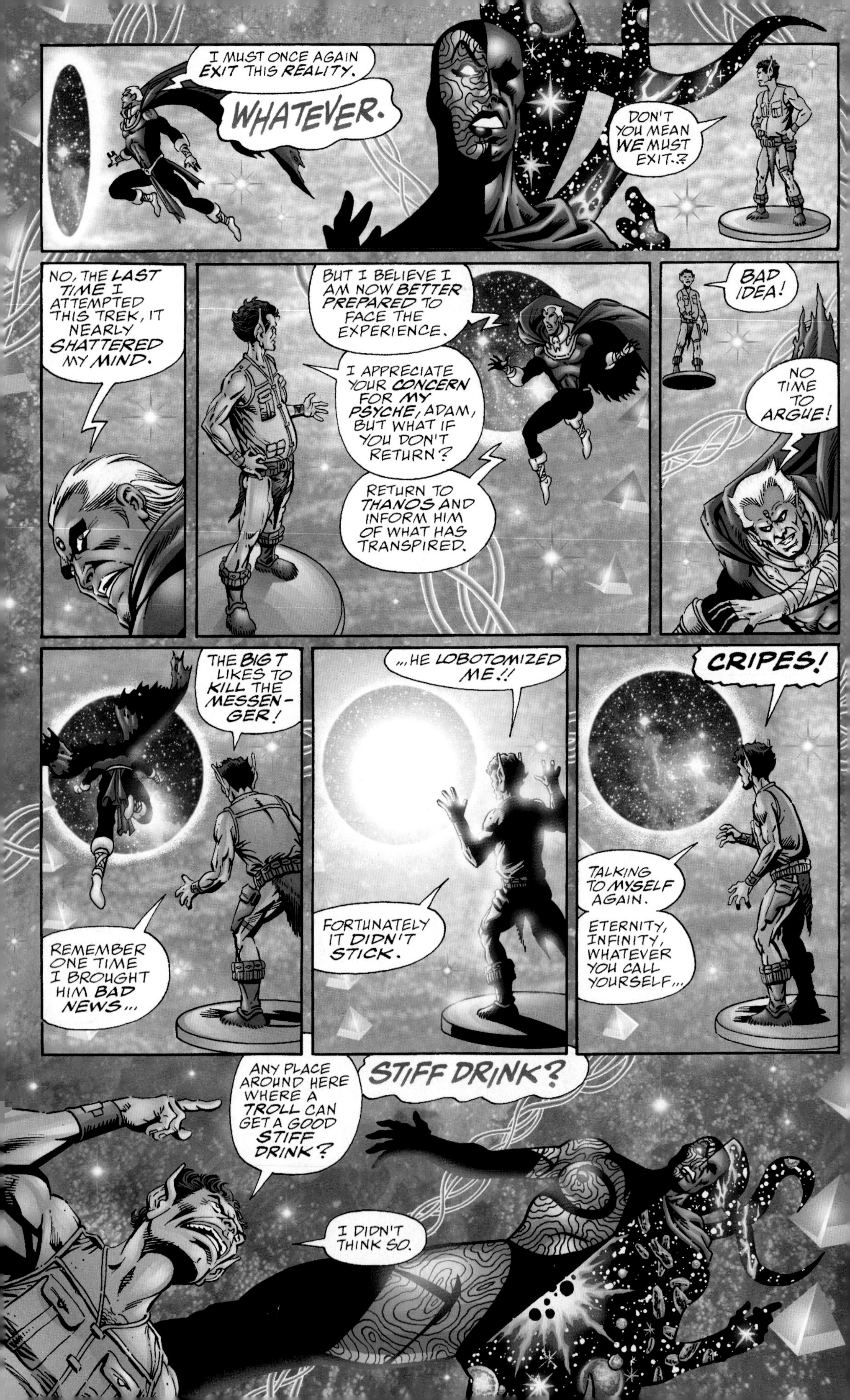
I MUST ONCE AGAIN EXIT THIS REALITY.
WHATEVER.
DON'T YOU MEAN WE MUST EXIT..?
NO, THE LAST TIME I ATTEMPTED THIS TREK, IT NEARLY SHATTERED MY MIND.
BUT I BELIEVE I AM NOW BETTER PREPARED TO FACE THE EXPERIENCE.
I APPRECIATE YOUR CONCERN FOR MY PSYCHE, ADAM, BUT WHAT IF YOU DON'T RETURN?
RETURN TO THANOS AND INFORM HIM OF WHAT HAS TRANSPIRED.
BAD IDEA!
NO TIME TO ARGUE!
THE BIG T LIKES TO KILL THE MESSEN-GER!
REMEMBER ONE TIME I BROUGHT HIM BAD NEWS...
...HE LOBOTOMIZED ME!!
FORTUNATELY IT DIDN'T STICK.
CRIPES!
TALKING TO MYSELF AGAIN.
ETERNITY, INFINITY, WHATEVER YOU CALL YOURSELF...
ANY PLACE AROUND HERE WHERE A TROLL CAN GET A GOOD STIFF DRINK?
STIFF DRINK?
I DIDN'T THINK SO.

ESCAPING THEIR *CURRENT* SITUATION SEEMED THE MOST APPROPRIATE *NEXT STEP* TO SPIDER-MAN AND CAPTAIN MARVEL.

AND SEEING HOW THE WEB-SLINGER WAS *INCAPABLE* OF FLIGHT...

...AND I'LL *RETURN* ONCE I'VE CONTACTED THE *AVENGERS.*

THE *FANTASTIC FOUR* MIGHT BE A *BETTER* BET.

RICHARDS HAS TONS OF EXPERIENCE WITH *INTER-DIMENSIONAL WEIRDNESS.*

MEANWHILE I'LL MAKE MYSELF *USEFUL* BY ENTERTAINING THE KIDS WITH SOME *WEB TRICKS.*

SPIDER-MAN, BETTER THAN A FOR-HIRE *PARTY CLOWN.*

MAYBE I CAN--

HUH?!

THAT CLEARLY *DIDN'T* WORK OUT SO WELL.

THE OL' *MOBIUS STRIP* DILEMMA?

OR MAYBE OUR PRISON IS *SPHERICAL.*

OR PERHAPS SOME VERY BASIC *LAWS* OF *PHYSICS* DON'T APPLY IN THIS VOID.

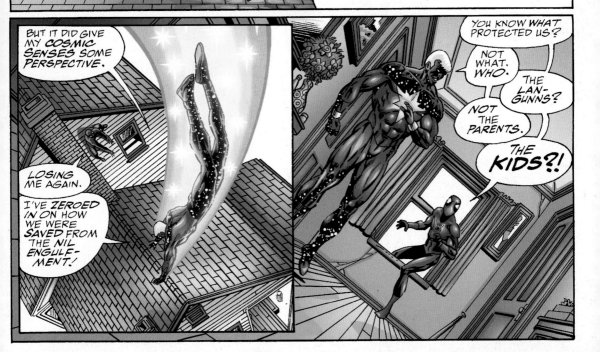

BUT IT *DID* GIVE MY *COSMIC SENSES* SOME *PERSPECTIVE.*

LOSING ME AGAIN.

I'VE *ZEROED IN* ON HOW WE WERE *SAVED* FROM THE *NIL* ENGULF-MENT!

YOU KNOW *WHAT* PROTECTED US?

NOT *WHAT.* *WHO.*

THE *LAN-GUNNS?*

NOT THE *PARENTS.*

THE *KIDS?!*

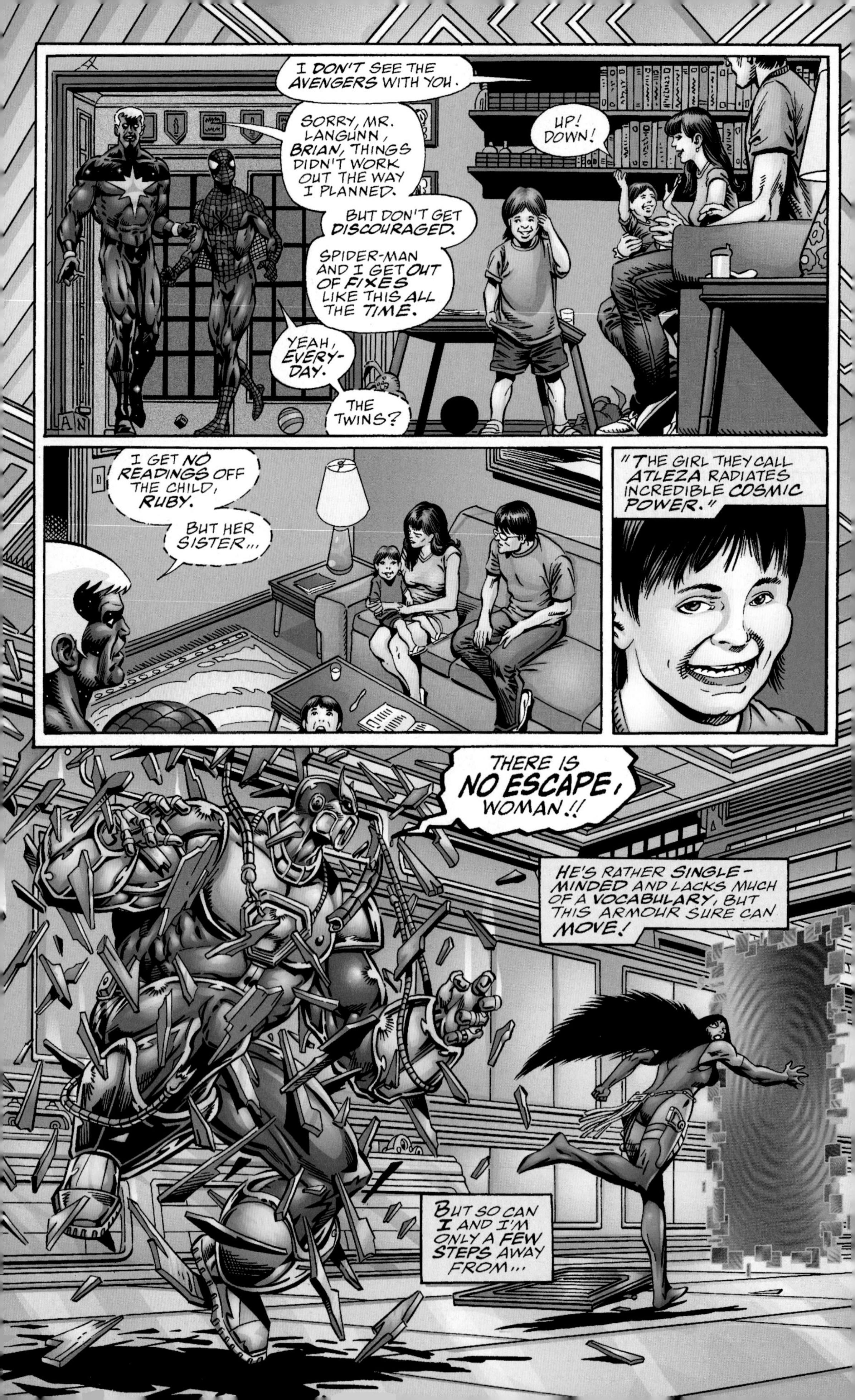
I DON'T SEE THE AVENGERS WITH YOU.
SORRY, MR. LANGUNN, BRIAN, THINGS DIDN'T WORK OUT THE WAY I PLANNED.
BUT DON'T GET DISCOURAGED.
SPIDER-MAN AND I GET OUT OF FIXES LIKE THIS ALL THE TIME.
YEAH, EVERY-DAY.
THE TWINS?
UP! DOWN!
I GET NO READINGS OFF THE CHILD, RUBY.
BUT HER SISTER...
"THE GIRL THEY CALL ATLEZA RADIATES INCREDIBLE COSMIC POWER."
THERE IS NO ESCAPE, WOMAN!!
HE'S RATHER SINGLE-MINDED AND LACKS MUCH OF A VOCABULARY, BUT THIS ARMOUR SURE CAN MOVE!
BUT SO CAN I AND I'M ONLY A FEW STEPS AWAY FROM...

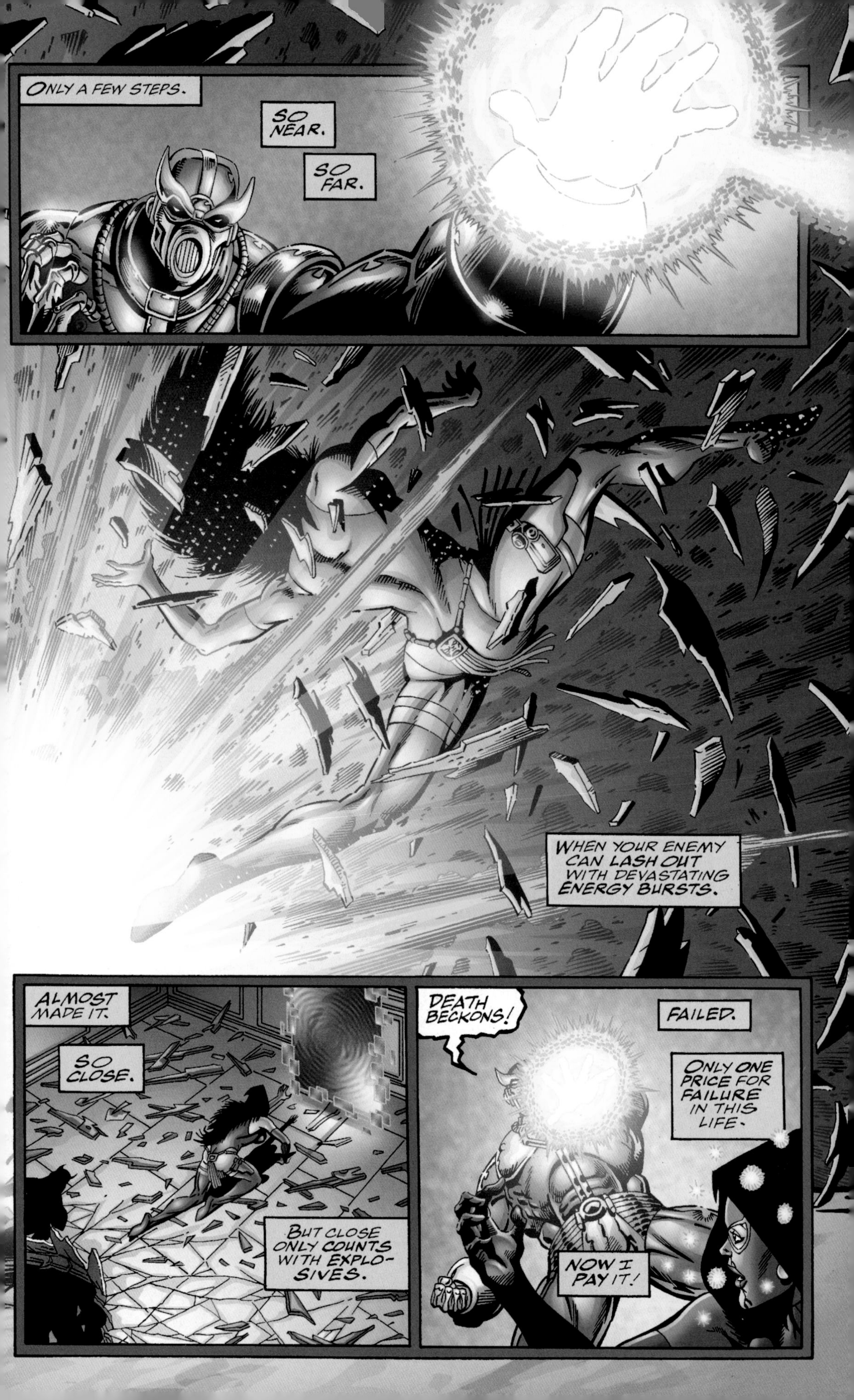
ONLY A FEW STEPS.
SO NEAR.
SO FAR.
WHEN YOUR ENEMY CAN LASH OUT WITH DEVASTATING ENERGY BURSTS.
ALMOST MADE IT.
SO CLOSE.
BUT CLOSE ONLY COUNTS WITH EXPLO-SIVES.
DEATH BECKONS!
FAILED.
ONLY ONE PRICE FOR FAILURE IN THIS LIFE.
NOW I PAY IT!

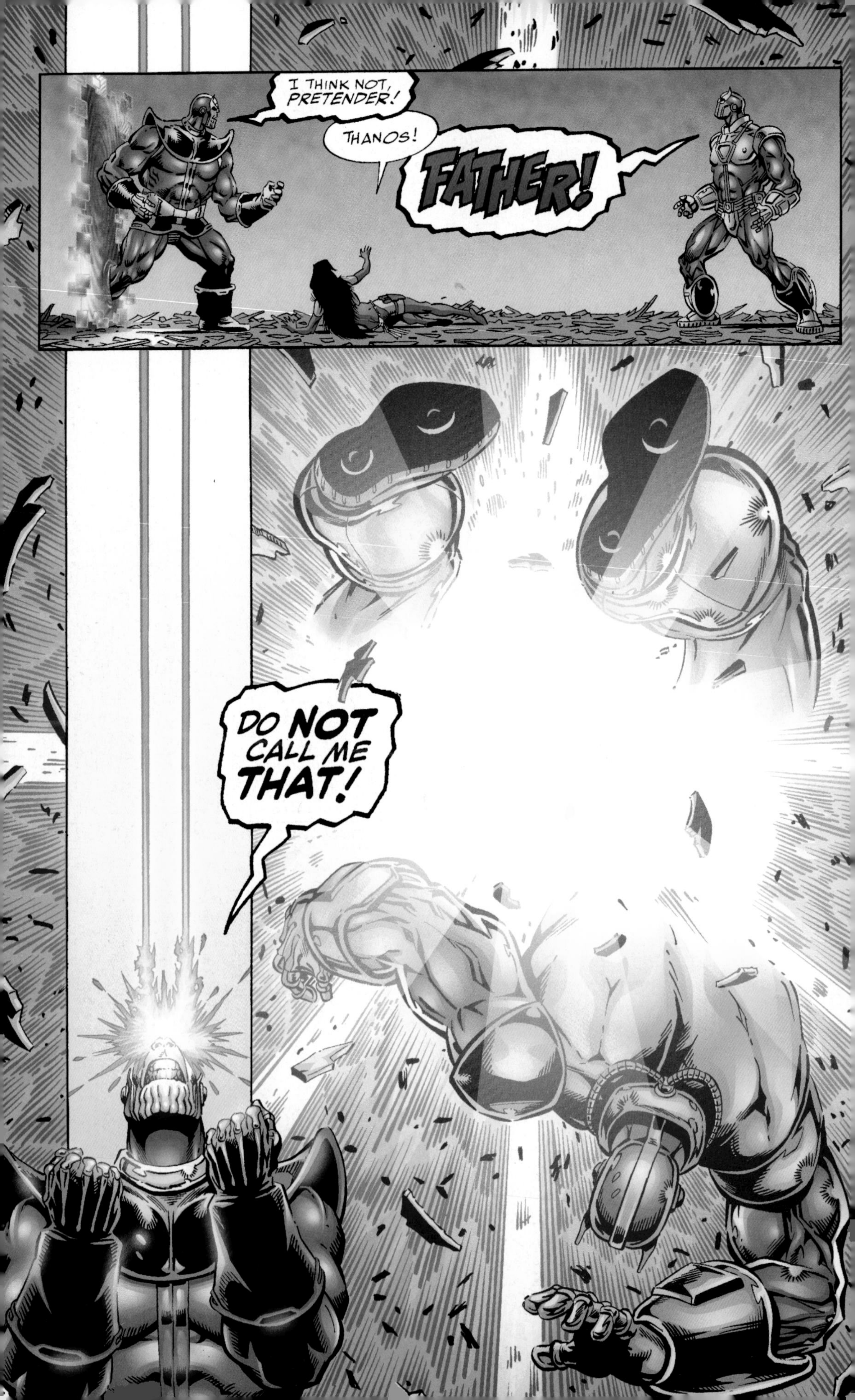
I THINK NOT, PRETENDER!
THANOS!
FATHER!
DO NOT CALL ME THAT!

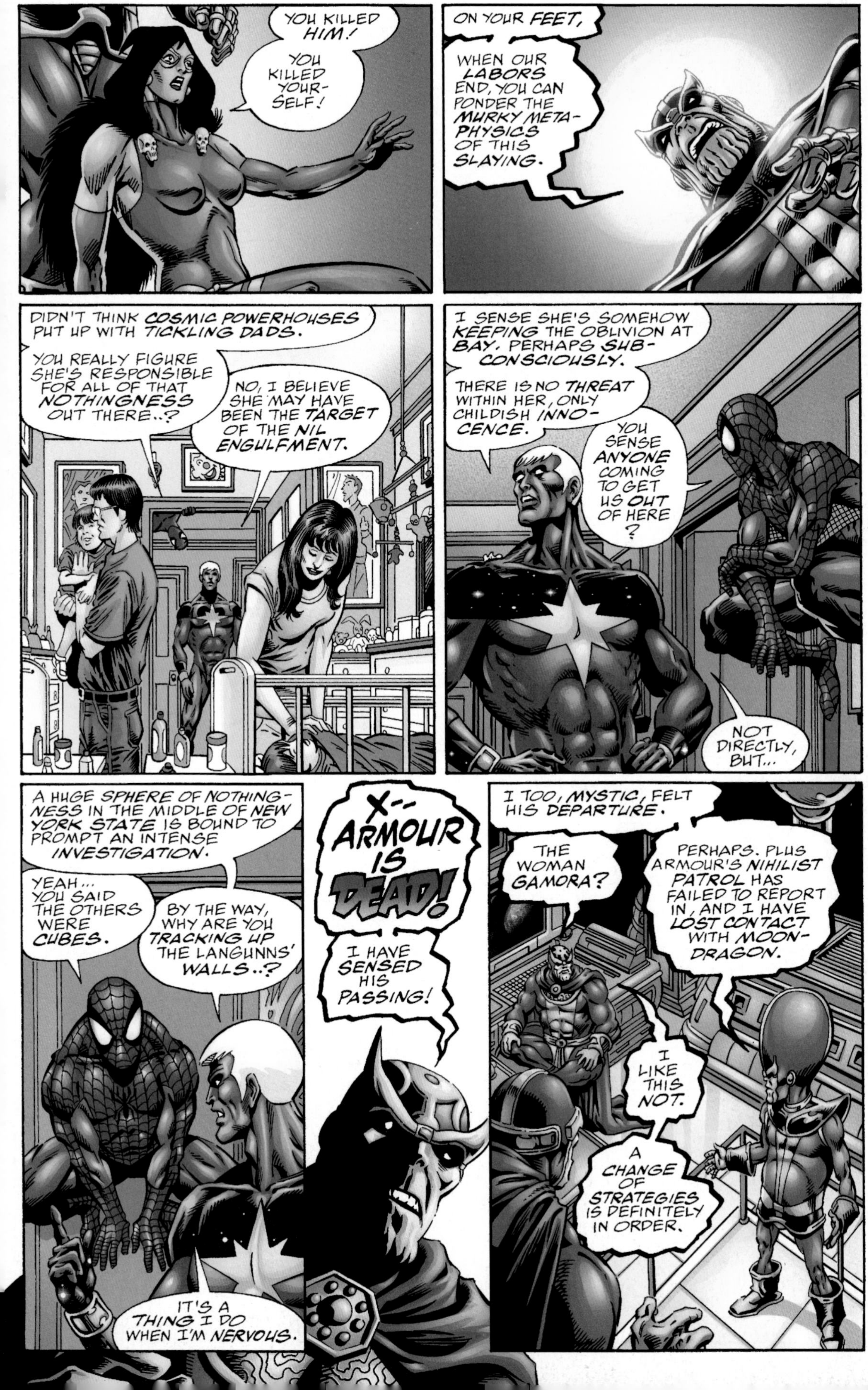
YOU KILLED HIM!
YOU KILLED YOURSELF!
ON YOUR FEET,
WHEN OUR LABORS END, YOU CAN PONDER THE MURKY METAPHYSICS OF THIS SLAYING.
DIDN'T THINK COSMIC POWERHOUSES PUT UP WITH TICKLING DADS.
YOU REALLY FIGURE SHE'S RESPONSIBLE FOR ALL OF THAT NOTHINGNESS OUT THERE..?
NO, I BELIEVE SHE MAY HAVE BEEN THE TARGET OF THE NIL ENGULFMENT.
I SENSE SHE'S SOMEHOW KEEPING THE OBLIVION AT BAY. PERHAPS SUBCONSCIOUSLY.
THERE IS NO THREAT WITHIN HER, ONLY CHILDISH INNOCENCE.
YOU SENSE ANYONE COMING TO GET US OUT OF HERE?
NOT DIRECTLY, BUT...
A HUGE SPHERE OF NOTHINGNESS IN THE MIDDLE OF NEW YORK STATE IS BOUND TO PROMPT AN INTENSE INVESTIGATION.
YEAH... YOU SAID THE OTHERS WERE CUBES.
BY THE WAY, WHY ARE YOU TRACKING UP THE LANGUNNS' WALLS..?
IT'S A THING I DO WHEN I'M NERVOUS.
X-- ARMOUR IS DEAD!
I HAVE SENSED HIS PASSING!
I TOO, MYSTIC, FELT HIS DEPARTURE.
THE WOMAN GAMORA?
PERHAPS. PLUS ARMOUR'S NIHILIST PATROL HAS FAILED TO REPORT IN, AND I HAVE LOST CONTACT WITH MOONDRAGON.
I LIKE THIS NOT.
A CHANGE OF STRATEGIES IS DEFINITELY IN ORDER.

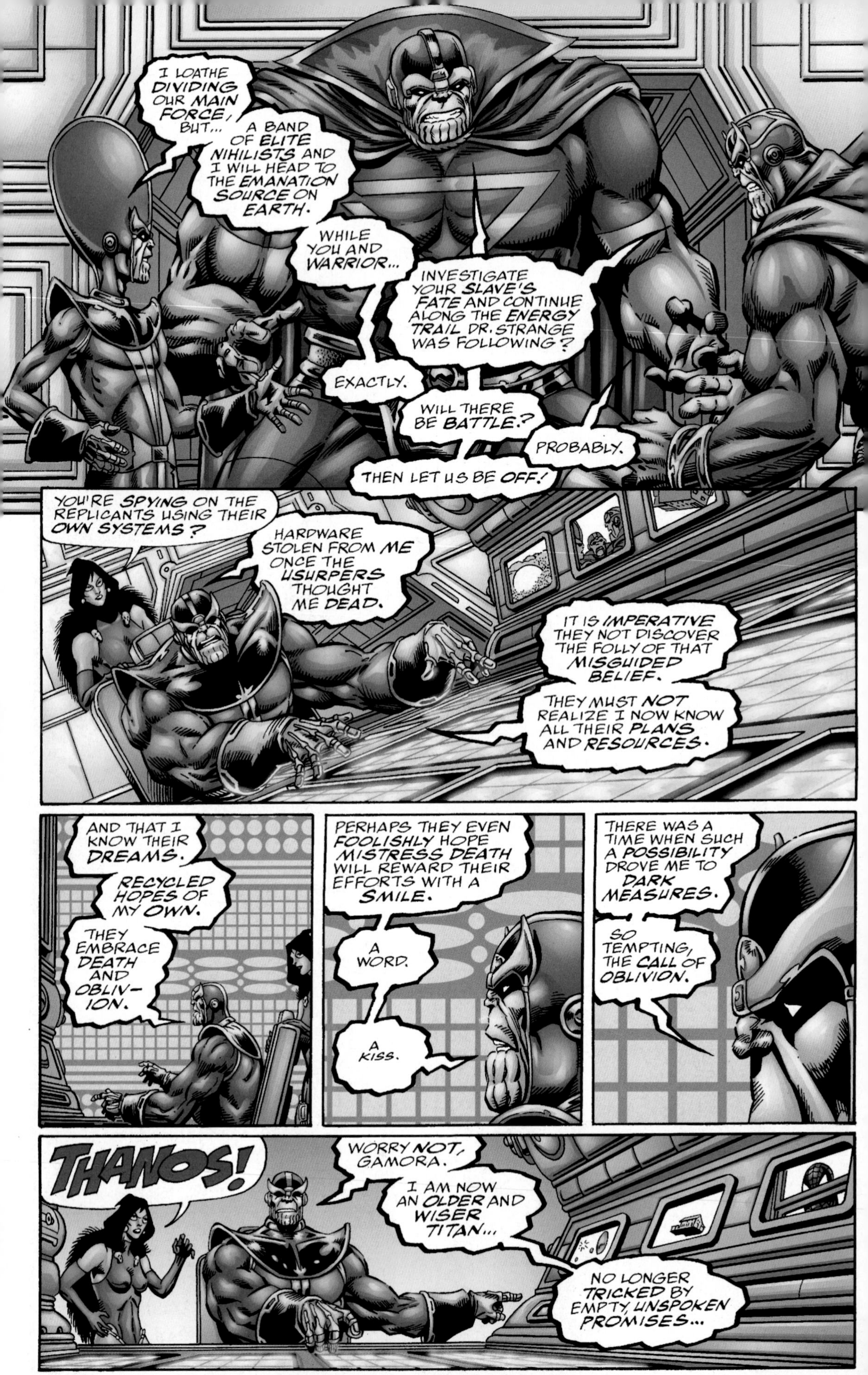
I LOATHE DIVIDING OUR MAIN FORCE, BUT...
A BAND OF ELITE NIHILISTS AND I WILL HEAD TO THE EMANATION SOURCE ON EARTH.
WHILE YOU AND WARRIOR...
INVESTIGATE YOUR SLAVE'S FATE AND CONTINUE ALONG THE ENERGY TRAIL DR. STRANGE WAS FOLLOWING?
EXACTLY.
WILL THERE BE BATTLE?
PROBABLY.
THEN LET US BE OFF!
YOU'RE SPYING ON THE REPLICANTS USING THEIR OWN SYSTEMS?
HARDWARE STOLEN FROM ME ONCE THE USURPERS THOUGHT ME DEAD.
IT IS IMPERATIVE THEY NOT DISCOVER THE FOLLY OF THAT MISGUIDED BELIEF.
THEY MUST NOT REALIZE I NOW KNOW ALL THEIR PLANS AND RESOURCES.
AND THAT I KNOW THEIR DREAMS.
RECYCLED HOPES OF MY OWN.
THEY EMBRACE DEATH AND OBLIVION.
PERHAPS THEY EVEN FOOLISHLY HOPE MISTRESS DEATH WILL REWARD THEIR EFFORTS WITH A SMILE.
A WORD.
A KISS.
THERE WAS A TIME WHEN SUCH A POSSIBILITY DROVE ME TO DARK MEASURES.
SO TEMPTING, THE CALL OF OBLIVION.
THANOS!
WORRY NOT, GAMORA.
I AM NOW AN OLDER AND WISER TITAN...
NO LONGER TRICKED BY EMPTY, UNSPOKEN PROMISES...

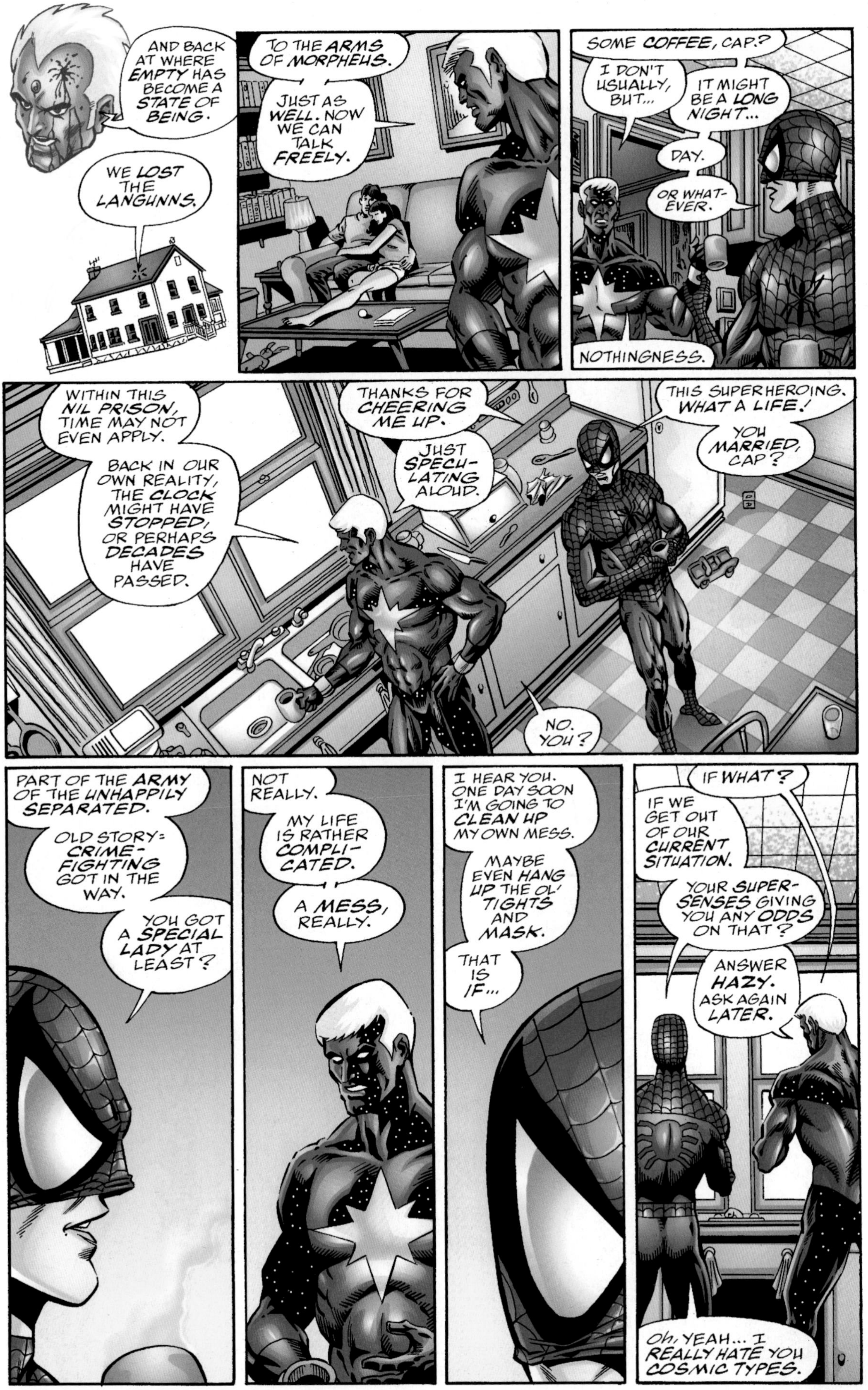
AND BACK AT WHERE EMPTY HAS BECOME A STATE OF BEING.
WE LOST THE LANGUNNS.
TO THE ARMS OF MORPHEUS.
JUST AS WELL. NOW WE CAN TALK FREELY.
SOME COFFEE, CAP.?
I DON'T USUALLY, BUT...
IT MIGHT BE A LONG NIGHT...
DAY.
OR WHAT-EVER.
NOTHINGNESS.
WITHIN THIS NIL PRISON, TIME MAY NOT EVEN APPLY.
BACK IN OUR OWN REALITY, THE CLOCK MIGHT HAVE STOPPED, OR PERHAPS DECADES HAVE PASSED.
THANKS FOR CHEERING ME UP.
JUST SPECU-LATING ALOUD.
THIS SUPERHEROING. WHAT A LIFE!
YOU MARRIED, CAP?
NO. YOU?
PART OF THE ARMY OF THE UNHAPPILY SEPARATED.
OLD STORY: CRIME-FIGHTING GOT IN THE WAY.
YOU GOT A SPECIAL LADY AT LEAST?
NOT REALLY.
MY LIFE IS RATHER COMPLI-CATED.
A MESS, REALLY.
I HEAR YOU. ONE DAY SOON I'M GOING TO CLEAN UP MY OWN MESS.
MAYBE EVEN HANG UP THE OL' TIGHTS AND MASK.
THAT IS IF...
IF WHAT?
IF WE GET OUT OF OUR CURRENT SITUATION.
YOUR SUPER-SENSES GIVING YOU ANY ODDS ON THAT?
ANSWER HAZY. ASK AGAIN LATER.
Oh, YEAH... I REALLY HATE YOU COSMIC TYPES.

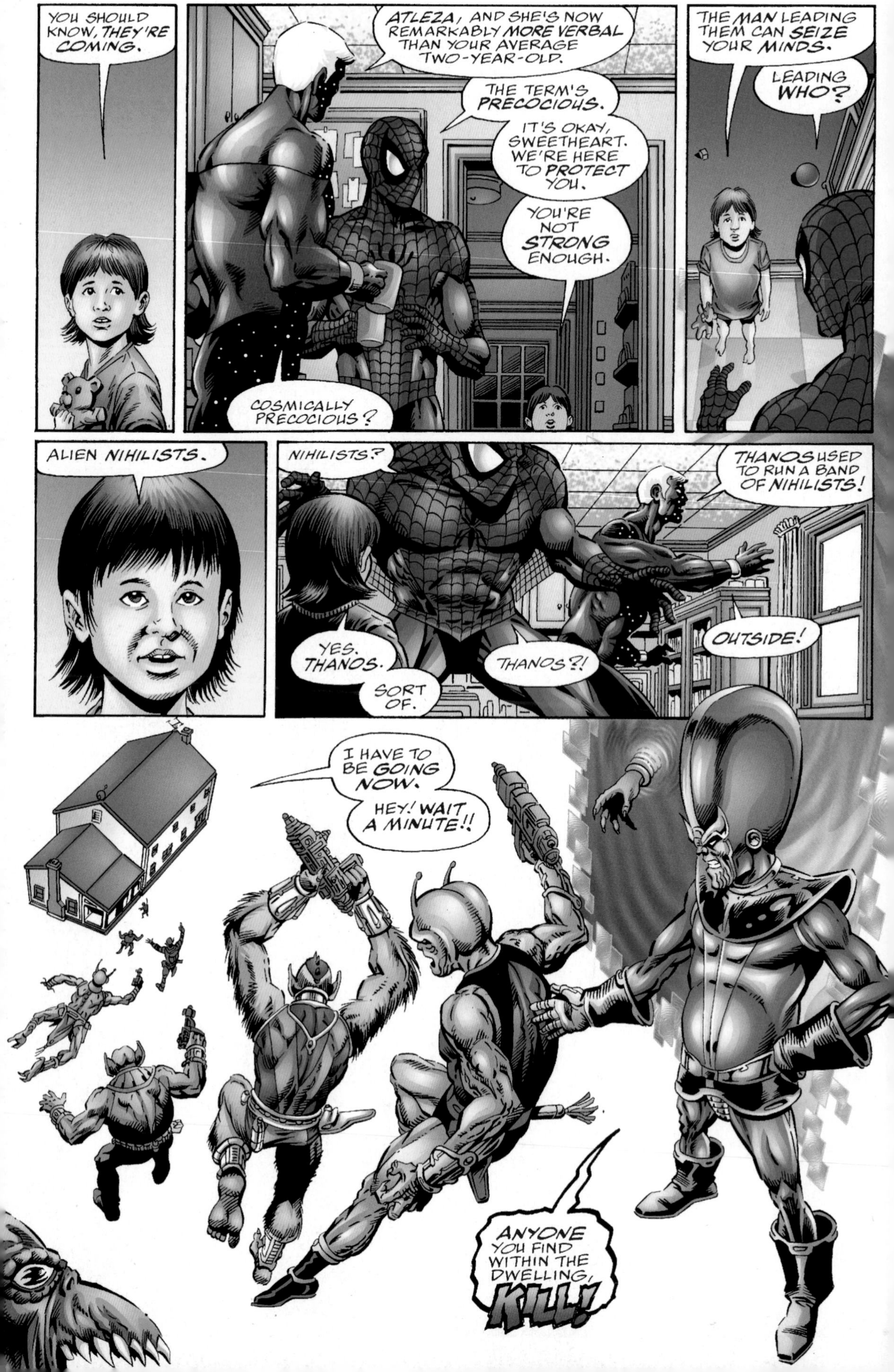
YOU SHOULD KNOW, THEY'RE COMING.
ATLEZA, AND SHE'S NOW REMARKABLY MORE VERBAL THAN YOUR AVERAGE TWO-YEAR-OLD.
THE TERM'S PRECOCIOUS.
IT'S OKAY, SWEETHEART. WE'RE HERE TO PROTECT YOU.
YOU'RE NOT STRONG ENOUGH.
COSMICALLY PRECOCIOUS?
THE MAN LEADING THEM CAN SEIZE YOUR MINDS.
LEADING WHO?
ALIEN NIHILISTS.
NIHILISTS?
THANOS USED TO RUN A BAND OF NIHILISTS!
YES. THANOS.
SORT OF.
THANOS?!
OUTSIDE!
I HAVE TO BE GOING NOW.
HEY! WAIT A MINUTE!!
ANYONE YOU FIND WITHIN THE DWELLING, KILL!

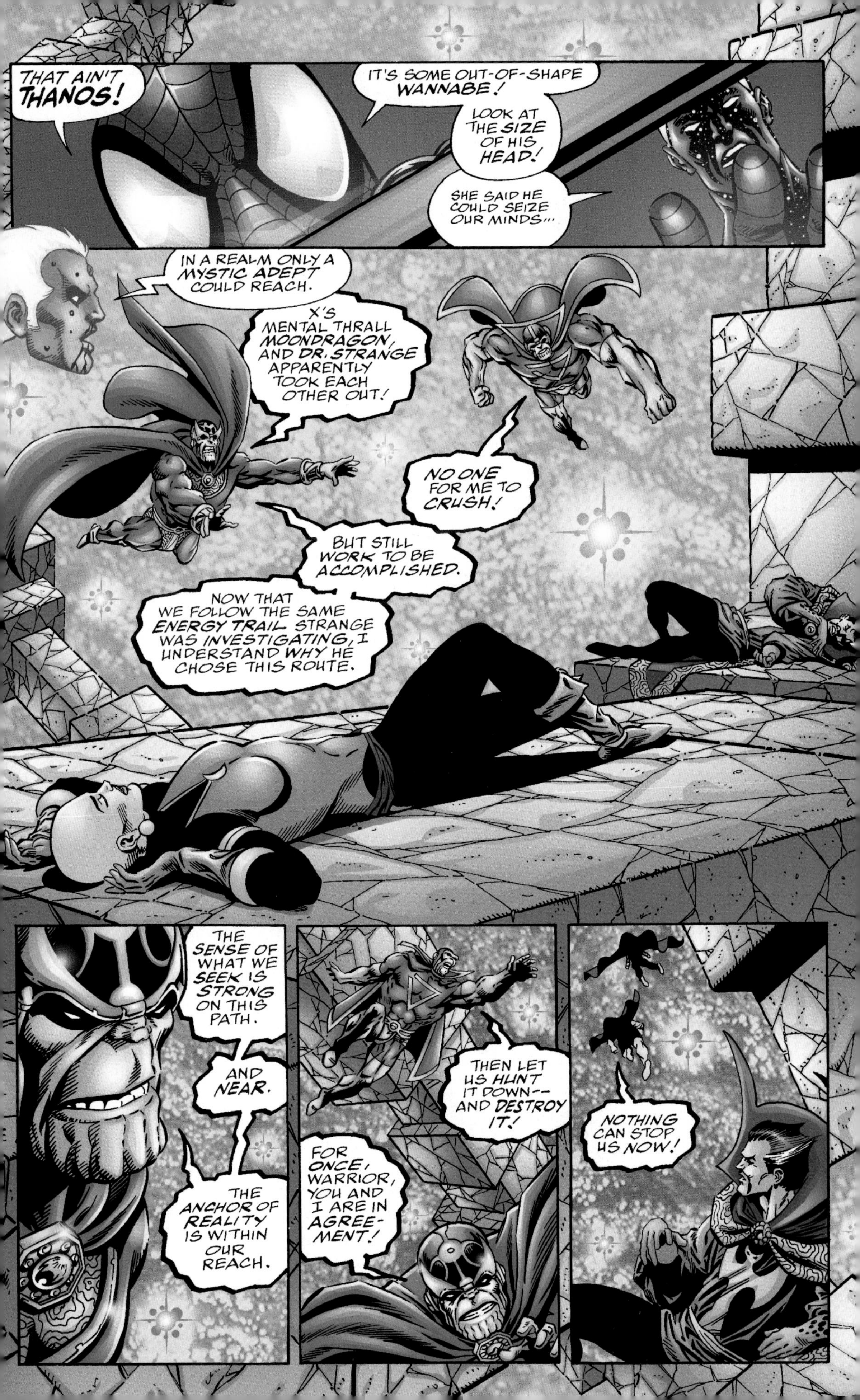

THAT AIN'T THANOS!
IT'S SOME OUT-OF-SHAPE WANNABE!
LOOK AT THE SIZE OF HIS HEAD!
SHE SAID HE COULD SEIZE OUR MINDS...
IN A REALM ONLY A MYSTIC ADEPT COULD REACH.
X'S MENTAL THRALL MOONDRAGON, AND DR. STRANGE APPARENTLY TOOK EACH OTHER OUT!
NO ONE FOR ME TO CRUSH!
BUT STILL WORK TO BE ACCOMPLISHED.
NOW THAT WE FOLLOW THE SAME ENERGY TRAIL STRANGE WAS INVESTIGATING, I UNDERSTAND WHY HE CHOSE THIS ROUTE.
THE SENSE OF WHAT WE SEEK IS STRONG ON THIS PATH.
AND NEAR.
THE ANCHOR OF REALITY IS WITHIN OUR REACH.
THEN LET US HUNT IT DOWN-- AND DESTROY IT!
FOR ONCE, WARRIOR, YOU AND I ARE IN AGREE-MENT!
NOTHING CAN STOP US NOW!

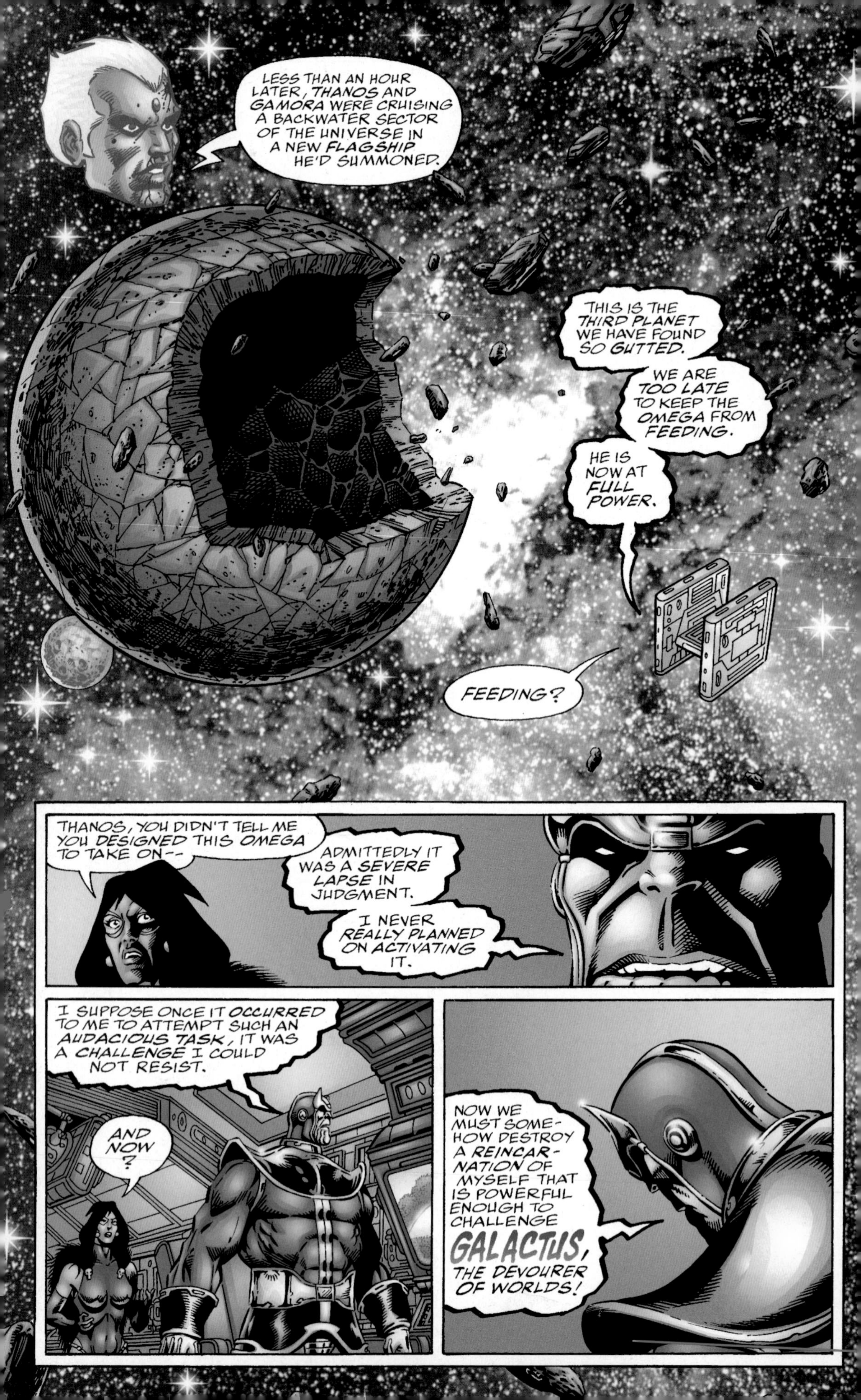
LESS THAN AN HOUR LATER, THANOS AND GAMORA WERE CRUISING A BACKWATER SECTOR OF THE UNIVERSE IN A NEW FLAGSHIP HE'D SUMMONED.
THIS IS THE THIRD PLANET WE HAVE FOUND SO GUTTED.
WE ARE TOO LATE TO KEEP THE OMEGA FROM FEEDING.
HE IS NOW AT FULL POWER.
FEEDING?
THANOS, YOU DIDN'T TELL ME YOU DESIGNED THIS OMEGA TO TAKE ON--
ADMITTEDLY IT WAS A SEVERE LAPSE IN JUDGMENT.
I NEVER REALLY PLANNED ON ACTIVATING IT.
I SUPPOSE ONCE IT OCCURRED TO ME TO ATTEMPT SUCH AN AUDACIOUS TASK, IT WAS A CHALLENGE I COULD NOT RESIST.
AND NOW?
NOW WE MUST SOME-HOW DESTROY A REINCAR-NATION OF MYSELF THAT IS POWERFUL ENOUGH TO CHALLENGE GALACTUS, THE DEVOURER OF WORLDS!

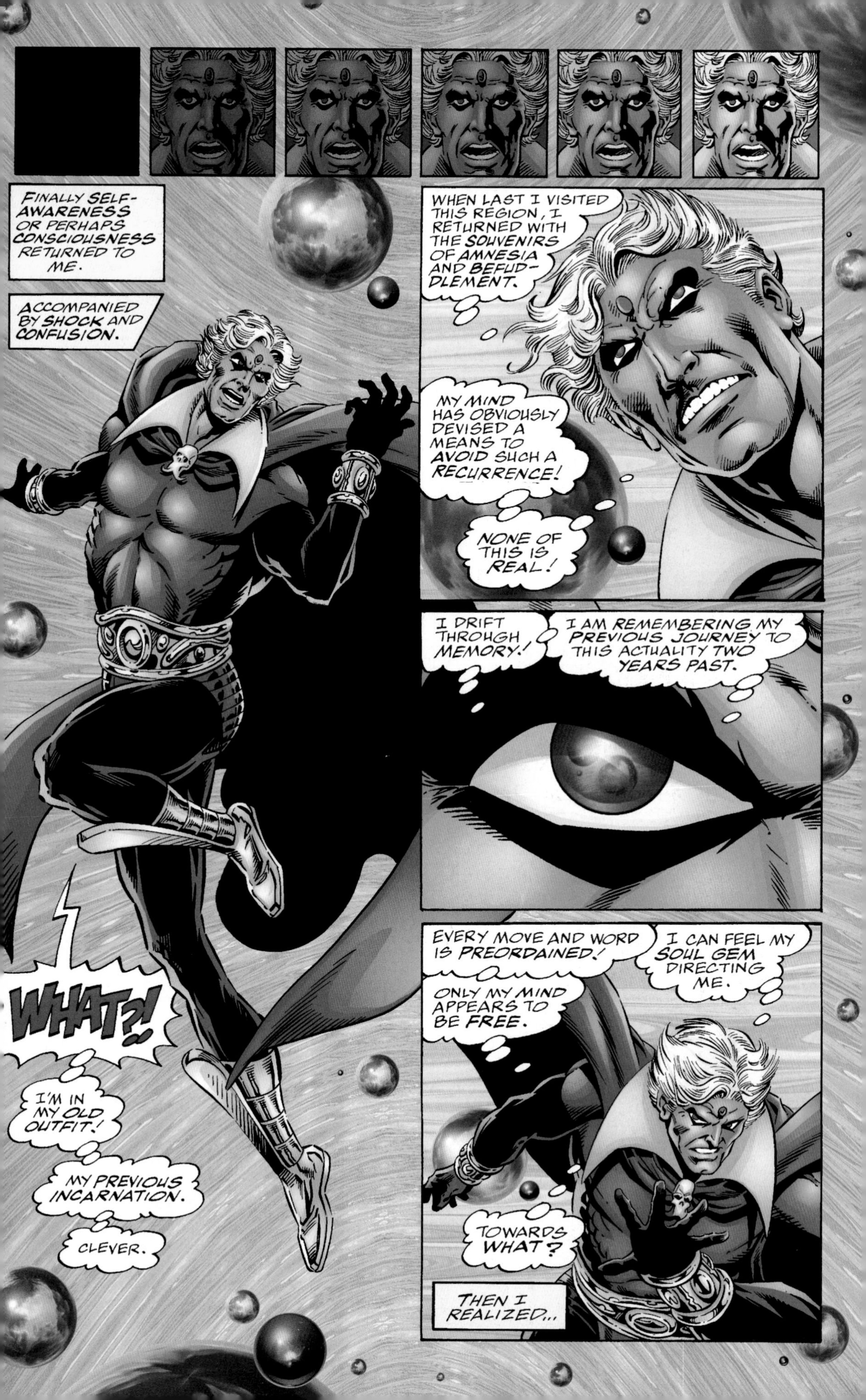
FINALLY SELF-AWARENESS OR PERHAPS CONSCIOUSNESS RETURNED TO ME.
ACCOMPANIED BY SHOCK AND CONFUSION.
WHAT?!
I'M IN MY OLD OUTFIT!
MY PREVIOUS INCARNATION.
CLEVER.
WHEN LAST I VISITED THIS REGION, I RETURNED WITH THE SOUVENIRS OF AMNESIA AND BEFUDDLEMENT.
MY MIND HAS OBVIOUSLY DEVISED A MEANS TO AVOID SUCH A RECURRENCE!
NONE OF THIS IS REAL!
I DRIFT THROUGH MEMORY!
I AM REMEMBERING MY PREVIOUS JOURNEY TO THIS ACTUALITY TWO YEARS PAST.
EVERY MOVE AND WORD IS PREORDAINED!
I CAN FEEL MY SOUL GEM DIRECTING ME.
ONLY MY MIND APPEARS TO BE FREE.
TOWARDS WHAT?
THEN I REALIZED...

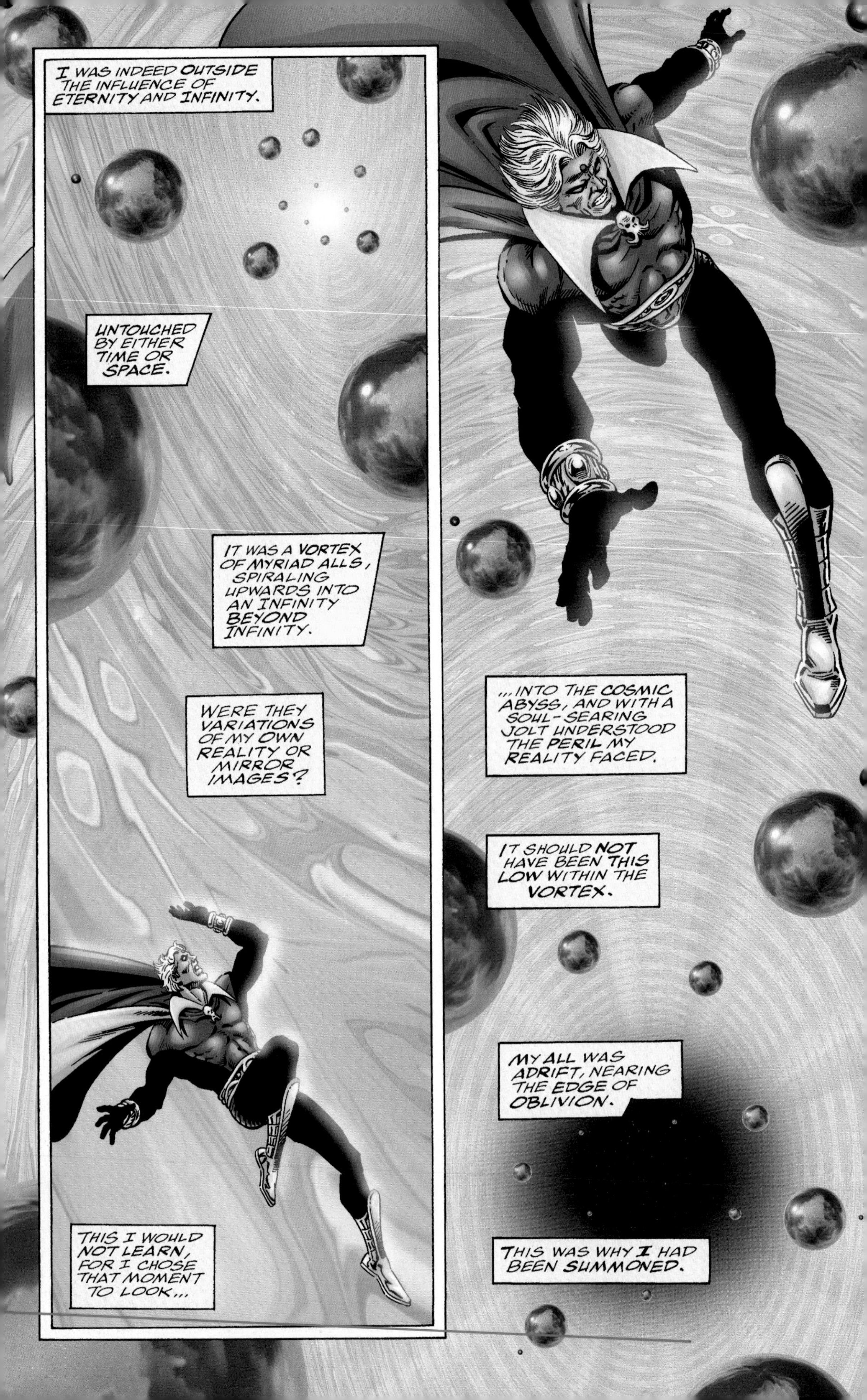
I WAS INDEED OUTSIDE THE INFLUENCE OF ETERNITY AND INFINITY.
UNTOUCHED BY EITHER TIME OR SPACE.
IT WAS A VORTEX OF MYRIAD ALLS, SPIRALING UPWARDS INTO AN INFINITY BEYOND INFINITY.
WERE THEY VARIATIONS OF MY OWN REALITY OR MIRROR IMAGES?
THIS I WOULD NOT LEARN, FOR I CHOSE THAT MOMENT TO LOOK...
...INTO THE COSMIC ABYSS, AND WITH A SOUL-SEARING JOLT UNDERSTOOD THE PERIL MY REALITY FACED.
IT SHOULD NOT HAVE BEEN THIS LOW WITHIN THE VORTEX.
MY ALL WAS ADRIFT, NEARING THE EDGE OF OBLIVION.
THIS WAS WHY I HAD BEEN SUMMONED.

THE SOUL GEM IGNORED MY HORROR AND SPURRED ME ON.

NOT BACK TO A FAMILIAR REALITY, BUT TO A HOVERING BLACK ORB.

THE INADEQUATE ANCHOR OF MY ACTUALITY.

INVITATION.

ACCEPTANCE.

ENTRANCE.

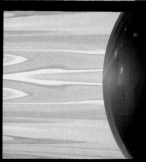

THE GEM HAS STRONG BONDS WITH THE CELESTIAL.

IT CAN STEAL SOULS.

THESE PURLOINED SPIRITS RESIDE WITHIN ME.

ARE A PART OF ME.

THEIR ENERGIES CAN BE UTILIZED.

FIERY ENERGY BLASTS...

...OR...

SIMPLE ILLUMINATION.

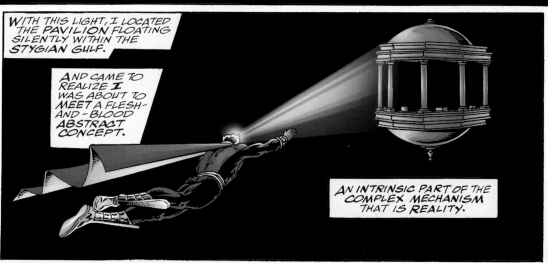

WITH THIS LIGHT, I LOCATED THE PAVILION FLOATING SILENTLY WITHIN THE STYGIAN GULF.

AND CAME TO REALIZE I WAS ABOUT TO MEET A FLESH-AND-BLOOD ABSTRACT CONCEPT.

AN INTRINSIC PART OF THE COMPLEX MECHANISM THAT IS REALITY.

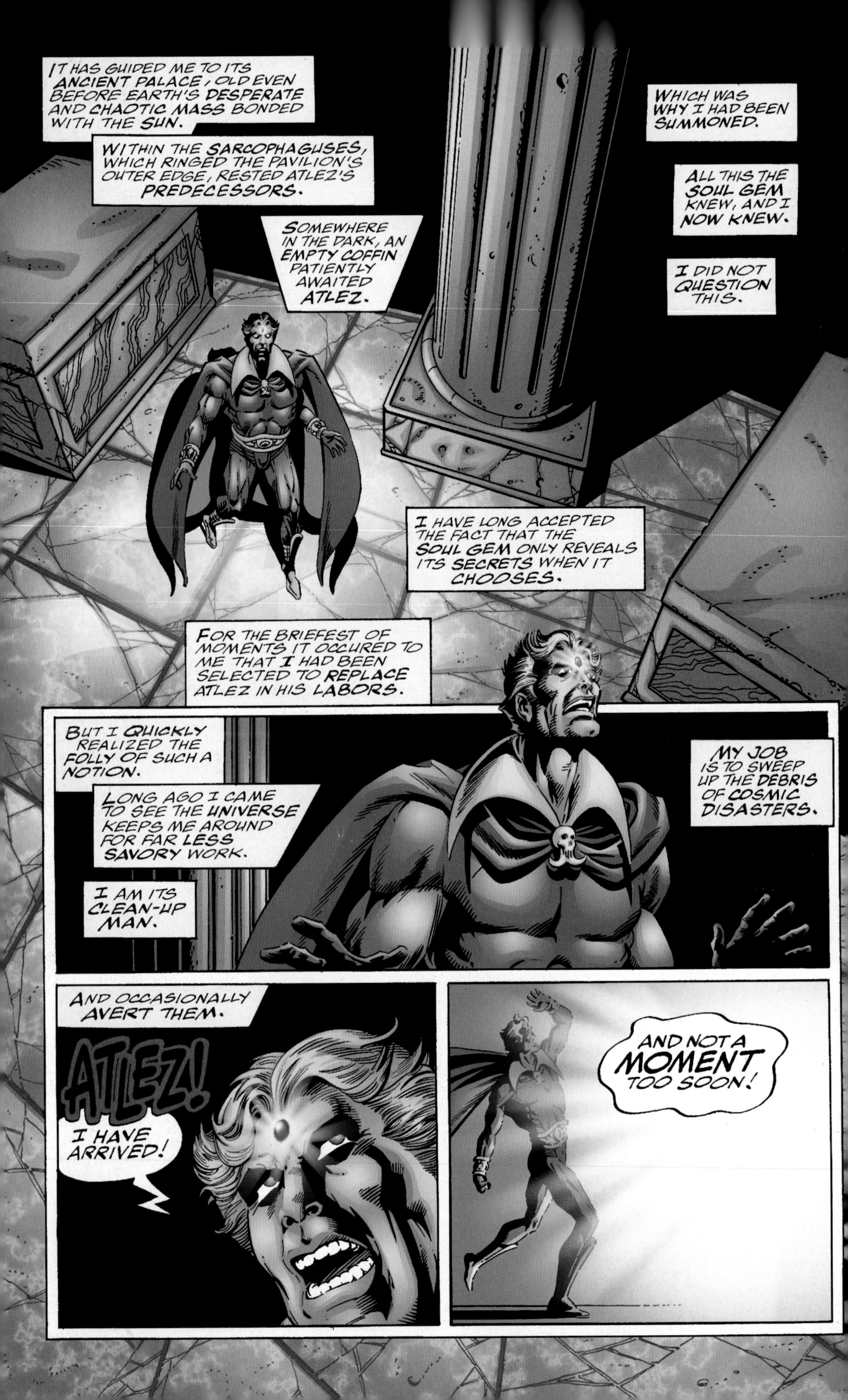
IT HAS GUIDED ME TO ITS ANCIENT PALACE, OLD EVEN BEFORE EARTH'S DESPERATE AND CHAOTIC MASS BONDED WITH THE SUN.
WITHIN THE SARCOPHAGUSES, WHICH RINGED THE PAVILION'S OUTER EDGE, RESTED ATLEZ'S PREDECESSORS.
SOMEWHERE IN THE DARK, AN EMPTY COFFIN PATIENTLY AWAITED ATLEZ.
WHICH WAS WHY I HAD BEEN SUMMONED.
ALL THIS THE SOUL GEM KNEW, AND I NOW KNEW.
I DID NOT QUESTION THIS.
I HAVE LONG ACCEPTED THE FACT THAT THE SOUL GEM ONLY REVEALS ITS SECRETS WHEN IT CHOOSES.
FOR THE BRIEFEST OF MOMENTS IT OCCURED TO ME THAT I HAD BEEN SELECTED TO REPLACE ATLEZ IN HIS LABORS.
BUT I QUICKLY REALIZED THE FOLLY OF SUCH A NOTION.
LONG AGO I CAME TO SEE THE UNIVERSE KEEPS ME AROUND FOR FAR LESS SAVORY WORK.
I AM ITS CLEAN-UP MAN.
MY JOB IS TO SWEEP UP THE DEBRIS OF COSMIC DISASTERS.
AND OCCASIONALLY AVERT THEM.
ATLEZ!
I HAVE ARRIVED!
AND NOT A MOMENT TOO SOON!

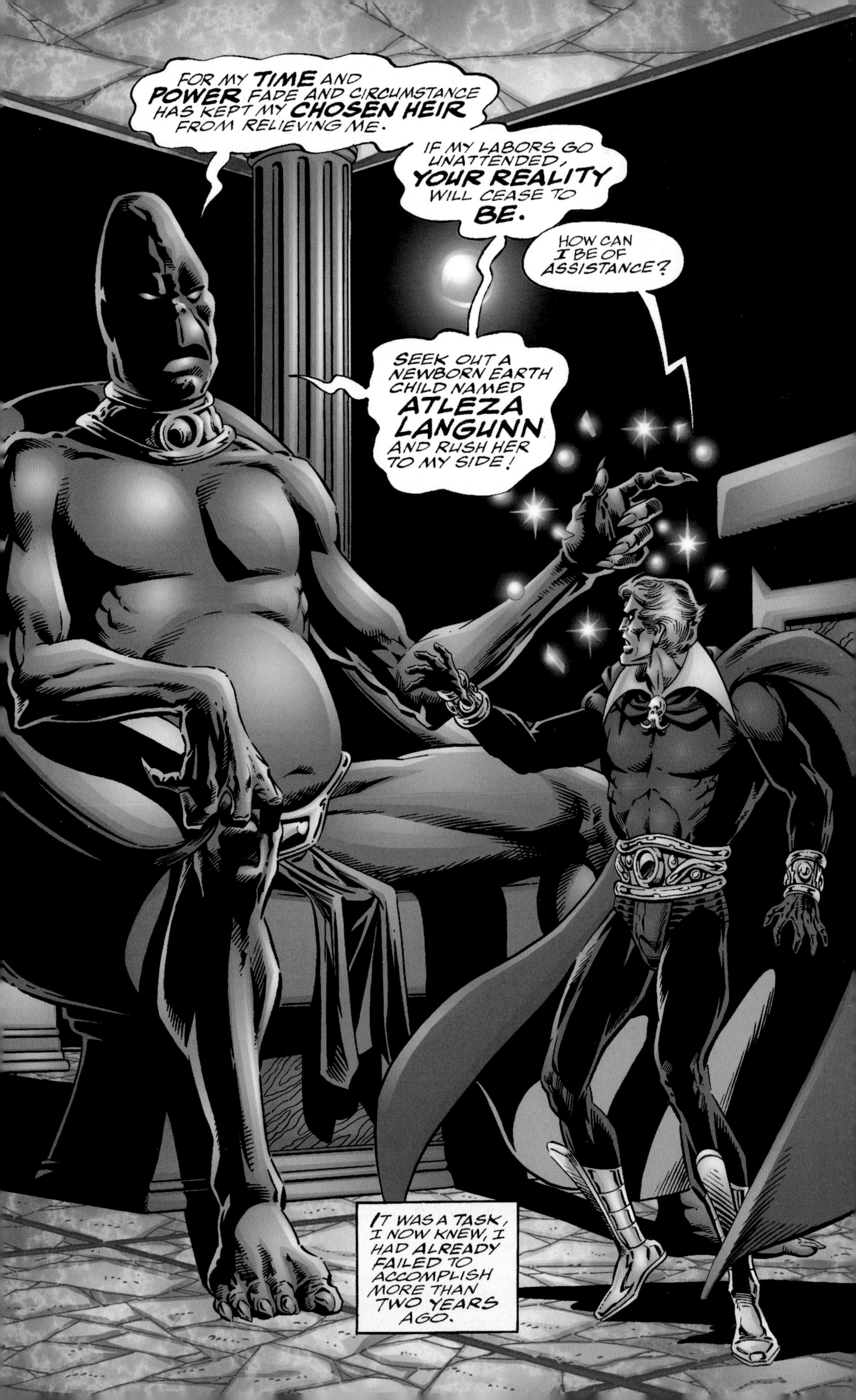
FOR MY TIME AND POWER FADE AND CIRCUMSTANCE HAS KEPT MY CHOSEN HEIR FROM RELIEVING ME.
IF MY LABORS GO UNATTENDED, YOUR REALITY WILL CEASE TO BE.
HOW CAN I BE OF ASSISTANCE?
SEEK OUT A NEWBORN EARTH CHILD NAMED ATLEZA LANGUNN AND RUSH HER TO MY SIDE!
IT WAS A TASK, I NOW KNEW, I HAD ALREADY FAILED TO ACCOMPLISH MORE THAN TWO YEARS AGO.

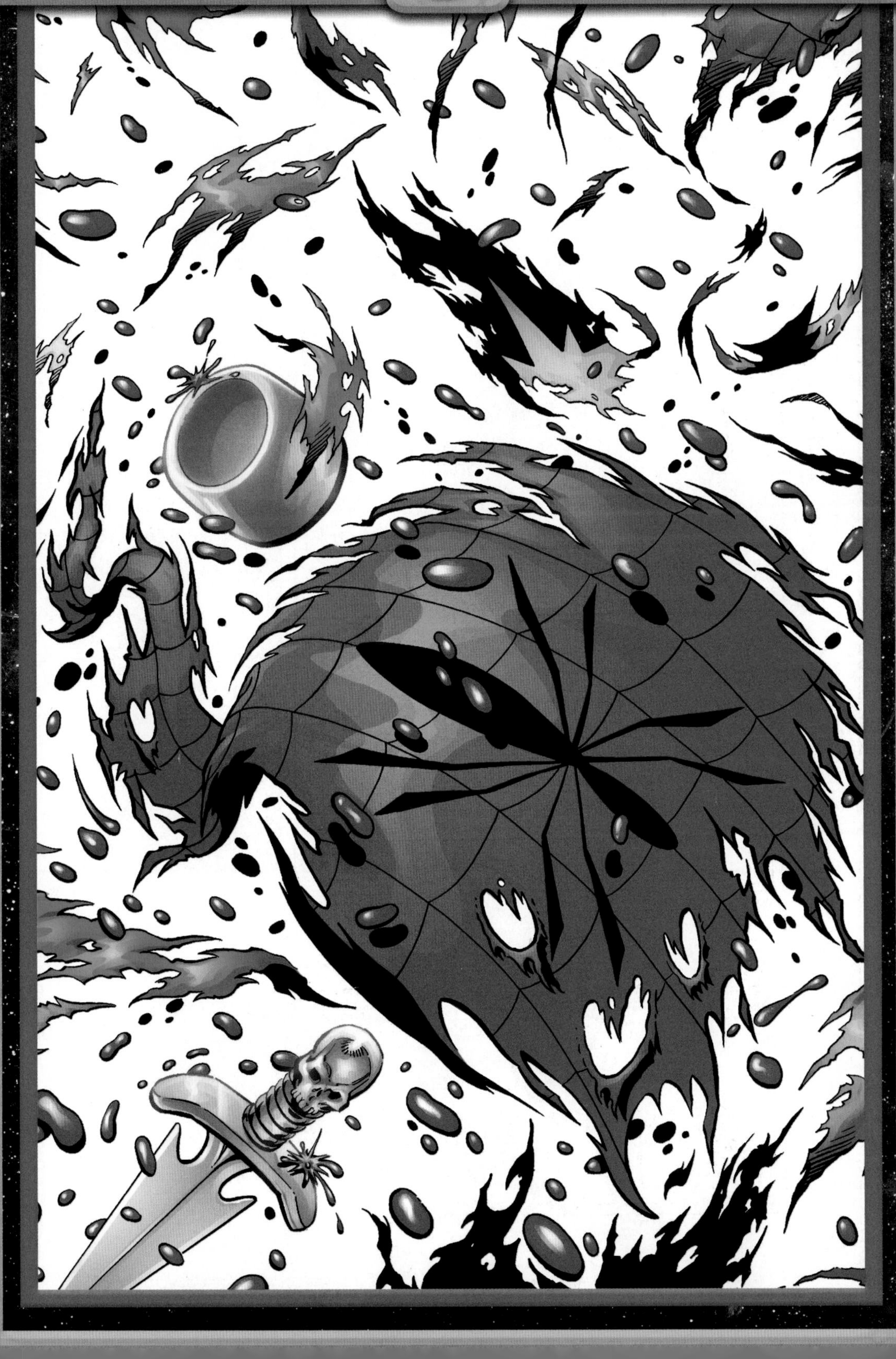

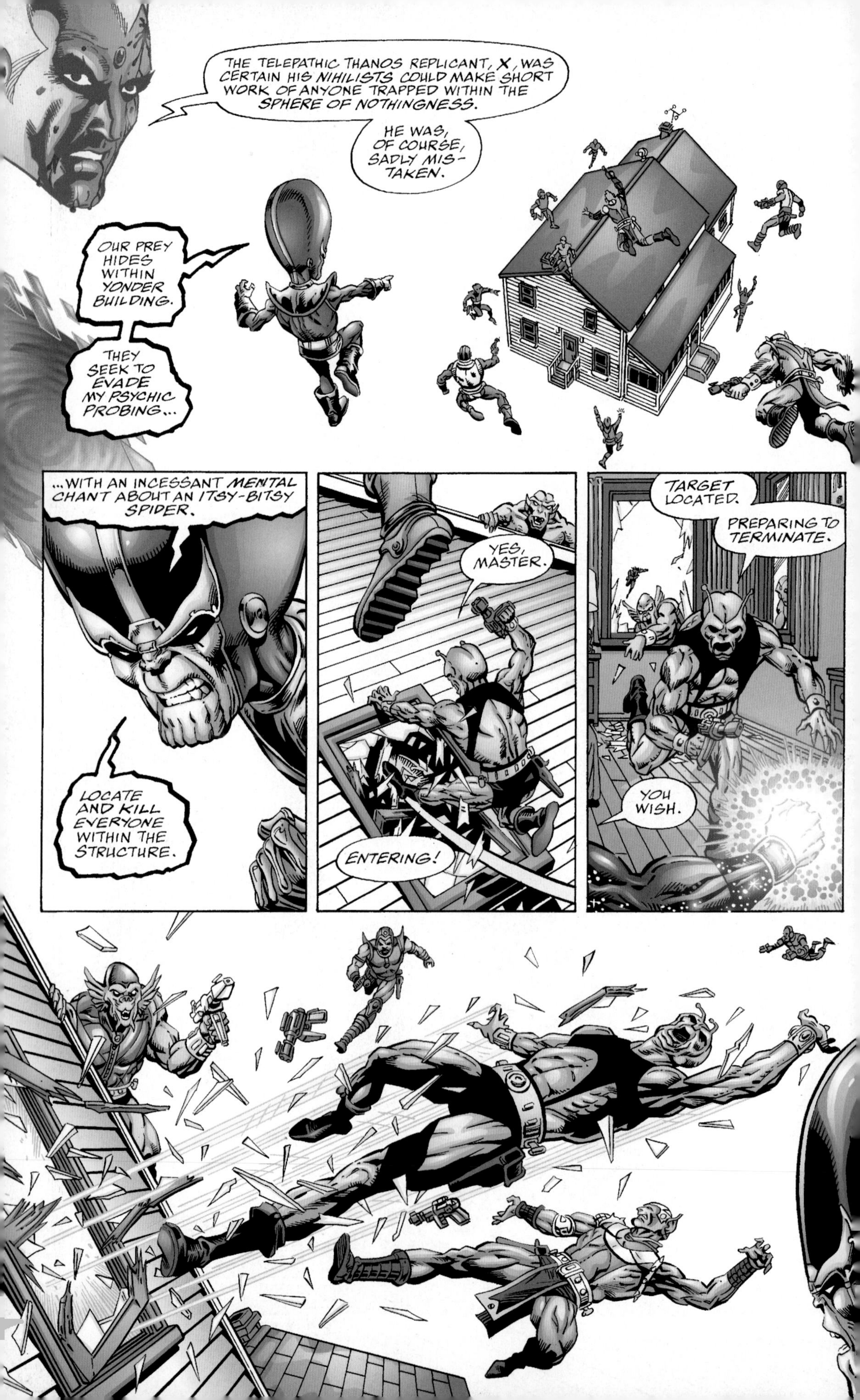
THE TELEPATHIC THANOS REPLICANT, X, WAS CERTAIN HIS NIHILISTS COULD MAKE SHORT WORK OF ANYONE TRAPPED WITHIN THE SPHERE OF NOTHINGNESS.
HE WAS, OF COURSE, SADLY MIS-TAKEN.
OUR PREY HIDES WITHIN YONDER BUILDING.
THEY SEEK TO EVADE MY PSYCHIC PROBING...
...WITH AN INCESSANT MENTAL CHANT ABOUT AN ITSY-BITSY SPIDER.
LOCATE AND KILL EVERYONE WITHIN THE STRUCTURE.
YES, MASTER.
ENTERING!
TARGET LOCATED.
PREPARING TO TERMINATE.
YOU WISH.

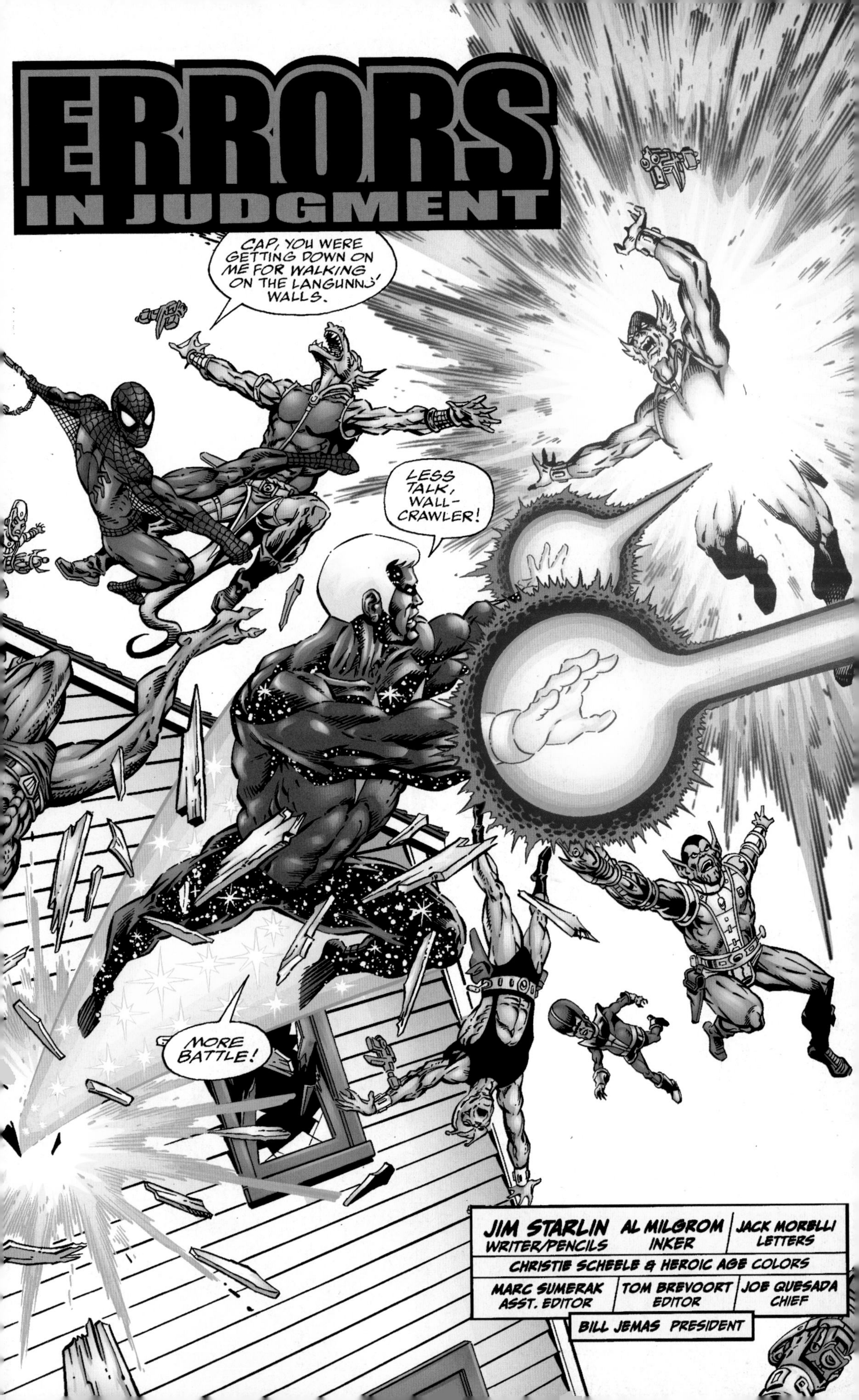
ERRORS IN JUDGMENT
CAP, YOU WERE GETTING DOWN ON ME FOR WALKING ON THE LANGUNNS' WALLS.
LESS TALK, WALL-CRAWLER!
MORE BATTLE!
JIM STARLIN WRITER/PENCILS
AL MILGROM INKER
JACK MORELLI LETTERS
CHRISTIE SCHEELE & HEROIC AGE COLORS
MARC SUMERAK ASST. EDITOR
TOM BREVOORT EDITOR
JOE QUESADA CHIEF
BILL JEMAS PRESIDENT

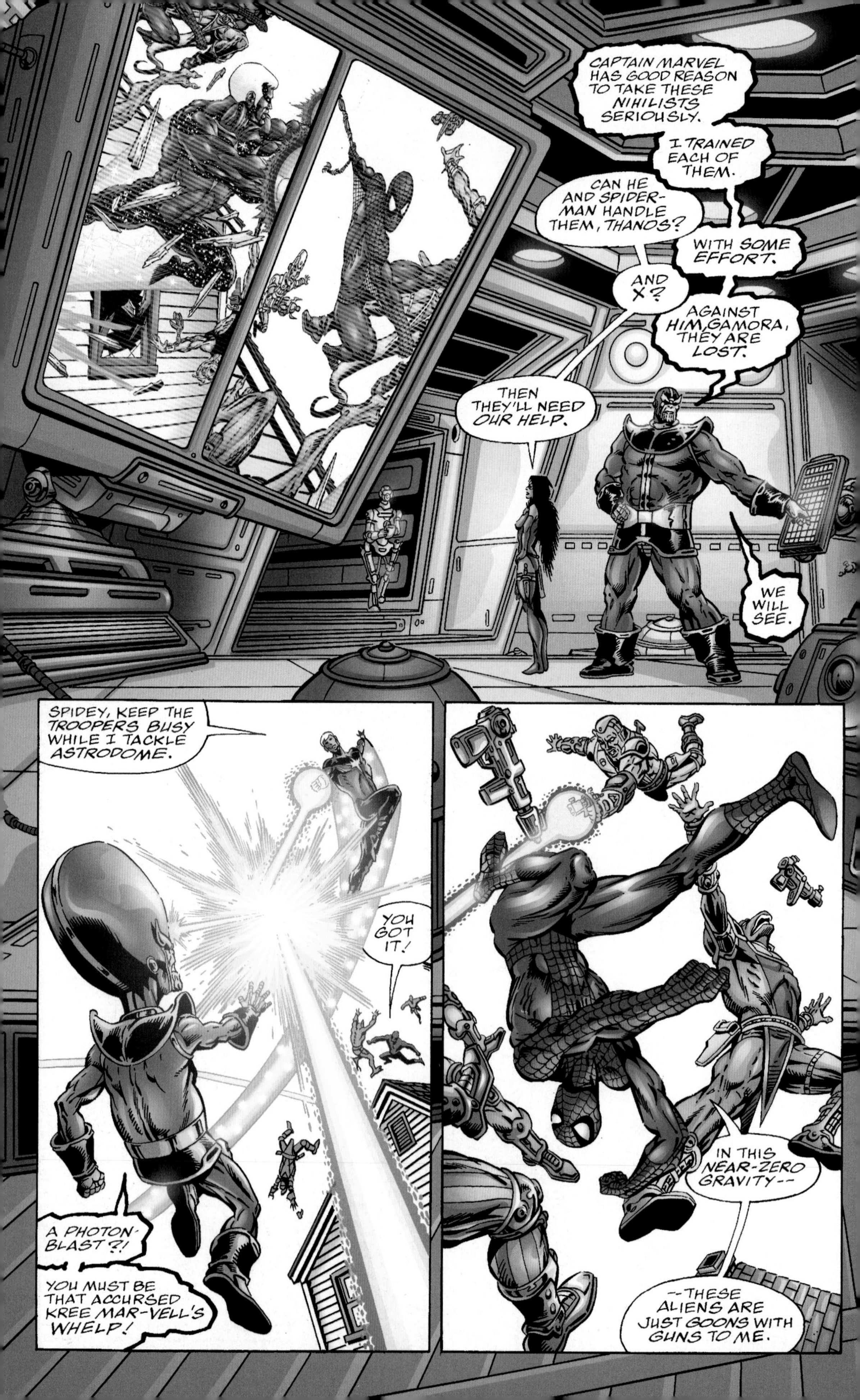
CAPTAIN MARVEL HAS GOOD REASON TO TAKE THESE NIHILISTS SERIOUSLY.
I TRAINED EACH OF THEM.
CAN HE AND SPIDER-MAN HANDLE THEM, THANOS?
WITH SOME EFFORT.
AND X?
AGAINST HIM, GAMORA, THEY ARE LOST.
THEN THEY'LL NEED OUR HELP.
WE WILL SEE.
SPIDEY, KEEP THE TROOPERS BUSY WHILE I TACKLE ASTRODOME.
YOU GOT IT!
A PHOTON-BLAST?!
YOU MUST BE THAT ACCURSED KREE MAR-VELL'S WHELP!
IN THIS NEAR-ZERO GRAVITY--
--THESE ALIENS ARE JUST GOONS WITH GUNS TO ME.

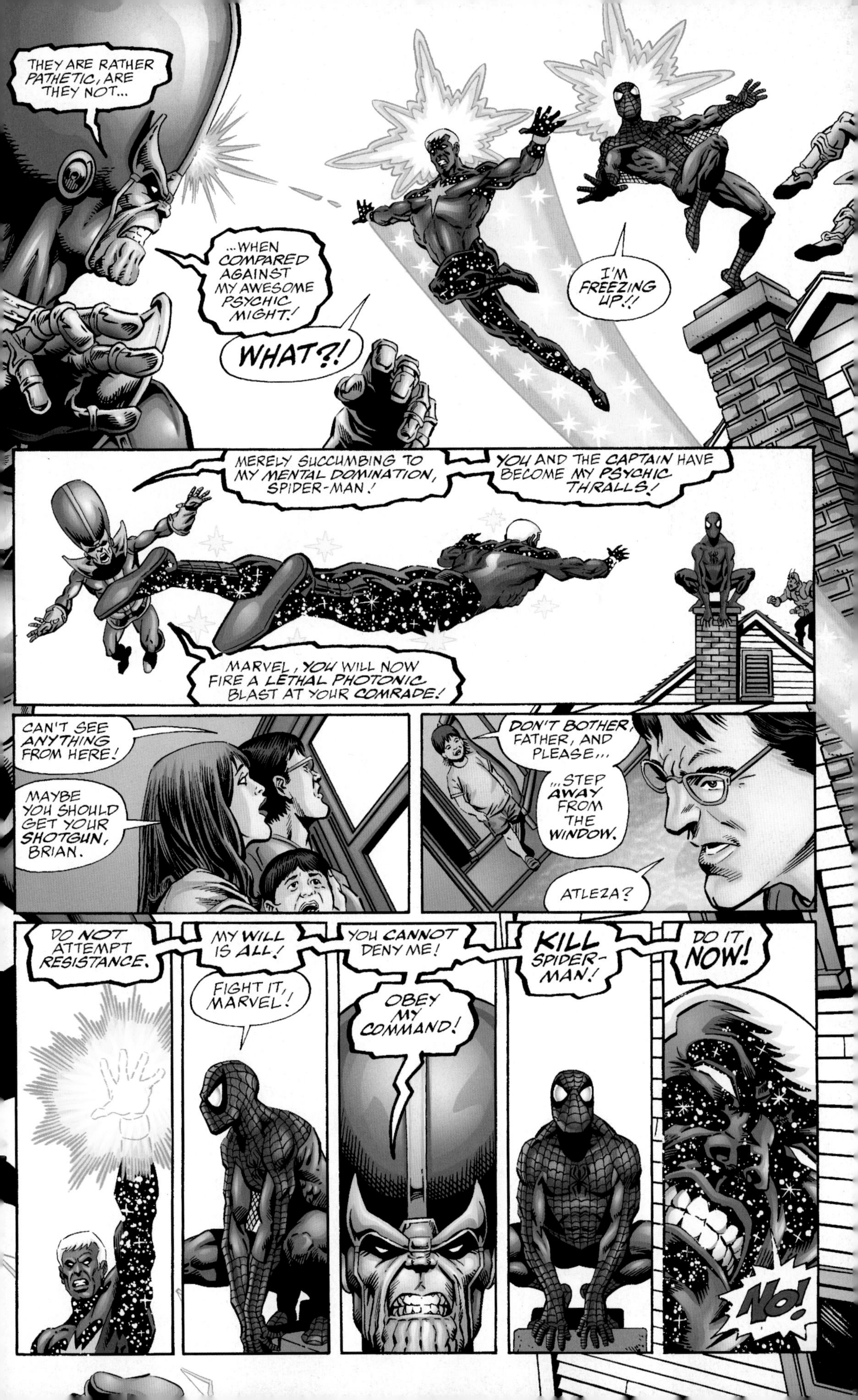
THEY ARE RATHER PATHETIC, ARE THEY NOT...
...WHEN COMPARED AGAINST MY AWESOME PSYCHIC MIGHT!
WHAT?!
I'M FREEZING UP!!
MERELY SUCCUMBING TO MY MENTAL DOMINATION, SPIDER-MAN!
YOU AND THE CAPTAIN HAVE BECOME MY PSYCHIC THRALLS!
MARVEL, YOU WILL NOW FIRE A LETHAL PHOTONIC BLAST AT YOUR COMRADE!
CAN'T SEE ANYTHING FROM HERE!
MAYBE YOU SHOULD GET YOUR SHOTGUN, BRIAN.
DON'T BOTHER, FATHER, AND PLEASE...
...STEP AWAY FROM THE WINDOW.
ATLEZA?
DO NOT ATTEMPT RESISTANCE.
MY WILL IS ALL!
FIGHT IT, MARVEL!
YOU CANNOT DENY ME!
OBEY MY COMMAND!
KILL SPIDER-MAN!
DO IT NOW!
NO!

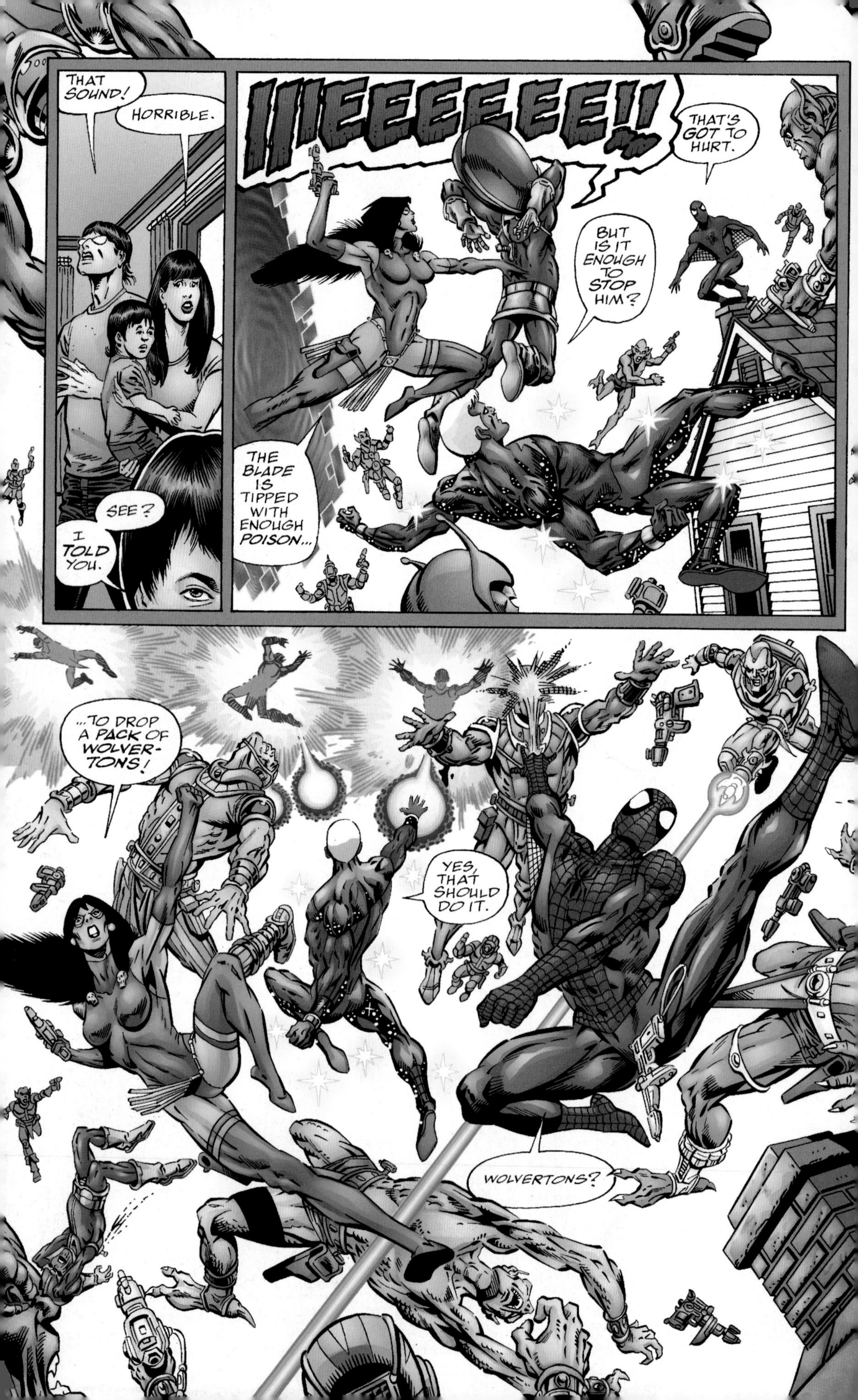
THAT SOUND!
HORRIBLE.
SEE?
I TOLD YOU.
IIIEEEEEEE!!
THAT'S GOT TO HURT.
BUT IS IT ENOUGH TO STOP HIM?
THE BLADE IS TIPPED WITH ENOUGH POISON...
...TO DROP A PACK OF WOLVER-TONS!
YES, THAT SHOULD DO IT.
WOLVERTONS?

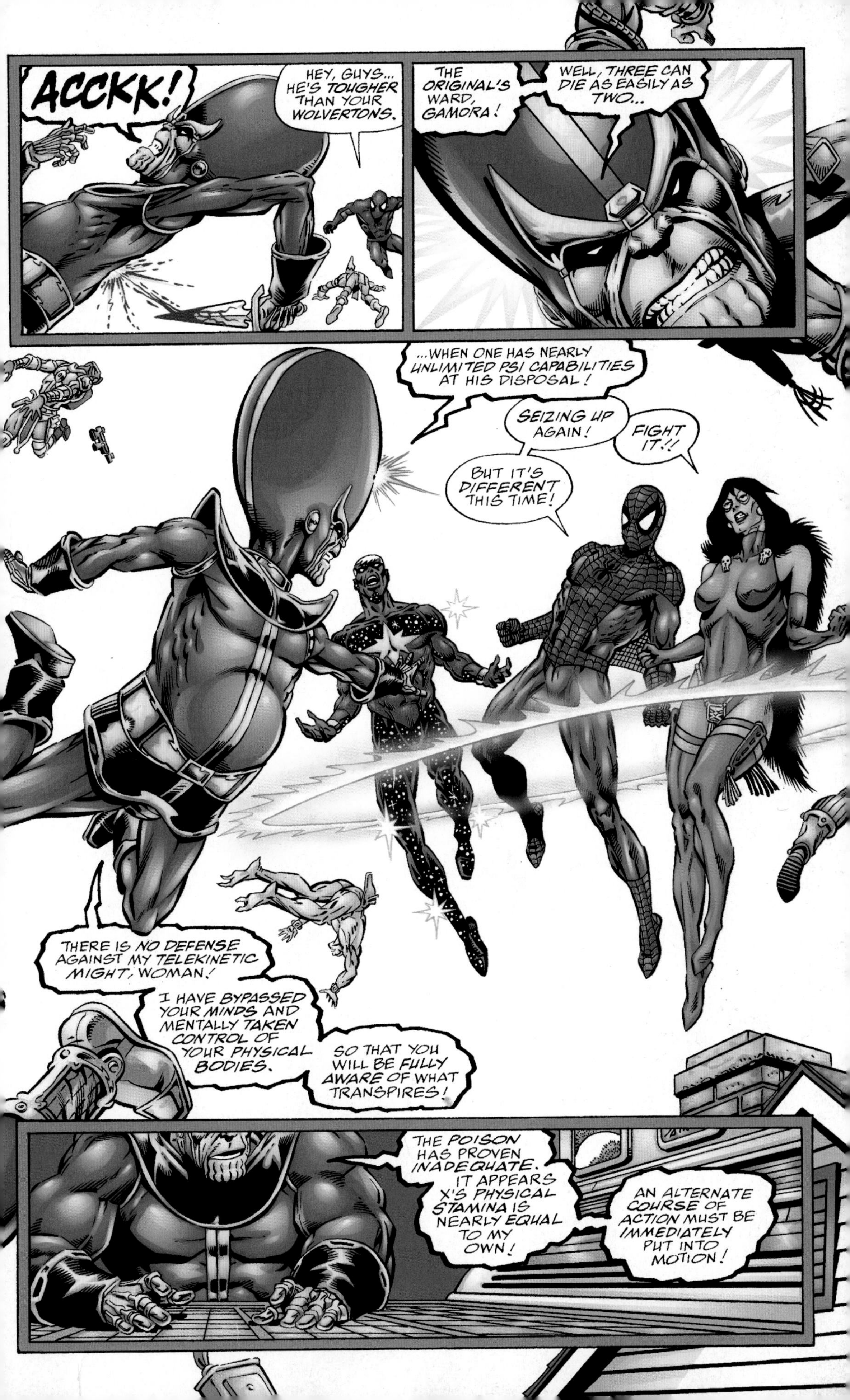
ACCKK!
HEY, GUYS... HE'S TOUGHER THAN YOUR WOLVERTONS.
THE ORIGINAL'S WARD, GAMORA!
WELL, THREE CAN DIE AS EASILY AS TWO...
...WHEN ONE HAS NEARLY UNLIMITED PSI CAPABILITIES AT HIS DISPOSAL!
SEIZING UP AGAIN!
FIGHT IT!!
BUT IT'S DIFFERENT THIS TIME!
THERE IS NO DEFENSE AGAINST MY TELEKINETIC MIGHT, WOMAN!
I HAVE BYPASSED YOUR MINDS AND MENTALLY TAKEN CONTROL OF YOUR PHYSICAL BODIES.
SO THAT YOU WILL BE FULLY AWARE OF WHAT TRANSPIRES!
THE POISON HAS PROVEN INADEQUATE. IT APPEARS X'S PHYSICAL STAMINA IS NEARLY EQUAL TO MY OWN!
AN ALTERNATE COURSE OF ACTION MUST BE IMMEDIATELY PUT INTO MOTION!

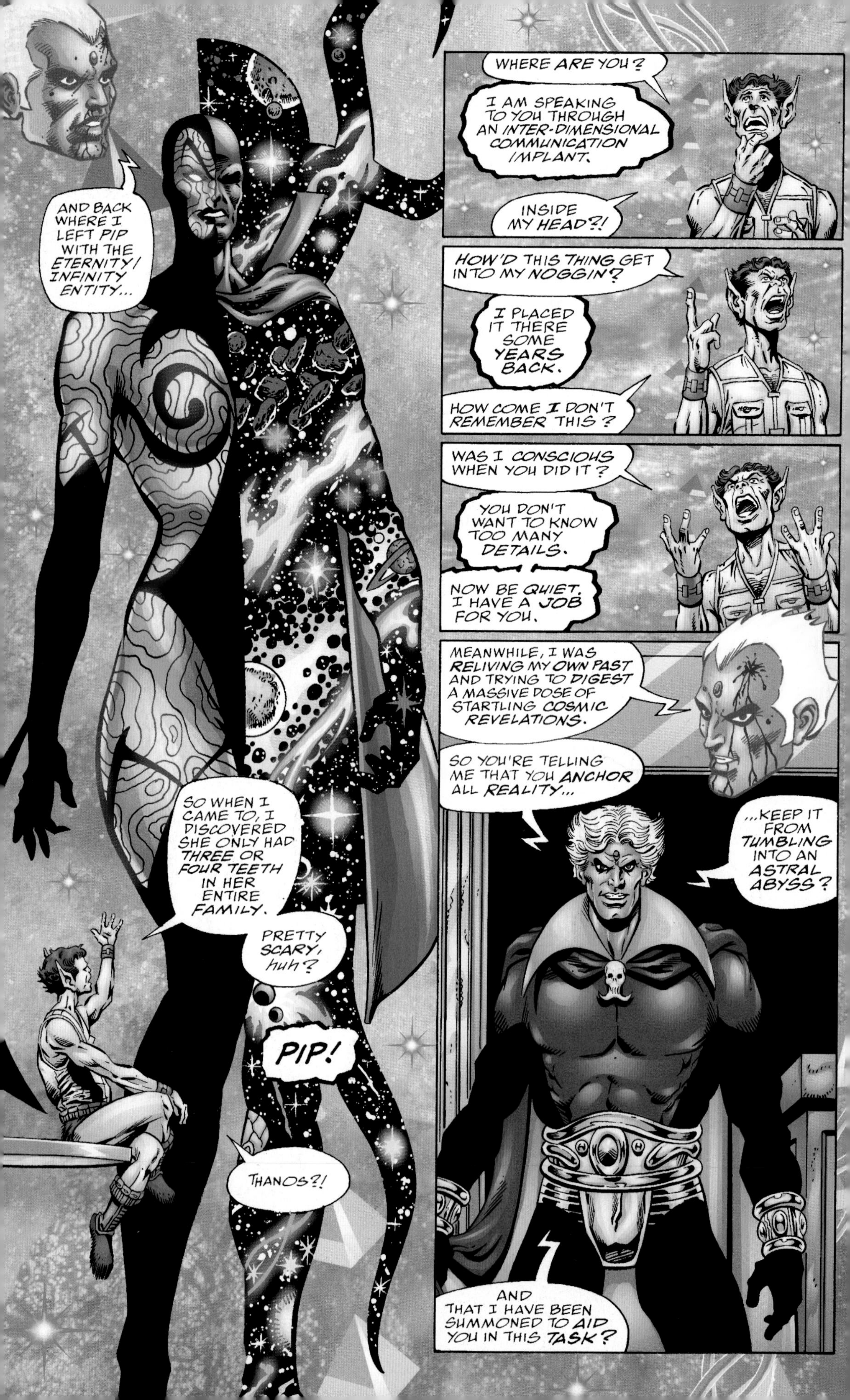

AND BACK WHERE I LEFT PIP WITH THE ETERNITY/ INFINITY ENTITY...
SO WHEN I CAME TO, I DISCOVERED SHE ONLY HAD THREE OR FOUR TEETH IN HER ENTIRE FAMILY.
PRETTY SCARY, huh?
PIP!
THANOS?!
WHERE ARE YOU?
I AM SPEAKING TO YOU THROUGH AN INTER-DIMENSIONAL COMMUNICATION IMPLANT.
INSIDE MY HEAD?!
HOW'D THIS THING GET INTO MY NOGGIN?
I PLACED IT THERE SOME YEARS BACK.
HOW COME I DON'T REMEMBER THIS?
WAS I CONSCIOUS WHEN YOU DID IT?
YOU DON'T WANT TO KNOW TOO MANY DETAILS.
NOW BE QUIET. I HAVE A JOB FOR YOU.
MEANWHILE, I WAS RELIVING MY OWN PAST AND TRYING TO DIGEST A MASSIVE DOSE OF STARTLING COSMIC REVELATIONS.
SO YOU'RE TELLING ME THAT YOU ANCHOR ALL REALITY...
...KEEP IT FROM TUMBLING INTO AN ASTRAL ABYSS?
AND THAT I HAVE BEEN SUMMONED TO AID YOU IN THIS TASK?

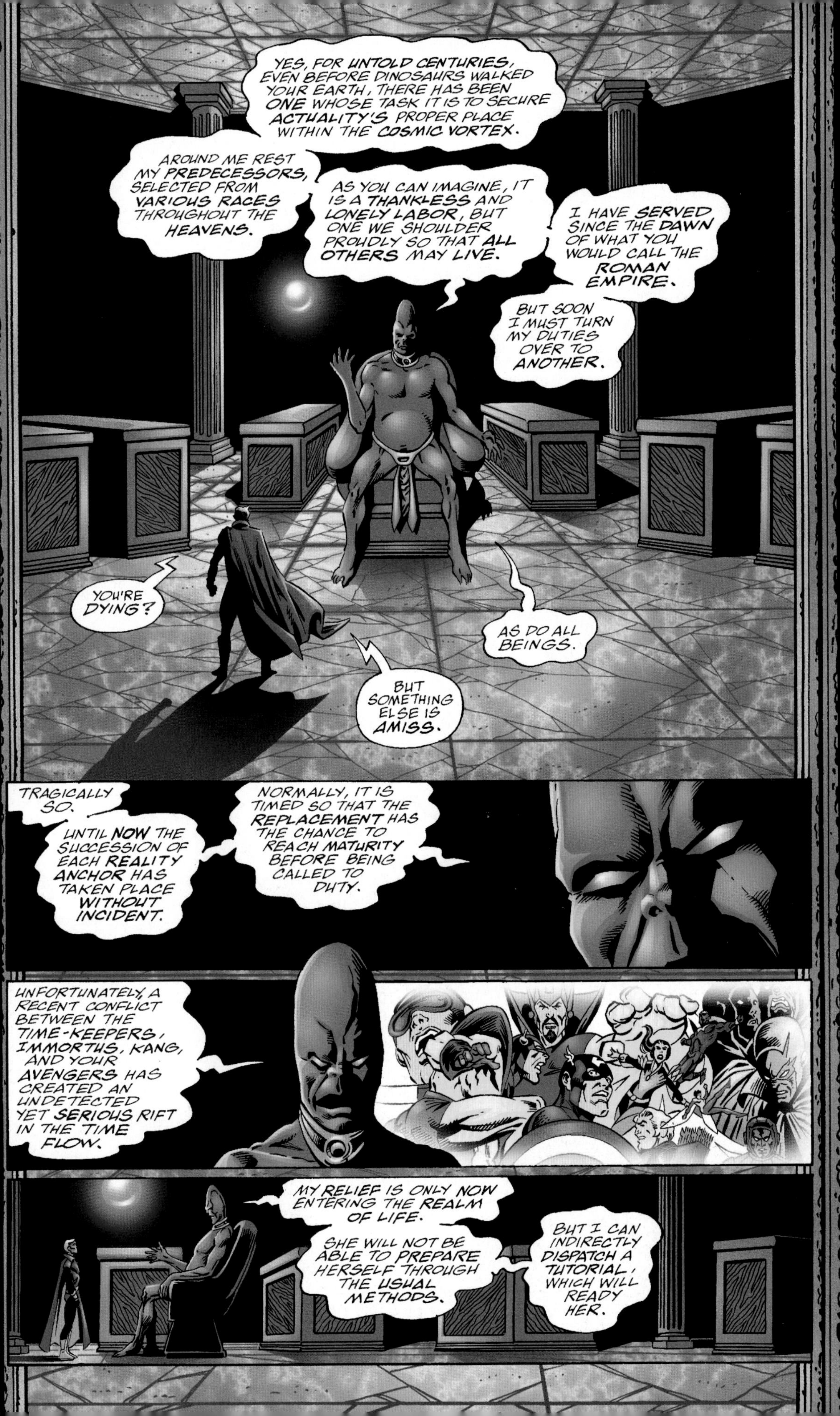
YES, FOR UNTOLD CENTURIES, EVEN BEFORE DINOSAURS WALKED YOUR EARTH, THERE HAS BEEN ONE WHOSE TASK IT IS TO SECURE ACTUALITY'S PROPER PLACE WITHIN THE COSMIC VORTEX.
AROUND ME REST MY PREDECESSORS, SELECTED FROM VARIOUS RACES THROUGHOUT THE HEAVENS.
AS YOU CAN IMAGINE, IT IS A THANKLESS AND LONELY LABOR, BUT ONE WE SHOULDER PROUDLY SO THAT ALL OTHERS MAY LIVE.
I HAVE SERVED SINCE THE DAWN OF WHAT YOU WOULD CALL THE ROMAN EMPIRE.
BUT SOON I MUST TURN MY DUTIES OVER TO ANOTHER.
YOU'RE DYING?
AS DO ALL BEINGS.
BUT SOMETHING ELSE IS AMISS.
TRAGICALLY SO.
UNTIL NOW THE SUCCESSION OF EACH REALITY ANCHOR HAS TAKEN PLACE WITHOUT INCIDENT.
NORMALLY, IT IS TIMED SO THAT THE REPLACEMENT HAS THE CHANCE TO REACH MATURITY BEFORE BEING CALLED TO DUTY.
UNFORTUNATELY, A RECENT CONFLICT BETWEEN THE TIME-KEEPERS, IMMORTUS, KANG, AND YOUR AVENGERS HAS CREATED AN UNDETECTED YET SERIOUS RIFT IN THE TIME FLOW.
MY RELIEF IS ONLY NOW ENTERING THE REALM OF LIFE.
SHE WILL NOT BE ABLE TO PREPARE HERSELF THROUGH THE USUAL METHODS.
BUT I CAN INDIRECTLY DISPATCH A TUTORIAL, WHICH WILL READY HER.

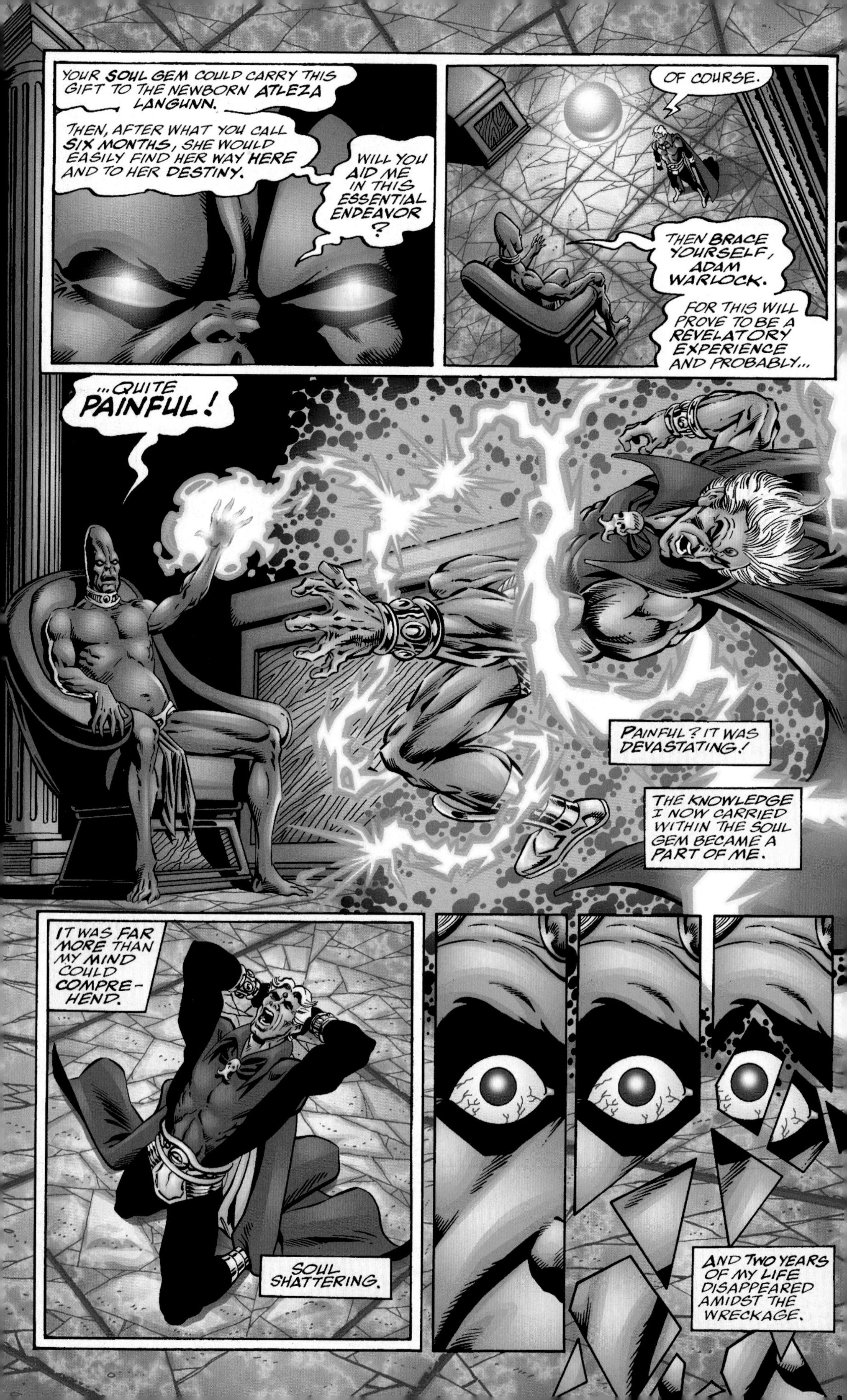

YOUR SOUL GEM COULD CARRY THIS GIFT TO THE NEWBORN ATLEZA LANGUNN.
THEN, AFTER WHAT YOU CALL SIX MONTHS, SHE WOULD EASILY FIND HER WAY HERE AND TO HER DESTINY.
WILL YOU AID ME IN THIS ESSENTIAL ENDEAVOR?
OF COURSE.
THEN BRACE YOURSELF, ADAM WARLOCK.
FOR THIS WILL PROVE TO BE A REVELATORY EXPERIENCE AND PROBABLY...
...QUITE PAINFUL!
PAINFUL? IT WAS DEVASTATING!
THE KNOWLEDGE I NOW CARRIED WITHIN THE SOUL GEM BECAME A PART OF ME.
IT WAS FAR MORE THAN MY MIND COULD COMPRE-HEND.
SOUL SHATTERING.
AND TWO YEARS OF MY LIFE DISAPPEARED AMIDST THE WRECKAGE.

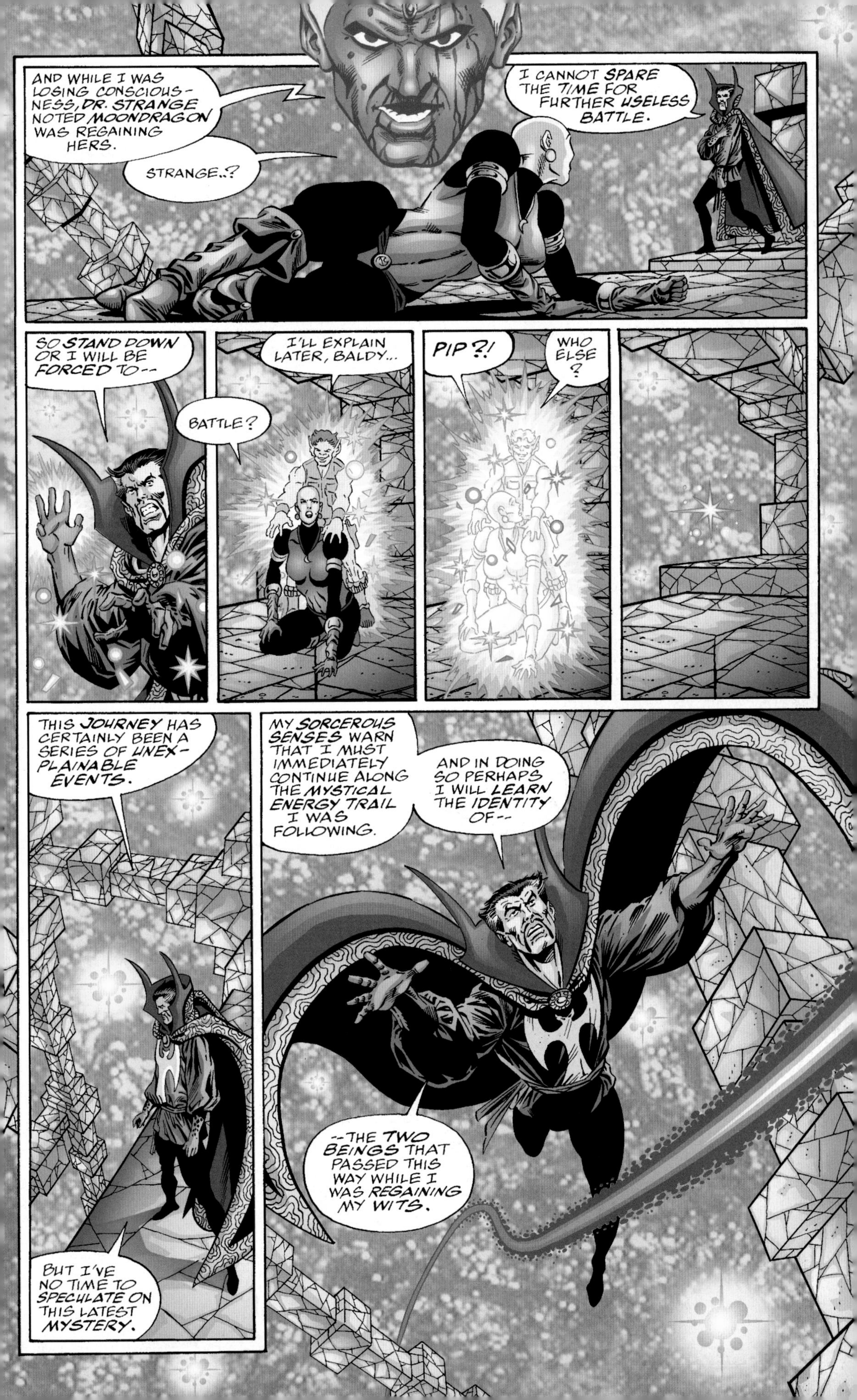
AND WHILE I WAS LOSING CONSCIOUS-NESS, DR. STRANGE NOTED MOONDRAGON WAS REGAINING HERS.
I CANNOT SPARE THE TIME FOR FURTHER USELESS BATTLE.
STRANGE..?
SO STAND DOWN OR I WILL BE FORCED TO--
BATTLE?
I'LL EXPLAIN LATER, BALDY...
PIP?!
WHO ELSE?
THIS JOURNEY HAS CERTAINLY BEEN A SERIES OF UNEX-PLAINABLE EVENTS.
BUT I'VE NO TIME TO SPECULATE ON THIS LATEST MYSTERY.
MY SORCEROUS SENSES WARN THAT I MUST IMMEDIATELY CONTINUE ALONG THE MYSTICAL ENERGY TRAIL I WAS FOLLOWING.
AND IN DOING SO PERHAPS I WILL LEARN THE IDENTITY OF--
--THE TWO BEINGS THAT PASSED THIS WAY WHILE I WAS REGAINING MY WITS.

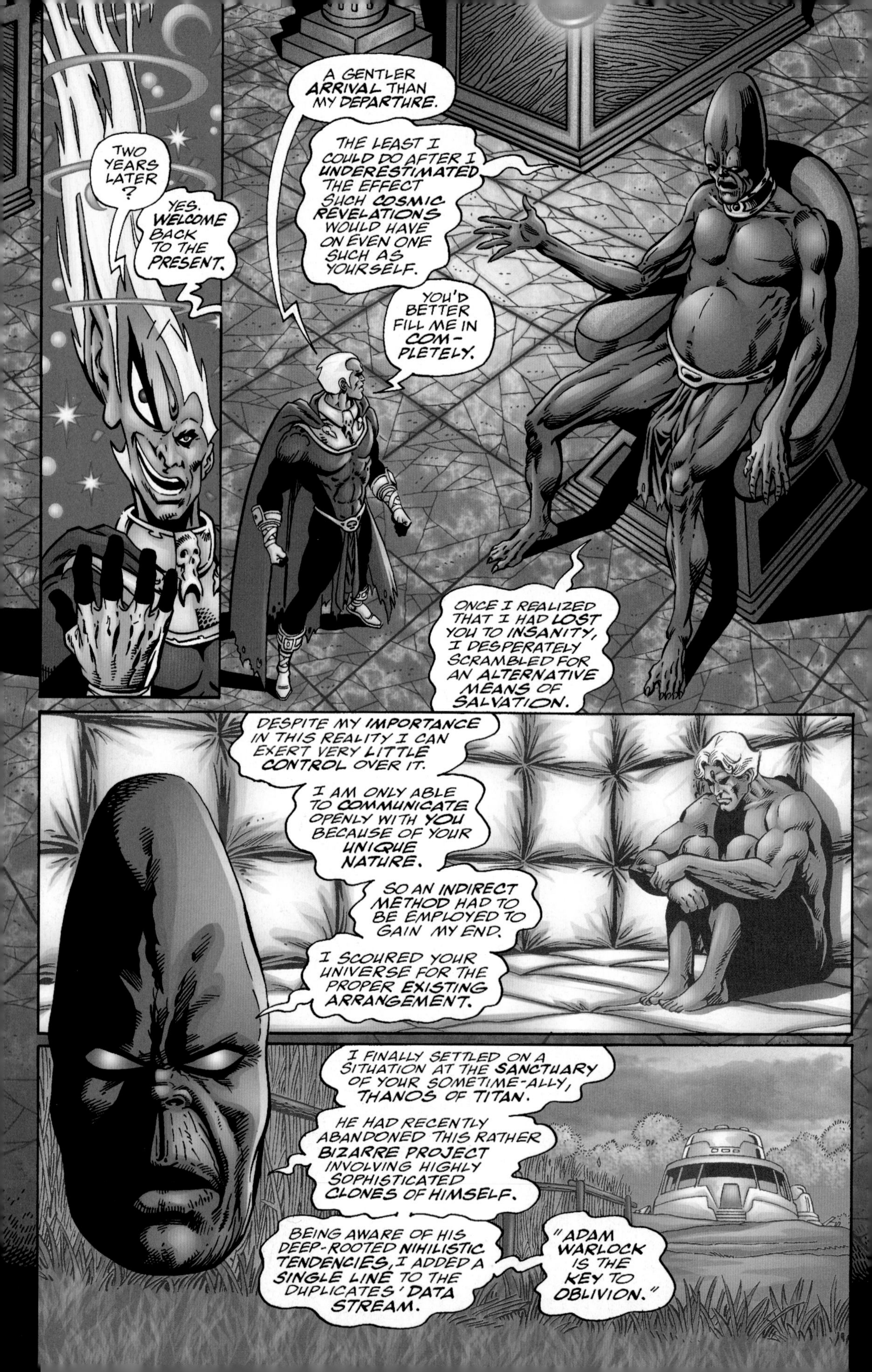
A GENTLER ARRIVAL THAN MY DEPARTURE.
THE LEAST I COULD DO AFTER I UNDERESTIMATED THE EFFECT SUCH COSMIC REVELATIONS WOULD HAVE ON EVEN ONE SUCH AS YOURSELF.
TWO YEARS LATER?
YES. WELCOME BACK TO THE PRESENT.
YOU'D BETTER FILL ME IN COMPLETELY.
ONCE I REALIZED THAT I HAD LOST YOU TO INSANITY, I DESPERATELY SCRAMBLED FOR AN ALTERNATIVE MEANS OF SALVATION.
DESPITE MY IMPORTANCE IN THIS REALITY I CAN EXERT VERY LITTLE CONTROL OVER IT.
I AM ONLY ABLE TO COMMUNICATE OPENLY WITH YOU BECAUSE OF YOUR UNIQUE NATURE.
SO AN INDIRECT METHOD HAD TO BE EMPLOYED TO GAIN MY END.
I SCOURED YOUR UNIVERSE FOR THE PROPER EXISTING ARRANGEMENT.
I FINALLY SETTLED ON A SITUATION AT THE SANCTUARY OF YOUR SOMETIME-ALLY, THANOS OF TITAN.
HE HAD RECENTLY ABANDONED THIS RATHER BIZARRE PROJECT INVOLVING HIGHLY SOPHISTICATED CLONES OF HIMSELF.
BEING AWARE OF HIS DEEP-ROOTED NIHILISTIC TENDENCIES, I ADDED A SINGLE LINE TO THE DUPLICATES' DATA STREAM.
"ADAM WARLOCK IS THE KEY TO OBLIVION."

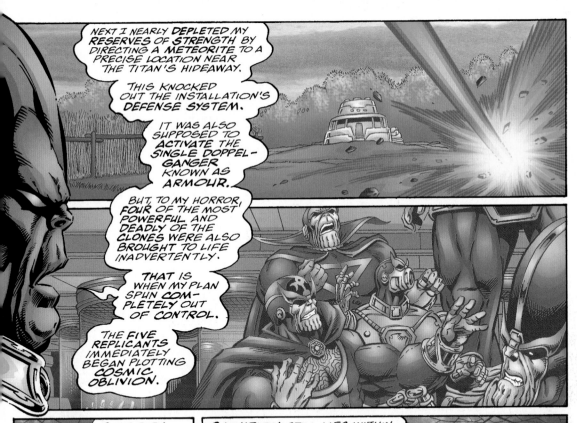

NEXT I NEARLY **DEPLETED** MY **RESERVES** OF **STRENGTH** BY DIRECTING A **METEORITE** TO A PRECISE LOCATION NEAR THE **TITAN'S** HIDEAWAY.

THIS KNOCKED OUT THE INSTALLATION'S **DEFENSE SYSTEM.**

IT WAS ALSO SUPPOSED TO **ACTIVATE** THE SINGLE **DOPPEL-GANGER** KNOWN AS **ARMOUR.**

BUT, TO MY HORROR, **FOUR** OF THE MOST **POWERFUL** AND **DEADLY** OF THE **CLONES** WERE ALSO BROUGHT TO LIFE **INADVERTENTLY.**

THAT IS WHEN MY PLAN SPUN **COM-PLETELY** OUT OF **CONTROL.**

THE **FIVE REPLICANTS** IMMEDIATELY BEGAN PLOTTING **COSMIC OBLIVION.**

SINCE THEN, THEIR EVERY **MOVE** HAS BROUGHT UNIVERSAL **DESTRUCTION** CLOSER TO **REALITY.**

HOW CAN THEY BE STOPPED?

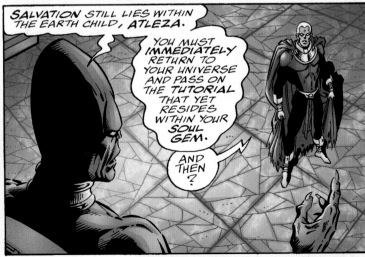

SALVATION STILL LIES WITHIN THE **EARTH** CHILD, **ATLEZA.**

YOU MUST **IMMEDIATELY** RETURN TO YOUR UNIVERSE AND PASS ON THE **TUTORIAL** THAT YET RESIDES WITHIN YOUR **SOUL GEM.**

AND THEN?

BRING ATLEZA BACK **HERE** TO TAKE UP HER DUTIES, FOR THE TIME LEFT TO ME CAN BE COUNTED IN **MINUTES.**

MAKE THAT **SECONDS!**

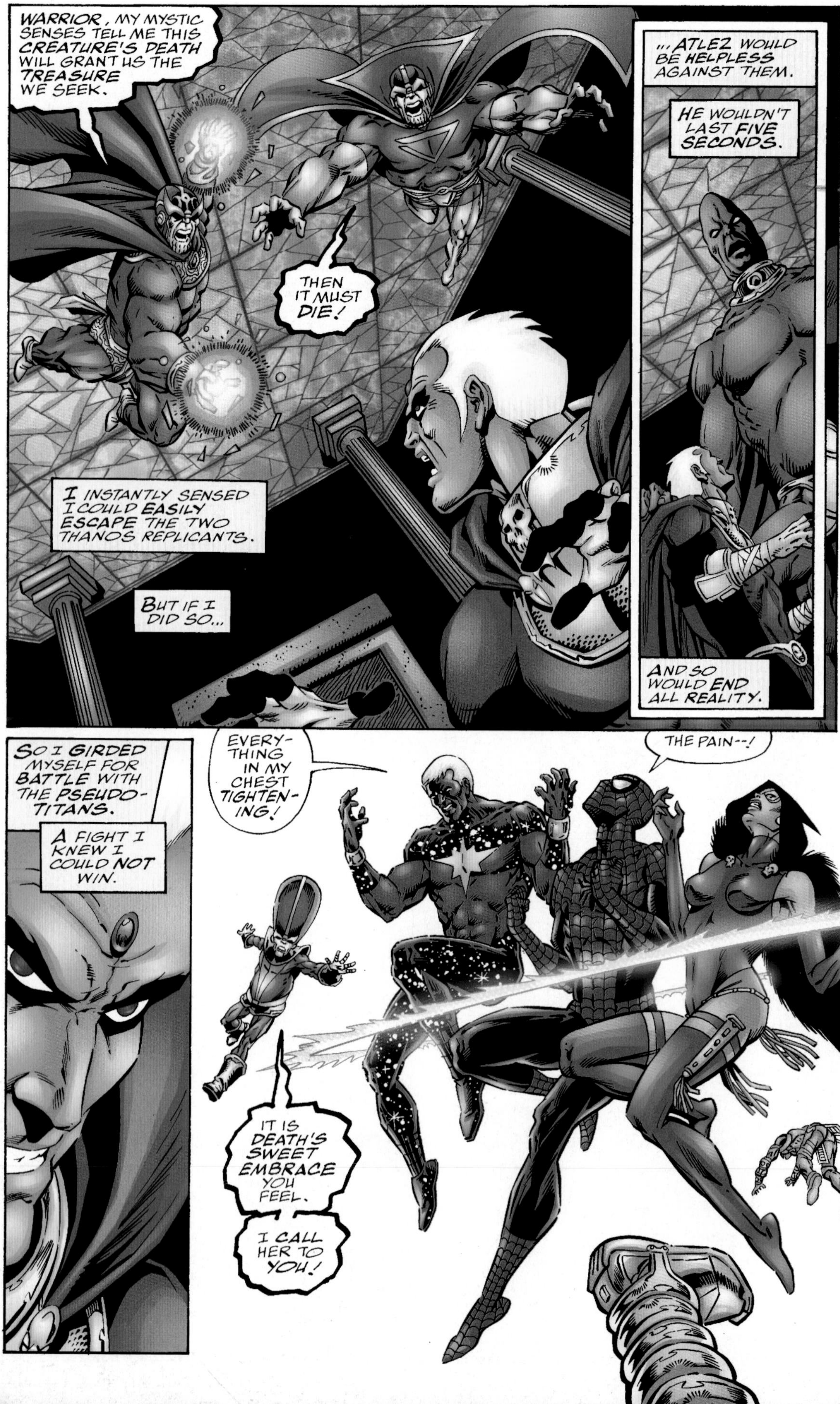
WARRIOR, MY MYSTIC SENSES TELL ME THIS CREATURE'S DEATH WILL GRANT US THE TREASURE WE SEEK.
THEN IT MUST DIE!
I INSTANTLY SENSED I COULD EASILY ESCAPE THE TWO THANOS REPLICANTS.
BUT IF I DID SO...
...ATLEZ WOULD BE HELPLESS AGAINST THEM.
HE WOULDN'T LAST FIVE SECONDS.
AND SO WOULD END ALL REALITY.
SO I GIRDED MYSELF FOR BATTLE WITH THE PSEUDO-TITANS.
A FIGHT I KNEW I COULD NOT WIN.
EVERY-THING IN MY CHEST TIGHTEN-ING!
THE PAIN--!
IT IS DEATH'S SWEET EMBRACE YOU FEEL.
I CALL HER TO YOU!

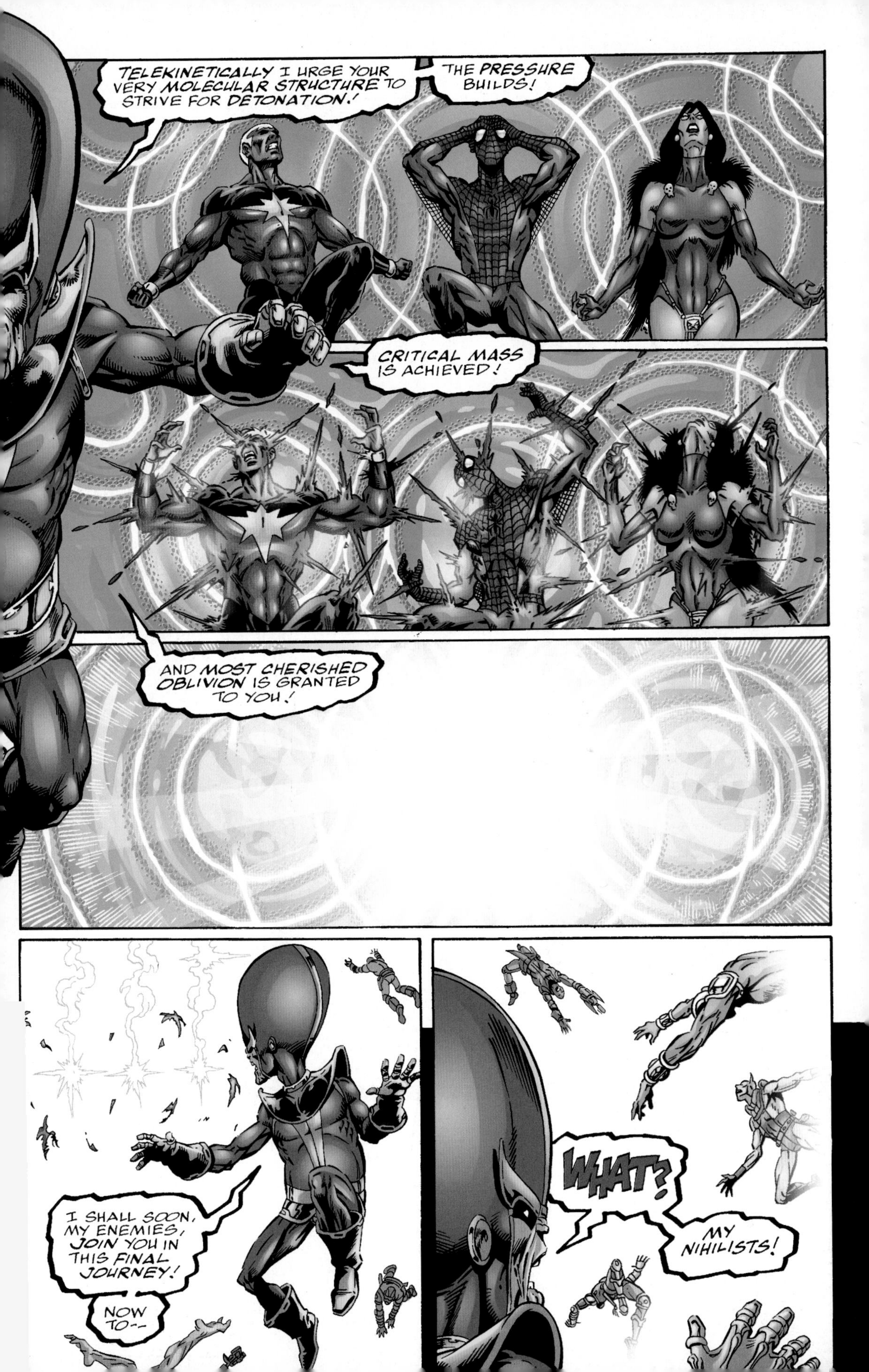

TELEKINETICALLY I URGE YOUR VERY MOLECULAR STRUCTURE TO STRIVE FOR DETONATION!
THE PRESSURE BUILDS!
CRITICAL MASS IS ACHIEVED!
AND MOST CHERISHED OBLIVION IS GRANTED TO YOU!
I SHALL SOON, MY ENEMIES, JOIN YOU IN THIS FINAL JOURNEY!
NOW TO--
WHAT?
MY NIHILISTS!

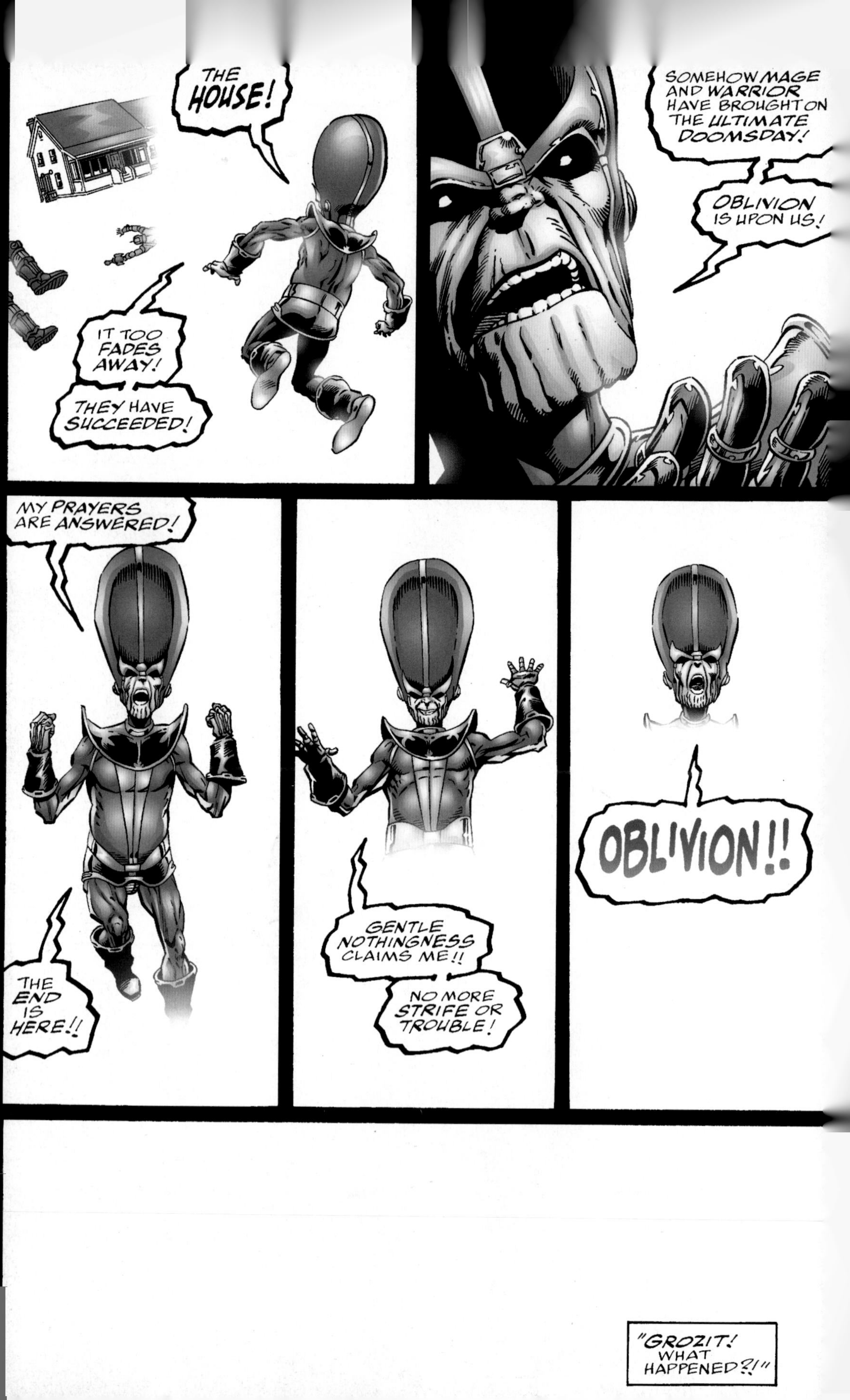
THE HOUSE!
IT TOO FADES AWAY!
THEY HAVE SUCCEEDED!
SOMEHOW MAGE AND WARRIOR HAVE BROUGHT ON THE ULTIMATE DOOMSDAY!
OBLIVION IS UPON US!
MY PRAYERS ARE ANSWERED!
THE END IS HERE!!
GENTLE NOTHINGNESS CLAIMS ME!!
NO MORE STRIFE OR TROUBLE!
OBLIVION!!
"GROZIT! WHAT HAPPENED?!"

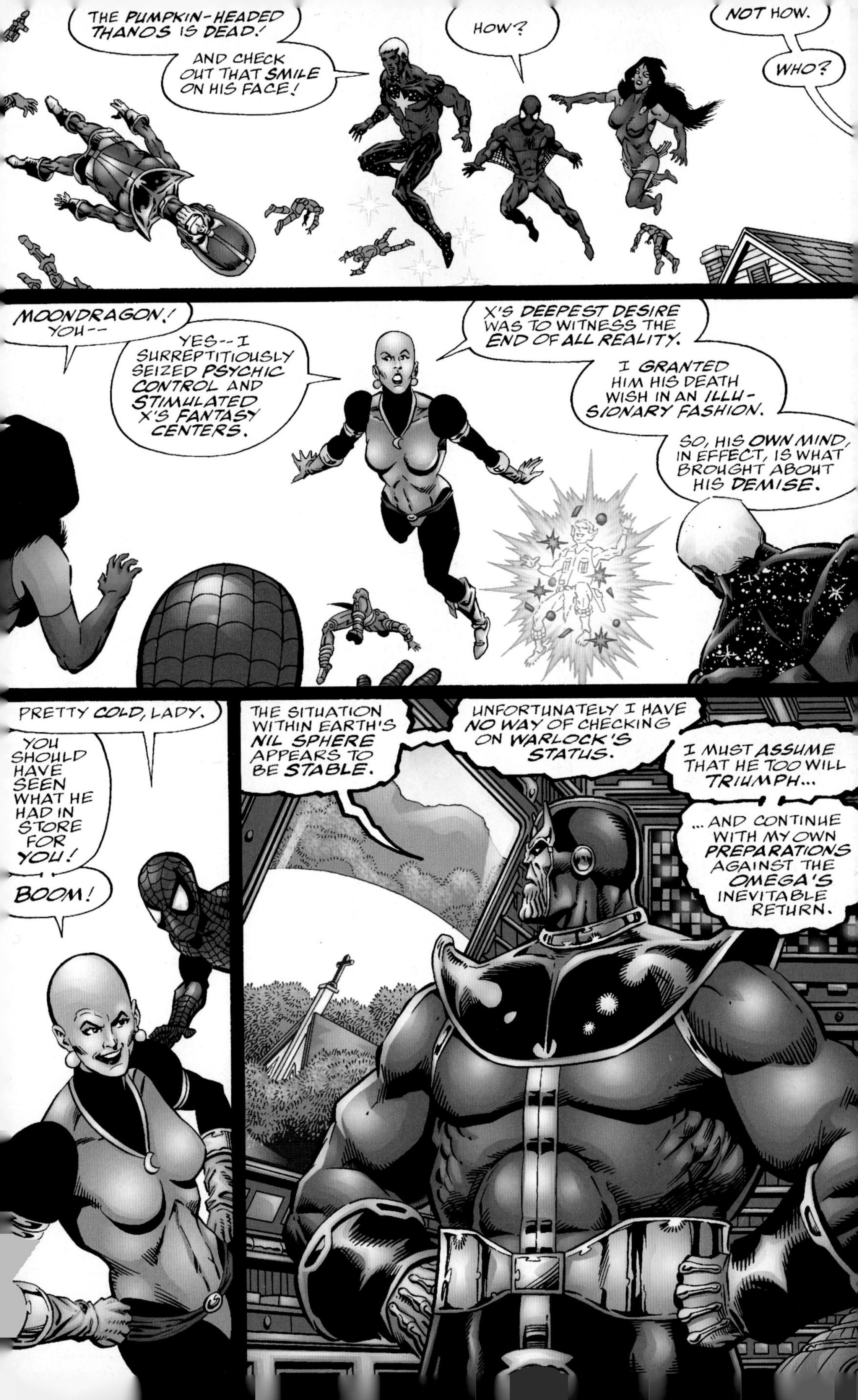
THE PUMPKIN-HEADED THANOS IS DEAD!
AND CHECK OUT THAT SMILE ON HIS FACE!
HOW?
NOT HOW.
WHO?
MOONDRAGON! YOU--
YES--I SURREPTITIOUSLY SEIZED PSYCHIC CONTROL AND STIMULATED X'S FANTASY CENTERS.
X'S DEEPEST DESIRE WAS TO WITNESS THE END OF ALL REALITY.
I GRANTED HIM HIS DEATH WISH IN AN ILLUSIONARY FASHION.
SO, HIS OWN MIND, IN EFFECT, IS WHAT BROUGHT ABOUT HIS DEMISE.
PRETTY COLD, LADY.
YOU SHOULD HAVE SEEN WHAT HE HAD IN STORE FOR YOU!
BOOM!
THE SITUATION WITHIN EARTH'S NIL SPHERE APPEARS TO BE STABLE.
UNFORTUNATELY I HAVE NO WAY OF CHECKING ON WARLOCK'S STATUS.
I MUST ASSUME THAT HE TOO WILL TRIUMPH...
...AND CONTINUE WITH MY OWN PREPARATIONS AGAINST THE OMEGA'S INEVITABLE RETURN.

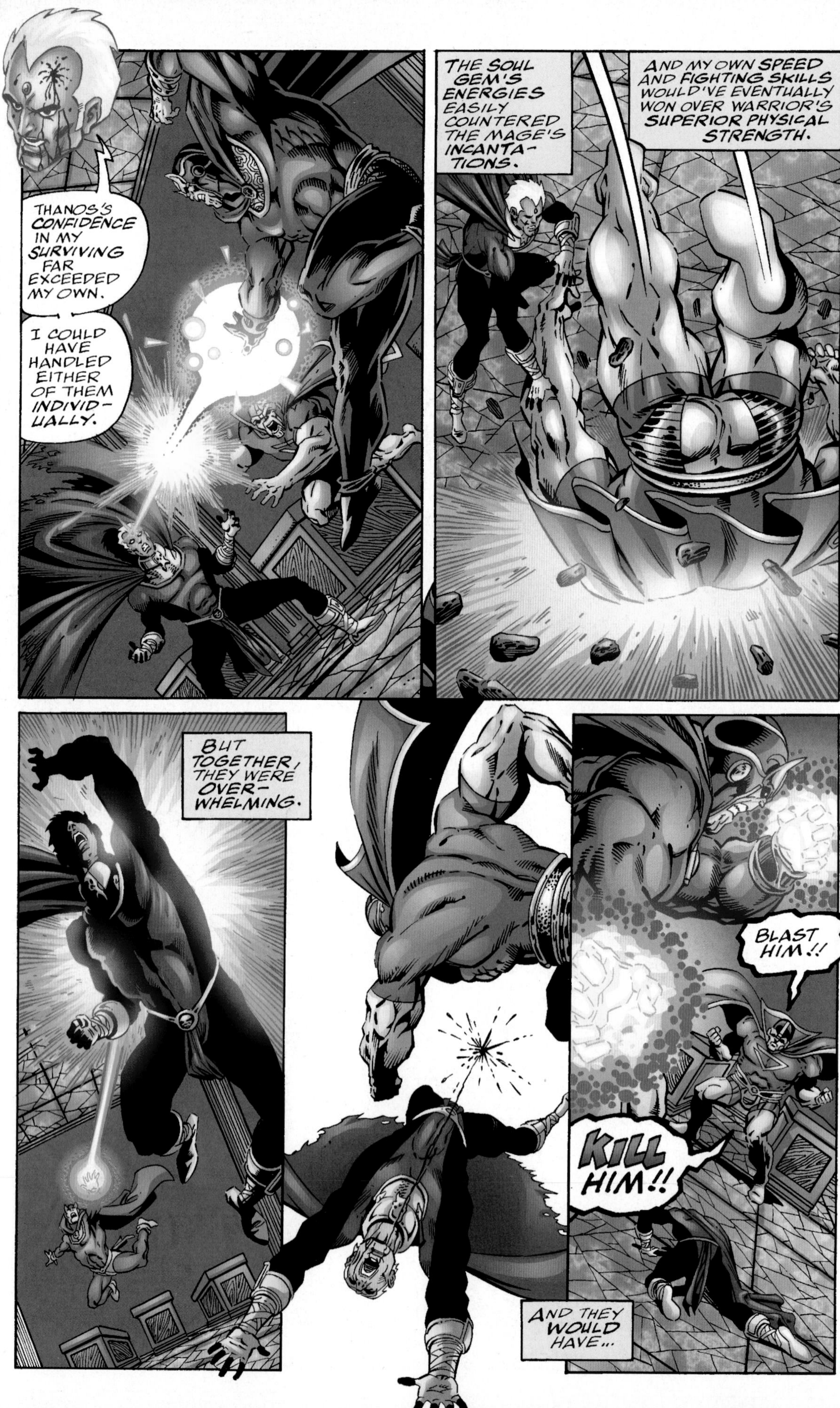
THANOS'S CONFIDENCE IN MY SURVIVING FAR EXCEEDED MY OWN.
I COULD HAVE HANDLED EITHER OF THEM INDIVIDUALLY.
THE SOUL GEM'S ENERGIES EASILY COUNTERED THE MAGE'S INCANTATIONS.
AND MY OWN SPEED AND FIGHTING SKILLS WOULD'VE EVENTUALLY WON OVER WARRIOR'S SUPERIOR PHYSICAL STRENGTH.
BUT TOGETHER, THEY WERE OVERWHELMING.
BLAST HIM!!
KILL HIM!!
AND THEY WOULD HAVE...

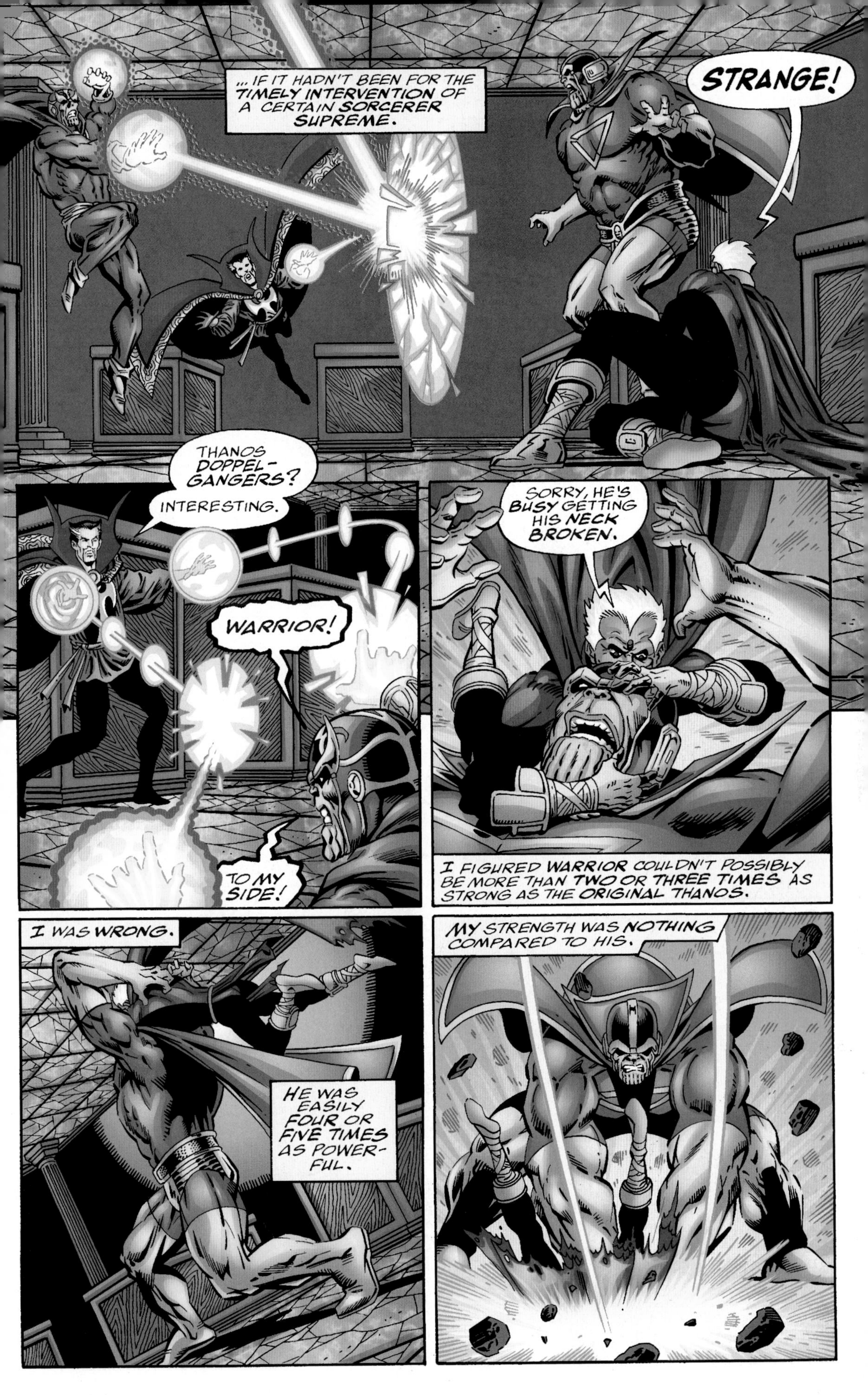
...IF IT HADN'T BEEN FOR THE TIMELY INTERVENTION OF A CERTAIN SORCERER SUPREME.
STRANGE!
THANOS DOPPEL-GANGERS?
INTERESTING.
WARRIOR!
TO MY SIDE!
SORRY, HE'S BUSY GETTING HIS NECK BROKEN.
I FIGURED WARRIOR COULDN'T POSSIBLY BE MORE THAN TWO OR THREE TIMES AS STRONG AS THE ORIGINAL THANOS.
I WAS WRONG.
HE WAS EASILY FOUR OR FIVE TIMES AS POWER-FUL.
MY STRENGTH WAS NOTHING COMPARED TO HIS.

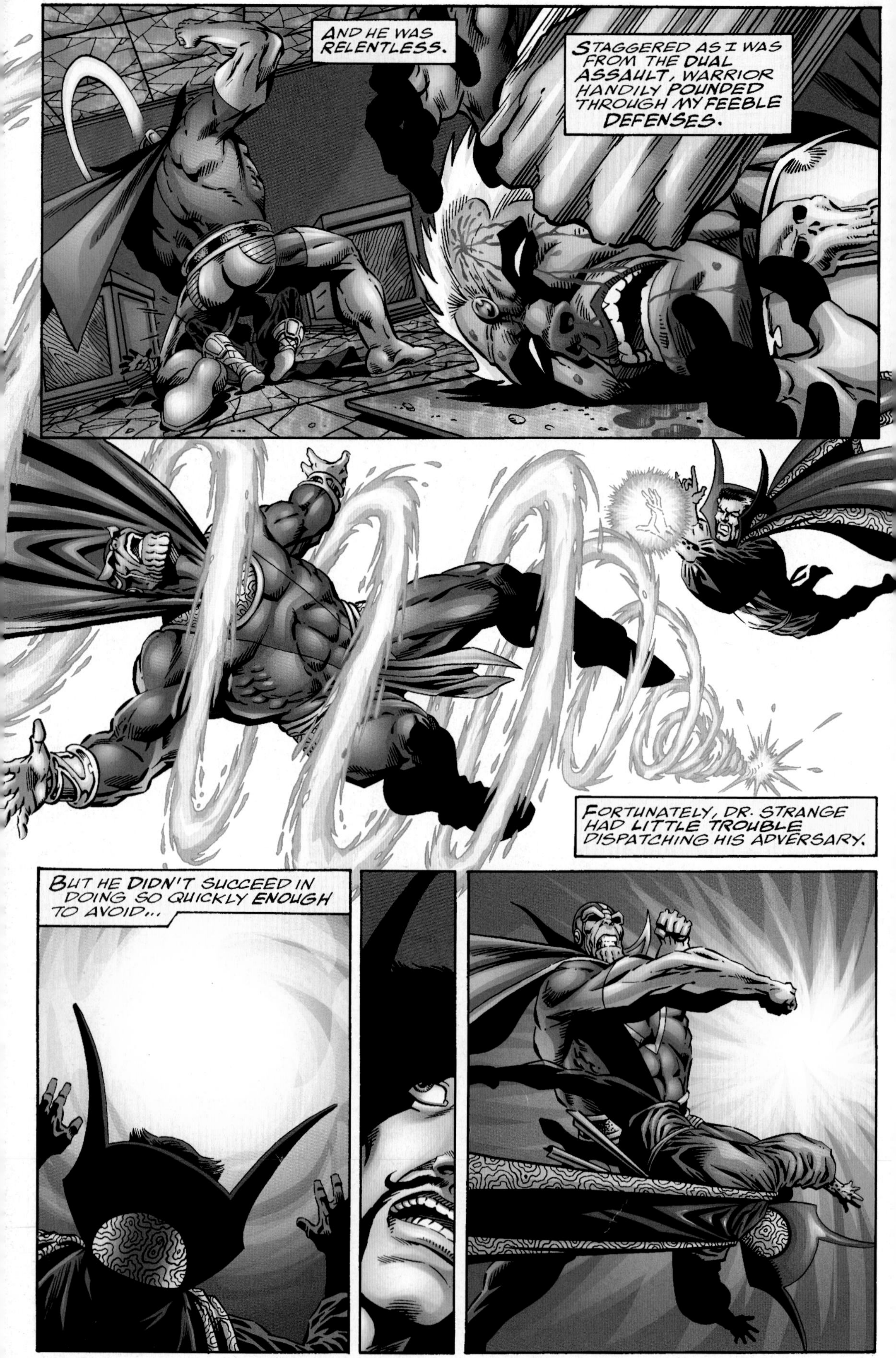
AND HE WAS RELENTLESS.
STAGGERED AS I WAS FROM THE DUAL ASSAULT, WARRIOR HANDILY POUNDED THROUGH MY FEEBLE DEFENSES.
FORTUNATELY, DR. STRANGE HAD LITTLE TROUBLE DISPATCHING HIS ADVERSARY.
BUT HE DIDN'T SUCCEED IN DOING SO QUICKLY ENOUGH TO AVOID...

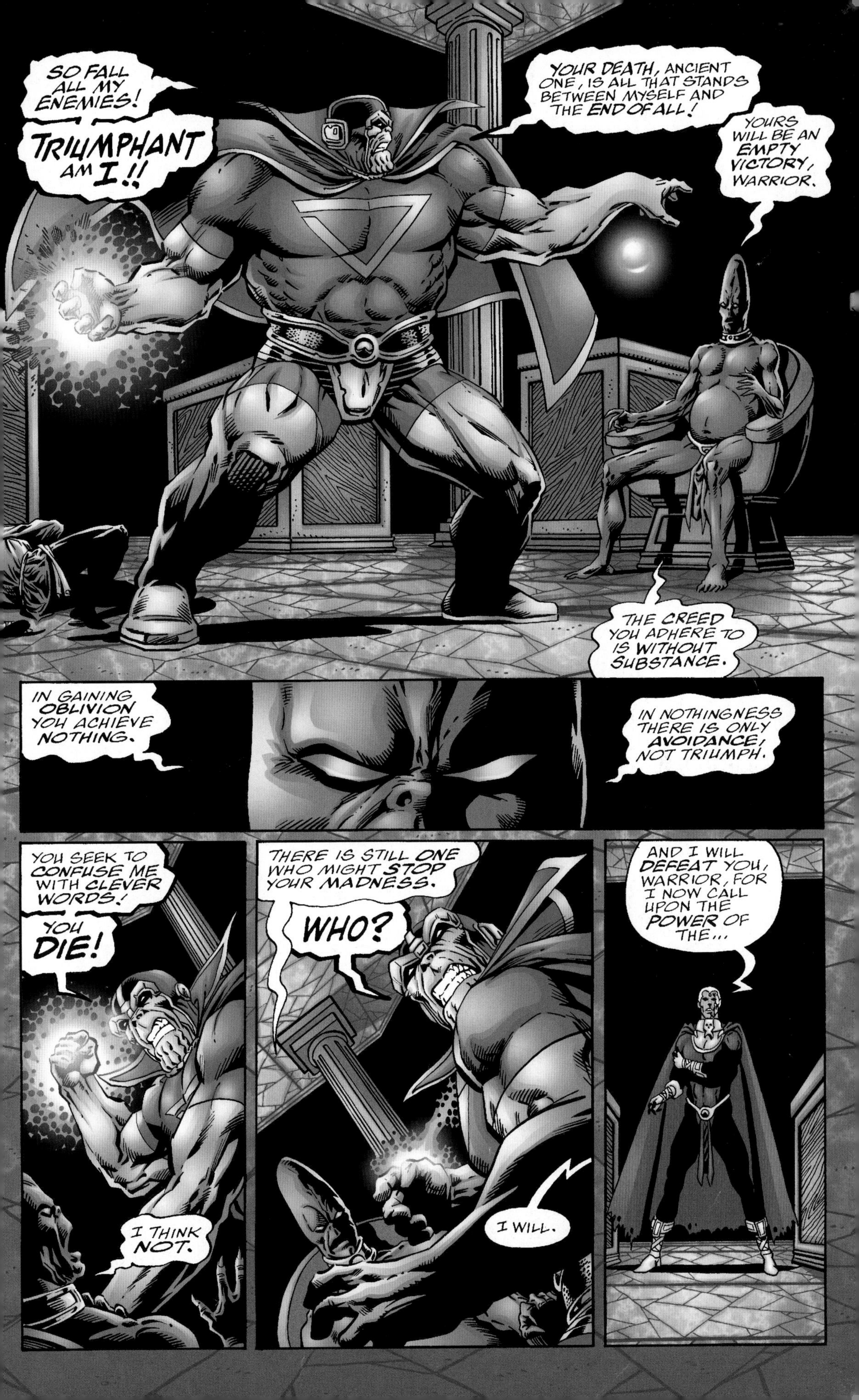
SO FALL ALL MY ENEMIES!
TRIUMPHANT AM I!!
YOUR DEATH, ANCIENT ONE, IS ALL THAT STANDS BETWEEN MYSELF AND THE END OF ALL!
YOURS WILL BE AN EMPTY VICTORY, WARRIOR.
THE CREED YOU ADHERE TO IS WITHOUT SUBSTANCE.
IN GAINING OBLIVION YOU ACHIEVE NOTHING.
IN NOTHINGNESS THERE IS ONLY AVOIDANCE, NOT TRIUMPH.
YOU SEEK TO CONFUSE ME WITH CLEVER WORDS!
YOU DIE!
I THINK NOT.
THERE IS STILL ONE WHO MIGHT STOP YOUR MADNESS.
WHO?
I WILL.
AND I WILL DEFEAT YOU, WARRIOR, FOR I NOW CALL UPON THE POWER OF THE...

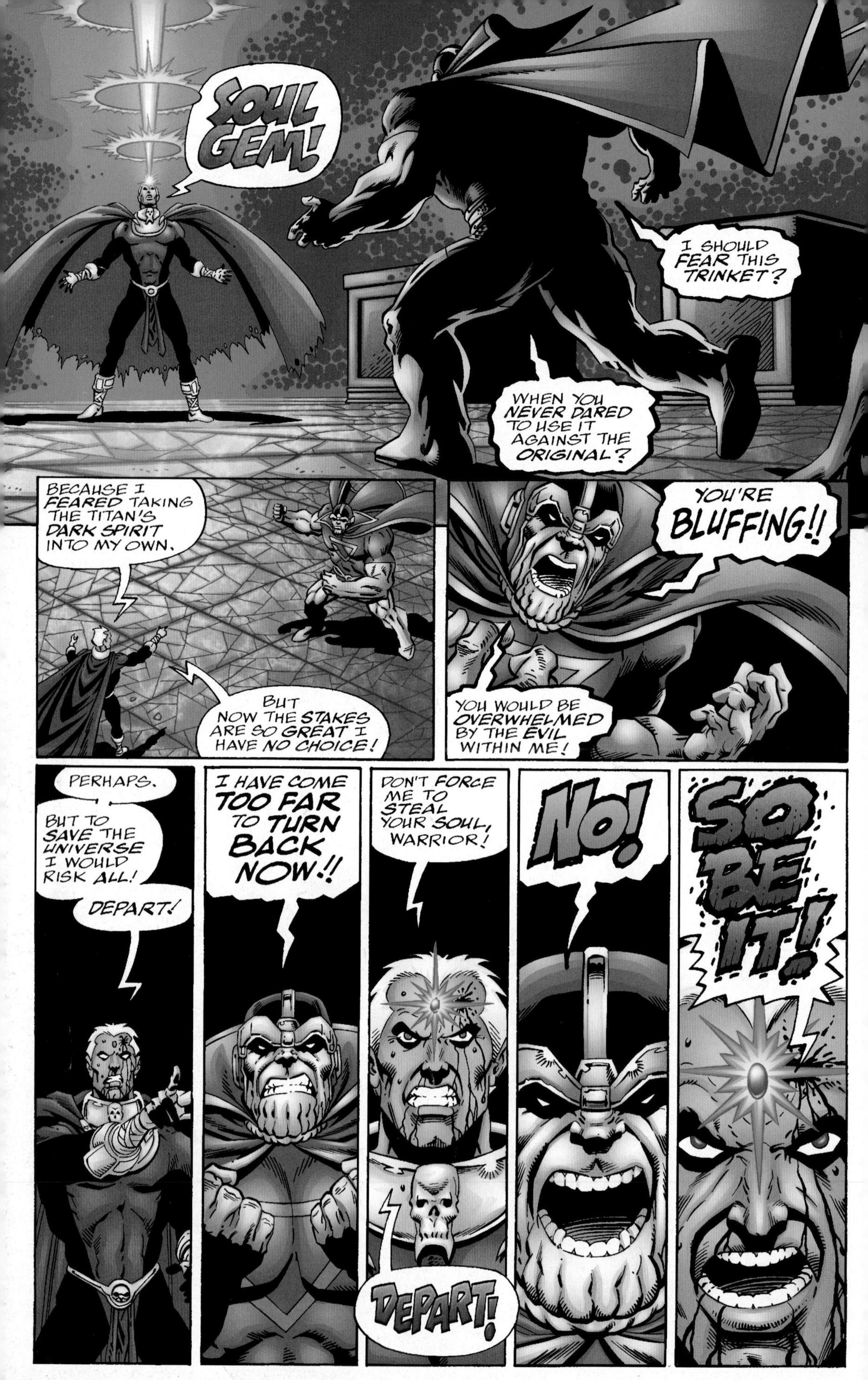
SOUL GEM!
I SHOULD FEAR THIS TRINKET?
WHEN YOU NEVER DARED TO USE IT AGAINST THE ORIGINAL?
BECAUSE I FEARED TAKING THE TITAN'S DARK SPIRIT INTO MY OWN.
BUT NOW THE STAKES ARE SO GREAT I HAVE NO CHOICE!
YOU'RE BLUFFING!!
YOU WOULD BE OVERWHELMED BY THE EVIL WITHIN ME!
PERHAPS.
BUT TO SAVE THE UNIVERSE I WOULD RISK ALL!
DEPART!
I HAVE COME TOO FAR TO TURN BACK NOW!!
DON'T FORCE ME TO STEAL YOUR SOUL, WARRIOR!
DEPART!
NO!
SO BE IT!

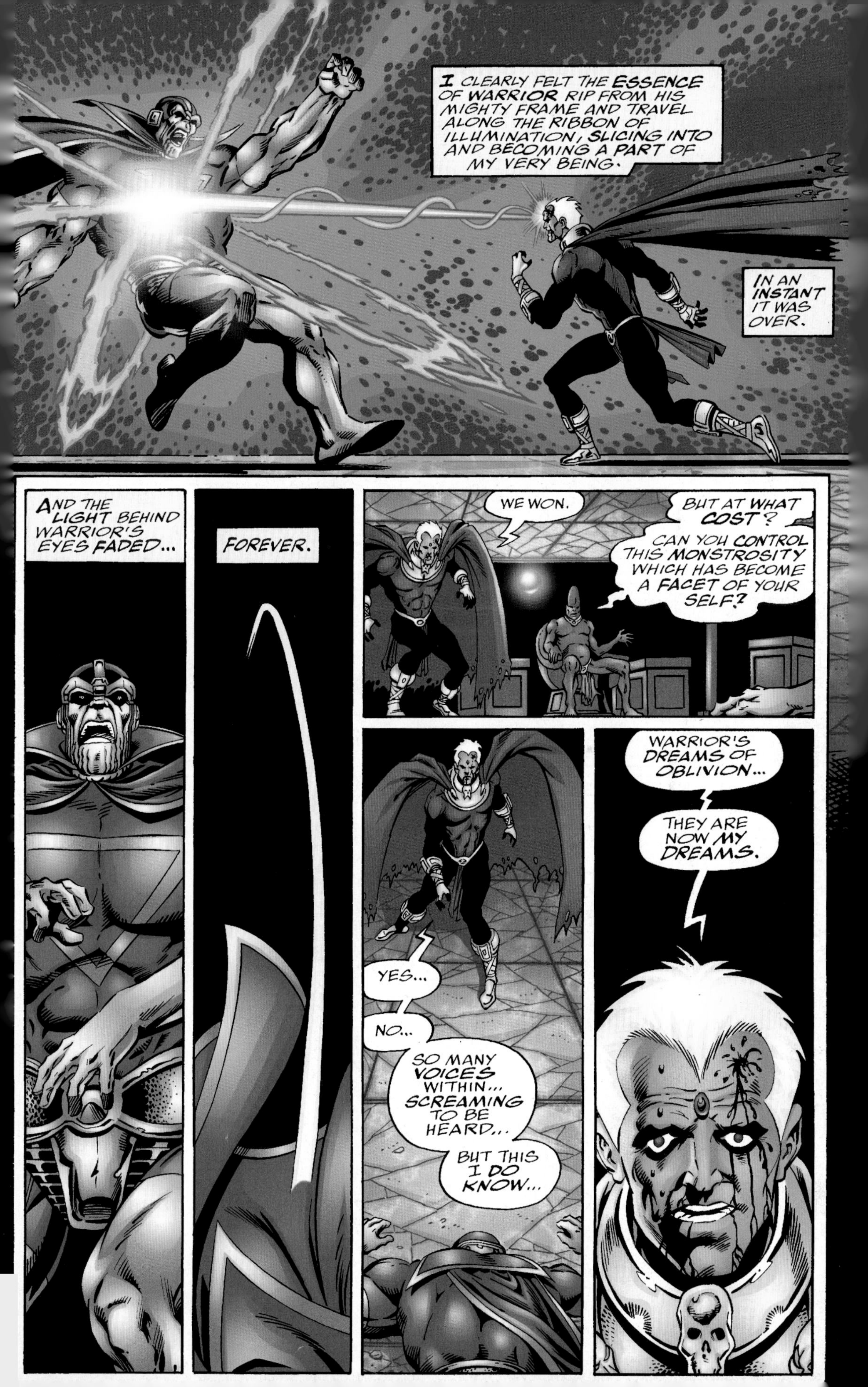
I CLEARLY FELT THE ESSENCE OF WARRIOR RIP FROM HIS MIGHTY FRAME AND TRAVEL ALONG THE RIBBON OF ILLUMINATION, SLICING INTO AND BECOMING A PART OF MY VERY BEING.
IN AN INSTANT IT WAS OVER.
AND THE LIGHT BEHIND WARRIOR'S EYES FADED...
FOREVER.
WE WON.
BUT AT WHAT COST?
CAN YOU CONTROL THIS MONSTROSITY WHICH HAS BECOME A FACET OF YOUR SELF?
YES...
NO...
SO MANY VOICES WITHIN... SCREAMING TO BE HEARD...
BUT THIS I DO KNOW...
WARRIOR'S DREAMS OF OBLIVION...
THEY ARE NOW MY DREAMS.

6

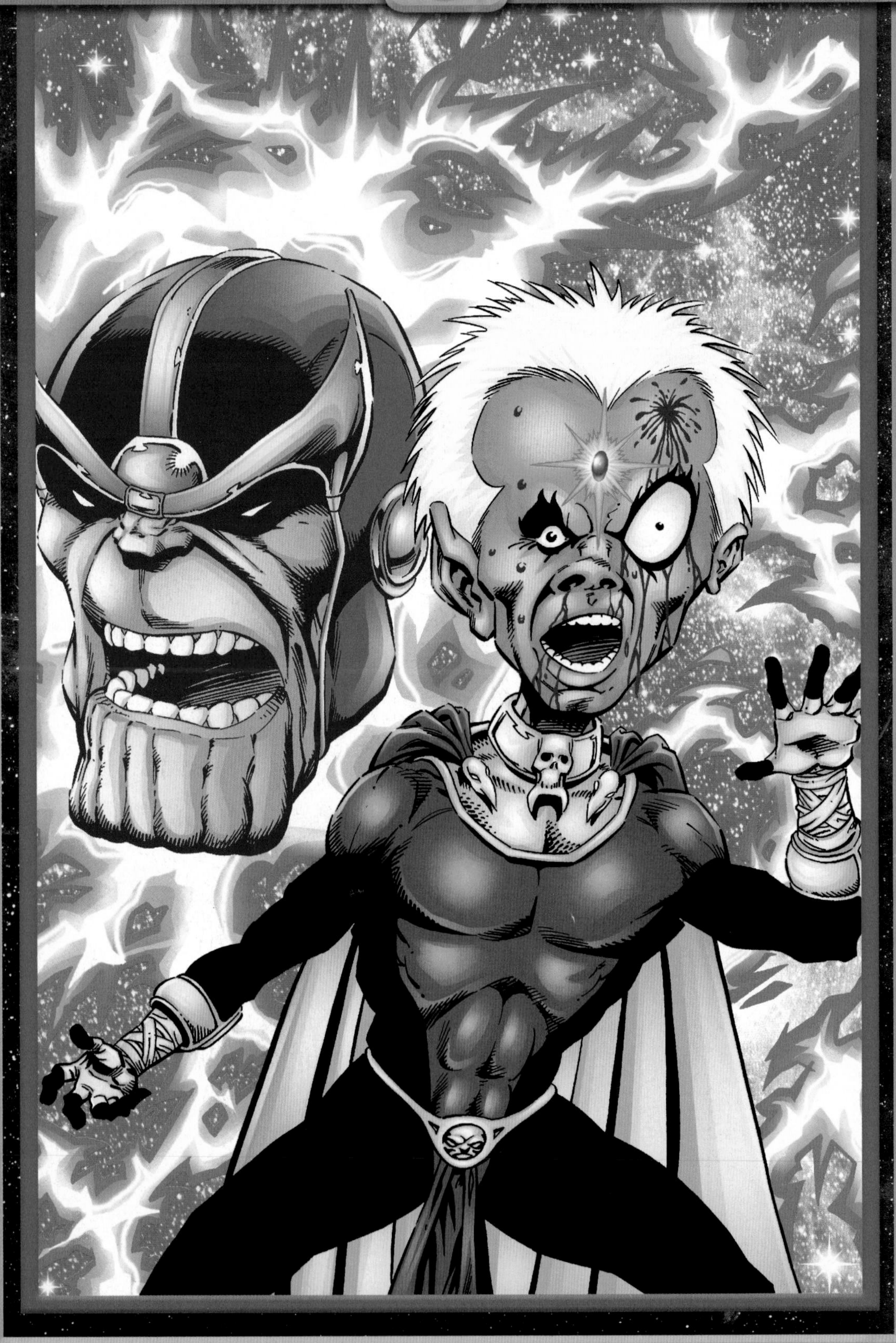

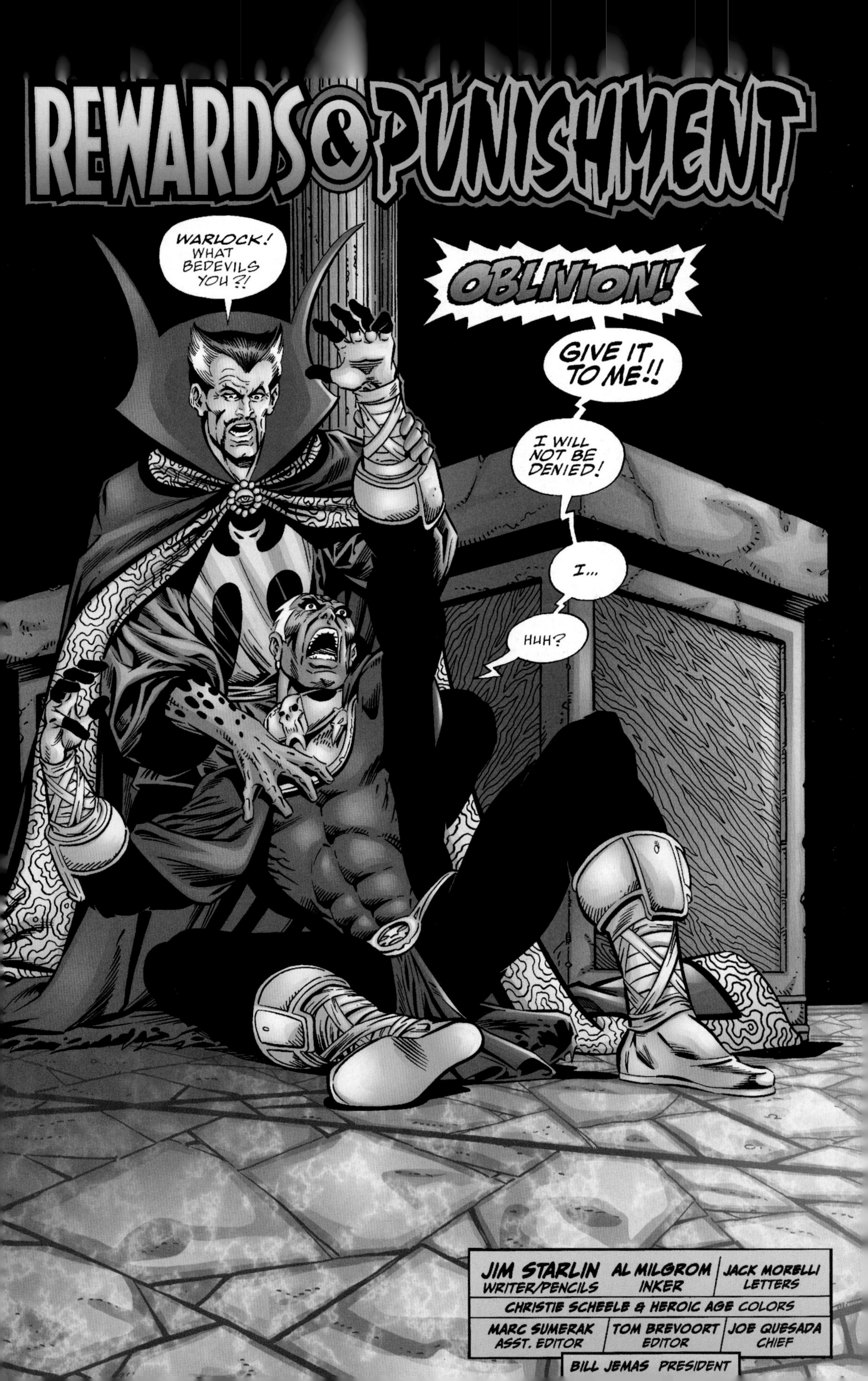
REWARDS & PUNISHMENT
WARLOCK! WHAT BEDEVILS YOU?!
OBLIVION!
GIVE IT TO ME!!
I WILL NOT BE DENIED!
I...
HUH?
JIM STARLIN WRITER/PENCILS
AL MILGROM INKER
JACK MORELLI LETTERS
CHRISTIE SCHEELE & HEROIC AGE COLORS
MARC SUMERAK ASST. EDITOR
TOM BREVOORT EDITOR
JOE QUESADA CHIEF
BILL JEMAS PRESIDENT

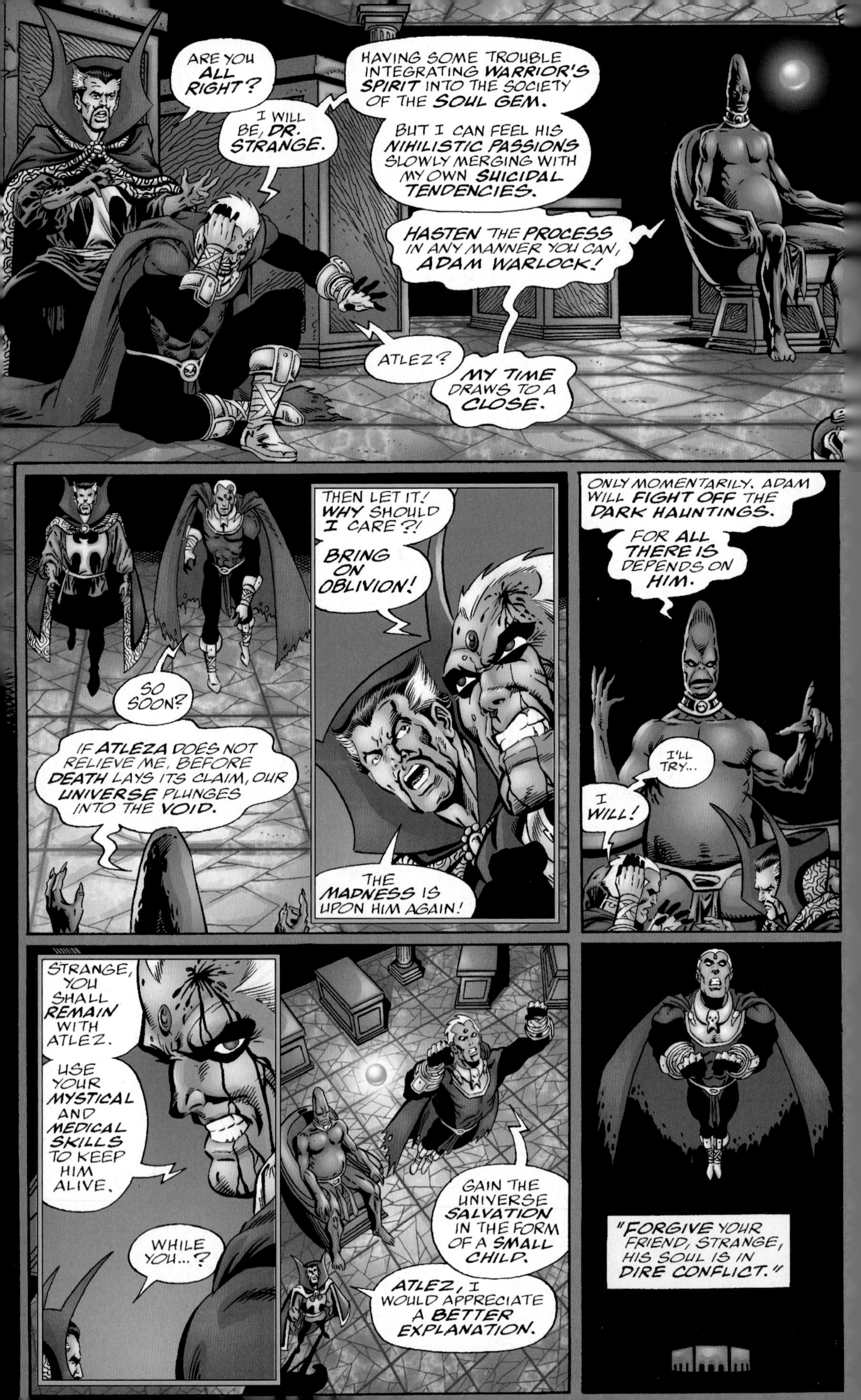
ARE YOU ALL RIGHT?
I WILL BE, DR. STRANGE.
HAVING SOME TROUBLE INTEGRATING WARRIOR'S SPIRIT INTO THE SOCIETY OF THE SOUL GEM.
BUT I CAN FEEL HIS NIHILISTIC PASSIONS SLOWLY MERGING WITH MY OWN SUICIDAL TENDENCIES.
HASTEN THE PROCESS IN ANY MANNER YOU CAN, ADAM WARLOCK!
ATLEZ?
MY TIME DRAWS TO A CLOSE.
SO SOON?
IF ATLEZA DOES NOT RELIEVE ME, BEFORE DEATH LAYS ITS CLAIM, OUR UNIVERSE PLUNGES INTO THE VOID.
THEN LET IT! WHY SHOULD I CARE?!
BRING ON OBLIVION!
THE MADNESS IS UPON HIM AGAIN!
ONLY MOMENTARILY. ADAM WILL FIGHT OFF THE DARK HAUNTINGS.
FOR ALL THERE IS DEPENDS ON HIM.
I'LL TRY...
I WILL!
STRANGE, YOU SHALL REMAIN WITH ATLEZ.
USE YOUR MYSTICAL AND MEDICAL SKILLS TO KEEP HIM ALIVE.
WHILE YOU...?
GAIN THE UNIVERSE SALVATION IN THE FORM OF A SMALL CHILD.
ATLEZ, I WOULD APPRECIATE A BETTER EXPLANATION.
"FORGIVE YOUR FRIEND, STRANGE, HIS SOUL IS IN DIRE CONFLICT."

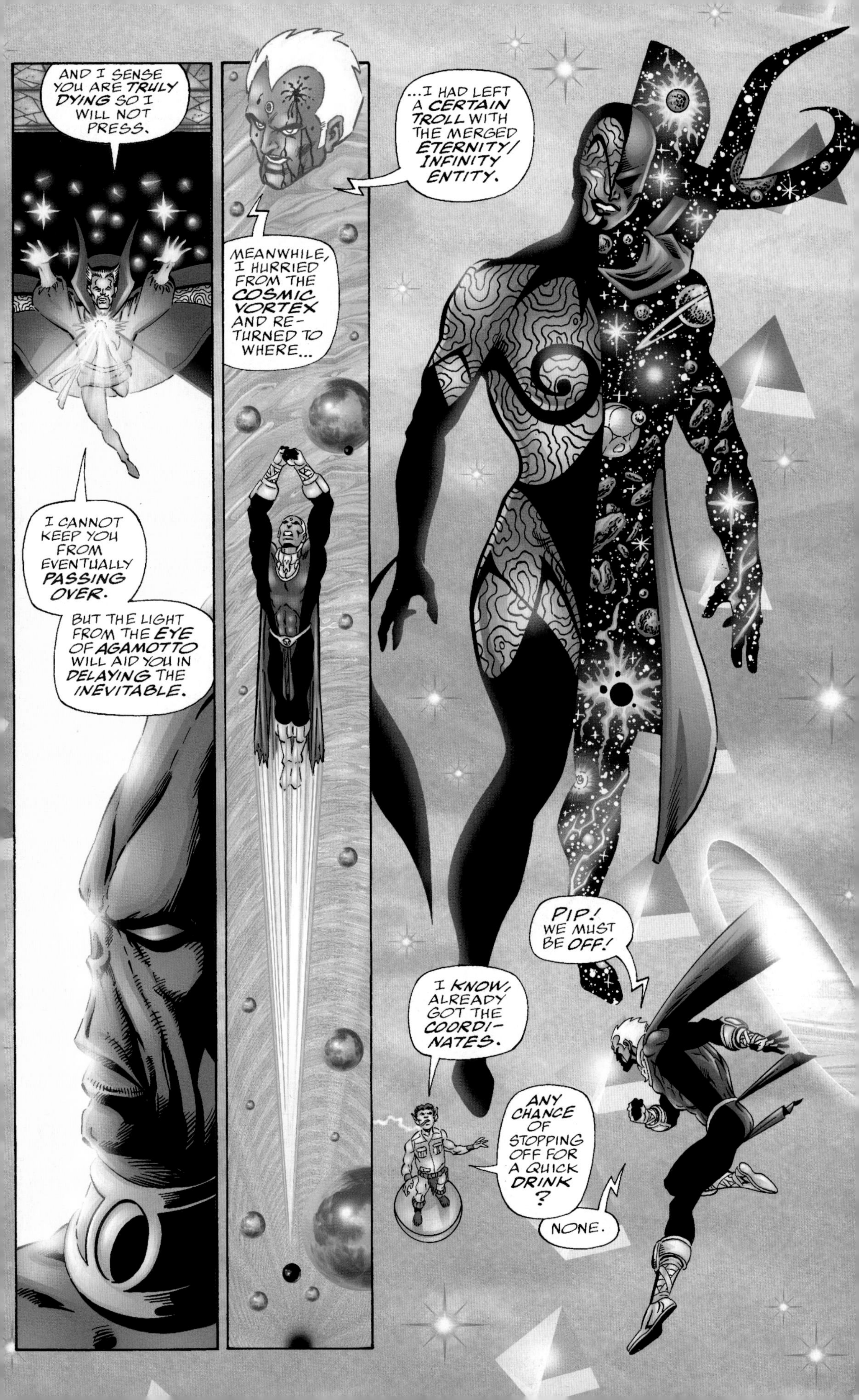
AND I SENSE YOU ARE TRULY DYING SO I WILL NOT PRESS.
I CANNOT KEEP YOU FROM EVENTUALLY PASSING OVER.
BUT THE LIGHT FROM THE EYE OF AGAMOTTO WILL AID YOU IN DELAYING THE INEVITABLE.
MEANWHILE, I HURRIED FROM THE COSMIC VORTEX AND RE-TURNED TO WHERE...
...I HAD LEFT A CERTAIN TROLL WITH THE MERGED ETERNITY/INFINITY ENTITY.
PIP! WE MUST BE OFF!
I KNOW, ALREADY GOT THE COORDI-NATES.
ANY CHANCE OF STOPPING OFF FOR A QUICK DRINK ?
NONE.

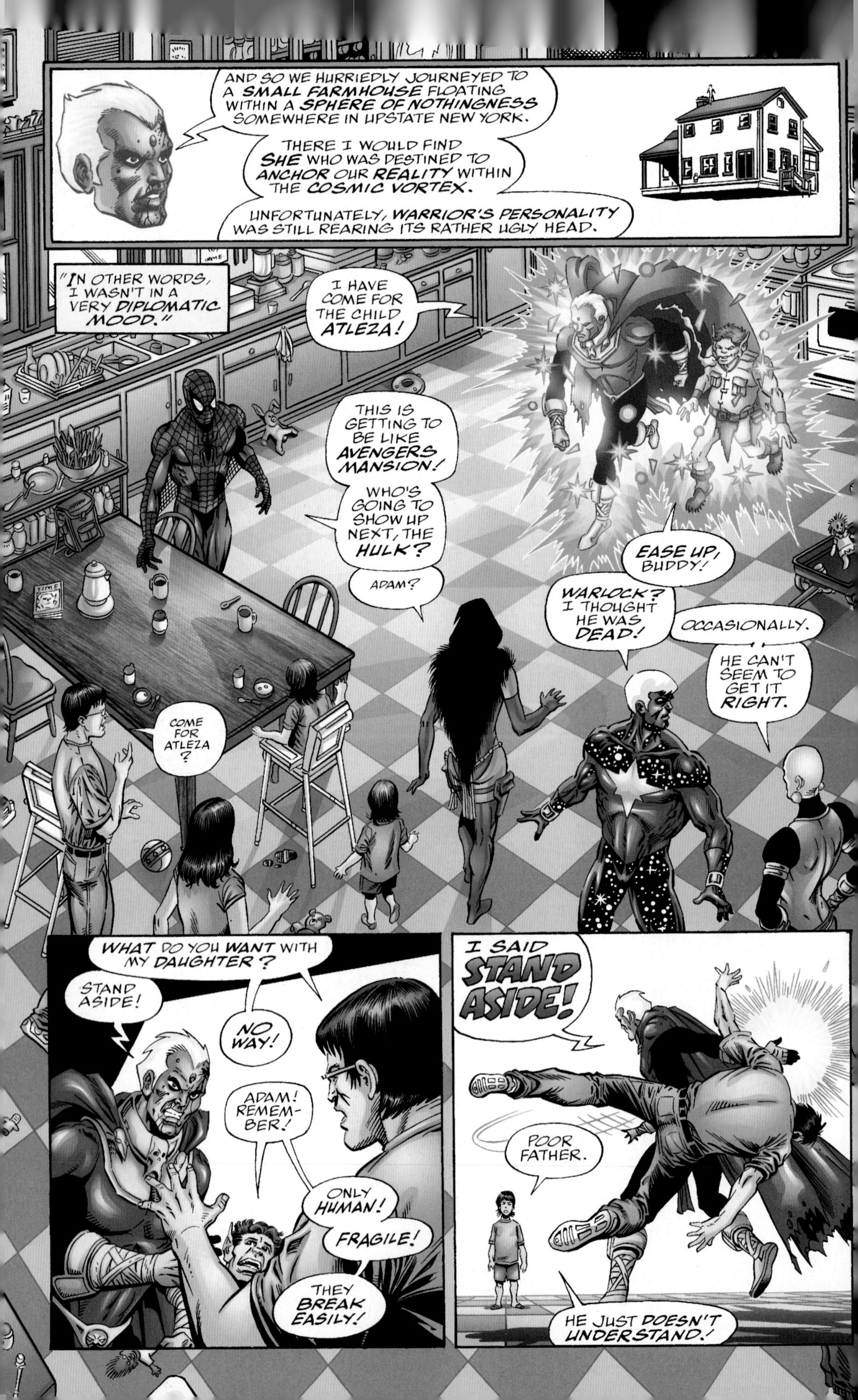

AND SO WE HURRIEDLY JOURNEYED TO A SMALL FARMHOUSE FLOATING WITHIN A SPHERE OF NOTHINGNESS SOMEWHERE IN UPSTATE NEW YORK.
THERE I WOULD FIND SHE WHO WAS DESTINED TO ANCHOR OUR REALITY WITHIN THE COSMIC VORTEX.
UNFORTUNATELY, WARRIOR'S PERSONALITY WAS STILL REARING ITS RATHER UGLY HEAD.
"IN OTHER WORDS, I WASN'T IN A VERY DIPLOMATIC MOOD."
I HAVE COME FOR THE CHILD ATLEZA!
THIS IS GETTING TO BE LIKE AVENGERS MANSION!
WHO'S GOING TO SHOW UP NEXT, THE HULK?
ADAM?
EASE UP, BUDDY!
WARLOCK? I THOUGHT HE WAS DEAD!
OCCASIONALLY.
HE CAN'T SEEM TO GET IT RIGHT.
COME FOR ATLEZA?
WHAT DO YOU WANT WITH MY DAUGHTER?
STAND ASIDE!
NO WAY!
ADAM! REMEMBER!
ONLY HUMAN!
FRAGILE!
THEY BREAK EASILY!
I SAID STAND ASIDE!
POOR FATHER.
HE JUST DOESN'T UNDERSTAND.

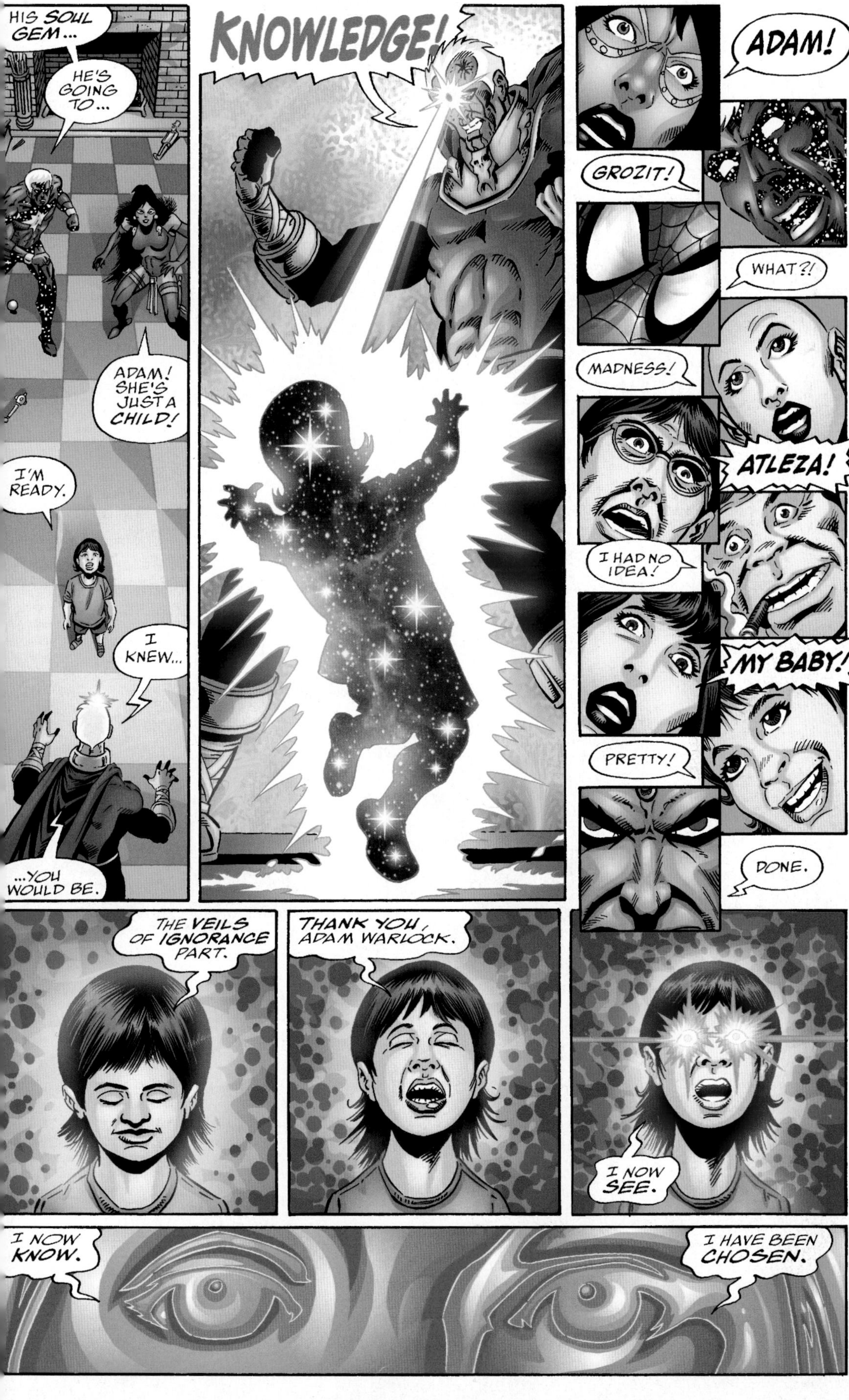
HIS SOUL GEM...
HE'S GOING TO...
ADAM! SHE'S JUST A CHILD!
I'M READY.
I KNEW...
...YOU WOULD BE.
KNOWLEDGE!
ADAM!
GROZIT!
WHAT?!
MADNESS!
ATLEZA!
I HAD NO IDEA!
MY BABY!
PRETTY!
DONE.
THE VEILS OF IGNORANCE PART.
THANK YOU, ADAM WARLOCK.
I NOW SEE.
I NOW KNOW.
I HAVE BEEN CHOSEN.

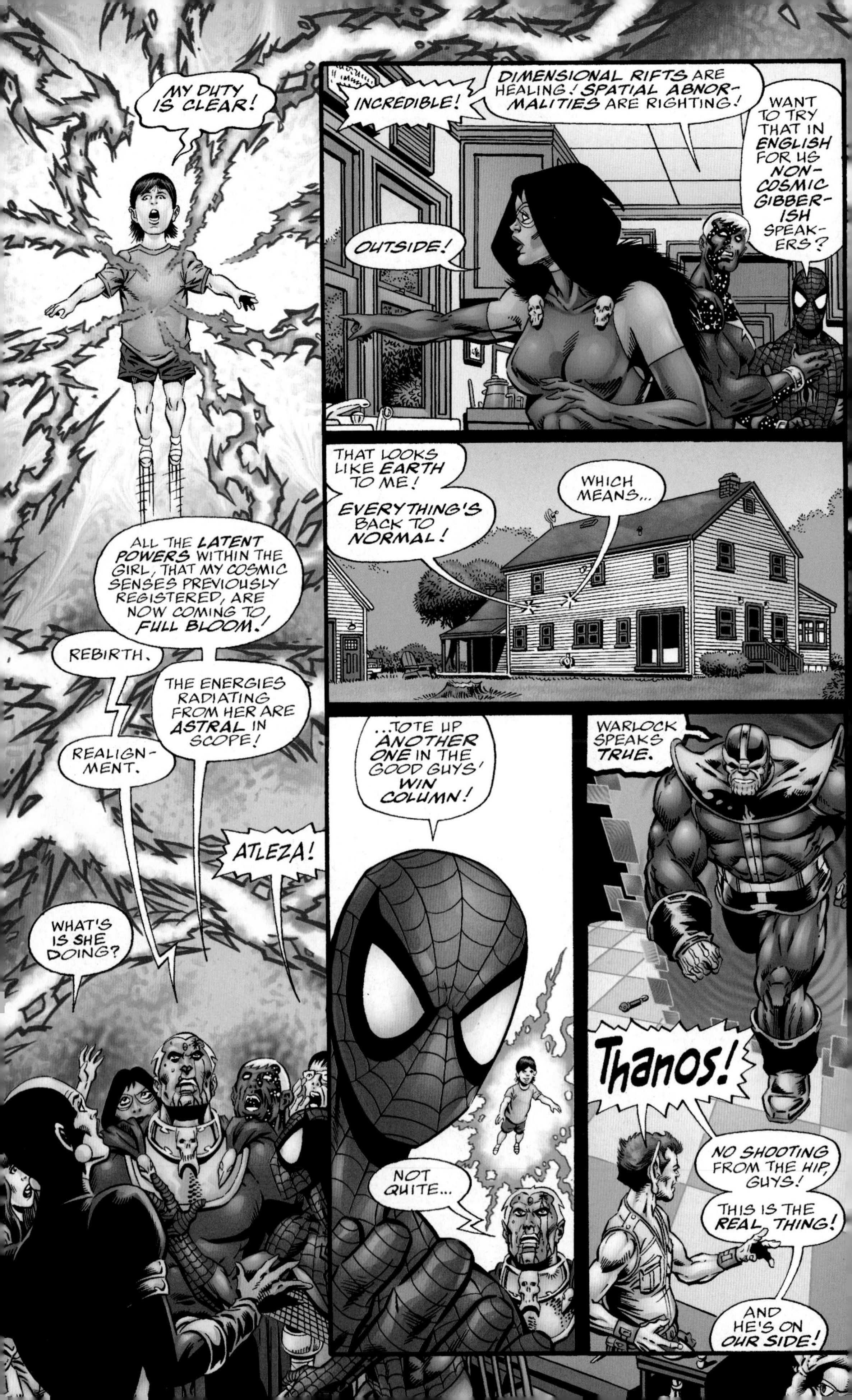
MY DUTY IS CLEAR!
INCREDIBLE!
DIMENSIONAL RIFTS ARE HEALING! SPATIAL ABNORMALITIES ARE RIGHTING!
OUTSIDE!
WANT TO TRY THAT IN ENGLISH FOR US NON-COSMIC GIBBERISH SPEAKERS?
THAT LOOKS LIKE EARTH TO ME!
EVERYTHING'S BACK TO NORMAL!
WHICH MEANS...
...TOTE UP ANOTHER ONE IN THE GOOD GUYS' WIN COLUMN!
NOT QUITE...
WARLOCK SPEAKS TRUE.
Thanos!
NO SHOOTING FROM THE HIP, GUYS!
THIS IS THE REAL THING!
AND HE'S ON OUR SIDE!
ALL THE LATENT POWERS WITHIN THE GIRL, THAT MY COSMIC SENSES PREVIOUSLY REGISTERED, ARE NOW COMING TO FULL BLOOM!
REBIRTH.
REALIGNMENT.
THE ENERGIES RADIATING FROM HER ARE ASTRAL IN SCOPE!
ATLEZA!
WHAT'S IS SHE DOING?

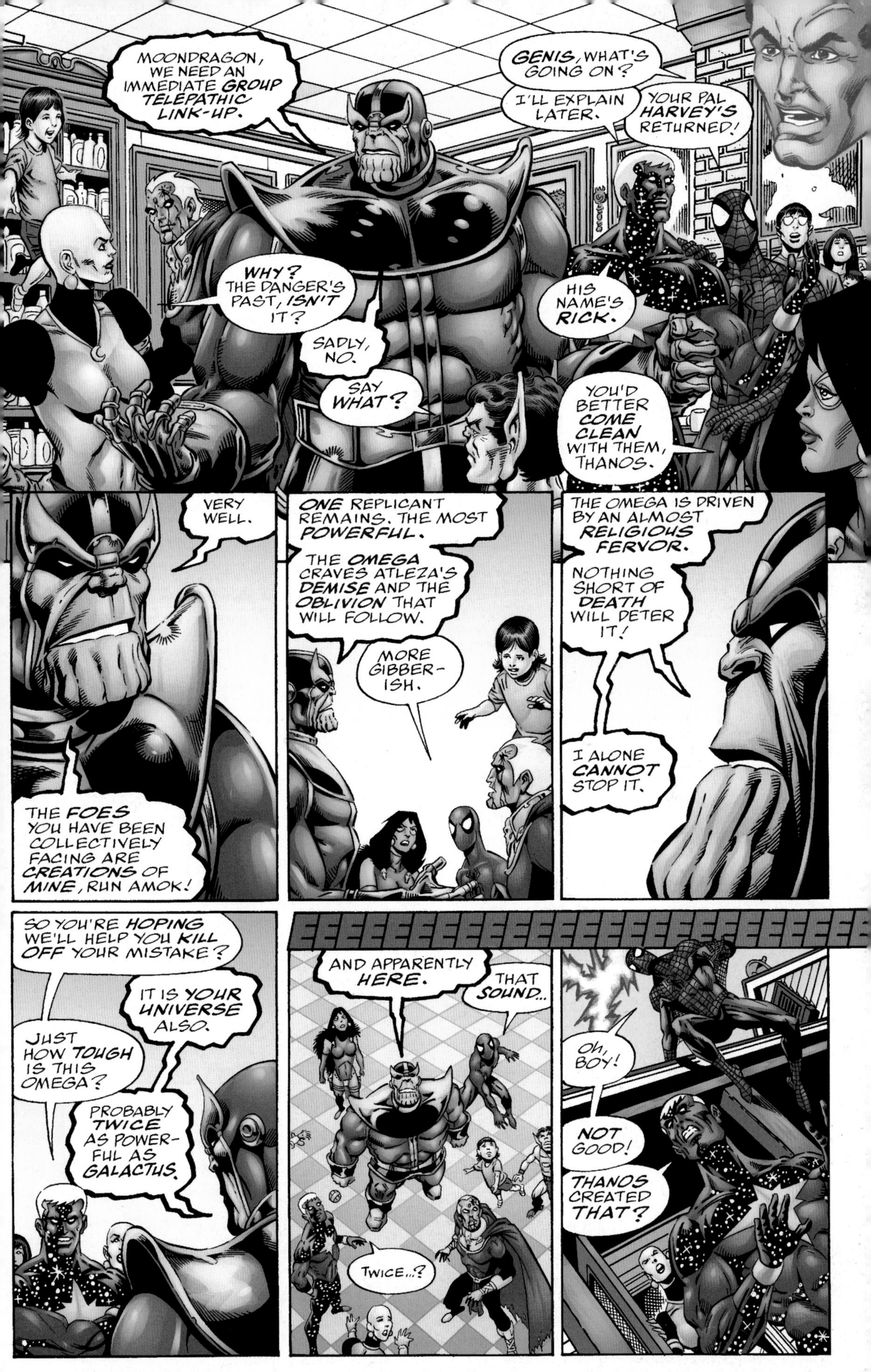
MOONDRAGON, WE NEED AN IMMEDIATE GROUP TELEPATHIC LINK-UP.
GENIS, WHAT'S GOING ON?
I'LL EXPLAIN LATER.
YOUR PAL HARVEY'S RETURNED!
WHY? THE DANGER'S PAST, ISN'T IT?
HIS NAME'S RICK.
SADLY, NO.
SAY WHAT?
YOU'D BETTER COME CLEAN WITH THEM, THANOS.
VERY WELL.
THE FOES YOU HAVE BEEN COLLECTIVELY FACING ARE CREATIONS OF MINE, RUN AMOK!
ONE REPLICANT REMAINS. THE MOST POWERFUL.
THE OMEGA CRAVES ATLEZA'S DEMISE AND THE OBLIVION THAT WILL FOLLOW.
MORE GIBBER-ISH.
THE OMEGA IS DRIVEN BY AN ALMOST RELIGIOUS FERVOR.
NOTHING SHORT OF DEATH WILL DETER IT!
I ALONE CANNOT STOP IT.
SO YOU'RE HOPING WE'LL HELP YOU KILL OFF YOUR MISTAKE?
IT IS YOUR UNIVERSE ALSO.
JUST HOW TOUGH IS THIS OMEGA?
PROBABLY TWICE AS POWER-FUL AS GALACTUS.
EEEEEEEEEEEEEEEEEEEEEEEEEEEEE
AND APPARENTLY HERE.
THAT SOUND...
TWICE...?
Oh, BOY!
NOT GOOD!
THANOS CREATED THAT?

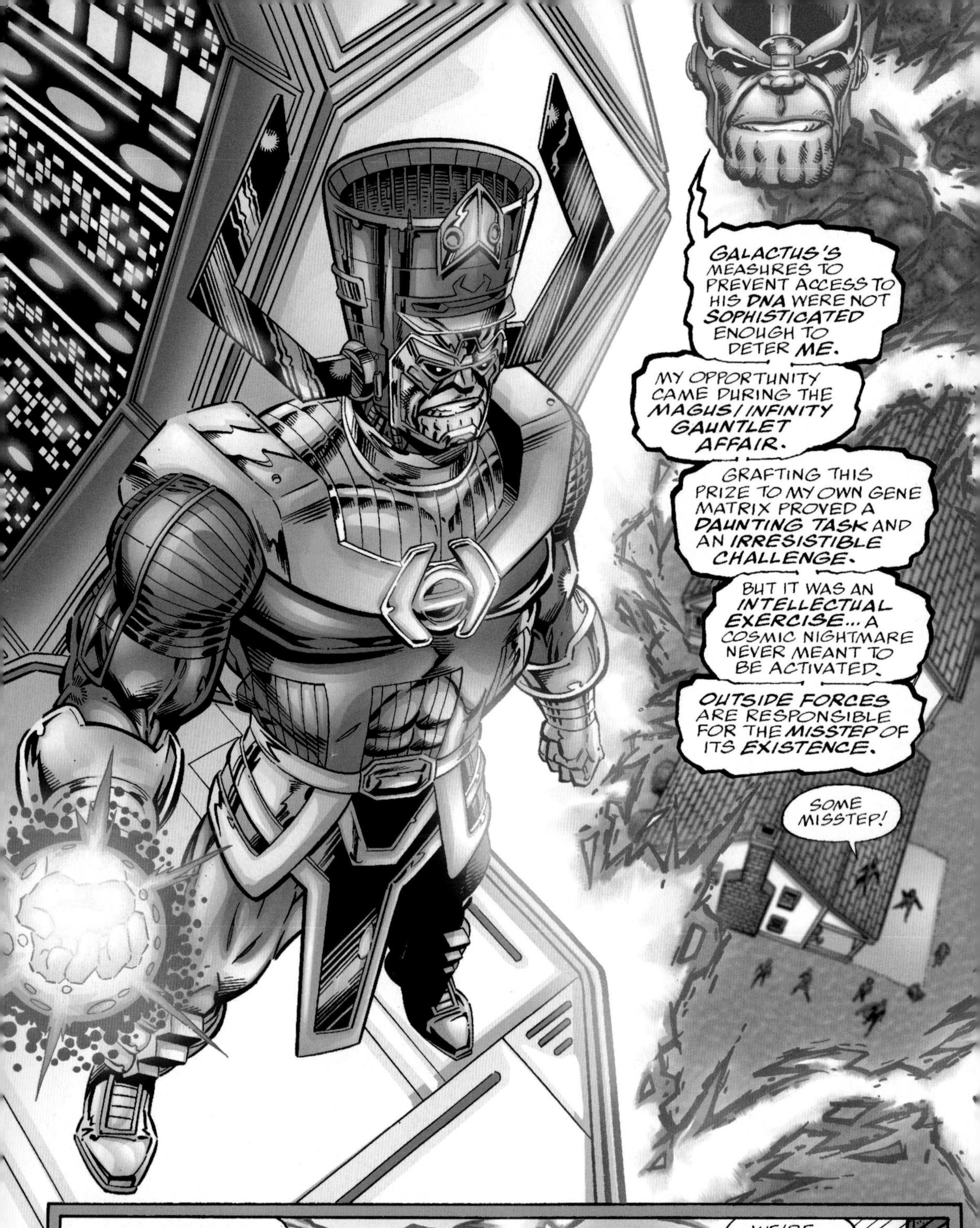
GALACTUS'S MEASURES TO PREVENT ACCESS TO HIS DNA WERE NOT SOPHISTICATED ENOUGH TO DETER ME.
MY OPPORTUNITY CAME DURING THE MAGUS/INFINITY GAUNTLET AFFAIR.
GRAFTING THIS PRIZE TO MY OWN GENE MATRIX PROVED A DAUNTING TASK AND AN IRRESISTIBLE CHALLENGE.
BUT IT WAS AN INTELLECTUAL EXERCISE... A COSMIC NIGHTMARE NEVER MEANT TO BE ACTIVATED.
OUTSIDE FORCES ARE RESPONSIBLE FOR THE MISSTEP OF ITS EXISTENCE.
SOME MISSTEP!

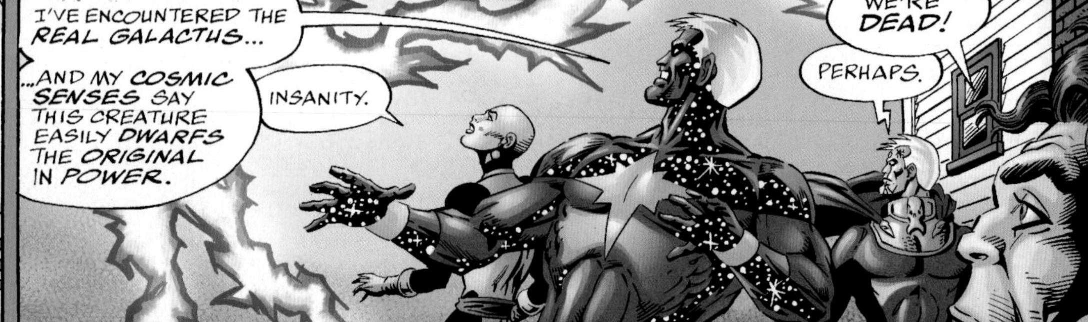
I'VE ENCOUNTERED THE REAL GALACTUS...
...AND MY COSMIC SENSES SAY THIS CREATURE EASILY DWARFS THE ORIGINAL IN POWER.
INSANITY.
WE'RE DEAD!
PERHAPS.

SURPRISE #1.

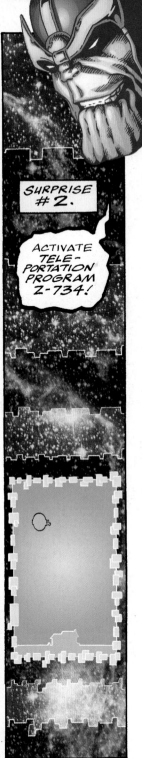

SURPRISE #2.

ACTIVATE TELE-PORTATION PROGRAM Z-734!

THERE WAS **NO** PREAMBLE TO THE OMEGA'S ASSAULT.

THANOS HADN'T BURDENED HIS FRANKENSTEIN WITH THE **GIFT OF SPEECH.**

WHY COMMUNICATE **VERBALLY** WHEN YOU WIELD SUCH **MIGHT?**

BUT WHEN DEALING WITH THE **MAD TITAN** ONE SHOULD **ALWAYS** EXPECT THE UNEX-PECTED.

A FORCE-FIELD! PROTECTING THE **HOUSE** AND US!

THIS HAS TO BE **THANOS'S** DOING!

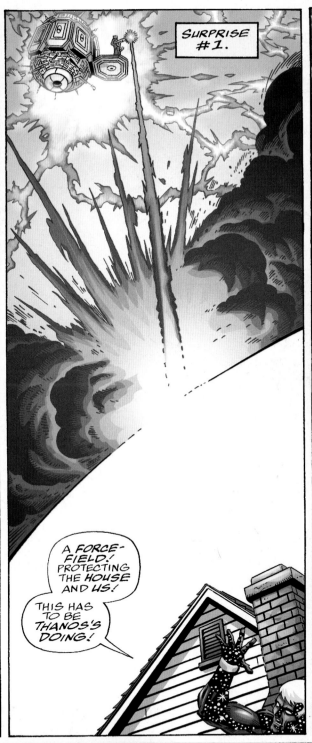

WHAT HAS THAT MANIAC DONE NOW?

WE'VE BEEN **TRANSPORTED** OFF **EARTH!**

MANIAC?

HEY! I DIDN'T DO THIS!

VERY CLEVER.

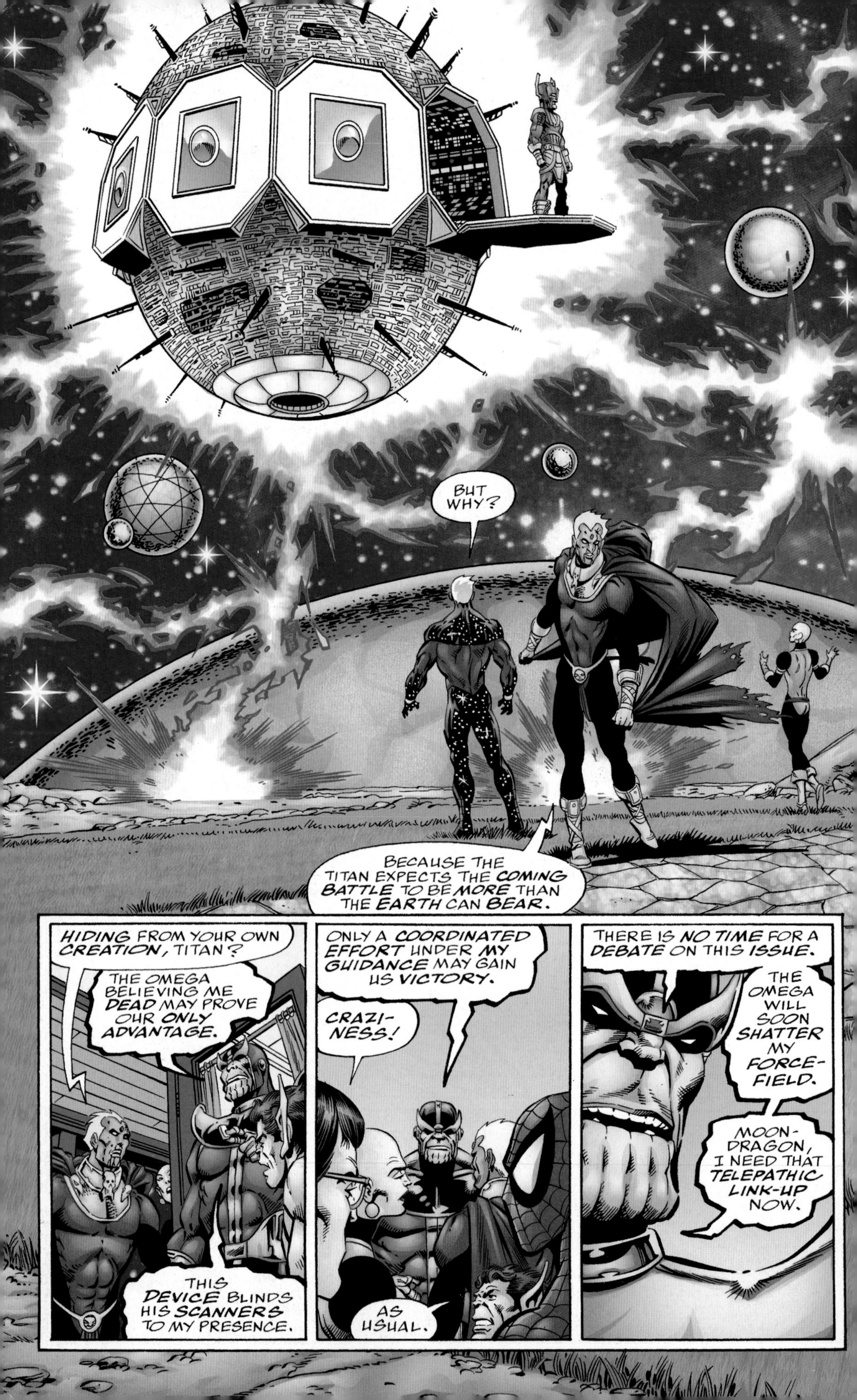
BUT WHY?
BECAUSE THE TITAN EXPECTS THE COMING BATTLE TO BE MORE THAN THE EARTH CAN BEAR.
HIDING FROM YOUR OWN CREATION, TITAN?
THE OMEGA BELIEVING ME DEAD MAY PROVE OUR ONLY ADVANTAGE.
THIS DEVICE BLINDS HIS SCANNERS TO MY PRESENCE.
ONLY A COORDINATED EFFORT UNDER MY GUIDANCE MAY GAIN US VICTORY.
CRAZINESS!
AS USUAL.
THERE IS NO TIME FOR A DEBATE ON THIS ISSUE.
THE OMEGA WILL SOON SHATTER MY FORCE-FIELD.
MOON-DRAGON, I NEED THAT TELEPATHIC LINK-UP NOW.

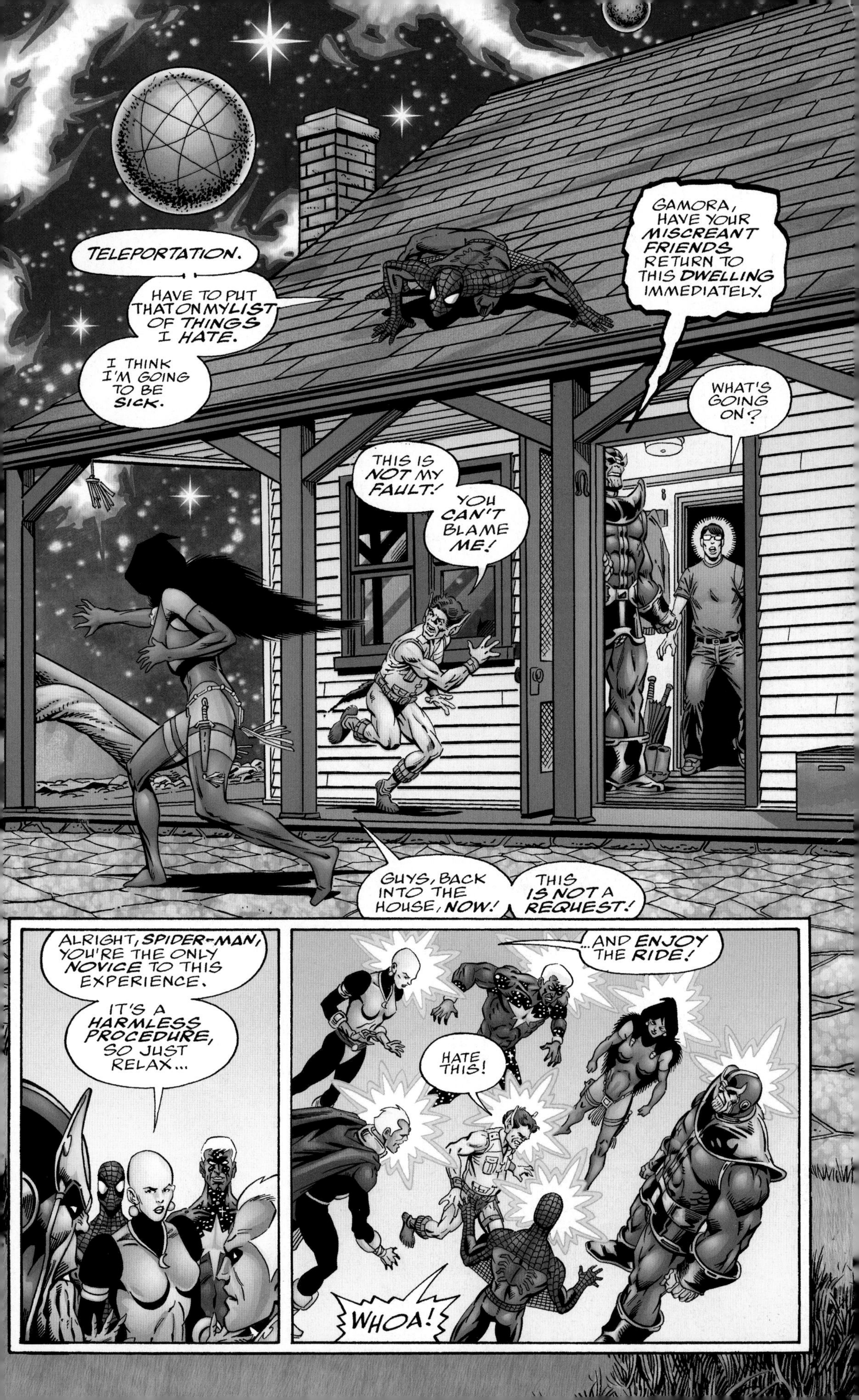
TELEPORTATION.
HAVE TO PUT THAT ON MY LIST OF THINGS I HATE.
I THINK I'M GOING TO BE SICK.
GAMORA, HAVE YOUR MISCREANT FRIENDS RETURN TO THIS DWELLING IMMEDIATELY.
WHAT'S GOING ON?
THIS IS NOT MY FAULT!
YOU CAN'T BLAME ME!
GUYS, BACK INTO THE HOUSE, NOW!
THIS IS NOT A REQUEST!
ALRIGHT, SPIDER-MAN, YOU'RE THE ONLY NOVICE TO THIS EXPERIENCE.
IT'S A HARMLESS PROCEDURE, SO JUST RELAX...
...AND ENJOY THE RIDE!
HATE THIS!
WHOA!

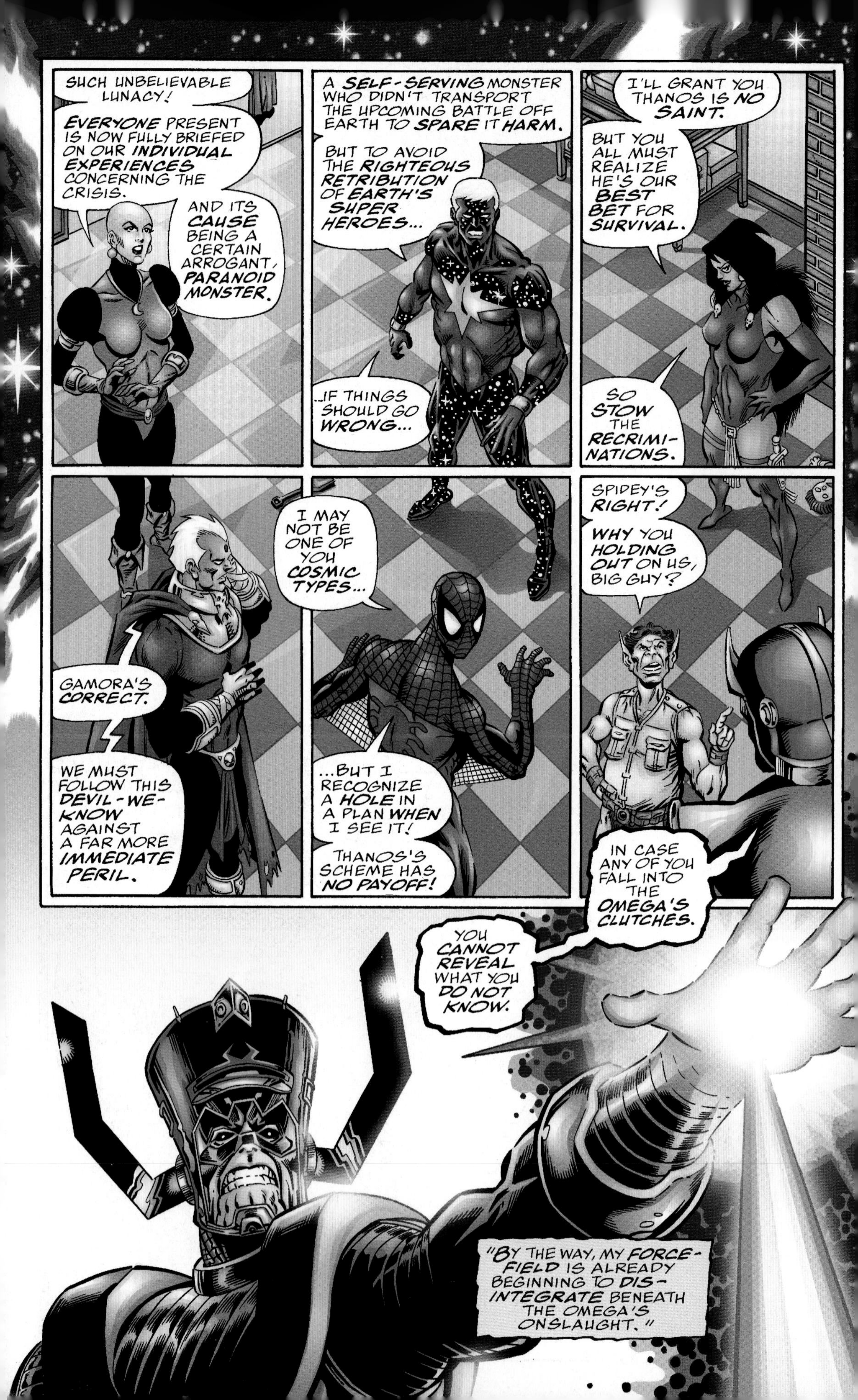
SUCH UNBELIEVABLE LUNACY!
EVERYONE PRESENT IS NOW FULLY BRIEFED ON OUR INDIVIDUAL EXPERIENCES CONCERNING THE CRISIS.
AND ITS CAUSE BEING A CERTAIN ARROGANT, PARANOID MONSTER.
A SELF-SERVING MONSTER WHO DIDN'T TRANSPORT THE UPCOMING BATTLE OFF EARTH TO SPARE IT HARM.
BUT TO AVOID THE RIGHTEOUS RETRIBUTION OF EARTH'S SUPER HEROES...
...IF THINGS SHOULD GO WRONG...
I'LL GRANT YOU THANOS IS NO SAINT.
BUT YOU ALL MUST REALIZE HE'S OUR BEST BET FOR SURVIVAL.
SO STOW THE RECRIMINATIONS.
GAMORA'S CORRECT.
WE MUST FOLLOW THIS DEVIL-WE-KNOW AGAINST A FAR MORE IMMEDIATE PERIL.
I MAY NOT BE ONE OF YOU COSMIC TYPES...
...BUT I RECOGNIZE A HOLE IN A PLAN WHEN I SEE IT!
THANOS'S SCHEME HAS NO PAYOFF!
SPIDEY'S RIGHT!
WHY YOU HOLDING OUT ON US, BIG GUY?
IN CASE ANY OF YOU FALL INTO THE OMEGA'S CLUTCHES.
YOU CANNOT REVEAL WHAT YOU DO NOT KNOW.
"BY THE WAY, MY FORCE-FIELD IS ALREADY BEGINNING TO DIS-INTEGRATE BENEATH THE OMEGA'S ONSLAUGHT."

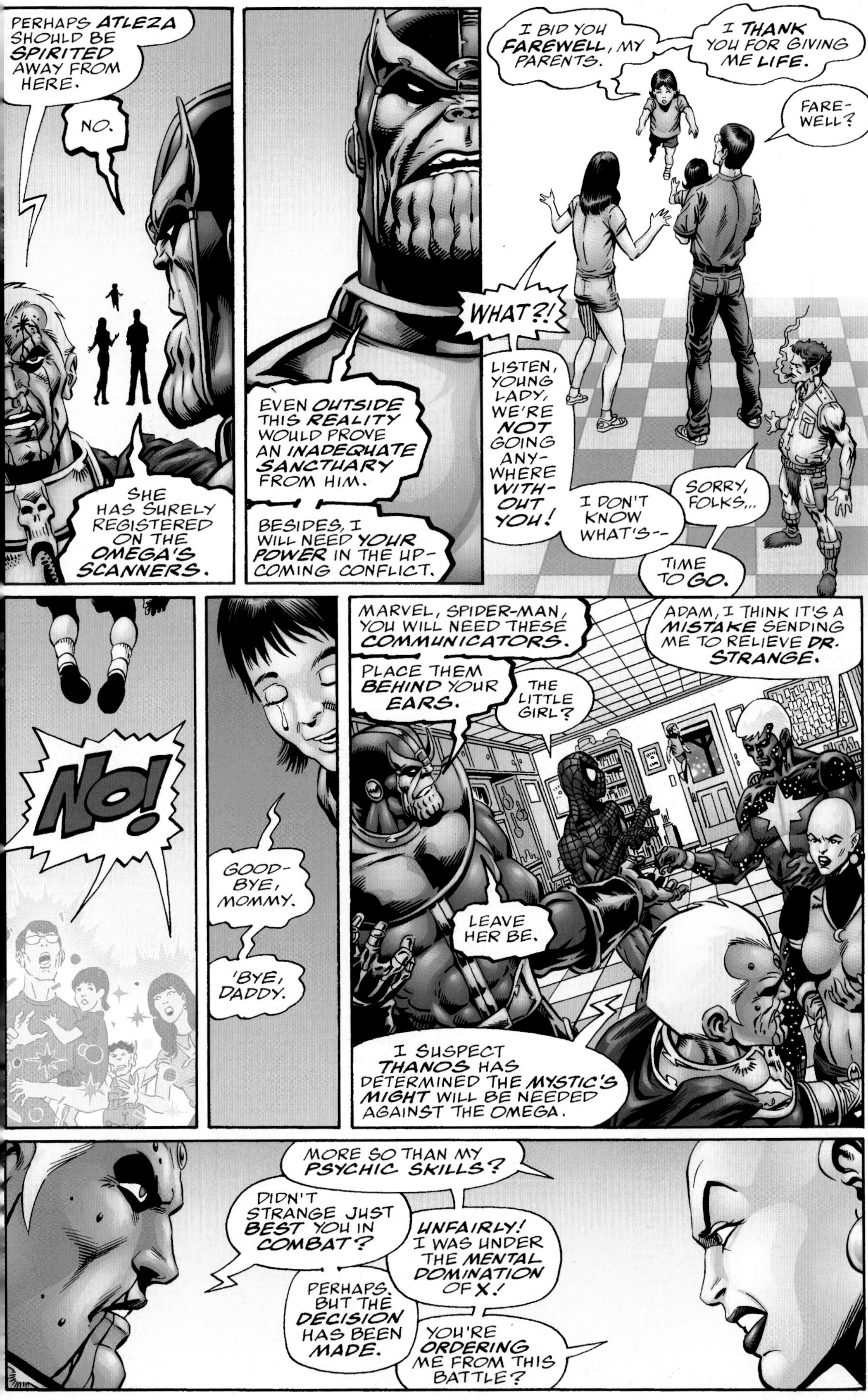
PERHAPS ATLEZA SHOULD BE SPIRITED AWAY FROM HERE.
NO.
SHE HAS SURELY REGISTERED ON THE OMEGA'S SCANNERS.
EVEN OUTSIDE THIS REALITY WOULD PROVE AN INADEQUATE SANCTUARY FROM HIM.
BESIDES, I WILL NEED YOUR POWER IN THE UP-COMING CONFLICT.
I BID YOU FAREWELL, MY PARENTS.
I THANK YOU FOR GIVING ME LIFE.
FARE-WELL?
WHAT?!
LISTEN, YOUNG LADY, WE'RE NOT GOING ANY-WHERE WITH-OUT YOU!
I DON'T KNOW WHAT'S--
SORRY, FOLKS...
TIME TO GO.
NO!
GOOD-BYE, MOMMY.
'BYE, DADDY.
MARVEL, SPIDER-MAN, YOU WILL NEED THESE COMMUNICATORS.
PLACE THEM BEHIND YOUR EARS.
THE LITTLE GIRL?
LEAVE HER BE.
ADAM, I THINK IT'S A MISTAKE SENDING ME TO RELIEVE DR. STRANGE.
I SUSPECT THANOS HAS DETERMINED THE MYSTIC'S MIGHT WILL BE NEEDED AGAINST THE OMEGA.
MORE SO THAN MY PSYCHIC SKILLS?
DIDN'T STRANGE JUST BEST YOU IN COMBAT?
UNFAIRLY! I WAS UNDER THE MENTAL DOMINATION OF X!
PERHAPS. BUT THE DECISION HAS BEEN MADE.
YOU'RE ORDERING ME FROM THIS BATTLE?

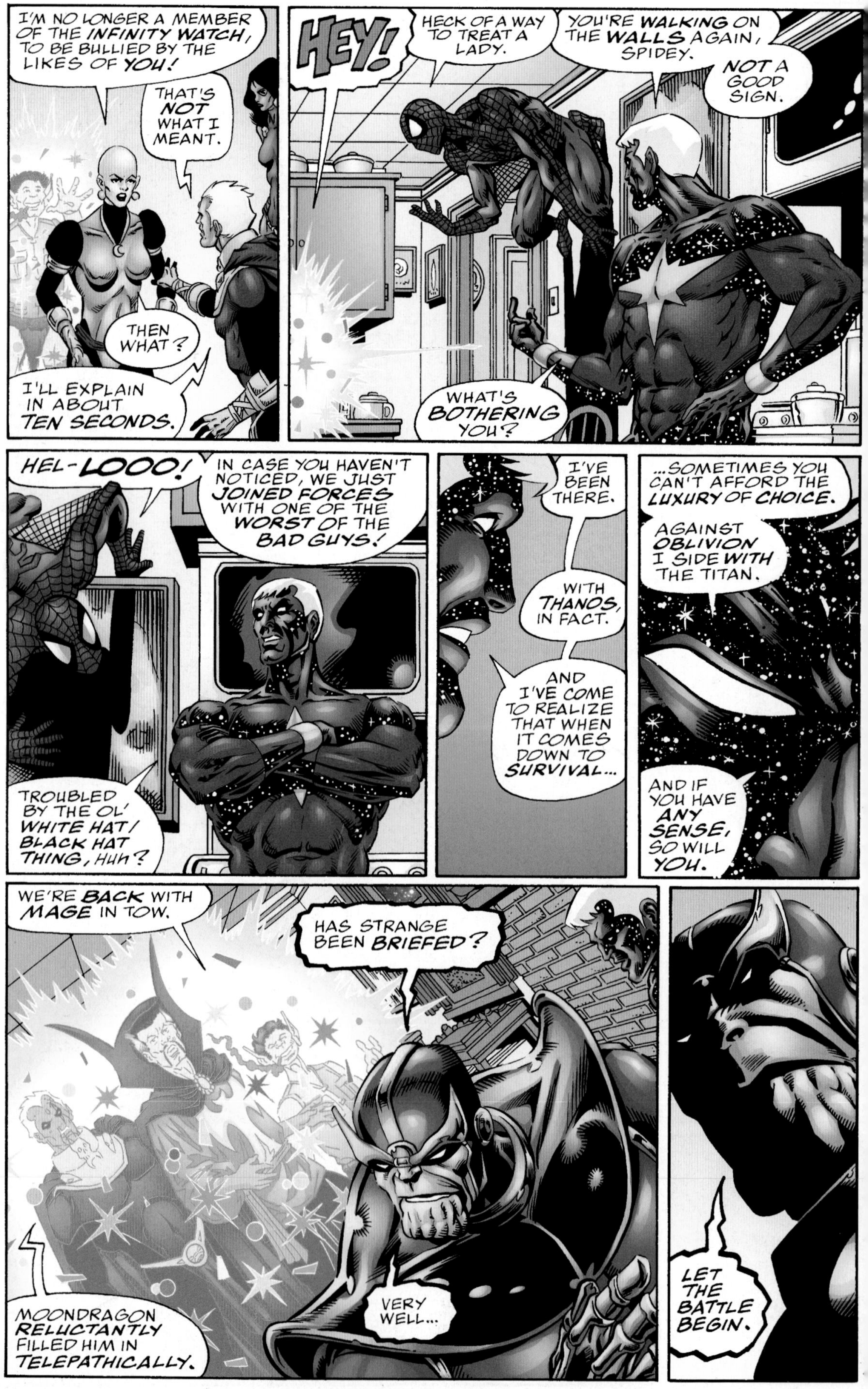

I'M NO LONGER A MEMBER OF THE INFINITY WATCH, TO BE BULLIED BY THE LIKES OF YOU!
THAT'S NOT WHAT I MEANT.
THEN WHAT?
I'LL EXPLAIN IN ABOUT TEN SECONDS.
HEY!
HECK OF A WAY TO TREAT A LADY.
YOU'RE WALKING ON THE WALLS AGAIN, SPIDEY.
NOT A GOOD SIGN.
WHAT'S BOTHERING YOU?
HEL-LOOO!
IN CASE YOU HAVEN'T NOTICED, WE JUST JOINED FORCES WITH ONE OF THE WORST OF THE BAD GUYS!
TROUBLED BY THE OL' WHITE HAT/ BLACK HAT THING, HUH?
I'VE BEEN THERE.
WITH THANOS, IN FACT.
AND I'VE COME TO REALIZE THAT WHEN IT COMES DOWN TO SURVIVAL...
...SOMETIMES YOU CAN'T AFFORD THE LUXURY OF CHOICE.
AGAINST OBLIVION I SIDE WITH THE TITAN.
AND IF YOU HAVE ANY SENSE, SO WILL YOU.
WE'RE BACK WITH MAGE IN TOW.
HAS STRANGE BEEN BRIEFED?
MOONDRAGON RELUCTANTLY FILLED HIM IN TELEPATHICALLY.
VERY WELL...
LET THE BATTLE BEGIN.

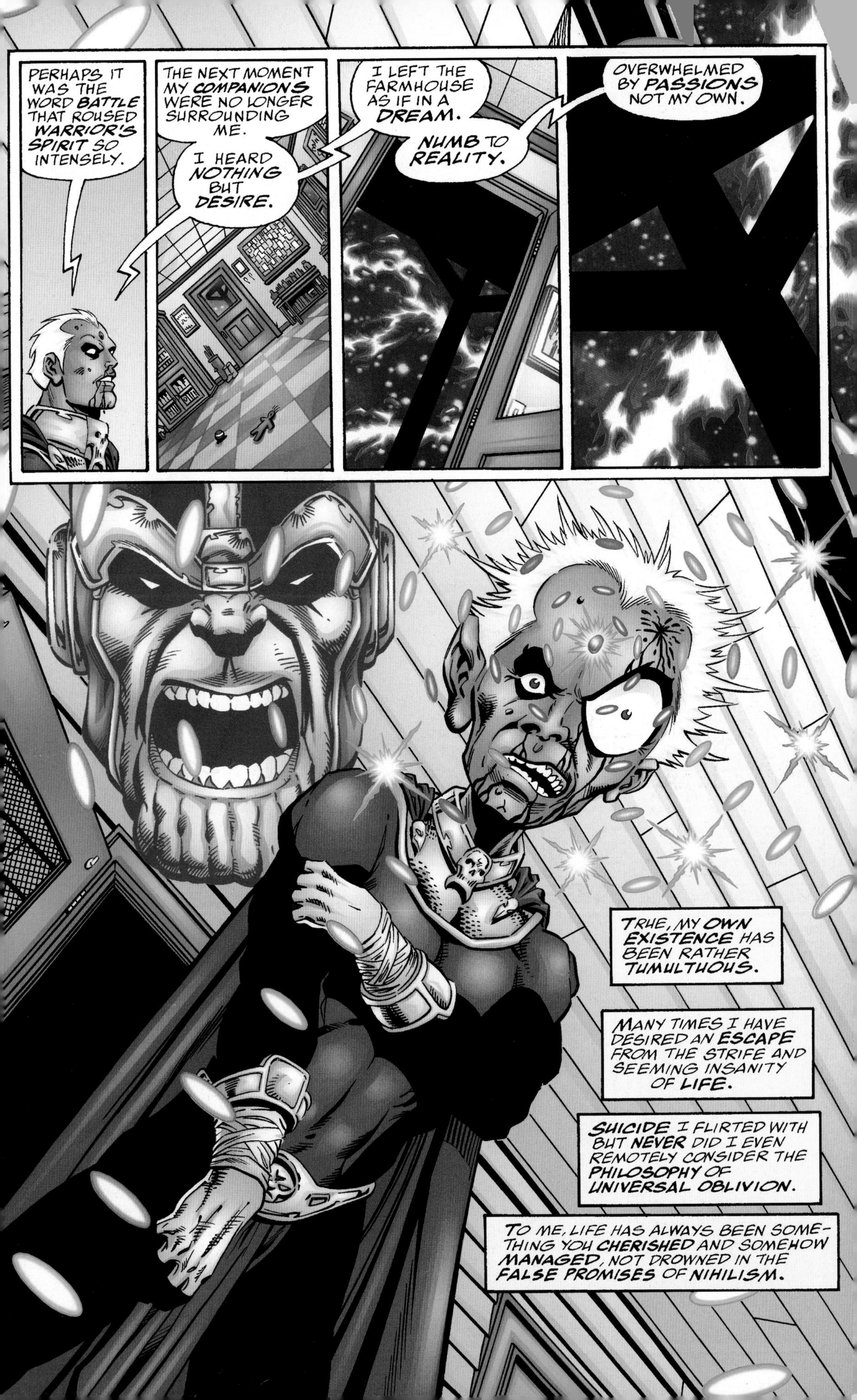
PERHAPS IT WAS THE WORD BATTLE THAT ROUSED WARRIOR'S SPIRIT SO INTENSELY.
THE NEXT MOMENT MY COMPANIONS WERE NO LONGER SURROUNDING ME.
I HEARD NOTHING BUT DESIRE.
I LEFT THE FARMHOUSE AS IF IN A DREAM.
NUMB TO REALITY.
OVERWHELMED BY PASSIONS NOT MY OWN.
TRUE, MY OWN EXISTENCE HAS BEEN RATHER TUMULTUOUS.
MANY TIMES I HAVE DESIRED AN ESCAPE FROM THE STRIFE AND SEEMING INSANITY OF LIFE.
SUICIDE I FLIRTED WITH BUT NEVER DID I EVEN REMOTELY CONSIDER THE PHILOSOPHY OF UNIVERSAL OBLIVION.
TO ME, LIFE HAS ALWAYS BEEN SOMETHING YOU CHERISHED AND SOMEHOW MANAGED, NOT DROWNED IN THE FALSE PROMISES OF NIHILISM.

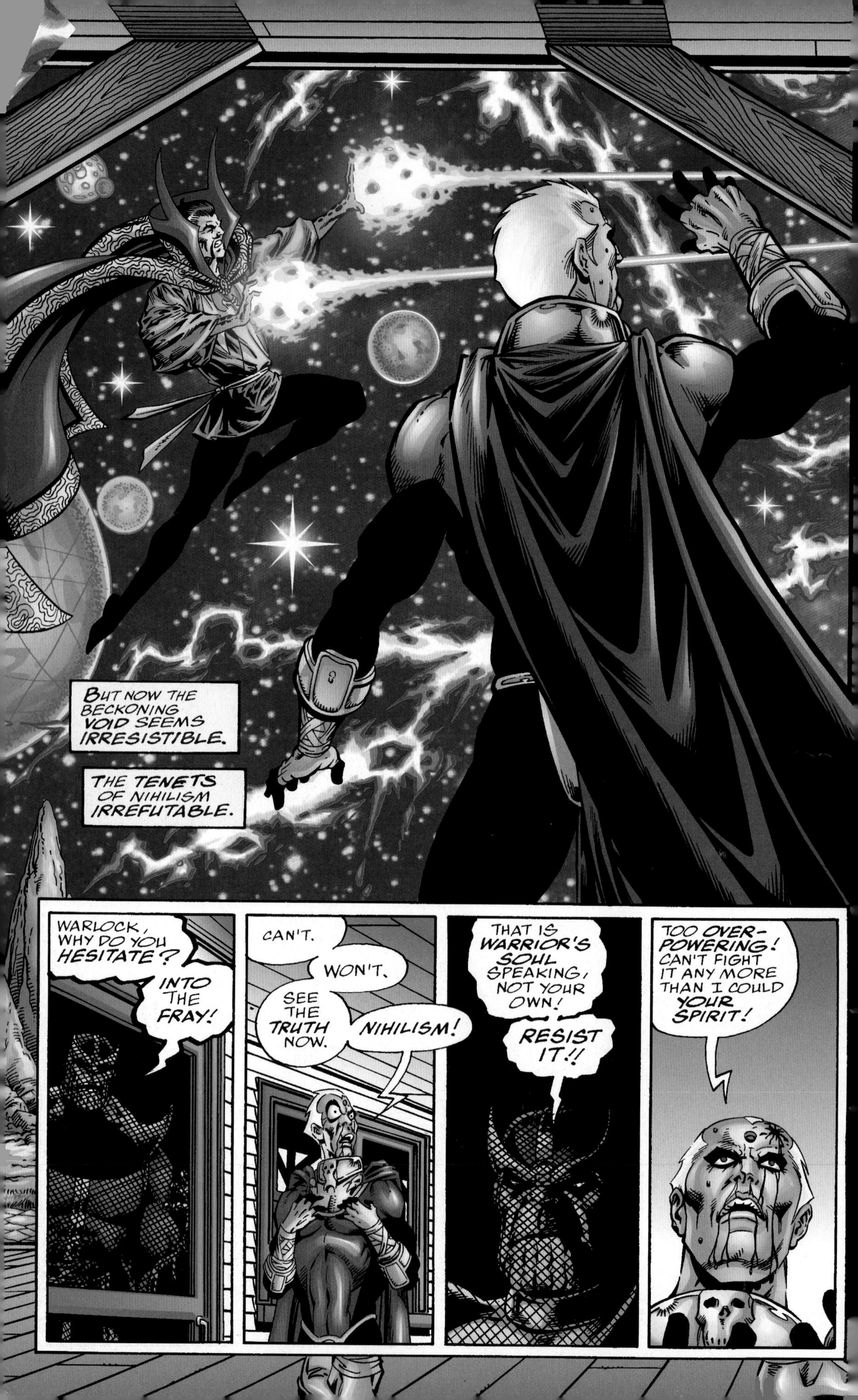
BUT NOW THE BECKONING VOID SEEMS IRRESISTIBLE.
THE TENETS OF NIHILISM IRREFUTABLE.
WARLOCK, WHY DO YOU HESITATE?
INTO THE FRAY!
CAN'T.
WON'T.
SEE THE TRUTH NOW.
NIHILISM!
THAT IS WARRIOR'S SOUL SPEAKING, NOT YOUR OWN!
RESIST IT!!
TOO OVER-POWERING! CAN'T FIGHT IT ANY MORE THAN I COULD YOUR SPIRIT!

WARLOCK, YOU ARE A *FOOL*.

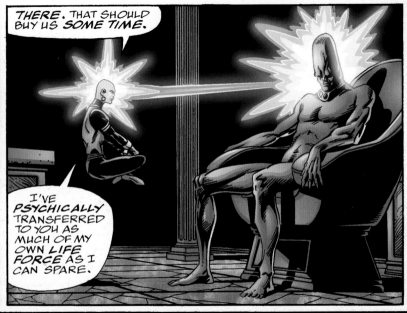

THERE. THAT SHOULD BUY US *SOME TIME.*

I'VE *PSYCHICALLY* TRANSFERRED TO YOU AS MUCH OF MY OWN *LIFE FORCE* AS I CAN SPARE.

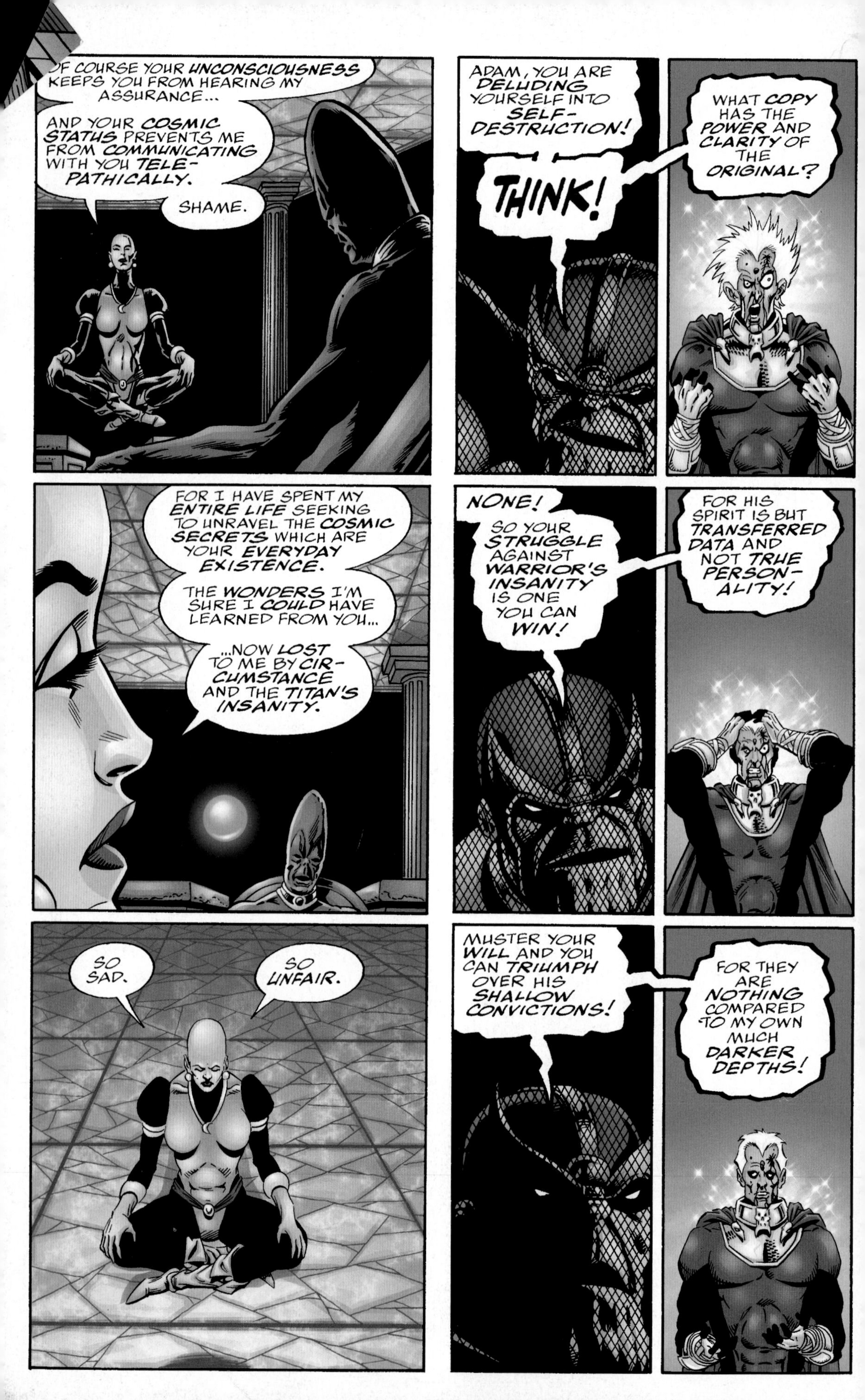
OF COURSE YOUR UNCONSCIOUSNESS KEEPS YOU FROM HEARING MY ASSURANCE...
AND YOUR COSMIC STATUS PREVENTS ME FROM COMMUNICATING WITH YOU TELE-PATHICALLY.
SHAME.
ADAM, YOU ARE DELUDING YOURSELF INTO SELF-DESTRUCTION!
THINK!
WHAT COPY HAS THE POWER AND CLARITY OF THE ORIGINAL?
FOR I HAVE SPENT MY ENTIRE LIFE SEEKING TO UNRAVEL THE COSMIC SECRETS WHICH ARE YOUR EVERYDAY EXISTENCE.
THE WONDERS I'M SURE I COULD HAVE LEARNED FROM YOU...
...NOW LOST TO ME BY CIR-CUMSTANCE AND THE TITAN'S INSANITY.
NONE!
SO YOUR STRUGGLE AGAINST WARRIOR'S INSANITY IS ONE YOU CAN WIN!
FOR HIS SPIRIT IS BUT TRANSFERRED DATA AND NOT TRUE PERSON-ALITY!
SO SAD.
SO UNFAIR.
MUSTER YOUR WILL AND YOU CAN TRIUMPH OVER HIS SHALLOW CONVICTIONS!
FOR THEY ARE NOTHING COMPARED TO MY OWN MUCH DARKER DEPTHS!

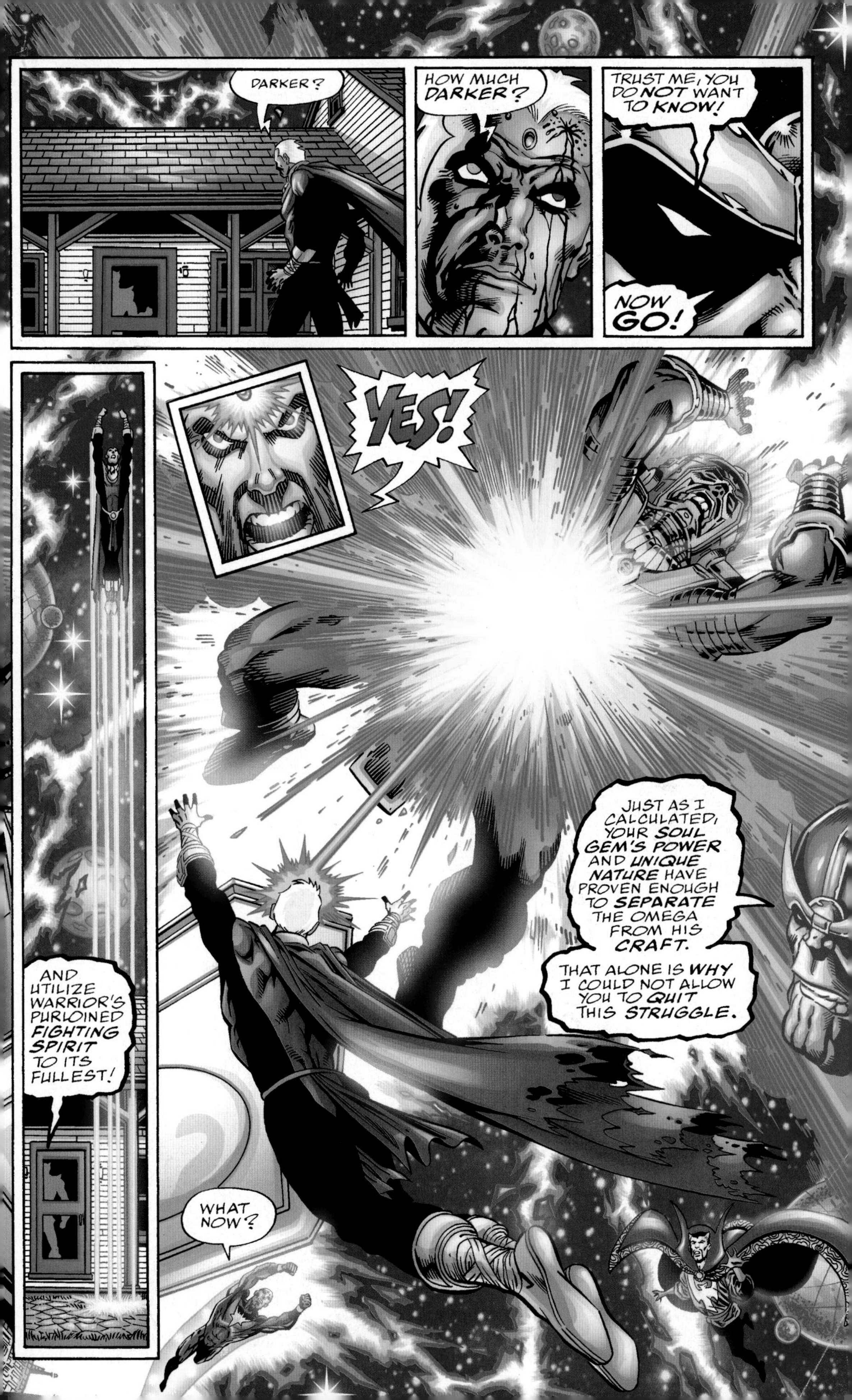
DARKER?
HOW MUCH DARKER?
TRUST ME, YOU DO NOT WANT TO KNOW!
NOW GO!
YES!
JUST AS I CALCULATED, YOUR SOUL GEM'S POWER AND UNIQUE NATURE HAVE PROVEN ENOUGH TO SEPARATE THE OMEGA FROM HIS CRAFT.
THAT ALONE IS WHY I COULD NOT ALLOW YOU TO QUIT THIS STRUGGLE.
AND UTILIZE WARRIOR'S PURLOINED FIGHTING SPIRIT TO ITS FULLEST!
WHAT NOW?

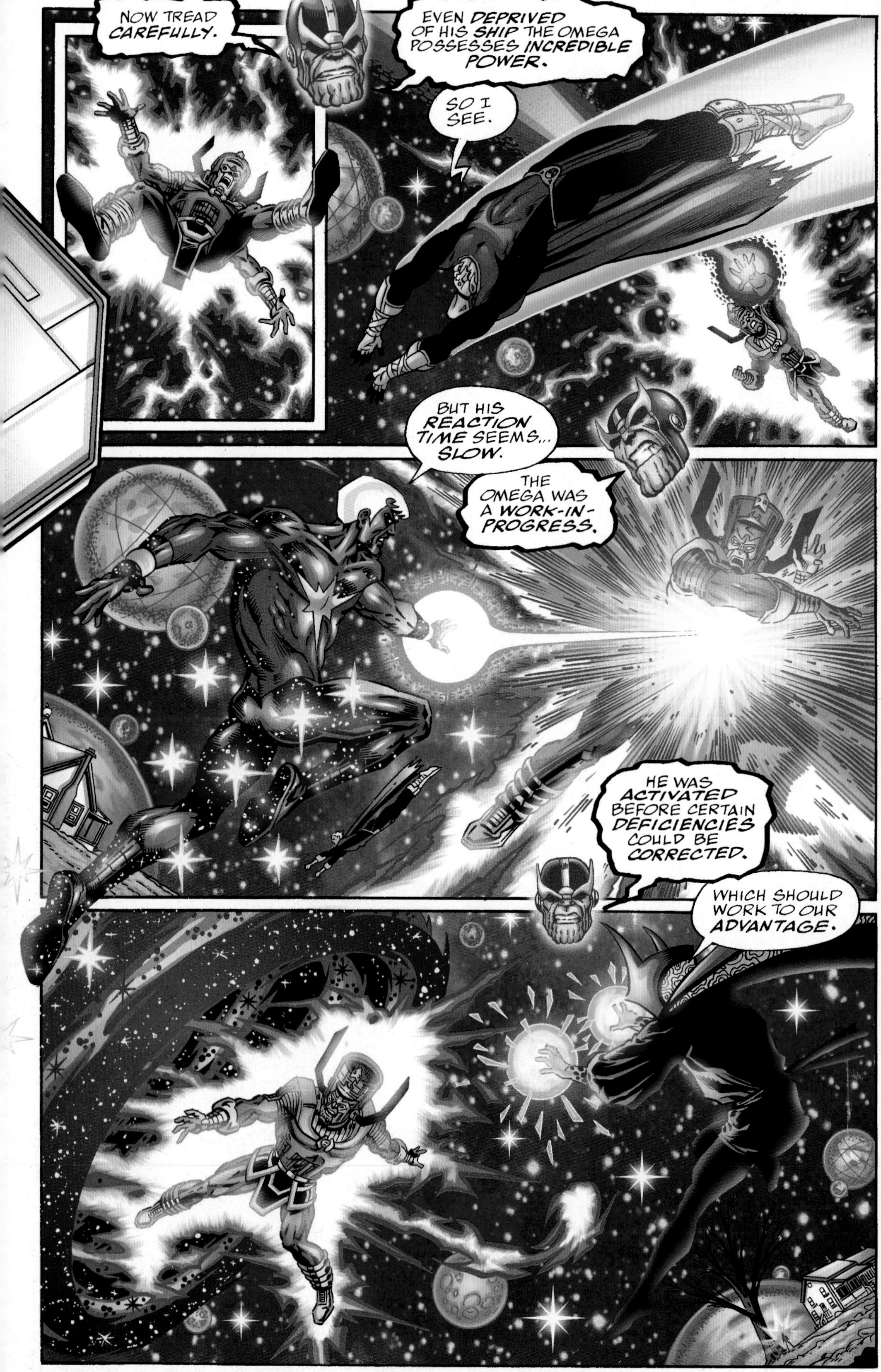
NOW TREAD CAREFULLY.
EVEN DEPRIVED OF HIS SHIP THE OMEGA POSSESSES INCREDIBLE POWER.
SO I SEE.
BUT HIS REACTION TIME SEEMS... SLOW.
THE OMEGA WAS A WORK-IN-PROGRESS.
HE WAS ACTIVATED BEFORE CERTAIN DEFICIENCIES COULD BE CORRECTED.
WHICH SHOULD WORK TO OUR ADVANTAGE.

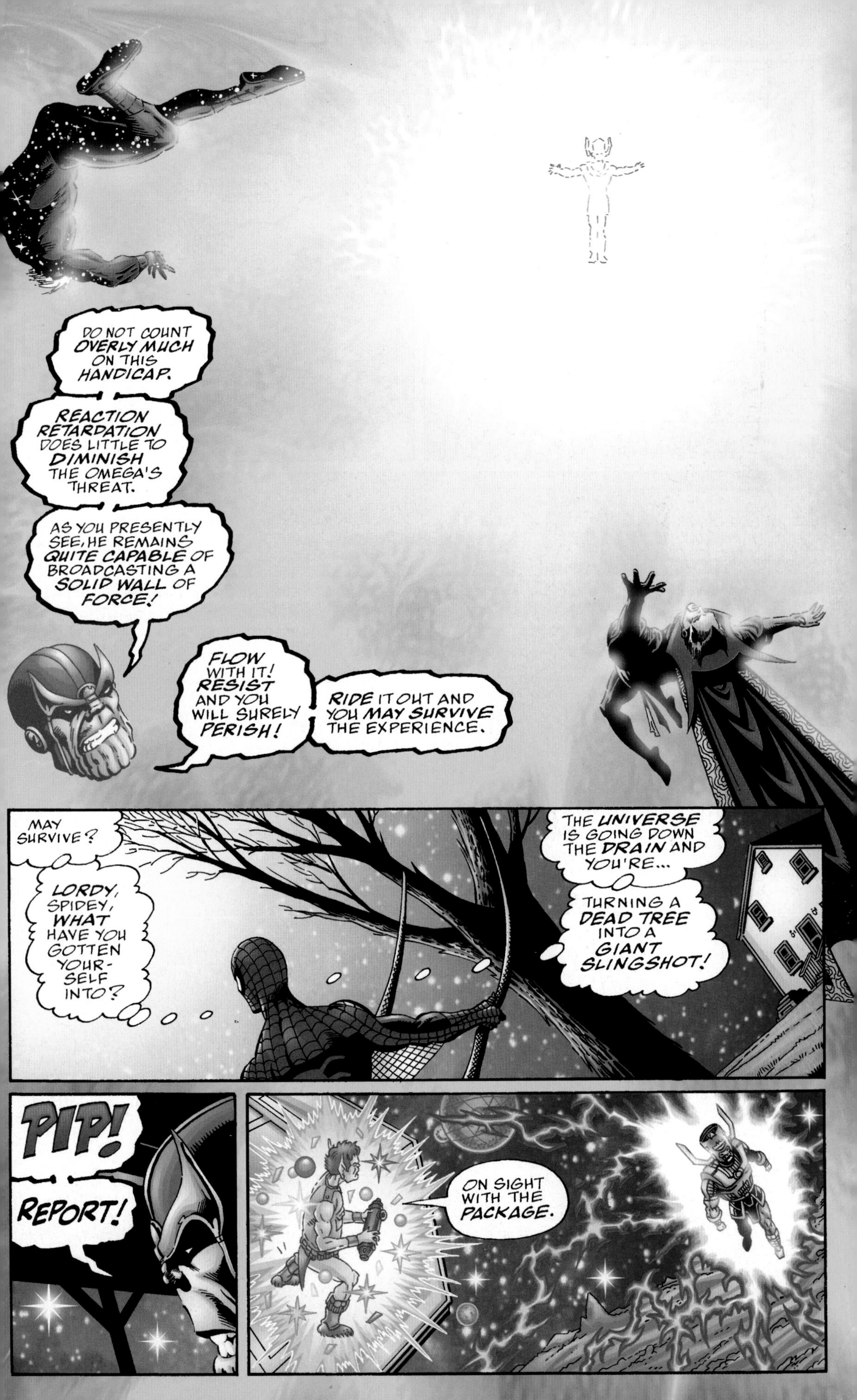
DO NOT COUNT OVERLY MUCH ON THIS HANDICAP.
REACTION RETARDATION DOES LITTLE TO DIMINISH THE OMEGA'S THREAT.
AS YOU PRESENTLY SEE, HE REMAINS QUITE CAPABLE OF BROADCASTING A SOLID WALL OF FORCE!
FLOW WITH IT! RESIST AND YOU WILL SURELY PERISH!
RIDE IT OUT AND YOU MAY SURVIVE THE EXPERIENCE.
MAY SURVIVE?
LORDY, SPIDEY, WHAT HAVE YOU GOTTEN YOURSELF INTO?
THE UNIVERSE IS GOING DOWN THE DRAIN AND YOU'RE...
TURNING A DEAD TREE INTO A GIANT SLINGSHOT!
PIP!
REPORT!
ON SIGHT WITH THE PACKAGE.

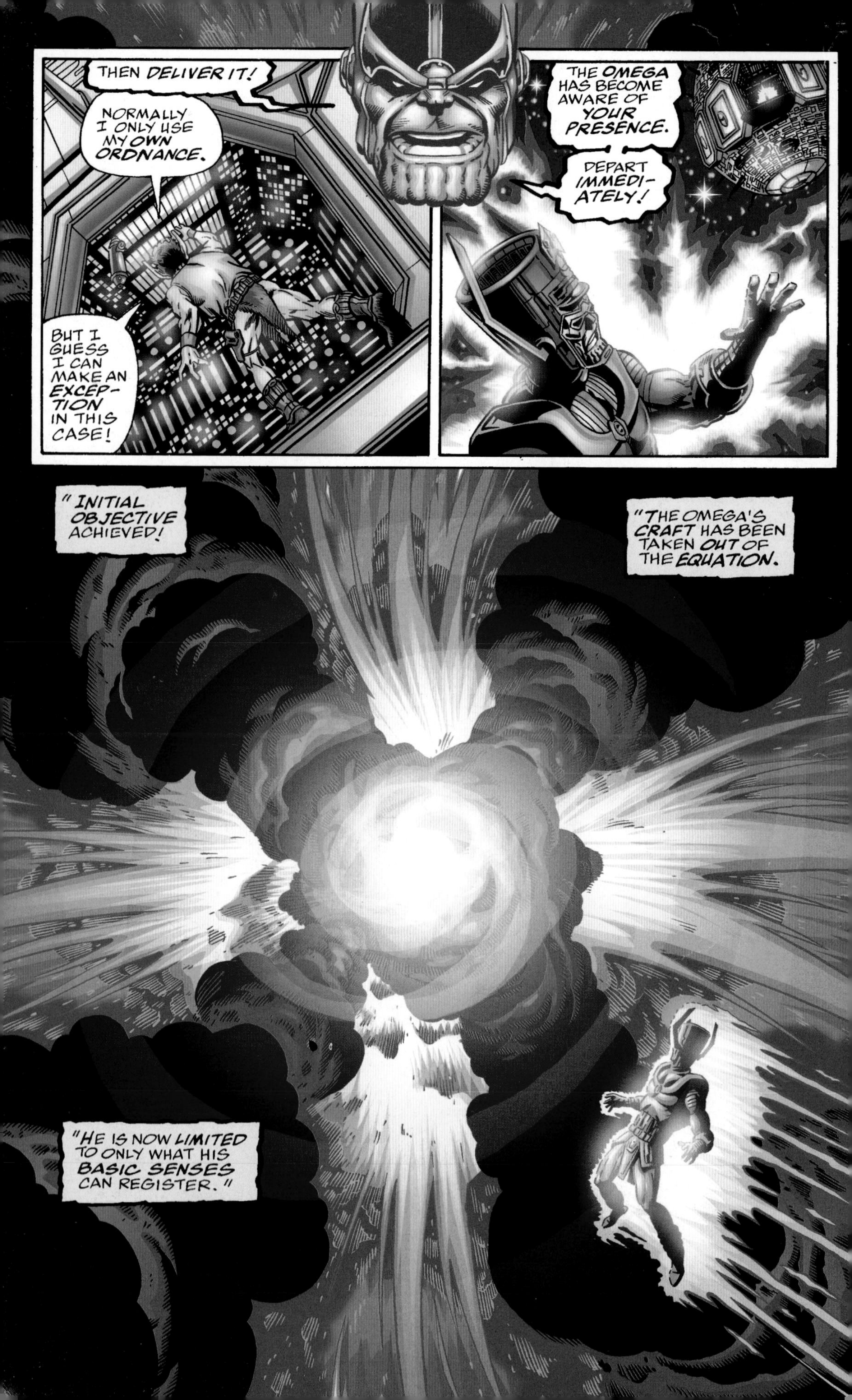

THEN DELIVER IT!
NORMALLY I ONLY USE MY OWN ORDNANCE.
BUT I GUESS I CAN MAKE AN EXCEPTION IN THIS CASE!
THE OMEGA HAS BECOME AWARE OF YOUR PRESENCE.
DEPART IMMEDIATELY!
"INITIAL OBJECTIVE ACHIEVED!
"THE OMEGA'S CRAFT HAS BEEN TAKEN OUT OF THE EQUATION.
"HE IS NOW LIMITED TO ONLY WHAT HIS BASIC SENSES CAN REGISTER."

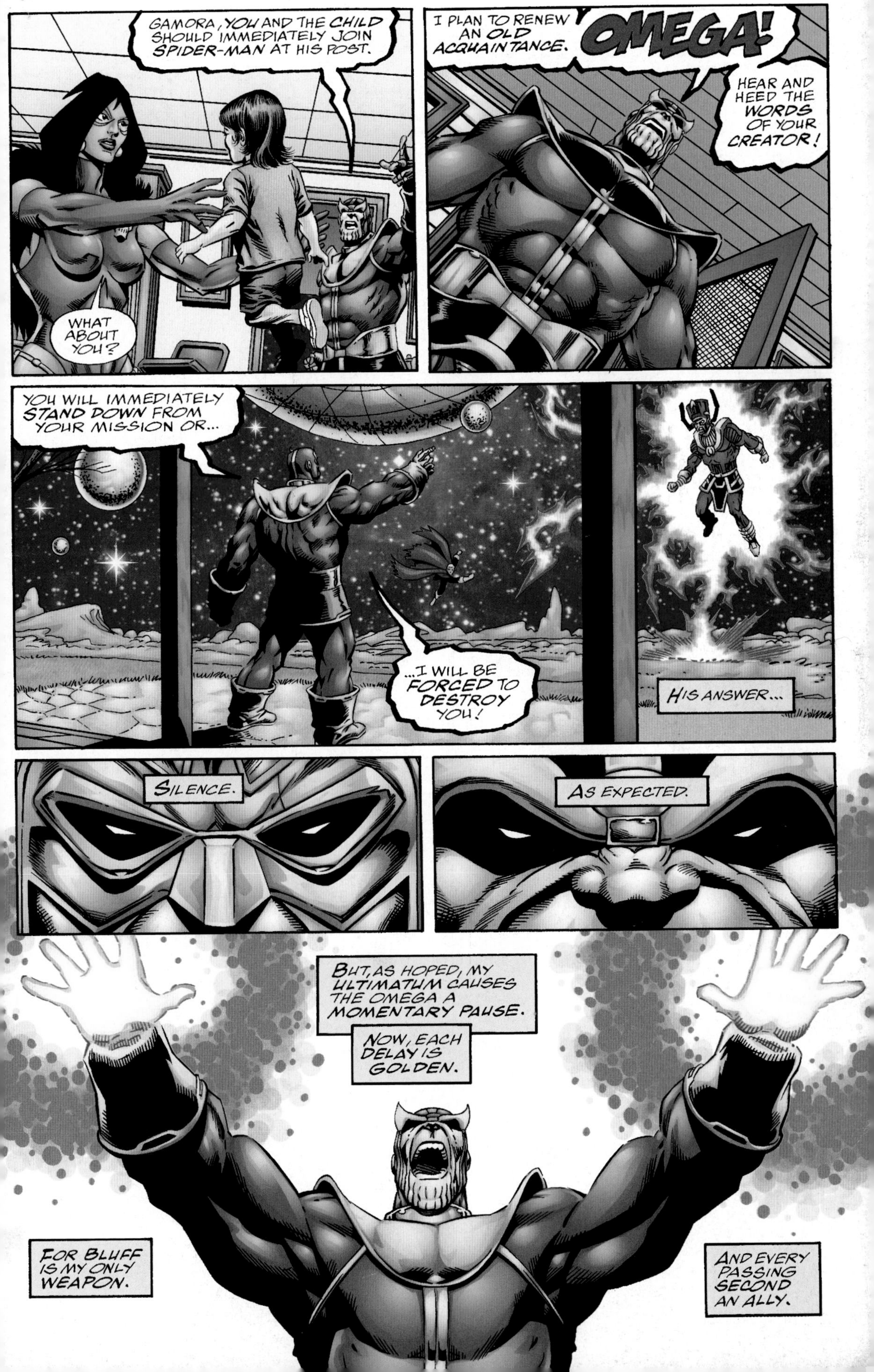
GAMORA, YOU AND THE CHILD SHOULD IMMEDIATELY JOIN SPIDER-MAN AT HIS POST.
WHAT ABOUT YOU?
I PLAN TO RENEW AN OLD ACQUAINTANCE.
OMEGA!
HEAR AND HEED THE WORDS OF YOUR CREATOR!
YOU WILL IMMEDIATELY STAND DOWN FROM YOUR MISSION OR...
...I WILL BE FORCED TO DESTROY YOU!
HIS ANSWER...
SILENCE.
AS EXPECTED.
BUT, AS HOPED, MY ULTIMATUM CAUSES THE OMEGA A MOMENTARY PAUSE.
NOW, EACH DELAY IS GOLDEN.
FOR BLUFF IS MY ONLY WEAPON.
AND EVERY PASSING SECOND AN ALLY.

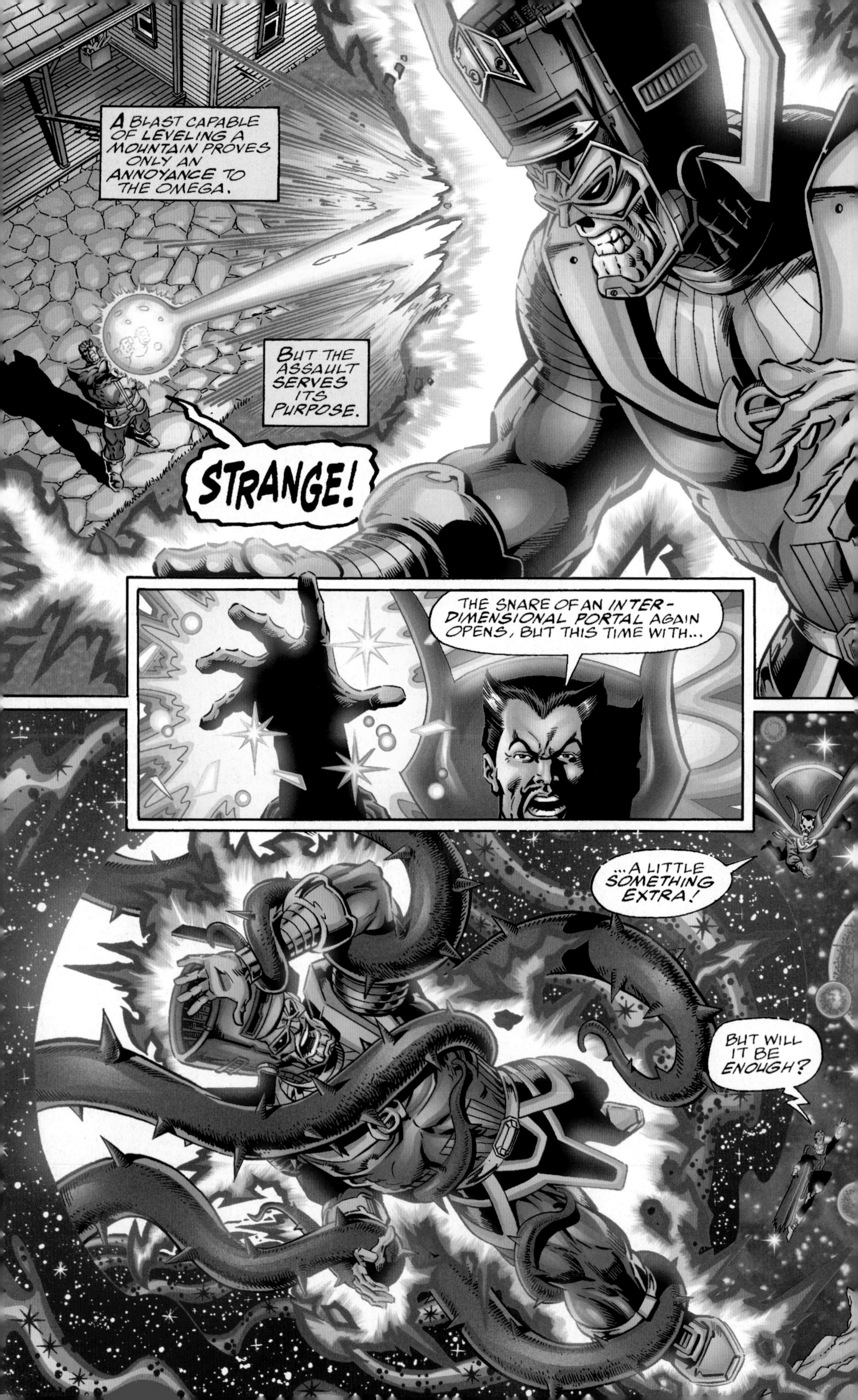
A BLAST CAPABLE OF LEVELING A MOUNTAIN PROVES ONLY AN ANNOYANCE TO THE OMEGA.
BUT THE ASSAULT SERVES ITS PURPOSE.
STRANGE!
THE SNARE OF AN INTER-DIMENSIONAL PORTAL AGAIN OPENS, BUT THIS TIME WITH...
...A LITTLE SOMETHING EXTRA!
BUT WILL IT BE ENOUGH?

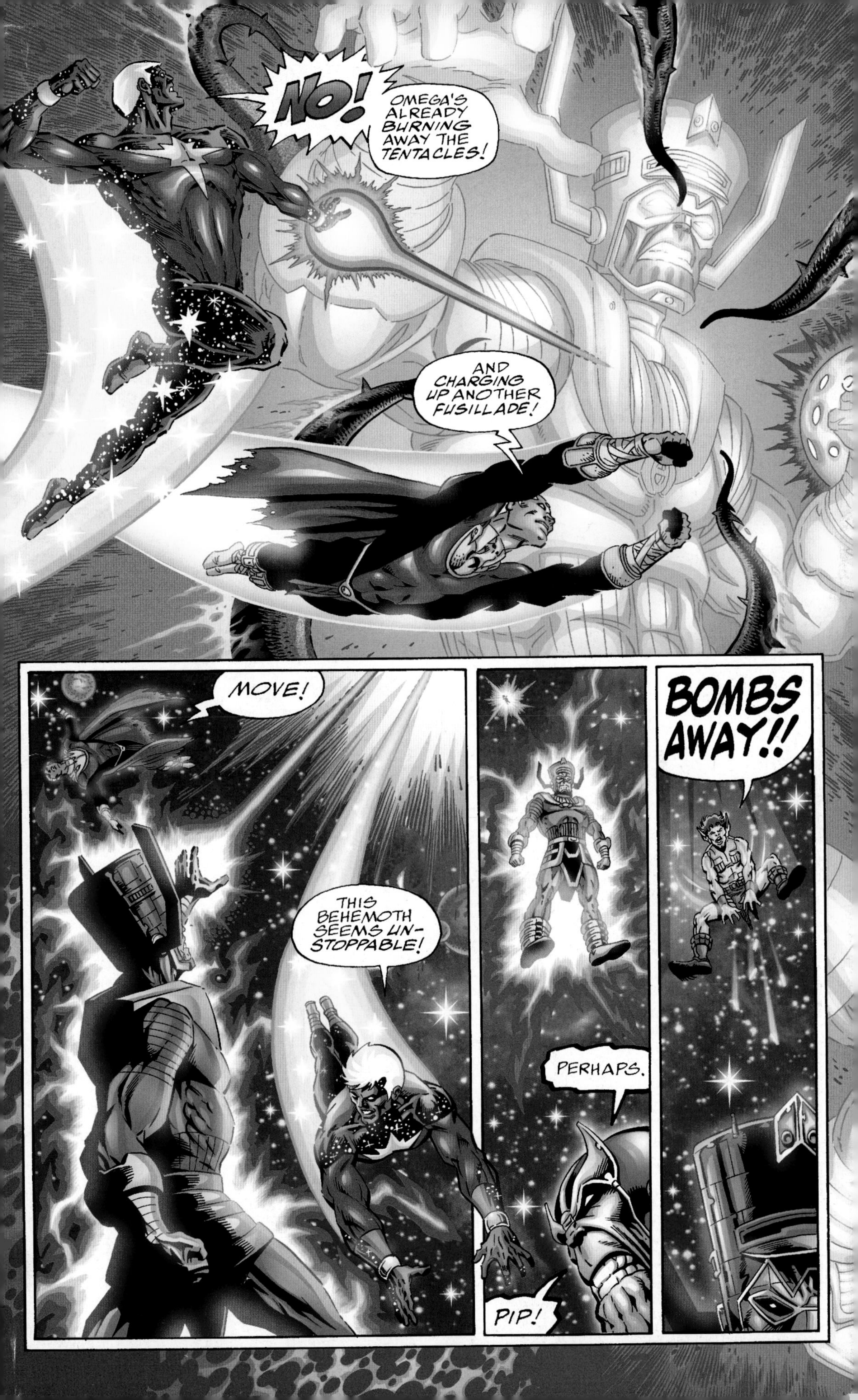
NO!
OMEGA'S ALREADY BURNING AWAY THE TENTACLES!
AND CHARGING UP ANOTHER FUSILLADE!
MOVE!
THIS BEHEMOTH SEEMS UN-STOPPABLE!
PERHAPS.
PIP!
BOMBS AWAY!!

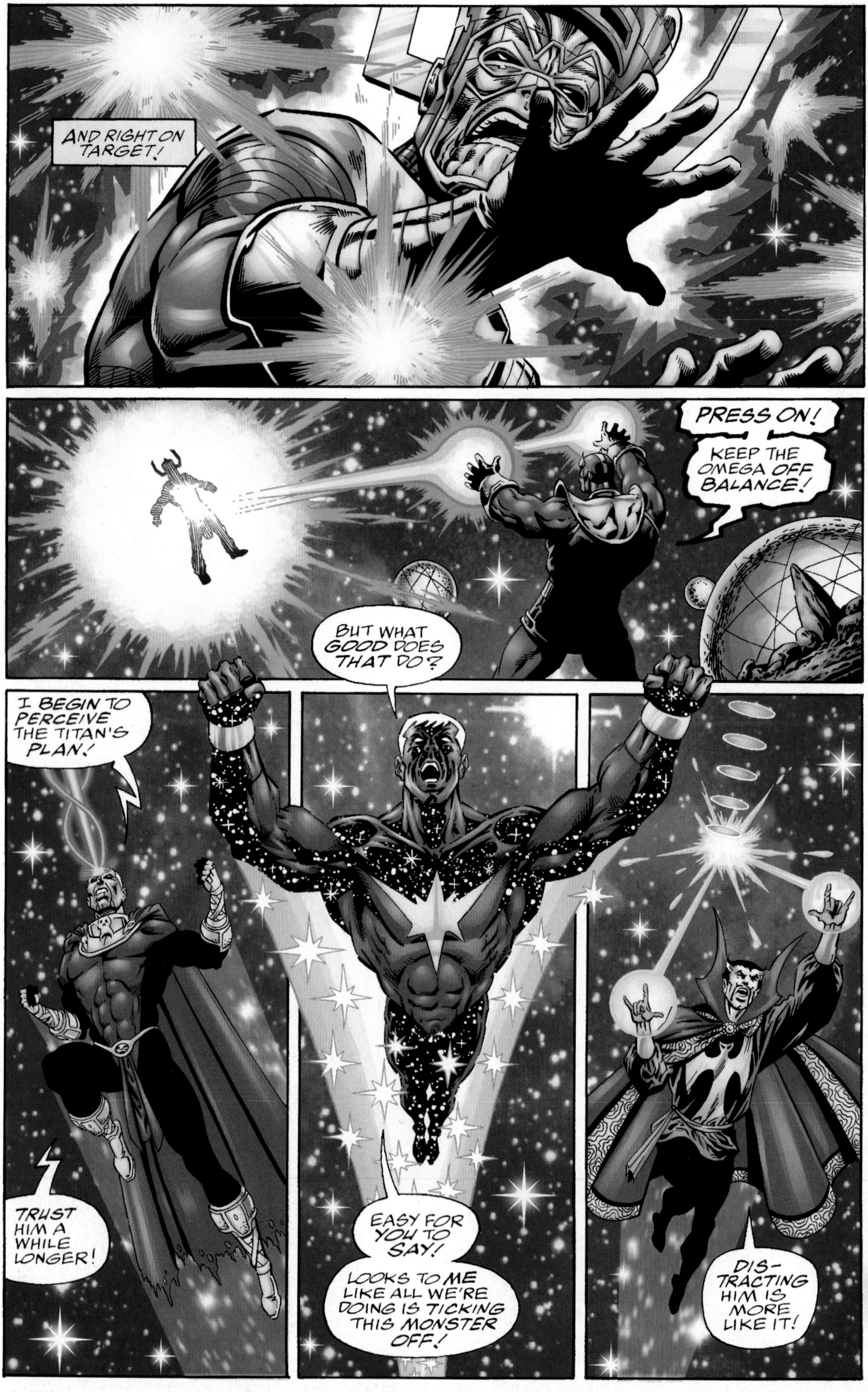
AND RIGHT ON TARGET!
PRESS ON!
KEEP THE OMEGA OFF BALANCE!
BUT WHAT GOOD DOES THAT DO?
I BEGIN TO PERCEIVE THE TITAN'S PLAN!
TRUST HIM A WHILE LONGER!
EASY FOR YOU TO SAY!
LOOKS TO ME LIKE ALL WE'RE DOING IS TICKING THIS MONSTER OFF!
DIS-TRACTING HIM IS MORE LIKE IT!

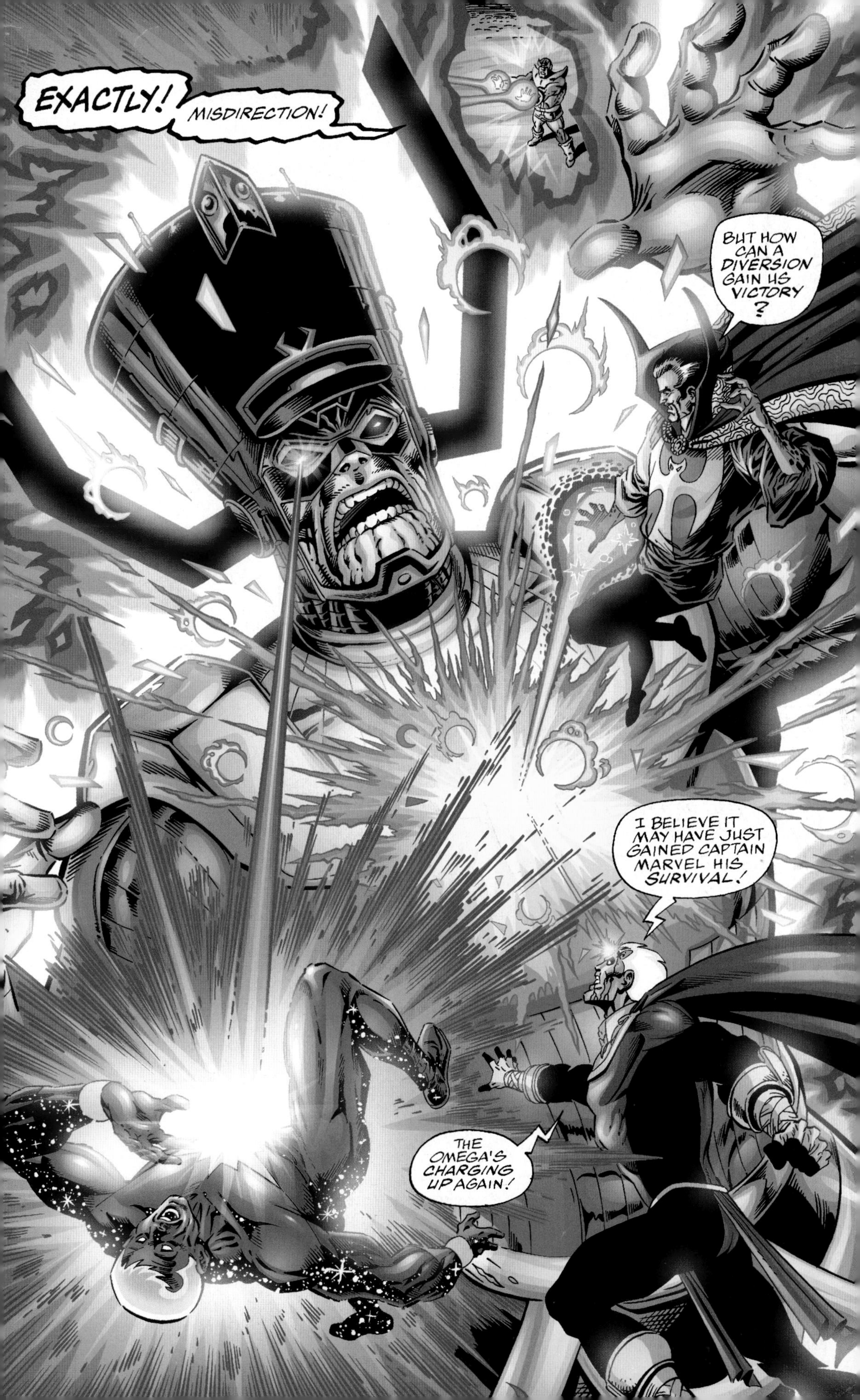
EXACTLY! MISDIRECTION!
BUT HOW CAN A DIVERSION GAIN US VICTORY?
I BELIEVE IT MAY HAVE JUST GAINED CAPTAIN MARVEL HIS SURVIVAL!
THE OMEGA'S CHARGING UP AGAIN!

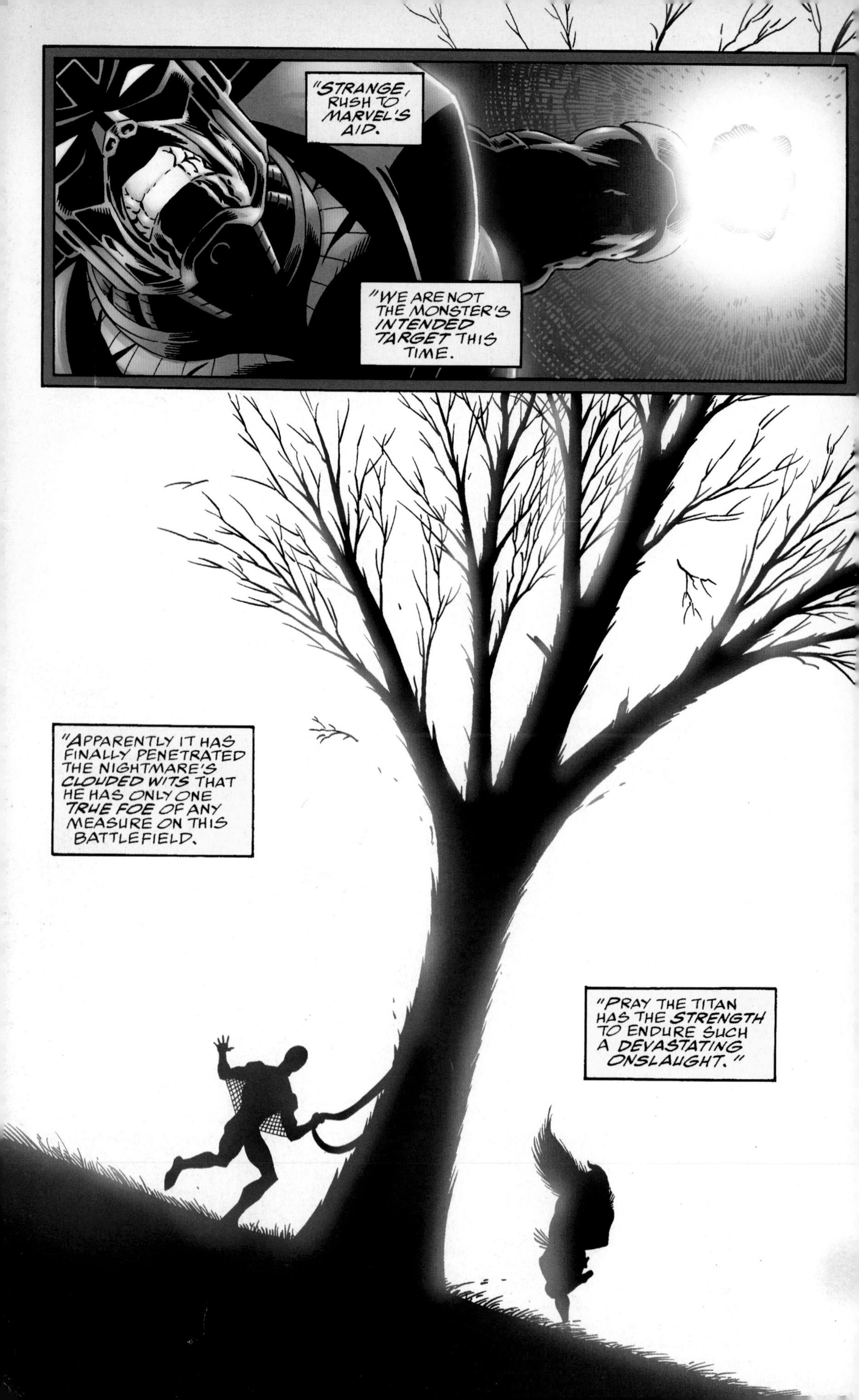
"STRANGE, RUSH TO MARVEL'S AID.
"WE ARE NOT THE MONSTER'S INTENDED TARGET THIS TIME.
"APPARENTLY IT HAS FINALLY PENETRATED THE NIGHTMARE'S CLOUDED WITS THAT HE HAS ONLY ONE TRUE FOE OF ANY MEASURE ON THIS BATTLEFIELD.
"PRAY THE TITAN HAS THE STRENGTH TO ENDURE SUCH A DEVASTATING ONSLAUGHT."

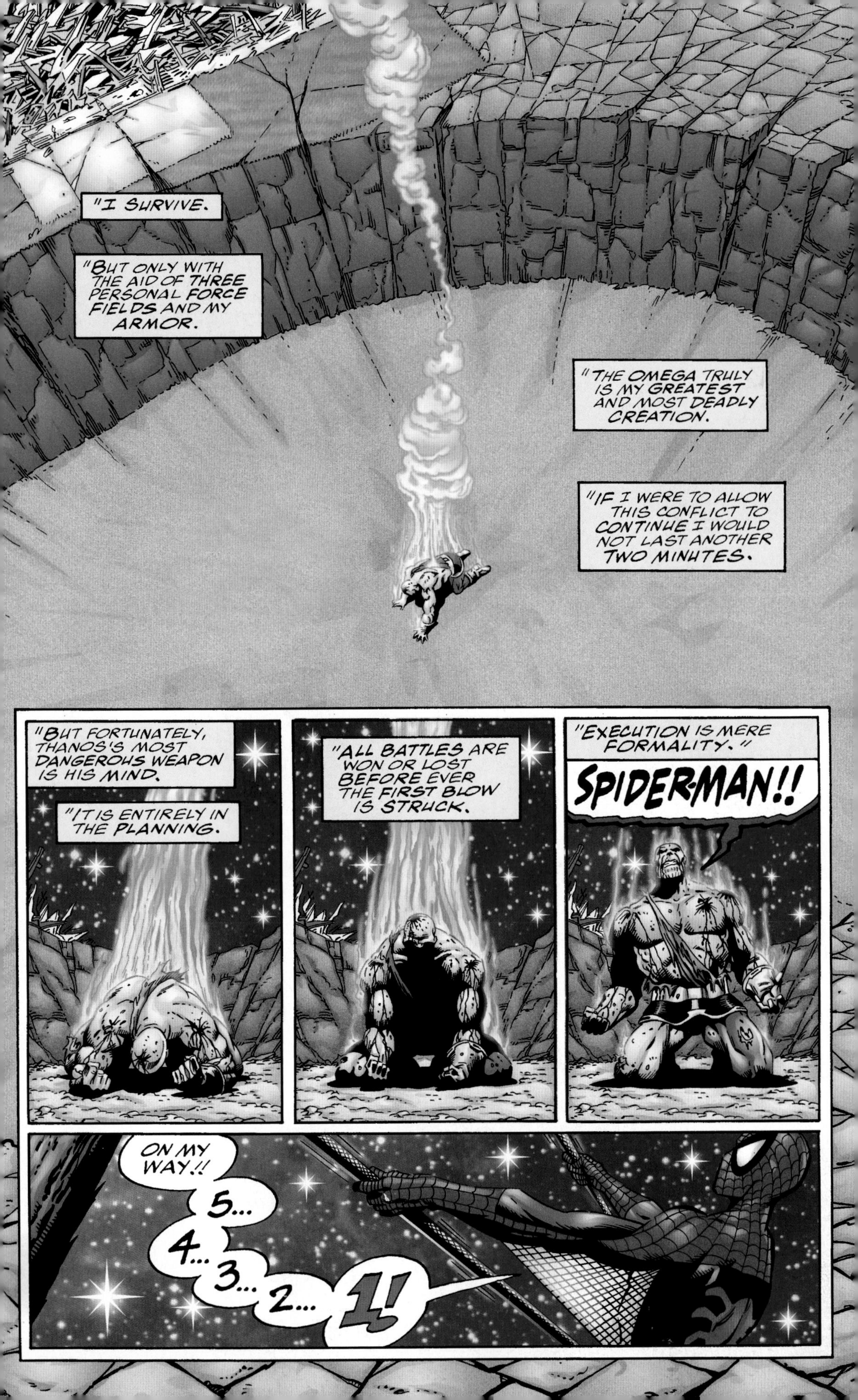
"I SURVIVE.
"BUT ONLY WITH THE AID OF THREE PERSONAL FORCE FIELDS AND MY ARMOR.
"THE OMEGA TRULY IS MY GREATEST AND MOST DEADLY CREATION.
"IF I WERE TO ALLOW THIS CONFLICT TO CONTINUE I WOULD NOT LAST ANOTHER TWO MINUTES.
"BUT FORTUNATELY, THANOS'S MOST DANGEROUS WEAPON IS HIS MIND.
"IT IS ENTIRELY IN THE PLANNING.
"ALL BATTLES ARE WON OR LOST BEFORE EVER THE FIRST BLOW IS STRUCK.
"EXECUTION IS MERE FORMALITY."
SPIDER-MAN!!
ON MY WAY!!
5...
4...
3...
2...
1!

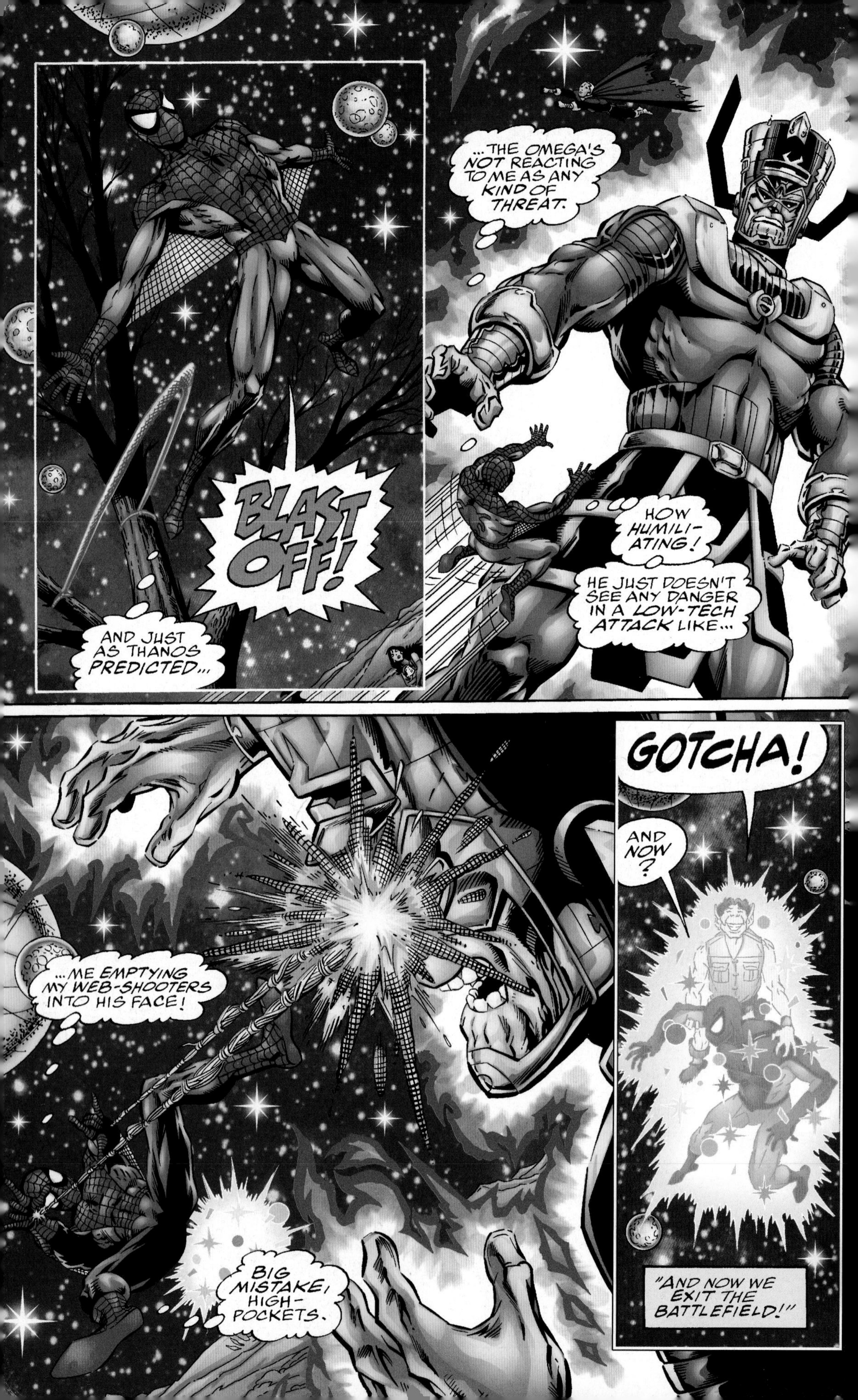
BLAST OFF!
AND JUST AS THANOS PREDICTED...
...THE OMEGA'S NOT REACTING TO ME AS ANY KIND OF THREAT.
HOW HUMILI-ATING!
HE JUST DOESN'T SEE ANY DANGER IN A LOW-TECH ATTACK LIKE...
...ME EMPTYING MY WEB-SHOOTERS INTO HIS FACE!
BIG MISTAKE, HIGH-POCKETS.
GOTCHA!
AND NOW?
"AND NOW WE EXIT THE BATTLEFIELD!"

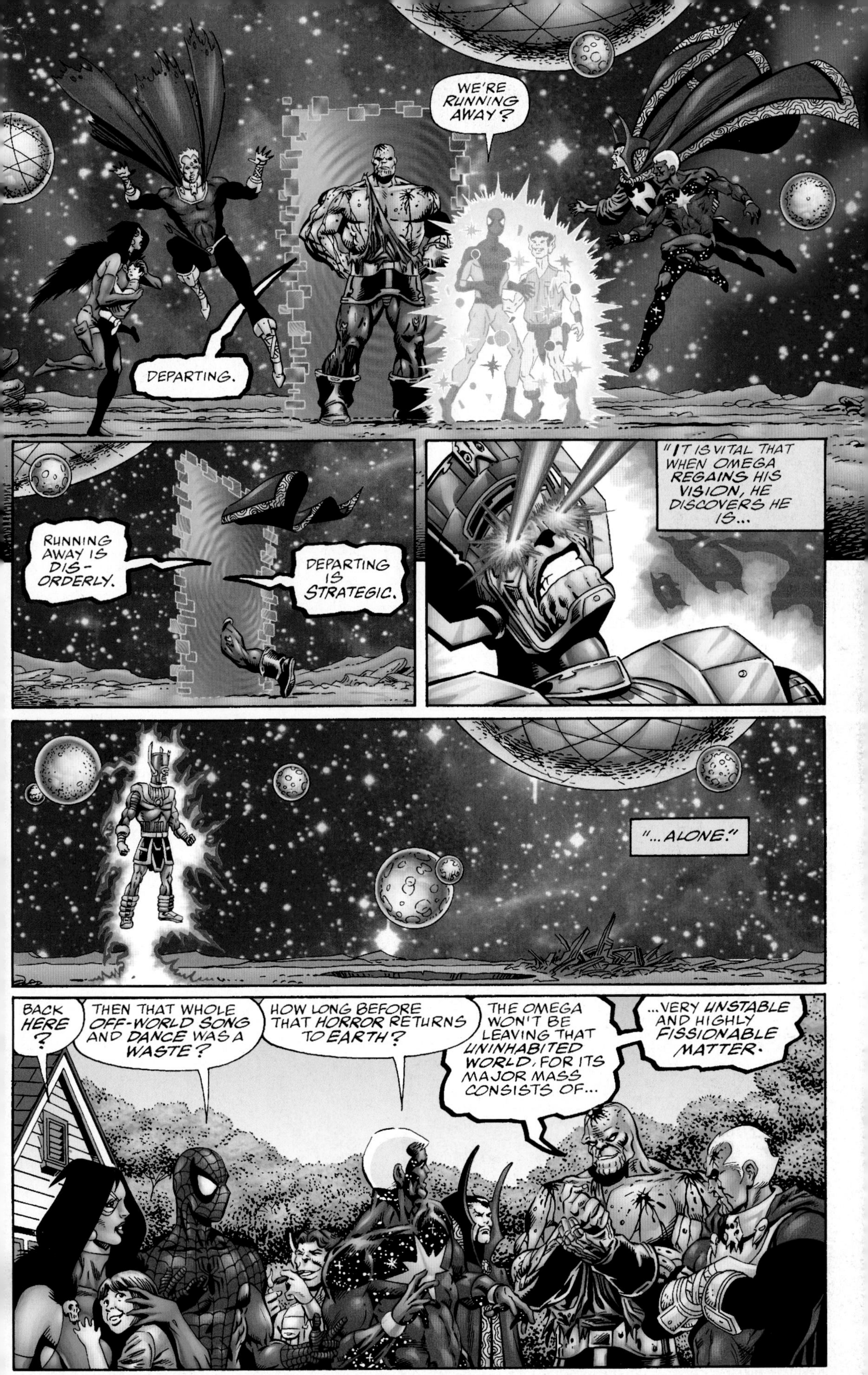
WE'RE RUNNING AWAY?
DEPARTING.
RUNNING AWAY IS DIS-ORDERLY.
DEPARTING IS STRATEGIC.
"IT IS VITAL THAT WHEN OMEGA REGAINS HIS VISION, HE DISCOVERS HE IS...
"...ALONE."
BACK HERE?
THEN THAT WHOLE OFF-WORLD SONG AND DANCE WAS A WASTE?
HOW LONG BEFORE THAT HORROR RETURNS TO EARTH?
THE OMEGA WON'T BE LEAVING THAT UNINHABITED WORLD, FOR ITS MAJOR MASS CONSISTS OF...
...VERY UNSTABLE AND HIGHLY FISSIONABLE MATTER.

"OUR SONG AND DANCE AND THE DESTROYING OF OMEGA'S CRAFT KEPT HIM FROM REALIZING THE PLANET WAS BEING SURROUNDED BY MY ARMADA OF REMOTE-CONTROLLED BATTLESHIPS.

"EVEN AS WE SPEAK, THE FLEET IS DIRECTING ITS ENTIRE ARSENAL AT THE WORLD, SPARKING A MASSIVE CHAIN REACTION WITHIN ITS DEPTHS.

"IF THE OMEGA STILL HAD HIS SHIP IT WOULD CONVERT THIS PLANET'S FIERY DEMISE INTO NOURISHMENT."

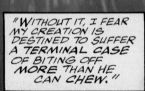

"WITHOUT IT, I FEAR MY CREATION IS DESTINED TO SUFFER A TERMINAL CASE OF BITING OFF MORE THAN HE CAN CHEW."

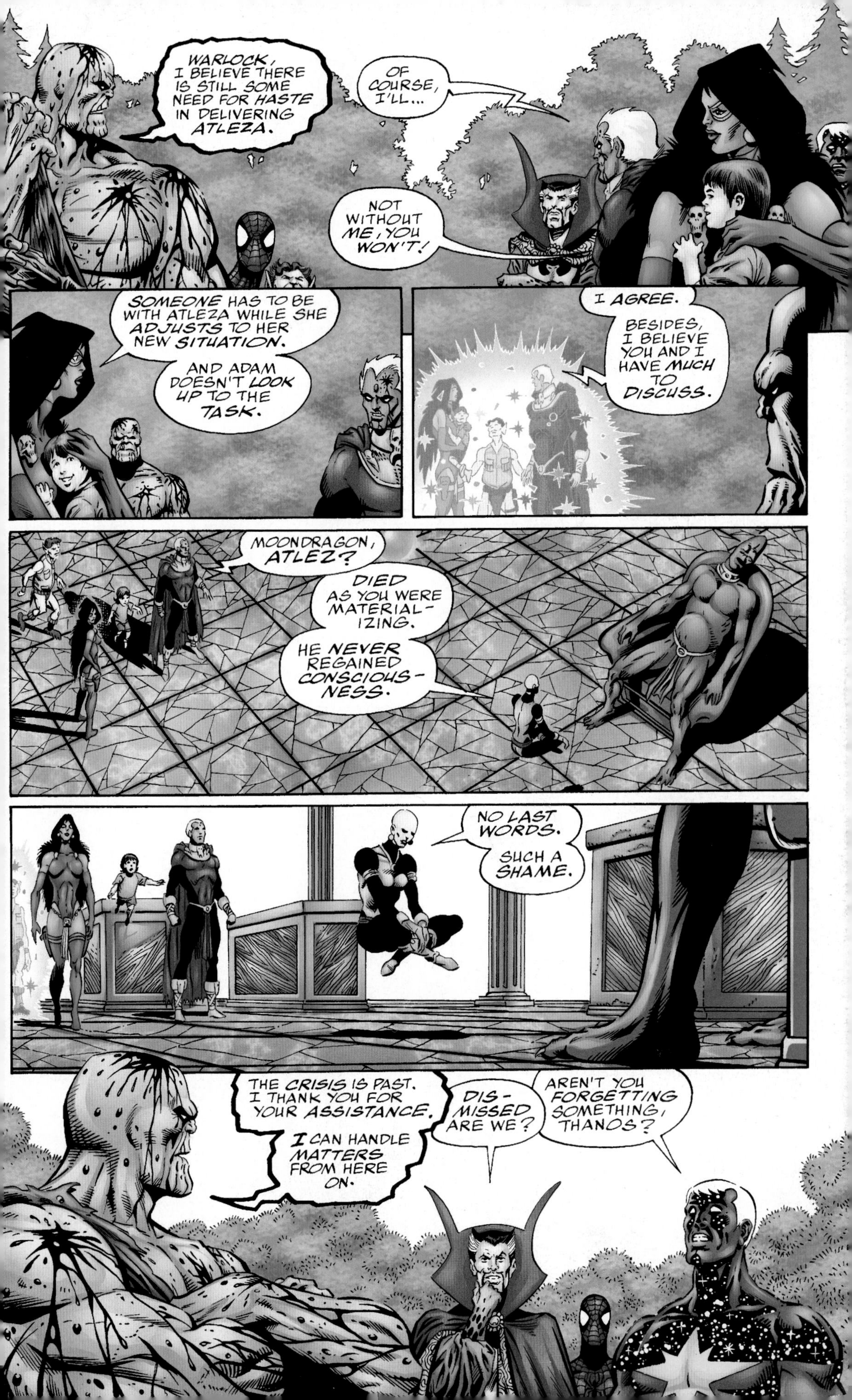
WARLOCK, I BELIEVE THERE IS STILL SOME NEED FOR HASTE IN DELIVERING ATLEZA.
OF COURSE, I'LL...
NOT WITHOUT ME, YOU WON'T!
SOMEONE HAS TO BE WITH ATLEZA WHILE SHE ADJUSTS TO HER NEW SITUATION.
AND ADAM DOESN'T LOOK UP TO THE TASK.
I AGREE.
BESIDES, I BELIEVE YOU AND I HAVE MUCH TO DISCUSS.
MOONDRAGON, ATLEZ?
DIED AS YOU WERE MATERIAL-IZING.
HE NEVER REGAINED CONSCIOUS-NESS.
NO LAST WORDS.
SUCH A SHAME.
THE CRISIS IS PAST. I THANK YOU FOR YOUR ASSISTANCE.
I CAN HANDLE MATTERS FROM HERE ON.
DIS-MISSED ARE WE?
AREN'T YOU FORGETTING SOMETHING, THANOS?

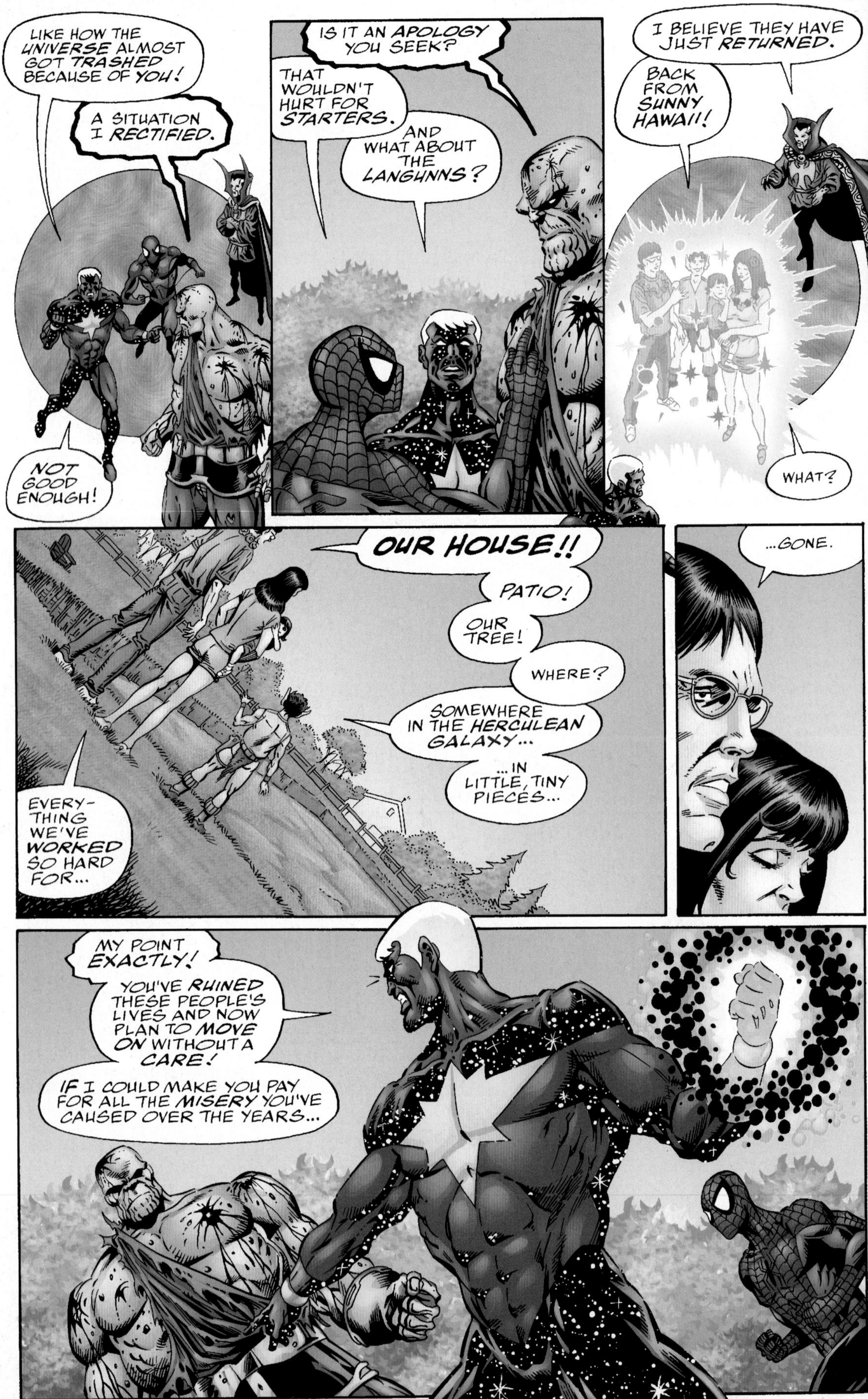
LIKE HOW THE UNIVERSE ALMOST GOT TRASHED BECAUSE OF YOU!
A SITUATION I RECTIFIED.
NOT GOOD ENOUGH!
IS IT AN APOLOGY YOU SEEK?
THAT WOULDN'T HURT FOR STARTERS.
AND WHAT ABOUT THE LANGUNNS?
I BELIEVE THEY HAVE JUST RETURNED.
BACK FROM SUNNY HAWAII!
WHAT?
OUR HOUSE!!
PATIO!
OUR TREE!
WHERE?
SOMEWHERE IN THE HERCULEAN GALAXY...
...IN LITTLE, TINY PIECES...
EVERY-THING WE'VE WORKED SO HARD FOR...
...GONE.
MY POINT EXACTLY!
YOU'VE RUINED THESE PEOPLE'S LIVES AND NOW PLAN TO MOVE ON WITHOUT A CARE!
IF I COULD MAKE YOU PAY FOR ALL THE MISERY YOU'VE CAUSED OVER THE YEARS...

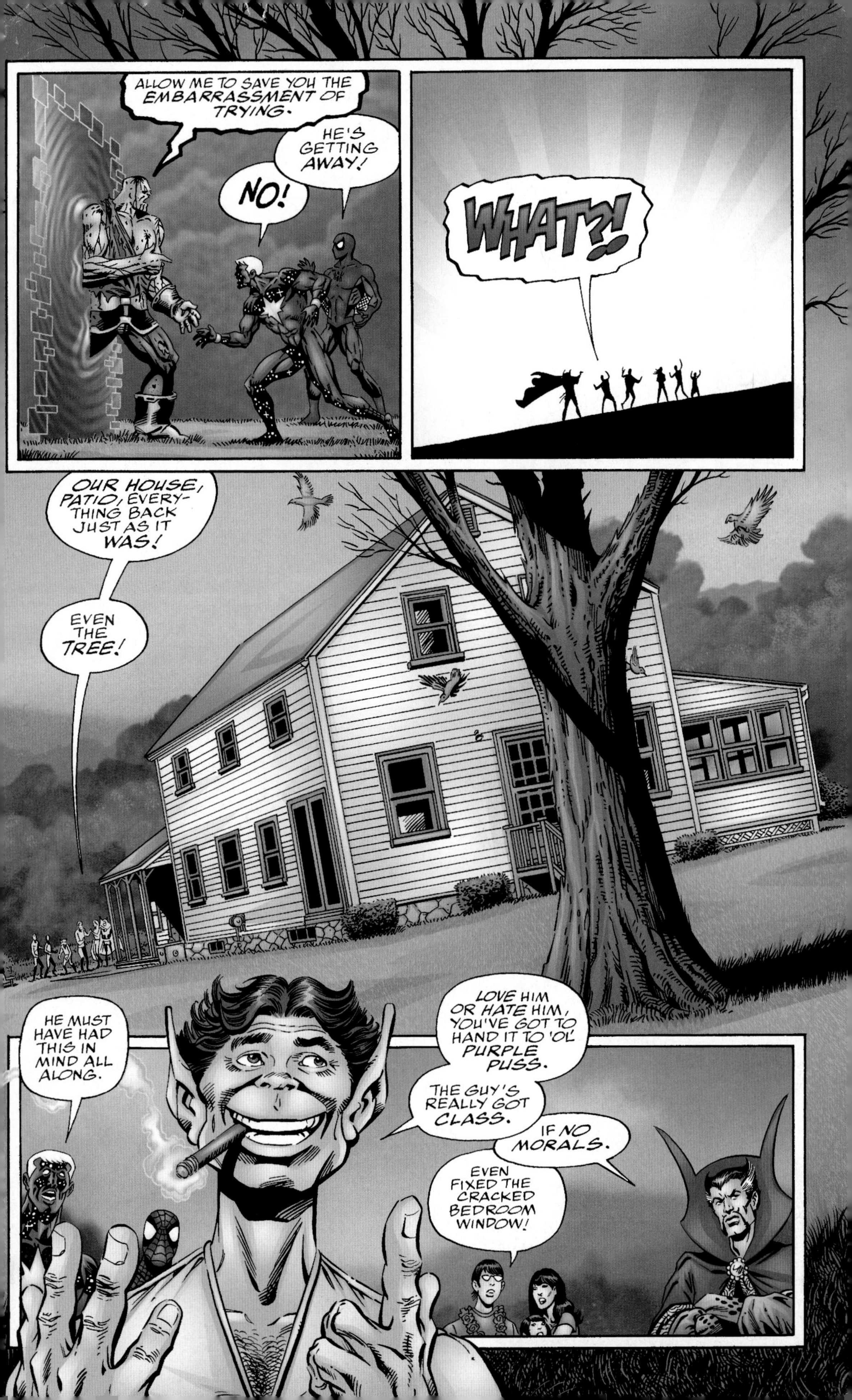
ALLOW ME TO SAVE YOU THE EMBARRASSMENT OF TRYING.
HE'S GETTING AWAY!
NO!
WHAT?!
OUR HOUSE, PATIO, EVERYTHING BACK JUST AS IT WAS!
EVEN THE TREE!
HE MUST HAVE HAD THIS IN MIND ALL ALONG.
LOVE HIM OR HATE HIM, YOU'VE GOT TO HAND IT TO 'OL' PURPLE PUSS.
THE GUY'S REALLY GOT CLASS.
IF NO MORALS.
EVEN FIXED THE CRACKED BEDROOM WINDOW!

AND SO, WITH *DISASTER* AT LEAST PRESENTLY *AVERTED*, THE UNIVERSE *RETURNS* TO ITS *NORMAL RHYTHM.*

ALL INVOLVED *RESUME* THEIR *LIVES*, DIGESTING AND ADJUSTING TO *SURVIVAL.*

"*SOME* WILL *STRUGGLE* WITH *LOSS* AND *CONFUSION.*

"*NO SIMPLE TASK.*

"*WHILE OTHERS* CARRY *LESS WEIGHT.*

"*THERE* WILL BE *CHERISHED REUNIONS.*

"*ONE TENDER...*

"*ANOTHER* A BIT MORE *ACRIMONIOUS.*

"*EXPLANATIONS* WILL NOT BE *EASY.*

"*BUT* THEY WILL BE *MADE*, AND *EVENTUALLY ACCEPTED.*

"*ONE* WILL RETURN TO HER *SEARCH* FOR *UNDERSTANDING* AND *TRUTH.*

"*WHILE ANOTHER...*

...SEEING *THANOS* WAS SO *HELPFUL*, I HAD TO LET HIM *ESCAPE*,...

AND THAT'S *HOW* I *SAVED* THE *UNIVERSE!*

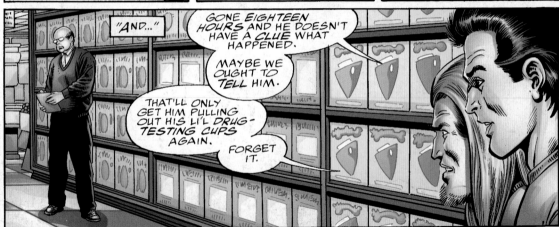

"*AND...*"

GONE *EIGHTEEN HOURS* AND HE DOESN'T HAVE A *CLUE* WHAT HAPPENED.

MAYBE WE OUGHT TO *TELL* HIM.

THAT'LL ONLY GET HIM PULLING OUT HIS LI'L *DRUG-TESTING CUPS* AGAIN.

FORGET IT.

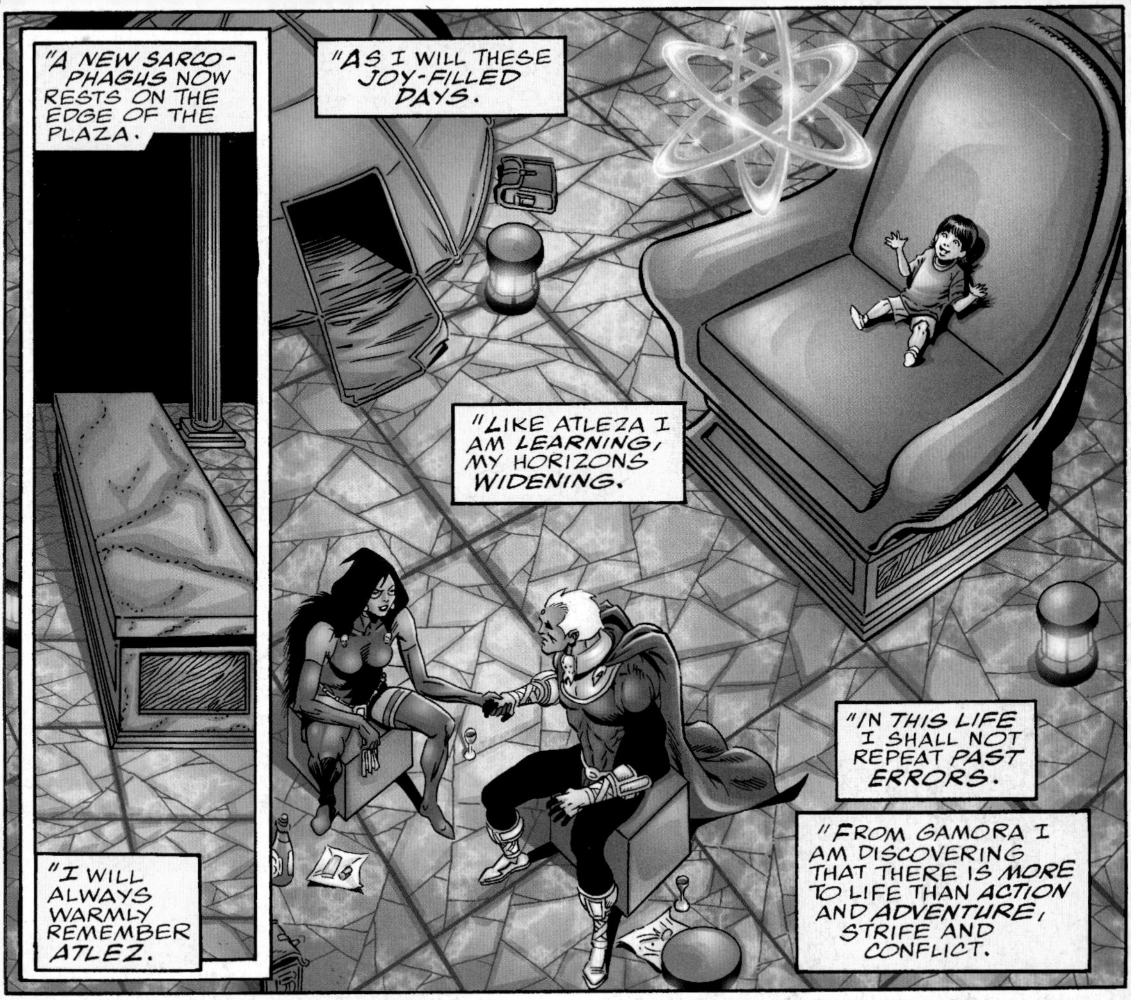
"A NEW SARCOPHAGUS NOW RESTS ON THE EDGE OF THE PLAZA.
"I WILL ALWAYS WARMLY REMEMBER ATLEZ.
"AS I WILL THESE JOY-FILLED DAYS.
"LIKE ATLEZA I AM LEARNING, MY HORIZONS WIDENING.
"IN THIS LIFE I SHALL NOT REPEAT PAST ERRORS.
"FROM GAMORA I AM DISCOVERING THAT THERE IS MORE TO LIFE THAN ACTION AND ADVENTURE, STRIFE AND CONFLICT.

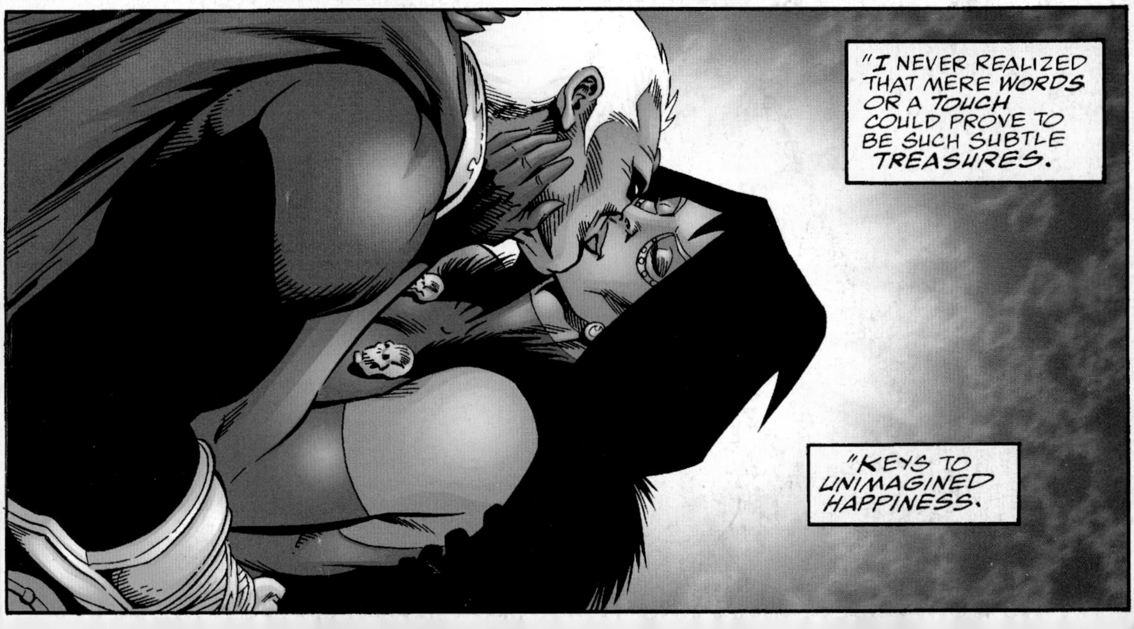
"I NEVER REALIZED THAT MERE WORDS OR A TOUCH COULD PROVE TO BE SUCH SUBTLE TREASURES.
"KEYS TO UNIMAGINED HAPPINESS.

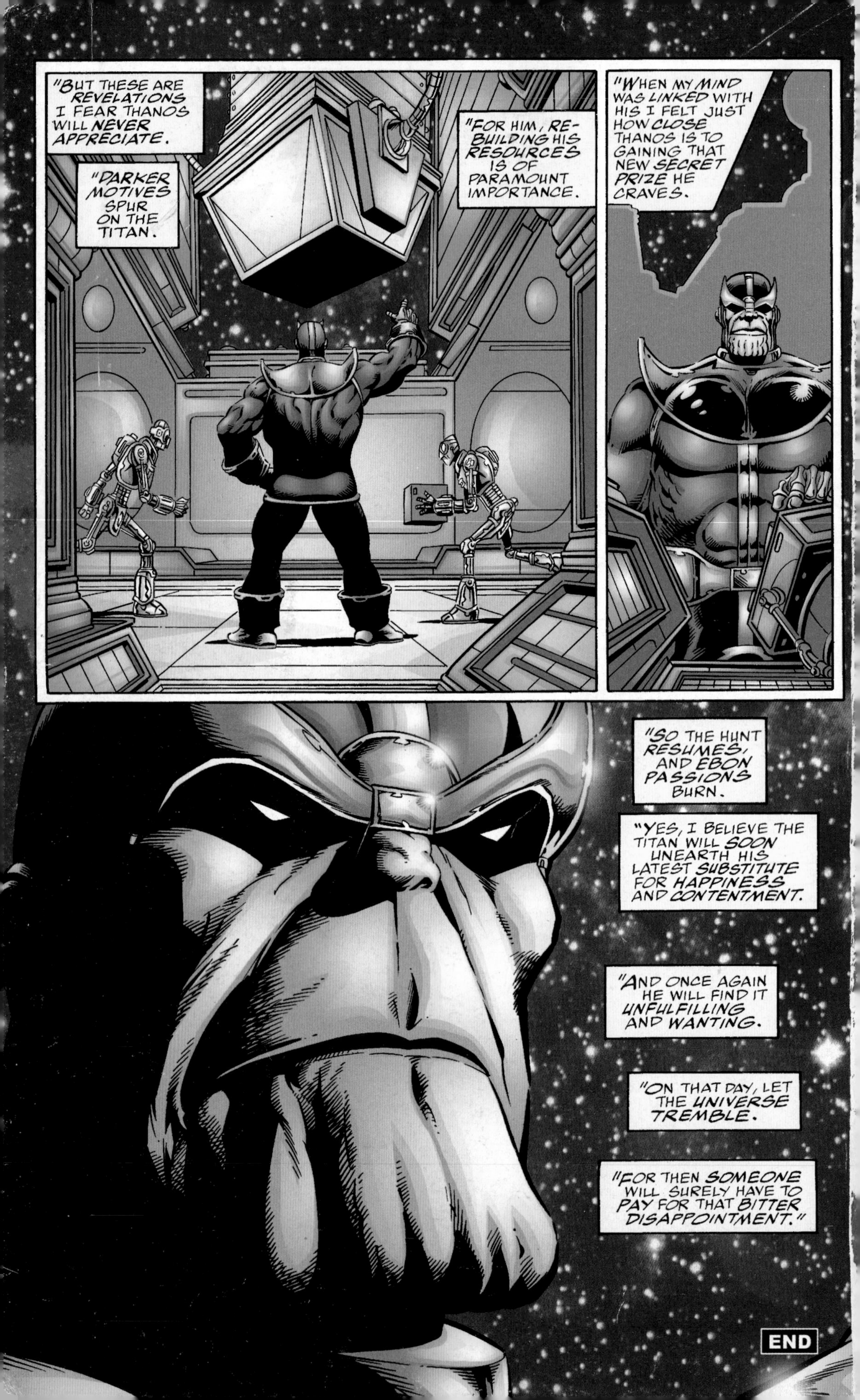
"BUT THESE ARE REVELATIONS I FEAR THANOS WILL NEVER APPRECIATE.
"DARKER MOTIVES SPUR ON THE TITAN.
"FOR HIM, RE-BUILDING HIS RESOURCES IS OF PARAMOUNT IMPORTANCE.
"WHEN MY MIND WAS LINKED WITH HIS I FELT JUST HOW CLOSE THANOS IS TO GAINING THAT NEW SECRET PRIZE HE CRAVES.
"SO THE HUNT RESUMES, AND EBON PASSIONS BURN.
"YES, I BELIEVE THE TITAN WILL SOON UNEARTH HIS LATEST SUBSTITUTE FOR HAPPINESS AND CONTENTMENT.
"AND ONCE AGAIN HE WILL FIND IT UNFULFILLING AND WANTING.
"ON THAT DAY, LET THE UNIVERSE TREMBLE.
"FOR THEN SOMEONE WILL SURELY HAVE TO PAY FOR THAT BITTER DISAPPOINTMENT."
END